RELIGIOUS VIOLENCE IN CONTEMPORARY JAPAN

*also by Ian Reader
and Published by the University of Hawai'i Press*

RELIGION IN CONTEMPORARY JAPAN

JAPANESE RELIGIONS
Past and Present
(with Esben Andreasen and Finn Stefánsson)

PRACTICALLY RELIGIOUS
Worldly Benefits and the Common Religion of Japan
(with George J. Tanabe, Jr.)

Religious Violence in Contemporary Japan

The Case of Aum Shinrikyō

IAN READER

UNIVERSITY OF HAWAI'I PRESS
HONOLULU

Published in North America by
University of Hawai'i Press
2840 Kolowalu Street
Honolulu, Hawai'i 96822

Printed in Great Britain

Library of Congress Cataloging-in-Publication Data

Reader, Ian, 1949–
    Religious violence in contemporary Japan: the case of Aum
Shinrikyō / Ian Reader.
        p.   cm.
    Includes bibliographical references and index.
    ISBN 0-8248-2339-7 (cloth) – ISBN 0-8248-2340-0 (pbk.)
    1. Oumu Shinrikyō (Religious organization)   2. Violence–Religious
aspects–Oumu Shinrikyō (Religious organization)   3. Terrorism–
religious aspects–Oumu Shinrikyō (Religious organization)
4. Terrorism–Japan.
    I. Title.
    BP605.088 R43   2000
    299'.93–dc21   00-023317
                                             CIP

Cover/jacket concept: The Japanese script, with three terms written vertically from right to left, indicates the words *shi* (death), *samadhi* (enlightenment) and *shinri* (truth). Aum equated *shi* and *samadhi*, using the Japanese phonetics for *samadhi* in conjunction with the ideogram for *shi*. *Shinri* was also part of the title of Aum Shinrikyō and was used to signify that the movement considered itself and absolute truth as being synonymous. *Designed and typeset by the Nordic Institute of Asian Studies*

For Philip

師

Contents

Acknowledgements

This book would not have been possible without the help, encouragement and support of many people over the past four and a half years since the Tokyo subway attack brought Aum Shinrikyō to world attention and triggered off my research into the movement. My colleagues at the Nordic Institute of Asian Studies (NIAS) in Copenhagen, where I was based during 1995–1998, deserve my thanks for their support. NIAS also provided me with some research funds out of its restricted budget to support a number of visits to Japan in 1996–1998 to collect material for this book and to conduct the interviews mentioned in it. I would like to thank the Directors of NIAS, Thommy Svensson and Robert Cribb, for their help and support. Gerald Jackson, Editor in Chief at NIAS, was instrumental in getting this project going, encouraging me to turn a long paper I wrote on Aum in late 1995 into the short book, *A Poisonous Cocktail*, that I wrote in early 1996 as a research report. Subsequently he encouraged me to develop the work further, and was instrumental in persuading me to produce this book. The rest of the publishing and editorial team at NIAS: Liz Bramsen, Leena Höskuldsson, Janice Leon, and Andrea Straub have all played their part in bringing this book to completion.

I would like also to thank the Japan Foundation Endowment Committee (JFEC) of the United Kingdom for their support at the beginning of the research that led to this book. I was in possession of a grant (No. 843) from the JFEC to visit Japan and research a different topic when the Aum affair exploded in spring 1995. The JFEC readily agreed, through the secretary John Hawthorne, to permit me to use some of the time I was to spend in Japan not on the topic for which the money was granted but on studying Aum. This initial help in effect seed-funded the project that has materialised in this book.

I am extremely fortunate in having as academic colleagues many people whom I would more accurately describe as friends, and to these I owe many debts and thanks. I wish to thank Shimazono Susumu from the University of Tokyo for his friendship and assistance, his kind and

pertinent critiques of my work, and his willingness to discuss the affair
in a series of conversations and meetings that have taken place in Tokyo,
Copenhagen and the USA – even during a memorable visit together to
Memphis, Tennessee where, while acting as pilgrims visiting cultural
centres of special importance (for me, Graceland, the home of Elvis
Presley, for him, Beale Street, the home of the Blues), we continued to
discuss Aum. Robert Kisala of Nanzan University has answered many
questions, provided feedback to many of my thoughts and ideas, and
has been extremely generous in passing on to me the transcript of an
interview he carried out with a former Aum member, and much other
information about Aum. Mark Mullins of Meiji Gakuin University has
also been most encouraging and has provided me with information and
engaged me in fruitful discussions. Kisala and Mullins, who have both
been generous with comments on this manuscript, are also editing a
book on the repercussions and aftermath of the Aum affair, a book that
will deal with areas that the present book is unable to deal with at any
length. Paul Swanson, also of Nanzan University, is to be thanked for
providing me with information in the earlier part of the affair and for
his perceptive comments about the logistical meanings of the Tokyo
attack. Watanabe Manabu of Nanzan University was especially helpful in
providing me with Aum and Aum-related publications and information.
Others who have been valuable sources of materials and information have
been Takeda Michio and Hoshino Eiki of Taishō University, Kashioka
Tomihide, now of Kyoto Women's University, Ben Dorman, at the time a
postgraduate student working at Nanzan and now at Tokyo University,
and Maekawa Michiko, a postgraduate student at Tokyo University. Two
doctoral students of mine, Jay Sakashita and Clark Chilson, have also
been generous with information and with comments and discussions of
the affair. I have benefited from various discussions with Robert Jay
Lifton, who has conducted interviews with former Aum members and
has worked on aspects of the affair, and have learnt much from his
insights. George Tanabe of the University of Hawaii deserves my thanks
for his friendship and understanding over my absences from the
mutual book project (since completed) that we were working on so that
I could conduct my Aum research. His intellectual stimulus and advice
have contributed greatly to my wider knowledge of the world of religion
and of Japan.

I would like to thank several institutions and colleagues for inviting
me to speak and present papers on various aspects of Aum and its uses
of violence. These opportunities have enabled me both to test out my
ideas and to gain critical feedback from audiences. In particular, I thank

Jackie Stone, Bob Sharf and Sharon Minichiello, who were responsible for invitations to present aspects of my research on Aum at seminars at the universities of Princeton, Michigan and Hawaii respectively.

This research would not have been completed without the assistance of a number of Japanese people who are, or were, members of Aum Shinrikyō, who agreed to participate in often long and searching interviews with me in October 1997 and January 1998 during my visits to Tokyo, and who answered all manner of intrusive questions and provided access to written materials otherwise unavailable to me. To them I also owe thanks for being prepared to discuss many issues that were difficult and painful to talk about, and which many of them are still struggling to come to terms with. Although some were arrested and held for a number of days by the police early on – largely in order to extricate any information they might have had about the movement – none of those I interviewed was charged with or convicted of any criminal activity in the affair. Some are struggling to start new lives for themselves outside of Aum and in a society they have found hard to accept, while others have retained their faith and seek to practise it in a society that is, unsurprisingly, not well disposed towards it. Some of those I spoke to preferred to be known under pseudonyms, due to the problems of being publicly associated with Aum, while others requested that I preserve their anonymity. Accordingly, I have done this with all of them, and merely refer to them as informants or interviewees in this book.

I also wish to thank numerous friends in Japan outside of academia, who have talked to me about Aum from the perspective of ordinary Japanese watching a remarkable affair unfolding. I refer in particular to representatives of a number of religious organisations, from established Buddhist temples to new religious movements, who were willing to talk about the repercussions of the Aum affair on religion in Japan in general, and about the effects of legal changes to the Religious Corporations Law (*Shūkyō hōjin hō*) in the aftermath of Aum. Many friends in Japan also talked to me about Aum and their perceptions of the movement, while extending to me their hospitality during my trips there: for this I am indebted to the Kaneko and Sando families of Tokyo and to Matsumoto Minoru and Noriko of Nagoya.

Outside of Japan I am grateful to many scholars working on new religious movements in general, who have helped develop my knowledge of such issues. Mary Maaga shared with me her work on the Jonestown case and helped me develop my understanding of millennialism and of the ways in which religious movements may produce violent results. Catherine Wessinger of Loyola University, New Orleans, a specialist on millennialist movements, has also provided advice and assisted me further in my understanding of millennialist movements. J. Gordon Melton of the University of California at Santa Barbara was kind enough to invite me to speak at a special session of the Society for the Scientific Study of Religions annual conference in November 1996 on religions and violence, and he has also provided much encouragement for my work. I wish to thank also Val Hamilton and Tessa Carroll of the University of Stirling for their help and support and for passing on relevant items of information.

Despite all this help and assistance, the volume that follows, and any errors that may be found in it, are my own, for which I take full responsibility.

My last and, as ever, greatest thanks are to my family. My wife Dorothy collected Aum-related materials for me on two visits to Japan, the first within weeks of the subway attack, and before I had had the chance to get out there. She has also listened, with great patience, to me talking for many hours on the subject and has provided her own insights and comments. More than that, she has put up with my obsessive fixation with my books and computer screens, with my absences in Japan while I gathered materials for the research, and in other places when I have lectured on this subject. Most stoically of all, she has endured my anti-social work schedules, insomnia, floor-pacing and habit of getting up in the middle of the night to turn the computer on and start writing. My children Rosie and Philip, aged 10 and 7, have had to put up with all of this as well and the fact that (as they put it to me on various occasions) the books I do write do not have interesting pictures and are 'boring'.

Dorothy, Rosie and Philip, then, have provided the stable and loving environment which has been so crucial in enabling me to deal with this painful and difficult topic. This book is dedicated to Philip, but it is written with a deep debt of gratitude to all of them.

オウム

Terms and Conventions

Like many religious organisations, Aum Shinrikyō had its own specialised vocabulary and it developed its own set of codes and meanings which were critical elements in its self-understanding. The uses Aum made of certain terms do not necessarily concur with what people outside the movement, and scholars, might understand by them. For example, Aum used much of the vocabulary of Buddhism, and considered itself to be a movement intent on restoring *genshi bukkyō* (original/early Buddhism) to the world. Scholars may have very different understandings of what constituted 'original Buddhism' from what Aum meant by the term, just as they might find Aum's own self-description as Buddhist and its adoption of Tibetan Buddhist terms and names to be highly problematic.

It is a major scholastic problem, in such circumstances, to decide how to deal with such terms. My decision has been to use Aum Shinrikyō's own vocabulary while describing the movement, and to not become engaged in discussions about the extent to which the concepts and terms that were so imbibed were mistakenly or incorrectly used or understood in Aum. The reasons for this are straightforward: my intention is to provide some insights into how Aum viewed the world and into what type of movement it was. This necessitates examining Aum's self-understandings, which shaped how it saw itself as a religious movement. The vocabulary it used was central to that self-understanding. Accordingly, I have used various terms in this book in the context, and with the understandings, that Aum placed on them.

Hence, when dealing with Aum and with Asahara Shōkō's teachings, I use terms from Buddhism such as Vajrayāna, Hinayāna, Mahāyāna (which Aum affixed to itself) in the same way that they are used in Aum discourse. I have not as a rule discussed whether and to what extent these uses might be erroneous. To have done that would have produced a different book and taken me down very different lines of enquiry.

There are some terms used in Aum that I have retained in their Japanese form, such as *shukkesha*, simply because it has been more convenient to do so. The term *shukke* literally means 'leaving one's home' and is the Japanese Buddhist term for becoming a monk or nun and renouncing the world. This is what Aum's faithful did: they became *shukkesha*, people who had renounced the world. I have decided to use this term throughout to refer to the people who did this in Aum, rather than make use of terms such as monks and nuns, or 'renunciates', a term I used in previous writings but with which I have not felt comfortable.

There are times when transcriptions from the Japanese – especially of borrowed terms and names written, in Aum's publications, in the Japanese katakana syllabary – may be problematic, and one occasionally finds more than one way in which such borrowed terms have been transcribed in Japanese. For example, the term *poa*, which will be discussed in this book and which refers to a critical concept within Aum – one taken, Aum claimed, from Tibetan Buddhism – may be found in several versions both in katakana and, in Aum's English publications, in romanised versions (e.g. *powa*, *phowa*). Where possible, I have attempted to maintain a consistency in transcriptions by keeping to one form of transcription for each term, but occasionally this has been impossible when citing different Aum sources that might use different transcription forms. I have also co-opted the word into English in a verbal form, because it was used as a verb in Japanese (*poa suru* – literally, to perform the act of *poa* which, as I discuss in the book, was shorthand in Aum for killing someone). I have used the term *poa*-ed in this context (as in 'Asahara ordered him to be *poa*-ed') to convey the manner in which Aum expressed such acts.

Names too pose a problem, in that some of those who had renounced the world were given what Aum termed 'holy names' (*hōrinēmu*). These names were only bestowed on those deemed to have attained certain levels of ascetic practice and spiritual insight (see Chapter 3), and they were generally based on Sanskrit names relating to disciples of or family members related to the historical Buddha. The names, however, are often inaccurately or eccentrically used by Aum and are extremely hard to transcribe into roman letters. Where possible I have avoided (for the sake of clarity) such names, which are frequently long and barely recognisable, and have tried as much as possible to keep to the Japanese names of Aum members, even though they had given up these names as products and elements of the material world that they rejected. Where it has been necessary to use one of these holy names, I have cited the romanised forms of them as given in Aum publications, and where possible I also give the person's Japanese name. Where I have been unable to find the romanised form of the holy name, I have transcribed them in the manner that appears to conform most closely to the

Japanese script. Often in Aum publications members are referred to by their holy names, and many of them published articles in Aum publications under their holy rather than given worldly names. When this has been the case I give both the holy name and the Japanese name of the person. Throughout this book I refer to Aum's leader as Asahara Shōkō. His name at birth was Matsumoto Chizuo, and that is the name by which reference is made to him in the trials under way in Japan. In indictments he is also referred to as *Asahara Shōkō koto Matsumoto Chizuo* (Matsumoto Chizuo, also known as Asahara Shōkō). Asahara is a religious name taken on by Matsumoto at the time when Aum Shinrikyō was founded, and it is that name under which he was known in and outside the movement, and under which he gave his sermons, published his books and so on. While in court, he is known and charged under his real, family name (a name he stated, in his first court appearance on 24 April 1996, that he had rejected – see Chapter 2). However, it was as Asahara Shōkō that he was known not only to his followers but, indeed, to the whole Japanese nation in the period after the subway attack. Since that name represented his religious personality, which is a primary focus of this book, this is the one I use throughout the book.[1]

A further problem arises with the numerous publications Aum produced, many of which are collections of Asahara's sermons, or compendia of his sermons along with testimonies of his followers. The assignation of authorship or editorship of these books is often unclear: for example, the various books (approximately 20 in all) in the series *Asahara Shōkō no sekai* [The World of Asahara Shōkō] consist of Asahara's sermons, and bear his name on the front cover in a manner indicative of a sole author. However, at the back of the book in the section where the publication date, publisher and so on are recorded, the books are accredited as being edited volumes produced by Aum Press or by an Aum editorial committee. Where there are conflicts or confusions such as this, I have referenced the work in the way that seems most logical and useful: thus, in the aforementioned series I have chosen to list Asahara as the author in the notes and bibliography. I have also divided the list of references into two sections, the first covering publications by Aum Shinrikyō, including those by Asahara, the second covering all other works referred to in the text.

I refer to the movement at the centre of this book as Aum Shinrikyō, rather than Aum Supreme Truth (the name it often used in English), since this is the name it adopted in Japan, where the core of the events described here occurred. For ease of reference, I abbreviate it to Aum.

When transcribing Japanese, however, as in Aum's publications, I use Oumu, as this is the romanised form of the movement's name in Japanese.

As is normal with books on Japanese matters, all Japanese names are in standard Japanese order of family name first followed by given name.

Long vowels are indicated by macrons (ō, ū) except in commonly used words and names that have become adapted into English (e.g. Tokyo, Shinto).

NOTE

1.   Others, such as the journalist and Aum critic Egawa Shōkō, also continue to refer to him in their writings as Asahara rather than Matsumoto, for similar reasons. Egawa admits to confused feelings regarding the person on trial as criminal (Matsumoto) and the person who assumed the aura of a religious leader (Asahara) but notes that in general she will use the name Asahara (Egawa 1997, pp. 1–3).

Abbreviations

I use a number of abbreviations for publications referred to frequently in this book. These are as follows:

Asahara VK *Vajrayāna Kōsu Kyōgaku shisutemu kyōhon* This is an undated, photocopied series of 57 lectures by Asahara, given between August 1988 and April 1994 (see Introduction) that was distributed, in xeroxed form, to Aum members who became *shukkesha*. In referring to this series, I cite also the number of the lecture in the series and the page number. Thus VK 18, p. 127 refers to Sermon 18 and page 127 in the *Vajra-yāna Kōsu Kyōgaku shisutemu kyōhon*.

KNS   Kumamoto Nichinichi Shinbun (ed.) 1995

KDT   Kyōdō Tsūshinsha Shakaibu (ed.) 1997

MNL   Mahayana Newsletter (Aum English language magazine)

MNS   Mainichi Shinbun Shakaibu (ed) 1996

TSS   Tōkyō Shinbun Shakaibu (ed) 1995

真理

Introduction

In March 1995 the Japanese new religion Aum Shinrikyō and its leader Asahara Shōkō achieved international notoriety as a result of the poison gas attack carried out on the Tokyo subway system. Shocking as it was, however, this was neither the first nor the last in a series of atrocities perpetrated by the movement (or more accurately, by highly placed members in Aum's hierarchy under the direction of Asahara) dating back at least to 1988. These ranged from beatings of members inside the movement and the secret disposal of bodies of followers who had died accidentally during the movement's harsh ascetic practices, to the murders of public opponents of the group and the manufacture and use of chemical weapons. The subway attack, using the poison gas sarin originally developed by the Nazis in the 1930s, led to a massive police investigation of Aum, which became the focus of public and mass media attention in Japan for months afterwards. The Aum affair (*Oumu jiken*), as it came to be known in Japan, also attracted the attention of law enforcement agencies around the world because it represented the first case of the use of weapons of mass destruction by a private organisation, and led to investigations into Aum's acquisition and use of chemical weapons by several such agencies and by the US Senate's Committee on Governmental Affairs.[1]

The investigations into Aum by the Japanese police and by other law enforcement agencies, and the prosecutions that have resulted from those investigations, have naturally centred on the criminal activities themselves and on the misdeeds committed by Aum followers. The media, too, while narrating in detail these crimes, have largely been concerned with highlighting or sensationalising the bizarre aspects of the affair and of Aum Shinrikyō itself. The general coverage of Aum in

1

the Japanese media depicted a movement that claimed to be religious but that had seemingly regarded the murder of its opponents as a legitimate course of action; that had developed doctrines to justify its murderous activities; that had acquired materials that were used to build chemical laboratories and make weapons of mass destruction; that had used illegal drugs such as LSD in its rituals; and that had engaged in the kidnapping and enforced incarceration of members who tried to leave it. The media also, in the stories and images it transmitted, portrayed Aum Shinrikyō as an introverted yet aggressive movement whose highly educated young followers had given up their belongings, families, careers and identities to follow a blind guru figure who claimed to be able to levitate, who transferred his spiritual power to his followers by way of initiation rituals that included drinking his bath water or blood (for which they paid large sums of money), who preached that apocalyptic war was about to engulf the world, and who complained that he and his movement were being attacked with poison gases by evil forces controlled by a vast conspiracy intent on world domination which included the US and Japanese governments.

Sensationalised as the above images might appear, perhaps the most extraordinary element in the case is that the details given above are by and large accurate. Journalists' accounts of the affair that talked of the 'incredible story of Aum'[2] in a sense attested to the fact that reality can sometimes appear stranger than fiction. It is not, however, the sensational nature of the affair that interests me *per se*, nor indeed the various crimes and illegal acts that Aum perpetrated. These have been discussed and outlined many times in accounts of the affair. My concern is not so much *what* happened as *why* it did. Aum Shinrikyō's origins were in a yoga and meditation group founded by Asahara in Tokyo in 1984. Eleven years later many of its senior members, while remaining committed practitioners of the spiritual disciplines they had learned in Aum, stood accused of mass murders and multiple criminal offences. Yet Asahara and his disciples, when they carried out these deeds,[3] saw themselves not as criminals or murderers but as highly trained religious practitioners acting to protect the movement's mission and to enhance its salvation activity (*kyūsai katsudō*) or plan (*kyūsai keikaku*), which sought to transform the world spiritually.

How did the movement's leaders get to this seemingly contradictory position of killing in the name of salvation? What did they mean by their mission of salvation, and why was it shot through not just with violent images but with increasingly violent deeds? How did the seemingly peaceful yoga and meditation group meeting in central Tokyo turn into an aggressive religious organisation based in a rural commune, engaging in rancorous disputes with its neighbours, killing its own members when they incurred the wrath of its leaders, and devoting its energies to manufacturing and using chemical weapons on the ordinary citizens of Japan? Why and how did its leader develop doctrines that justified his movement's crimes? What was the appeal of Aum Shinrikyō and why did those who joined it because of its spiritual teachings earnestly continue to embrace it and devote themselves so wholeheartedly to it when it turned violent? How could Aum devotees board subway trains with the intention of releasing lethal poisonous gases that would cause death and injury on a massive scale, and yet see it as part of a religious mission?

These are the main issues that this book seeks to examine. Its purpose, in other words, is to discuss the factors underlying the production of violence in and by Aum Shinrikyō and to ask why the movement developed as it did in the period leading up to the 20 March 1995 attack and the subsequent arrest of Asahara and many of his followers. In examining these issues I have naturally had to make some choices about what to include and what to omit. Given the sheer amount of information that has become available through the Japanese media and the various Aum-related trials that have been going on in Japan since 1995, anyone approaching the affair is likely to be swamped with data. Consequently it is as important to emphasise what this book is *not* about as what it is about. While I provide a general outline of the events that took place during the affair, and look at some of the people involved and their actions, my intention is not to provide a narrative (sensationalised or otherwise) of who did what and when, to go into minute detail on every criminal activity Aum committed, or to describe the processes whereby members of Aum acquired various materials that were used for making chemical weapons and for building laboratories. Other accounts that focus on such details of the affair already exist,[4] while the continuing trials of Aum members in Japan, and the extensive reporting of them in the newspapers, in books and on the Internet continue to provide us with detailed accounts of the events and of Aum's deeds.[5] What concerns me most is to provide an interpretation not so much of how the sequence of crimes occurred but *why* they did. Equally, I do not discuss to any degree the aftermath or the repercussions of the affair in Japan, which have given rise to numerous other questions and issues, such as the legal position of religious movements in Japan in the wake of the affair. Nor do I pay attention to such questions as why several hundred members of Aum Shinrikyō, despite the revelations about their movement's criminality and their guru's involvement in mass murder, con-

tinue to venerate him and to devote themselves to the movement.[6] These
are all important issues and topics that require major studies in their
own right, and merit far more extensive discussion than would be possible
within the context of this volume.[7]

Some comment is required about my writing a second book on the
development of the Aum affair and on the factors behind Aum's violence.
As some readers will be aware, in 1996 I published a short volume entitled
A Poisonous Cocktail? Aum Shinrikyō's Path to Violence.[8] That volume was
researched, written and published within a year of the subway attack, as
an immediate response to the affair and because, as a scholar working
on religion in modern Japan, I felt it important to attempt an initial
academic analysis at a time when much of the information being disseminated was highly sensationalised. At that time I recognised that that
was a preliminary account, a 'first stage in more extensive discussions
and analyses of the affair',[9] and that as further information and material
became available, it would become possible to gain a more comprehensive
understanding of what drove Aum to develop as it did. As new and
critical materials have become available to me (including xeroxed texts
of a series of Asahara's sermons given to disciples, and on which I draw
extensively, and a large supply of Asahara's books and other Aum publications), and as I have been afforded the opportunity to speak to former
and current members of Aum, and to attend the courts and watch some
of the trials in progress, my analysis of the affair has developed further.
Moreover kind comments by colleagues and reviewers have alerted me
to deficiencies in that early analysis, in particular in terms of the ways in
which Aum's doctrines provided the legitimation for its violence, an
element of the affair that I had tended to overlook in my emphasis on
Aum's structure and attitudes as a communal and millennialist movement that believed that an apocalypse was imminent.[10] I have now come
to believe that the seeds of Aum's violence were more deeply rooted in
its basic doctrines, in the movement's image of itself, in its self-
proclaimed mission and in the personality of its founder, than I had
discussed in that book. In particular, in emphasising the structure of
the movement, I paid less attention than I ought to have to Aum's
doctrines. As Jamie Hubbard has recently argued, doctrine is an issue
that has been rather neglected in the study of Japanese new religions,
which have widely been portrayed as concerned primarily or wholly with
practice and as being devoid of doctrinal sophistication.[11] Hubbard's
argument is in effect reaffirmed in Shimazono Susumu's book on Aum,
which highlights some of the doctrinal issues underlying Aum's violence
– an argument with which I wholeheartedly concur. Accordingly Asahara's

teachings and Aum's doctrinal orientations receive greater attention here than they did in my earlier work. Equally, in that work I focused largely on later developments in Aum and paid relatively little attention to Asahara's own background and to the earlier years of his movement. I have attempted to rectify this imbalance in this book, and while I naturally continue to pay attention to the later period of Aum's development, I also discuss in some detail Aum's roots and critical aspects of its earlier history which, as this book argues, were central to the path of violence it followed.

In the light of the new materials that had become available to me, I originally intended simply to revise and update my earlier book. However, the more I looked at the affair and the more I considered the revisions I felt were necessary, the more I realised that a new book was developing, one that, while not refuting the contents of *A Poisonous Cocktail?*, would be more comprehensive and that would enhance its analyses, right some of its imbalances, and correct some minor errors, while also making some further comments in the broader context of religious violence in general.

Thus, in Chapter 1, I argue that the Aum affair can best be understood and analysed in the context of religious violence. In so doing I discuss a seemingly bizarre incident, in which a punishment meted out to a disaffected follower in 1993 resulted in his death. In showing why the punishment was deemed necessary by Aum and how the death was dealt with, I discuss how this incident manifested and reflected many of the doctrines and themes prevalent in Aum's worldview, and how the movement's religious beliefs and practices could lead to and justify the use of violence.

From there, in Chapters 2 and 3, I turn to a more detailed account of Aum and of its founder. Like many other Japanese new religions, Aum was essentially a creation of its founder: Asahara Shōkō was the source of inspiration in Aum and the focus of its faith. It was Asahara who formed and taught its doctrines and practices, and who instigated and oversaw its activities and crimes. In Chapter 2, I discuss Asahara's life, experiences and personality, especially in the context of the Japanese religious and cultural milieu of the late 1970s and the 1980s in which he developed his religious ideas. I also look at Asahara's self-image because this is highly important in understanding how he related to the rest of the world. In Chapter 3, I give a brief account of Aum's early history, largely up to 1988, and discuss its nature as a religious organisation.

Ideas, thoughts, doctrines and practices, even if they help (as in Aum's case) to create a confrontational ethic, do not of themselves kill;

nor do they create the circumstances in which theoretical views are put into practice as criminal acts. Asahara was the primary instigator of Aum's activities but he did not commit any murders himself or personally manufacture the chemical weapons used in Aum's crimes: it was his loyal devotees who, following his orders, did so. It was they who, by joining Aum and offering devotion to Asahara, supported his claims as a guru and invested him with spiritual authority. Accordingly, it is important when studying Aum to analyse the identity of the followers and their motivations. This is the intention of Chapter 4, which examines Asahara's followers, their reasons for joining and remaining faithful to Aum, their experiences, and their attitudes towards Asahara.

In the next chapters the focus switches to Aum's experiences, especially in the years between 1988 and 1995, which is the period encompassed by its known crimes. I look at developments in Aum's teaching and at various events that occurred both inside the movement and between it and the wider society, and that further shaped the movement's worldview. As Chapter 5 shows, the period between late summer 1988 (when Asahara began to emphasise the importance of absolute obedience to himself as guru) and mid-1990 (when, after a series of public exposés and a humiliating public loss of face, Asahara first considered deploying weapons of mass destruction) was a critical stage in the movement's development. It was in this period that Aum became deeply alienated from Japanese society and increasingly convinced that the world would descend into apocalyptic war. It also developed an increasingly elitist view of the world as it began to judge people outside of Aum as unworthy of salvation. During this period, too, Aum committed its first criminal acts, including murders that only came to light several years later as a result of the police investigations after the subway attack. Among the issues that will be examined in Chapter 5 are how unforeseen events played a role in shaping doctrines, and how growing conflicts with the outside world (provoked in great part by Aum's stark division of the world into good and evil) began to produce a rampant persecution complex in Aum.

These themes are continued in Chapters 6 and 7, which examine Aum in the period from 1990 onwards. Chapter 6 looks largely at the period up to spring 1993 when Aum began to engage in manufacturing chemical weapons in earnest, and at the various changes that occurred in its outlook during this period. It especially examines how Aum developed rural communes and, in so doing, came into conflict with its neighbours and became embroiled in numerous legal cases. This conflict with the outside world served to heighten Aum's increasing alienation from mainstream society. In this period Aum's millennialism and its belief in the coming of an apocalyptic war, coupled with its emphasis on the role and power of Asahara as a prophet, intensified. In discussing these issues, I also look at Asahara's conviction that there was a conspiracy against Aum, in which various hostile forces were plotting to destroy his movement (a theme that dominates many of his later sermons).

In this nexus of conspiracy theories and growing concerns about the imminence of a final war of death and destruction, one finds an intensification of the legitimation of violence found within Asahara's teaching, as well as a growing interest in, and concern for, the means of destruction. These issues are further discussed in Chapter 7 which shows how Aum moved on to a war footing, devoting resources to the manufacture of weapons and committing numerous acts of violence inside and outside the movement. This chapter looks also at the underlying patterns of Aum's violence, the question of whether the movement had a co-ordinated plan and strategy in its violence, and asks what its real intentions were in carrying out the subway and other attacks.

In the concluding chapter, I turn again to an overview of the affair, seeking to outline the factors that contributed to Aum's uses of violence. In so doing I make reference here (as elsewhere in the book) to other cases in which religious movements of recent times have engaged in acts of violence (either internally, by conducting group suicides) or externally (by attacking perceived opponents). In doing this I assert that while Aum was a Japanese religious organisation, the affair should not be viewed solely as a Japanese phenomenon but one that is of great significance for scholars of religion in general. The main elements in Aum's path to violence are based in the movement's nature as a religion, and hence the most effective means of understanding the Aum affair is in the context of the study of religion. The Conclusion, in other words, reaffirms the argument made in Chapter 1, and views the case of Aum Shinrikyō as a study in religious violence.

1 A Death in the Culture of Coercive Asceticism – Killing for Salvation, Religious Violence and Aum Shinrikyō

A POTENTIAL DEFECTION AND ITS MEANINGS

In May 1997 Ōuchi Sanae, a woman in her thirties who had been a high-ranking figure in Aum Shinrikyō, testified in court in the trial of Ishii Hisako, another woman of similar age and high rank in Aum. The trial was one of the many that have taken place in Japan since the spring of 1995 resulting from the Japanese police investigations into Aum after the Tokyo subway attack of 20 March 1995. Aum Shinrikyō was generally considered to be one of the 'new' new religions of Japan that had come into prominence in the 1980s, most particularly in urban areas and with a particular appeal for younger, educated Japanese.[1] Originally founded as a small yoga and meditation group in 1984 by Asahara Shōkō, the movement's partially blind and charismatic leader, it had, by 1995, developed into a highly structured and hierarchic movement of perhaps 10,000 followers in Japan,[2] of whom around 1,200, or just over 10 per cent, had renounced the world to become *shukkesha* (a general term in Aum for those who had 'left the world', severed ties with their families, and become nuns or monks in Aum's religious system). It had a number of centres in the Mount Fuji region in Shizuoka and Yamanashi prefectures, with a commune near the village of Kamikuishiki in Yamanashi, some two hours from Tokyo, where Aum had erected numerous buildings known in the movement as *satian* (this term being the movement's Japanised rendition of the Sanskrit word *satyam*, or truth).[3] While some of the *satian* were used for legitimate religious purposes as halls of worship and living quarters for the movement's *shukkesha*, others, it transpired, had more sinister uses. Satian 7 (each had been assigned a number) turned out to have harboured laboratories and plants where the poison gases used in the subway attack were produced.

Aum was already suspected of a number of criminal activities, including the murder and kidnapping of opponents, when the subway attack occurred, triggering police raids on the Kamikuishiki commune and other Aum centres. As a result, evidence began to emerge of various crimes and illegal activities that went back at least to 1988, and hundreds of Aum members were arrested, including Asahara (who was arrested on 16 May 1995, almost eight weeks after the subway attack) and his closest associates. They were charged with various offences including murder, and were brought to trial.

In the trial in question, Ishii was charged with the illegal disposal of the corpse of an Aum practitioner who had died in June 1993 during severe ascetic training ordered by Asahara. Ōuchi was appearing as a witness in the trial and her testimony provided a chilling insight into the atmosphere and attitudes within Aum at this time – attitudes that were central to Aum's uses of violence and espousal of the means of mass destruction. Ishii and Ōuchi were close disciples of Asahara and had been with the movement since its earliest days. Both held high positions in Aum, Ishii as head of Aum's finance 'ministry' in the quasi or alternative 'government' that it had established in June 1994,[4] and Ōuchi as second in charge of the 'ministry' overseeing new disciples. In addition to their having renounced the world as *shukkesha*, they both possessed 'holy names' (*hōrinēmu*); these names had their origins in Sanskrit, and were bestowed by Asahara on practitioners who had reached the higher levels of Aum's rigidly structured hierarchy. The two women had powerful reputations in Aum as seasoned ascetic practitioners. Ishii was the first in the movement and Ōuchi the second to be accredited with attaining the awakening of the *kundalini*,[5] a stage of yoga development that, according to Aum's system of practice, unleashed immense spiritual energy and awareness.

As will be discussed in later chapters, Aum had developed a highly structured and intensely hierarchical ranking system which related to its belief that there were various levels of existence and of consciousness, and that success at different levels of ascetic practice enabled the practitioner to enter these different realms. Members 'challenged' these various stages in their practice, and success (which was normally verified by Asahara as a result of the experiences disciples had during their practice) could lead to promotions on Aum's hierarchic spiritual ladder. At the top of this spiritual hierarchy was Asahara himself, who was referred to as the 'ultimately liberated one' (*saishu gedatsusha*) and as the 'Spirit of Truth: his Holiness the Master' (*shinri no mitama saisei*).[6]

Ishii was the highest-ranked practitioner in the spiritual hierarchy below Asahara, considered to be capable of carrying out spiritual initiations. She was one of only five members who held the rank and title *seitaishi* ('sacred grand teacher'),[7] while Ōuchi held the next rank below this, that of *seigoshi* ('sacred awakened teacher'). Besides her prowess as an ascetic practitioner and teacher (she gave various lectures and teachings to Aum disciples, and published numerous articles and volumes of her spiritual experiences),[8] Ishii had great control over the movement's finances and was central to Aum's administration. She had also for some time, although this was not widely known outside Aum's upper echelons, been Asahara's lover, and had borne three children in the 1990s, all presumed to be his, although it appears that this relationship had ended some time before the subway attack.[9]

She had also previously been imprisoned in the service of Aum, having been arrested and incarcerated in October 1990 along with Aoyama Yoshinobu, Aum's chief lawyer, and other officials on suspicion of violations of the Japanese land registry laws in relation to Aum's purchase of land at Namino in Kumamoto prefecture in southern Japan. This was one of many incidents (to be discussed in subsequent chapters) in which Aum came into conflict with mainstream society and demonstrated contempt for its laws. Basically Aum operated with wholly different perspectives and in a different moral universe from that of mainstream society, regarding its own interests and religious imperatives as being above or not bounded by the law of the land. This attitude was amply illustrated by Ōuchi's testimony in the trial of Ishii Hisako in May 1997.

According to Ōuchi, a 25-year-old Aum disciple, Ochi Naoki, had voiced doubts about his continued faith in Aum and had decided to quit the movement in the summer of 1993. Defections had been a matter of grave worry to Asahara for some time, and he had expressed fears that the very existence of the movement would be threatened as a result.[10] This feeling had become increasingly pronounced by 1993, which was a period that has been described by an Aum member as one of increasing paranoia.[11]

Aum had a polarised view of the world, in which the forces of good and evil were ranged against each other in a cosmic struggle. The origins of this polarisation were founded in Asahara's early religious conviction that he had been entrusted with a sacred mission to lead the forces of good in a war against evil. Aum had come to regard the world at large as corrupt and spiritually polluted, described by Asahara as being a 'den of evil' (*akugō no sōkutsu*)[12] and 'nothing but a cesspit'.[13] This profound rejection of the everyday world was one of the bases upon which Aum's system of world renunciation had been founded: members of the movement were deeply critical of the materialistic world and sought liberation from it. Aum did not just regard the everyday world as a hindrance to liberation, however: it saw it as a pernicious force that could pull down all those who lived in it. By 1993 this view was so strong that commune members who considered leaving were forcibly detained to 'save' them from 'falling' into the realms of evil, while Aum made concerted attempts to 'rescue' people from the world of evil by persuading or cajoling lay members to renounce the world and enter Aum's communal life as *shukkesha*.

Unsurprisingly in such a paranoid atmosphere, there were many who did try to leave, and this led to numerous incidents of forced detention, violence and maltreatment, as well as kidnappings in which defectors were forcibly brought back to Aum's premises. In the period from 1993 until the police raids in March 1995, numerous dissident followers were incarcerated by Aum at Kamikuishiki. There were two primary concerns behind this forcible resistance to defections and the kidnapping of defectors.

The first of these related to a belief that had first manifested itself in Asahara's thoughts in the latter part of the 1980s but that eventually became an overarching theme colouring his entire view of the world: the notion that Aum was surrounded by hostile forces and that a vast conspiracy bent on world domination was seeking to destroy Aum as part of its fiendish plans. It was seeking to destroy Aum because, in Asahara's aforementioned vision of sacred struggle, Aum was the only force left standing between the conspirators (who included the US and Japanese governments, the Freemasons, the Jews and numerous others) and their evil intentions.[14] The agents of this conspiracy, he stated in numerous sermons in 1993 and 1994, were not only using poisonous weapons against Aum but were also gathering information on the movement through the use of spies. This fear, that Aum was surrounded by conspirators intent on destroying it and was being infiltrated by spies, is indicative of the paranoid siege mentality in which Aum's leadership had come to exist. Thus defecting members were seen either as spies seeking to spread news of Aum's activities to the movement's enemies or as renegades who would spread false rumours and stories about what went on at Aum's commune at Kamikuishiki. As events have shown, there were clearly plentiful reasons for Aum's leadership to fear what defectors might say about its internal affairs because it was heavily engaged in a number of illegal activities, including the manufacture of various weapons of mass destruction that later were put to use against the Japanese public. By 1994 the fears about spying were such that Aum's leadership had started interrogating and using truth drugs on members whom they suspected (almost certainly erroneously) of being 'spies'. In one case in 1994, a person so accused was interrogated, deemed to have been a spy, and then killed on Asahara's orders. Asahara and four devotees have been charged for that case[15]

The second reason why defections were so abhorred was rooted in Aum's view of the world beyond its borders as evil. In leaving Aum and returning to the outside world, the defector was in effect considered to be descending into certain doom and spiritual destruction. The term used in Aum for leaving the movement was *gekō* (going down),[16] a term that implies descent into lower realms. This concept was closely linked to Aum's beliefs about the transmigration of souls and of rebirths in different realms.

According to Aum, the universe was multi-dimensional, consisting of various realms: the realm of desire, the realm of form and the realm of non-form, each of which was subdivided into a number of different spiritual levels. Humans exist in the realm of form, which is divided into six levels, the lowest of which are various hells. Above the human world and the realm of form is the realm of non-form, which can only be entered by those with high levels of consciousness and spiritual practice. Souls transmigrate at death and can ascend or descend through the realms depending on the deeds of the person in this life. Such movement was determined by the laws of karma (*karuma no hōsoku*), a critical concept in Asahara's teachings which refers to one's accumulated merits and demerits in life, and to how this balance of merits and demerits (or good deeds and sins) determines the realm in which one is reborn.[17]

Such beliefs about transmigration, rebirth and different realms of existence were present in Aum from early in its development and reflect some of its most constant and central doctrinal attitudes. In Aum's view, the task of the religious practitioner was to accrue spiritual merits and raise his/her consciousness so as to be able to ascend into higher realms. At death the spirits of the dead would be judged and, depending on their karmic status, would either be allowed rebirth into higher realms of consciousness or be cast into the lower realms and hells. It was Aum's belief that Asahara, as a supremely enlightened being, could intercede on behalf of the spirits at death and help them attain a better rebirth.[18] Hence it was one of the attractions of the movement that it offered members the hope of salvation in the form of escape from such a fate after death, provided they engaged in spiritual practices under its guidance.[19] However, although it offered its followers the hope of ascent to higher realms, Aum had an essentially negative view of transmigration, for it saw the most likely path at death to be a downward one to the lower realms, rather than one leading up to higher stages of consciousness.

This negative view was rooted in Aum's views of the laws of karma. This notion has played an important role in the thinking of many Japanese new religions of Buddhist persuasion. While karma can imply the potential for a better rebirth and have positive connotations, it has more often been conceived of in negative terms by the Japanese new religions. For example Agonshū, to which Asahara belonged for a period in the early 1980s and from which he imbibed many ideas, talks of the necessity of 'cutting karma' (*karuma o kiru*) and of 'escape from the bonds of karma' (*karuma kara no dasshutsu*), terms which imply an inherently negative view of karmic forces.[20] Aum's view was, if anything, even more negative: the power of the evil passions (*bonnō*) and the corrupt nature of the human world meant that simply living in this world caused one to absorb all manner of negative data and impulses from it – influences that invariably dragged one downwards. The normative patterns of the laws of karma, then, led downwards into lower realms at death while retribution for evil deeds could also strike people in this life.[21] This bleak view of the negative aspects of karma and of the corrupting ways of the world became progressively more pronounced in Asahara's teaching: in sermons in 1993 and 1994, for example, he preached that Japan was swamped with bad 'data' (*dēta*) a term that Asahara used to refer to the general cultural and social impulses of society, which were intrinsically evil and corrupting. Hence, just by living in society one accumulated bad karmic forces which would inevitably cause one to fall into the three miserable realms or hells (*sanakushu*, the realms of hell, of animal spirits and of hungry ghosts) at death.[22] The way to avoid this and to attain the salvation of a higher rebirth was through spiritual and ascetic practices that erased the negative effects of karma and enabled one to avoid retribution for one's deeds. According to Aum, it was only through devotion to Asahara as guru that people could avoid this fate.

Thus leaving Aum and returning to the 'corrupt' world was tanta-mount to embarking on a journey directly to the lowest hells. This was an especially critical issue by the time of Ochi's planned defection because Aum had increasingly come to believe that a final apocalyptic war would soon erupt to destroy much of humanity. Asahara's sermons were, in 1993 and 1994, infused with dramatic images of Armageddon (a term that entered Aum's vocabulary in autumn 1988), which, he prophesied, would engulf the world before the end of the century. At this final hour only Aum's highly trained spiritual practitioners who were capable of eradicating their karma could survive.[23]

Asahara's special role as guru and source of spiritual nourishment was founded not just in the fact that he had established the movement and developed its doctrines, but in his status, according to Aum, as a wholly liberated being and spiritual teacher who could guide his followers to liberation and transmit spiritual energy and power to them.

As well as guiding their meditation and interceding on their behalf after death, Asahara could supposedly assist his followers to avoid or shed their bad karma and acquire positive transcendent powers through mystically charged rituals of initiation. These involved the transfer of the guru's powers and consciousness to the disciple. Initiation, according to Asahara, was 'a special method of practice which causes the transfer of energy in those mysterious areas which we cannot understand simply by listening to or studying the Buddhist law (*hō*), or that changes one's consciousness.'[24] Initiation, besides being critical to Aum's doctrines and practices and reinforcing the bonds between disciple and teacher, proved to be one of the most controversial aspects of Aum. It provided a major source of income: followers paid large sums for their initiations and this fact, as well as the forms some of these initiations took – including drinking quantities of Asahara's blood – became widely reported in the media and led to criticisms and charges that Aum was exploiting its members. Initiation, in other words, was a central element in Aum's system and practices, but one that generated controversy and exacerbated the tensions between the movement and its critics.

Through asceticism, initiations and devotion to their guru, Aum followers sought to purify themselves of the corrupting influences of the world, to cast off their karma (*karuma otoshi*) and to remove the corrupt 'data' that had accumulated in their minds, replacing it with the positive energy and pure, uncorrupted data, which came from and were manifested in the mind of the guru.[25] This principle was affirmed through the concept of 'cloning the guru' (*guru no kurōnka o suru*),[26] in which devotees sought to reprogram their minds by erasing their inherent thought patterns and replacing them with those of the guru. They did this through such practices as fasting, meditating, listening repeatedly to tapes of Asahara chanting prayers and delivering sermons, or wearing a form of electronic headgear known as the PSI ('Perfect Salvation Initiation') unit, which had been developed by Aum technicians in 1994 in order to implant Asahara's thought patterns into the disciple.

While Aum members who have used these PSI units have stated that these techniques had positive, calming effects on them,[27] such activities were seen in a very different light by the media and general public. After the police raids and extensive media coverage of Aum in the spring of 1995, the images of Aum devotees wearing PSI units on their heads, coupled with evidence that Aum had utilised excessive saturation practices to 'clone' the guru on to the disciple, gave rise to allegations that Aum had 'brainwashed' its devotees into becoming mere pawns of their master.[28] In reality the situation was not as simple as the charges of 'brainwashing' (itself a problematic concept that has been widely critiqued in academic studies of new religions) would imply.[29] Members had willingly engaged in such practices because they wanted to break free from the effects and influences of a society they regarded as corrupt, while there also existed within Aum an enormous pressure to devote oneself wholly to the guru, and an extremely paranoid mentality which forced disciples to look inward and construct a new reality for themselves based around Aum's principles and its guru's ways of thinking.

In order to shed karma and escape from the influences of this world, Aum members engaged in severe ascetic practices that involved harsh bodily mortification. The body was considered to be polluted and in need of cleansing before the spirit could ascend to higher realms.[30] This belief in the polluted nature of the body thus paralleled Aum's beliefs in the spiritually polluted and corrupt nature of the phenomenal world: both were in need of spiritual cleansing. Testing the body to its limits and overcoming its physical shortcomings were important activities in the movement, testimony to the spiritual attainment and powers of the practitioner, who acquired higher status in the movement as a result. Those who were successful in such ascetic practices eventually formed a hierarchy in Aum, marked out by special forms of dress and titles. Ascetic practice thus was important to Aum not merely as a means of attaining liberation but as a symbol of its members' spiritual superiority over other beings. It was also central to Aum's self-assured belief that it was different from, and superior to, other religious groups, which it harshly criticised for their failure to perform ascetic practices.[31]

This attitude contributed to the development of a culture of coercive asceticism in Aum whereby those who were reluctant to perform ascetic practices were forced to do so (for their own sake, according to Aum's logic). This type of thinking appears to have developed in the second half of 1988, for it was at this time that people close to Asahara who shied from austerities were 'encouraged' to do them. Potential defectors were considered to be even more in need of such encouragement, since their apparent desire to leave Aum represented a direct rejection of Aum's belief system with its absolute faith in the guru and his capacity to lead all to salvation. Such potential defectors were in danger of acquiring the negative karma of denying the truth, and were considered to be deluded, captivated by the evils of the material world and hence headed for the hells. They had to be rescued through force if necessary: moreover, because they had in effect challenged Asahara's authority as the guru by trying to leave, they also had to be punished for their sins.

THE PUNISHMENT AND DEATH OF OCHI NAOKI

This was the fate that befell Ochi who, by expressing his desire to leave Aum was confessing to a grave karmic sin. Asahara ordered that Ochi be made to undergo karmic cleansing through ascetic practices, and this order was readily carried out by Asahara's willing deputies led by Ōuchi. The practice enforced on Ochi was that of inverted suspension: having his legs bound with rope and being suspended upside down. This was a form of torture that had been used to force Christian missionaries to renounce their faith (or, if they did not, to undergo a slow death) in Japan in the late sixteeenth and early seventeenth centuries.[32] It is not, as far as I know, used as an ascetic practice in Japan,[33] other than in Aum. Ochi was not the only person to undergo this practice, for as Ōuchi's court testimony shows, some seven or eight others were also doing it at the same time. Normally, it appears that the period of suspension used in Aum was around 90 minutes, with rest periods in between: however, in order to punish Ochi, Asahara ordered the periods of suspension to be far longer. When Ochi attempted to struggle, Ōuchi and another follower bound him more tightly around the hands as well, and left him suspended.

Some time later, it appears, Ōuchi was summoned by a fellow disciple who told her Ochi had ceased breathing: Ōuchi then called on Ishii for help and she, in order not to disturb the other practitioners in the room, announced that Ochi had entered *samadhi* (enlightenment). In Buddhist terms *samadhi* equates to the cessation of desire, but (in an example of how Aum adapted Buddhist ideas within its own frames of reference) in Aum it was equated with the ability to cease breathing for extended periods of time while the mind and spirit continued to function, as it were, without the need of the physical body. Aum, in other words, equated death (i.e. the stopping of breathing and the demise of the physical body) with *samadhi*, or enlightenment: indeed, in various Aum publications the Japanese ideogram for death *shi* was given the same reading as *samadi*.[34] Hence death itself, as the cessation of desire and attachment to the body, contained the potential for transformation to higher states of consciousness – a notion that contributed to Aum's seemingly cavalier attitude to the lives of those whose paths crossed it.

Ochi had indeed died, and so his body was cut down and moved to Ishii's room. Later Ishii informed the other practitioners present that Ochi had recovered consciousness and had left the commune to return to secular life (*gekō*). She then had his body incinerated and his ashes flushed away down a drain. Since disposing of a body without proper legal procedures is a crime in Japan, Ishii was charged with this felony: in February 1999 she was found guilty and sentenced to three years and eight months in prison. Ironically Ōuchi, who actually bound Ochi and contributed directly to his death, has not been arraigned because the lack of a body means that the cause of death cannot be established. Hence it has been deemed impossible, in Japanese legal terms, to determine the extent of her culpability.[35]

Ōuchi, shocked at an incident which had happened under her auspices, took counsel with Asahara, who told her to forget the matter. She then spoke with Jōyu Fumihiro, who was one of the highest placed figures in Aum (like Ishii, he was one of the five members who had reached the rank of *seitaishi*) and who, in the days after the Tokyo subway attack, became well known in Japan as Aum's spokesman dealing with the media. Jōyu reassured Ōuchi by telling her that while it was best for people to achieve liberation while alive, it was not at all a bad thing for them to be liberated, as Ochi had been, through dying in a practice initiated by the guru (Asahara): indeed, Jōyu informed her, this was a case where the practice of *poa* had occurred.[36]

The term *poa* (also written as *powa* or *phowa*)[37] is a critical one in Aum, and like many of the other concepts introduced here, it will feature throughout this book. It was, according to Aum, a concept imbibed from Tibetan Buddhism relating to transmigration and rebirth. While the soul's passage to different realms after death was based on karmic merits and demerits earned in life, it could be assisted to attain a higher spiritual realm through the transference of spiritual merit by the living (in particular advanced spiritual practitioners such as the guru).[38]

As guru, Asahara performed *poa* rituals for the recently departed, and there are various written accounts in which Aum disciples have spoken of Asahara's ability to perform this task. Iida Eriko, one of Asahara's earliest disciples, for example, spoke of how, when he became aware

17

that a female disciple had died in an accident, Asahara entered into a state of meditation through which he was able to guide the deceased's spirit to a higher spiritual realm.[39] He also conducted *poa* seminars to train his disciples to do the same and to develop in them the capacity to intercede on behalf of the recently departed. To be able to conduct *poa* rituals was thus a hallmark of advanced Aum practitioners.

Again, various testimonies by Aum members show how deep the beliefs in the efficacy of this practice were. Claiming that it was a sign of the liberated being (*gedatsusha*) that he could eradicate the bad karma of a deceased spirit and lead it to a better rebirth, the Aum devotee Kanai Ryōko has recorded how Milarepa (the holy name, taken from the name of the great Tibetan Buddhist teacher, of Niimi Tomomitsu, a leading figure in Aum's hierarchy) had performed a *poa* ritual for her father when he died of cancer in an Aum hospital facility. Kanai expressed her gratitude to Niimi for the compassion he showed in doing this and stated that the ritual had eased her father's transition to the next world while assuaging her own grief at her father's demise.[40] In many ways Niimi's compassionate performance of this ritual is illustrative of the paradoxical nature of a movement that sought to save its followers from falling into the hells yet ended up killing them. As subsequent investigations have disclosed, the compassionate Niimi who was able to soothe the grief of a young woman whose father had just died, was deeply implicated in Aum's crimes: he had, for example, been one of those who interrogated and killed the aforementioned 'spy' executed in Aum in 1994.

In the ways in which it was used here, the concept of *poa* might appear little different from standard Buddhist practices of performing ritual services for the recently dead to assist them in the passage to the world beyond, and as ritual intercessions of merit transfer between the living and the dead. Such practices are a staple element in traditional Japanese Buddhism, one of whose main social roles has been in caring for the dead and the recently bereaved.[41] However, whatever nuances and meanings *poa* might originally have had in Tibetan Buddhism, or whatever similarities it might have had to standard Japanese ritual practices, in Aum's interpretation it came to take on other, more sinister, nuances. Not only was it used in the context of intercession after death: it also acquired a more active dimension, signifying intercession in life to save people from acquiring further negative karma that would hinder them at death. In other words, *poa* came to mean not simply an act of merit transfer after death but a practice of intercession before-hand in order to 'save' the unworthy by 'transforming' their spirits so they could enter a higher spiritual realm. More bluntly, it was used in Aum as a metaphor for killing or having someone killed.

The theoretical justification for this process was that by interceding in a person's life in such ways, the guru was erasing that person's bad karma and preventing him or her from accumulating more of it, which would inevitably occur if s/he continued to live in this corrupt world. In cases where the spirit would (in Aum's view) otherwise fall into the hells at death because of the courses of action the person concerned was following in this world, there was 'no other way' than to *poa* them (*poa shika nai*), a term used on more than one occasion by Asahara when ordering the deaths of those who had angered him. In such terms the term came to indicate, within the framework of Asahara's thinking, the 'right' of the guru to perform this service on others for the sake of their souls.[42]

Such 'killing for salvation' became a dominant activity within Aum, directed at external enemies and internal dissidents alike. The concept of *poa* also, as the Ochi case shows, was used to put a good light on unforeseen deaths and to suggest that people such as Ochi had benefited *because* they had died in ascetic practice ordered by the guru. It could, in other words, be used to cover up, explain away or put a good gloss on accidental and unforeseen deaths.

THE OCHI INCIDENT: THEMES AND MEANINGS

The death of Ochi Naoki only came to light some time after the Tokyo subway attack because Ōuchi Sanae, under arrest on other charges, confessed the incident to her lawyer. Bizarre as the case is – a member of a religious movement bound and hung upside down by colleagues supposedly intent on saving his soul and assisting in his spiritual development – it was only one in an extraordinary series of deeds and activities carried out by Aum. The incident contains numerous motifs that are relevant for the study of the movement and the affair: it demonstrates, for example, how Aum's attitudes, beliefs and practices created the circumstances in which brutality could develop and flourish, and in which violence and death became part of its spiritual landscape. It also shows that Aum's acts of violence and the disregard for human life were not just directed outside the movement at the Japanese public.

This was a movement that killed its own members when they fell foul of the expectations or incurred the wrath of their leaders. Indeed, it is quite possible that the number of deaths that occurred inside Aum exceeded those caused by Aum outside the movement. Ochi's was not the first such death. The first, as far as is known, was Majima Terayuki, whose accidental death while doing austerities ordered by Asahara in autumn 1988 played a major part in triggering Aum's criminal activities (see below, Chapter 5), and there is evidence, backed by stories from repentant members such as Ōuchi, that there were several, and perhaps dozens more who, like Ochi and Majima, died accidentally or, like the 'spy' mentioned earlier, were killed deliberately. Hayashi Ikuo, a doctor and former Aum devotee now serving a life sentence for crimes including the subway attack, has testified that at least three devotees had died during the 'Christ initiation' used in Aum from mid-1994 onwards, which involved the ingestion of the hallucinogenic drug LSD along with repeated immersions in hot water. In all, according to Egawa Shōko, as many as 46 Aum members may have died in various ways inside Aum.[43]

The manner in which Ochi died exhibits the stark and brutal attitude to life held by Aum's leaders by this period. Having died unexpectedly, Ochi was disposed of in a degrading, subhuman way: no longer a potentially enlightened being or part of Aum's self-proclaimed mission of spreading religious truths to the world, he lost all human dignity, dying bound and trussed, his body burnt and ashes flushed away. While this was of course done to cover up the evidence of his death, the incident also showed the callous view of Aum's hierarchy towards those who had fallen short in the tasks, assignments and austerities set them. If they failed to measure up to the demands placed on them, or failed to show sufficient faith, they could be cast aside with impunity. This almost casual perception of the disposability of people was certainly underpinned by the emphasis placed on the inevitability of death and the imminence of a final cataclysm that would decimate humanity.

The incident illustrates many of the concepts and ideas that played a part in the internal and external violence of Aum. Through the incident, for example, we are able to get an insight into Aum's views of transmigration and karma, its polarised worldview, its emphasis on extreme asceticism as a means of escape from the repercussions and downward momentum of karmic law, its belief in the polluted nature of the body and of society, and its emphasis on the absolute authority of the guru. Added to these were other such vital beliefs and concepts as *poa* and the imminence of a final destructive war, which played their part in developing a framework in which Aum came to use violence and see it as justified. One can also see in the incident (and in the concepts that helped frame and bring it about) evidence of a siege mentality, fired by fears of fragmentation resulting from defections, that had become prominent in Aum in later years, and in which Aum's leaders were gripped by a sense of paranoia and by the belief that they were surrounded by enemies who were persecuting and conspiring against the movement. Aum had by the summer of 1993 created its own thought world, beliefs and modes of operation that set it apart from and in antithesis to mainstream society whose values it rejected.

The incident also draws attention to the role of Asahara, who, as the leader of Aum, bears the prime responsibility for the affair. It was he who established Aum and its doctrines, produced the legitimations it used to underpin its violence, and ordered his disciples to go out and kill or to commit barbaric acts such as the punishment meted out to Ochi Naoki. The role of Asahara will naturally be discussed at length in this book. Yet, as this incident illustrates, Asahara did not act alone: his disciples, and especially those in the upper echelons of Aum, were willing and active participants. They were ready to carry out his orders and supported his doctrines which turned murder into a form of salvation, and they were willing to treat their fellow beings with cruel contempt as a result.

It was they, too, who enabled Asahara to become a religious leader by giving him their support and unflinching devotion. While Asahara, like the leaders of many new religions, was clearly charismatic and inspirational in the eyes of his followers, it was they who reinforced and in a sense helped create this charisma through their support. As has been widely recognised in studies of religious behaviour and of the relationships between followers and leaders, charisma is always a 'relational term'[44] that is dependent not merely or primarily on the nature and person of those who assert themselves as religious leaders, but on the ways in which such claims are received and supported by those that follow them. It was because Asahara was able to attract a coterie of highly committed followers who regarded him as their guru and who gave him their unstinting devotion, that he was able to function as a religious leader. As the Ochi incident shows, it was through the activities of his followers and disciples that the seeds of violence inherent in Asahara's teaching were nurtured and blossomed. The willingness of Ōuchi and her helpers to bind and tie a struggling man, of Ishii to dispose of the body and explain away the deceased's absence to other practitioners, and of Jōyu to provide an interpretation of the death that absolved Aum of any hint of guilt and to turn the deed into a meritorious act, all show not only how readily Asahara's disciples went along with and hence reinforced his teachings, but how they actively set out to enact them, even at the cost of the lives of their fellow beings and fellow practitioners.

The affair would not have occurred without the complicit activities of the members of Aum, and particularly those who had ascended through

Aum's hierarchy to form an elite group close to Asahara. This inner elite were members of the *kanbu*, the administrative and executive group who implemented Asahara's orders and who advised him and ran Aum. They had ascended Aum's hierarchy because of their ascetic attainments and their extreme loyalty in a movement that regarded absolute devotion to the guru as a central tenet of faith. They had been rewarded with various ranks, titles and holy names for this, as well as other privileges not accorded to ordinary followers.[45] It was this group of people, such as Ishii, Hayashi Ikuo and Niimi Tomomitsu, who carried out the various crimes of which the movement stands accused, and who put Asahara's orders into action. As such, their role will be considered in this book, as will the attitudes of Asahara's followers in general, and the reasons why they chose to follow and give credence to Asahara and bestow charismatic authority on him.

MURDER ON THE SUBWAY: 20 MARCH 1995

The themes evident in the Ochi incident were manifested in Aum's most infamous act, the subway attack of 20 March 1995, in which five Aum devotees boarded five morning rush-hour trains scheduled to converge around Kasumigaseki, the subway station close to the National Diet and various ministries as well as the National Police Agency headquarters. Each devotee carried a sharpened umbrella and plastic bags filled with liquid poisons. Each stabbed the bags with their umbrellas so as to release the poisonous gases on the trains: the plan was to bring chaos to the city and to inflict as much damage as possible at the heart of the Japanese government and police force. The method of delivery of the gas was rather crude and the attack itself and the materials used were hastily planned and prepared. Although the devotees who were engaged in making chemical and other weapons for Aum have been depicted in the media as highly trained and brilliant scientists, the reality, as the subway attack shows, was somewhat different.

The attack had been organised over the two previous days, during which time two Aum devotees, Endō Seiichi and Tsuchiya Masami, who both had some training in chemistry, had made a quantity of the nerve gas sarin – a substance gas that had been previously used by Aum in the central Japanese town of Matsumoto on 27 June 1994, killing seven people and injuring many others. Evidence subsequently emerged to show that it had been involved in trying to make sarin for some years before the attack. Sarin had, in fact, featured prominently in Aum's consciousness from spring 1993 onwards, when Asahara began to claim

22

that Japan was beset by enemies that were conspiring to destroy it, and that the country should arm itself with sarin to defend itself.[46] He subsequently also claimed that the gas was being used against him and his movement by an evil conspiracy that included the Japanese government and that was intent on destroying him and Aum.[47]

Thankfully, because of its hasty preparation and Aum's technological deficiencies, the sarin that was produced in March 1995 was only around 30 per cent pure – a fact that saved the lives of several thousand travellers, for sarin in its pure concentrated form is highly lethal. The damage was cleared quite rapidly and later on the afternoon of 20 March the Tokyo subway was running at full capacity again. Even so, the results were horrific, with 12 people dead and thousands injured, both physically and, in the long term, also emotionally. Even two years after the raids, a sizeable percentage of the victims reported continuing lethargy, eye problems and other physical repercussions, while many still suffered from emotional distress and fears.[48]

The graphic images of the events on the Tokyo subway were rapidly disseminated around the world. Despite the fact that no-one claimed responsibility for the act, widespread talk and unofficial briefings in Japan immediately suggested Aum's involvement.[49] This general suspicion appeared to be confirmed two days later when, on 22 March, massive military-style raids were carried out on Aum premises throughout Japan, involving thousands of law enforcement agents wearing gas-masks and carrying batons and riot shields. The size and scope of the raids suggested a degree of advance planning that appeared to pre-date the Tokyo attack, a point that was later confirmed.

Indeed, Aum had been under grave suspicion for some time of being involved in the Matsumoto attack, and newspaper reports at the beginning of January 1995 had publicly broadcast this fact.[50] There was widespread speculation that a police raid on Aum was imminent, especially after the abduction of a 68-year-old public notary Kariya Kiyoshi in broad daylight from a Tokyo street on 28 February 1995. Kariya had been engaged in a dispute with Aum relating to his sister, a wealthy Aum devotee who had donated much money to the movement but who, fearing it was intent on taking everything she had, had subsequently decided to leave and had gone into hiding. Kariya was abducted because Aum's leaders believed that he knew where his sister was, and wanted to extract this fact from him. He was taken to Kamikuishiki, where, in the course of interrogations over the whereabouts of his sister, he was injected with drugs intended to make him talk but which, instead, caused his death. His body was then, like Ochi's, incinerated and hastily disposed of.

Evidence surrounding the abduction led the police to Aum and, while the movement was under suspicion of involvement with chemical weapons and with the Matsumoto attack, it was in connection to the Kariya kidnap that a warrant for raids on Aum had been served. Whether the raids had been specifically planned for earlier than 22 March is unclear, although various journalists' accounts show that there was a general expectation of a raid on Aum occurring on or around 20 March.[51] It appears also that Aum's leaders had learnt of this impending raid and that the attack on the subway was a pre-emptive strike aimed at stopping the police action by throwing Tokyo into mass confusion.

The subway attack, then, was not planned as part of a co-ordinated strategy of violence but as an ad hoc preventative measure designed to protect Aum and safeguard what it saw as its spiritual mission. The attack demonstrated with stark clarity just how ready Aum was to carry out acts of mass murder to protect itself and to further its own ends. The evidence uncovered in the raids on the movement illustrated this point further, showing that over a number of years (dating back, it would appear, to the spring of 1990) it had been engaged in attempts to produce various weapons of mass destruction, from biological weapons such as anthrax and botulism, to chemical ones such as nerve gases, which it had used not only in the mass attacks in Matsumoto and Tokyo, but also in attacks on individuals who were seen as opponents of the movement.[52]

Although Aum's leaders initially denied all involvement in the attack, gradually various members of the movement began to confess and to provide the police with enough evidence to develop a comprehensive picture of violence and criminality which included not only murders and abductions, but also extortion and forced detention, and the manufacture of weapons of mass destruction as well as illegal hallucinogenic and other drugs that were used in Aum's religious initiations. Eventually over 180 members of Aum Shinrikyō were arrested and charged with a variety of crimes, including murder and conspiracy to commit murder, in a litany of criminal activity and behaviour that extended back several years. Some have been convicted and sentenced to long periods in prison: Asahara's wife, Tomoko, for example, has received a seven-year prison sentence for her involvement in the killing of a dissident member; Hayashi Ikuo, the first of the subway attackers to be sentenced, has received a life sentence; and Okazaki Kazuaki, who participated in the murder of the Sakamoto family in November 1989 (see below, Chapter 5) was, on 23 October 1998, sentenced to death for that crime. Many others are still on trial and it is likely that further death sentences might be passed on several of those accused of murder.[53]

Asahara was arrested on 16 May 1995, and charged eventually with 17 criminal activities, including conspiracy to murder in the Tokyo and Matsumoto attacks, and involvement in the murder of various other enemies and dissident members of Aum. His trial began on 24 April 1996 and is expected to continue for a decade or more as the Japanese legal system is extremely slow. As of August 1999 Asahara had made over 120 appearances in court, and given that his lawyers are closely challenging or questioning every piece of evidence and every witness, it would appear that several hundred more appearances will be necessary before the trial can be concluded. The verdict, however, appears to be in no doubt. Japanese court cases invariably end with guilty verdicts, and given the weight of evidence against him, the death sentence seems inevitable. Although he has largely denied involvement or guilt in the network of crimes of which he is accused, many of his closest associates have made full confessions that have implicated him specifically in ordering the murders and of implementing the plans to make weapons.

A POLITICAL TERRORIST GROUP OR A CRIMINAL ORGANISATION?

The shocking nature of Aum's crimes appeared (certainly in the im-mediate aftermath of the sarin attack) to be incomprehensible except, perhaps, when viewed through the lens of political terrorism and of criminal extortion and organised crime. The images of bombs on aeroplanes and in public places have become part of the conceptual understandings of our age and have made us accustomed to politically motivated terrorism, so perhaps it was inevitable that an immediate assumption was that Aum was primarily a political terror group with criminal orientations. Other crimes perpetrated by Aum, such as its apparently extortionate extraction of funds from Kariya Kiyoshi's sister, made it look like other well-known organisations centred on criminality and bent on extortion and power. The revelations of Aum's wrongdoings make it hard *not* to regard it as a movement with criminal attitudes and behaviour. However, this criminality was underpinned and in a sense created by its religious orientations and views, rather than the other way around. In other words, Asahara did not create a religious move-ment primarily as a stratagem for getting rich, running a criminal organisation, achieving political power or carrying out political terrorism, but virtually the reverse: criminality and terror emerged in Aum out of its primary orientations as a religion, a point already illustrated by the account of the death of Ochi Naoki and the context in which it occurred.

NERVE CENTRES AND SYMBOLIC MEANINGS

It would be erroneous to consider Aum primarily as political in nature, even though Aum did engage sporadically in the world of politics, disastrously contesting political elections in 1990. Asahara had dreams and delusions of grandeur, envisioning himself as a spiritual leader who would emerge to lead the world after Armageddon. His view of the world was centred on the notion of spiritual leadership, and Aum had established, in June 1994, an 'alternative government' with distinctly theocratic orientations and with Asahara at it apex, styled as the 'sacred master/ emperor' (*shinsei hōō*). Nonetheless Aum's opposition to the existing order was expressed not in political terms through images of a conflict between political forces with differing agendas of how to organise society, but in religious ones, through a confrontation between the opposing moral forces of good and evil. In this confrontation Asahara visualised himself as leading the forces of good in a final war to exterminate evil and to establish a new spiritual realm in a scenario that was clearly located on a religious rather than a political axis: he was a sacred hero and messiah with a mission to save the world. Viewed from within its polarised worldview, Aum was beset by enemies who represented the forces of evil and who sought to destroy it. Some of these opposing forces were, as will be seen in later chapters, real, such as groups that had formed in opposition to Aum's activities, including the parents of Aum members and people who lived close to Aum centres. However many were imaginary.

In Asahara's teachings these conflicts and confrontations with his (real or imaginary) opponents were not placed in a political framework. Aum's actual political orientations and intentions in the present world were obscure; especially after its election debacle it had largely turned its back on the wider world, and expressed few if any political opinions. Nor did it appear to have any form of political strategy, agenda or vision for the new order that would appear after the final war. Moreover, unlike many political terror groups, it did not carry out violent acts and then claim responsibility for them so as to create publicity for a political cause or agenda. Nor did it express any specific political goals or aims in the name of which it carried out its attacks. Although the subway attack contained a dramatic symbolism, its violence was of an unrestrained type, potentially capable of killing massive numbers of people – a type of action more commonly associated, as Bruce Hoffman has argued, with religious groups that resort to violence in the furtherance of a religiously based agenda, than with overtly political terror movements.[54]

While the subway attack certainly expressed a dramatic political symbolism, it was a symbolism that was subsumed by a powerful religious message. At the centre of the sarin attack was Kasumigaseki subway station, which is close by the Japanese National Diet building and several key government agencies and ministries. It therefore stands at the nerve centre of Japanese public life, and one could suggest that the use of nerve gases to paralyse the nerve centre of Japan was thus an act highly charged with symbolic meanings.[55]

According to an Aum magazine published very shortly before the attack, Kasumigaseki station and the nearby Nagatachō station were deep enough to be used as a shelter in case of war. As a safe shelter beneath the Diet building, the station could be used to protect the politicians and senior members of the government in the case of nuclear attack.[56] Here, too, its symbolism was not lost on Aum, as the following comment by Toyoda Tōru (who, barely three months later was to be one of those who planted sarin on the subway) makes clear. Speaking in an Aum radio broadcast on 25 December 1994, Toyoda stated that it would be impossible for individuals to survive Armageddon, for any means of defending oneself required resources beyond the scope of individuals, while the Japanese government

> is far from being able to protect us, as you can see from the fact that only the subway station near the Diet Building has enough depth to be used as a shelter. When we calmly consider this situation, we find that the best thing to do is renounce worldly life and become a monk or nun of an organization with a serious approach to salvation.[57]

The *potential* political implications of this statement are striking. That the only place where one could be physically safe from cataclysmic attacks, according to Aum, is under the government's own buildings, suggests that the government had made a safe shelter for itself and did not really care about its citizens. Perhaps more striking is the fact that this comment, in referring to the subway station near the Diet building, is speaking of the place which bore the focus of Aum's March attack, viz. Kasumigaseki station. Hence the station stood as a symbol not just of the nerve-centre of government but of the lack of regard by the government and the political and bureaucratic elite for its own citizens. Moreover, an attack on that location could make a telling point. If an attack could be carried out in the one place supposedly safe from the ravages of a nuclear cataclysm, what would this mean both for the government's own sense of reassurance, and for the sense of well-being and trust its citizens could have in public safety in general?[58]

However, despite the potential political symbolism of an inadequate government and of a strike at its nerve-centre, the dominant message in Toyoda's statement is religious. There is no political call to arms, no cry to replace the government with a more competent, caring one. Rather, he affirms that the *only* possible course of action left is a religious one, of renouncing the world and becoming a monk or nun in a religious order (presumably, although not explicitly stated, in Aum). If the attack on the subway had political symbolism as well as practical intentions, it was produced by a movement whose orientations were primarily religious and whose notions of struggle with the existing order were framed in and conditioned by religious images.

A STUDY IN RELIGIOUS VIOLENCE

Aum was registered as a religious organisation in Japan and, as such, had satisfied the authorities that it exhibited the requisite attributes of a religion. As commentators such as Michael Pye have subsequently discussed, it manifested various elements that are widely recognised as characteristics of religions: for example, views of the nature of the world and of the destiny of individuals within it; practices designed to advance the spiritual consciousness of adherents; concepts of death and what lies beyond; a sense of belonging to a specific community with a spiritual purpose and centred on a leader who was considered to wield sacred authority.[59]

Aum's behaviour was founded in its religious characteristics, which underpinned the movement's self-constructed visions in which it saw itself as morally above the temporal concerns of the world and its legal systems, a beacon of spiritual truth surrounded by the 'cesspit' of the mundane world. Its worldview was centred on religious images, concepts and practices. In order to discuss the Aum affair, it is necessary to recognise this, and to consider Aum's activities as crimes committed by a religious movement in the course of its existence as a religion, and in some cases, in order to protect itself and preserve what it saw as its religious mission. In describing and analysing the worldview that formed the background to Aum's crimes, and that provided the mental space within which they could develop and be committed, I am treating the Aum affair as a case of religious violence: a series of linked criminal acts, many of them producing or centred on violent behaviour, carried out by a religious movement and spurred by religious motifs and images.

This approach may not find favour with everyone. There may be some people who, from their particular backgrounds and attitudes to the field of religion, will not be happy at my discussing Aum Shinrikyō in such a way, as a *religious* movement. In the immediate aftermath of the sarin attack, there were some scholars who felt that Aum could not have been a religious movement, because of its recourse to violence and because of its apparent aspirations to form a government, and because of the sheer enormity of its actions.[60] Some may argue that religion is an inherently 'good' thing, and that hence any deviance from such goodness and purity cannot be 'true' religion. This type of argument was implicit in much of the Japanese media treatment of the affair and in subsequent debates which questioned whether such movements should be termed 'religions' or, instead, be labelled 'cults' and considered as false religions.[61]

Such attitudes, however, are based on a narrow and one-dimensional view of religion and on value judgements that are incapable of being academically or intellectually sustained. Religion, I would argue, is an inclusive, value-neutral category that is certainly capable of containing and expressing 'good' elements: it does not, however, necessarily *have* to contain them, and nor is it limited to them. There is nothing in this inclusive nature which prevents religion from having violent, bad or negative qualities and it is important, in my view, not merely to recognise this point but also to pay attention to the potentially 'bad' qualities of religion if any serious analysis that takes account of its multi-dimensional nature is to be undertaken. This point has been made by David C. Rapoport in his statement that religion may 'have an *essential* violence-reducing element, but it also has a violence-producing dimension, one that is *equally* essential'.[62] Shimazono Susumu, in his analysis of Aum Shinrikyō, has equally drawn attention to the religious motifs and doctrines that underpinned Aum's activities, and has discussed the affair in terms of the potential of religion to generate violence.[63] Brian K. Smith makes this point tellingly also when he states that the

> insistence on the ironic and conciliatory nature of religion ... is disingenuous, shallow, and hopelessly myopic in light both of recently scholarly work on the subject and of the historical and ongoing fact of religious violence. To dismiss the latter as merely a perversion of 'true' religion is simultaneously naïve and arrogant. Religious violence, in all its many forms, must be accounted for *as religious* and not merely wished away as external to some self-proclaimed ideal form of the true nature of religion.[64]

Mark Juergensmeyer has emphasised this view in different terms when, in stating that 'violence has always been endemic to religion',[65] he points to the prevalence of symbols of violence, destruction and death in religious traditions: the crucifixion images of Christianity (which, as will be seen, also came into play in Aum Shinrikyō), the symbols of martyrdom in Islam, and the wars and battles narrated in Hindu epic myths 'indicate that in virtually every tradition images of violence occupy as central a place as portrayals of non-violence'.[66]

If the images of violence are normally symbolic, and have an important preventative element, allowing, as Juergensmeyer puts it 'the urges to conquer to be channelled into the harmless rituals of drama',[67] they also can become all too real: the cosmic war of good and evil as manifested in images and epics can become real war. As Juergensmeyer again notes, there is a link between the images of cosmic struggle and war on the symbolic level, and conflicts in the real world. The image of cosmic struggle as outlined in sacred texts and epics pits good against evil, truth against falsehood, faith against disbelief, and sacred order against profane disorder: in this epic struggle, truth, faith and goodness vanquish the disorders of the profane world and impose a sacred order on it. Such images of triumph and struggle can also be transposed on to the real world and articulated by religious leaders in the context of actual struggles that seek to impose a religious order on the world at large or on specific enemies. Juergensmeyer cites, for example, the rhetoric of militant religious leaders such as the Sikh militant Jernail Singh Bhindranwale, the Iranian leader Ayatollah Khomeini, Sri Lankan Buddhist leaders, and right-wing Jewish activists such as Rabbi Meir Kahane, all of whom have been associated with the commission of acts of war or violence that they have justified and legitimated in religious terms. What is common to all of these, he notes, is that the 'enemy' in this cosmic struggle is ill-defined and vague: it is the response to and the fight against the 'enemy' that is of paramount importance.[68]

This creation of a polarising set of opposites as a central image in religion and in religious violence is reiterated by Smith in his review of the work of Regina M. Schwartz,[69] who shows how the creation of self-identities through shared beliefs implicitly requires the formation of 'others' that are thus transformed into or depicted as an opposing force that worships (from the viewpoint of such created self-identities) 'false' gods. Smith comments that it is

> precisely the authority religion assumes and wields that accounts for both the production and legitimation of violence. Violence is authorized by religion because religion is inherently absolutist in the type of authorita-

tive claims it makes and the all-encompassing nature of its demands on its followers.[70]

These points can be seen in the all-encompassing demands of Aum on its members that led to Ochi's death and the doctrinal explanations that were produced to justify the enforced asceticism and to account for that death. Aum Shinrikyō was fired by images of a sacred, cosmic struggle which was transposed to the real world, and in which it envisioned itself as being attacked by, and needing to fight against, the forces of evil. It had a mission to eradicate bad karma so as to improve the spiritual nature of this world, and that mission became one of actual conflict. Aum created a series of others – enemies against whom it had to fight in order to achieve its mission and to impose its sacred order on an evil world. The precise identity of that enemy was ill-defined, although, as will be seen in later chapters, as Aum's conspiracy theories escalated, this category eventually grew to include anyone who was not a devotee of Aum. Aum framed its view of the world in terms similar to those cited above by Juergensmeyer, of a war between good and evil, a heroic struggle by the forces of truth with sacred mission to fight against the forces of falsehood. In this context it is appropriate to note that the word *shinri* in Aum's title means 'truth' and that the word *shinri* was used often by Asahara in a dual sense, referring simultaneously to his movement and the truth, which were, in Aum's worldview, inseparable. Fighting for the truth and fighting for Aum were thus one and the same thing.

As such the Aum Shinrikyō affair is shot through with images of religious struggle and violence, and this is the context in which it will be discussed in the ensuing chapters. In the next chapter I shall turn to the figure who was central to the construction of Aum's vision of religious struggle and conflict: its founder and leader, Asahara Shōkō.

尊師

2 Compassionate Cruelty and the Cosmic Struggle – The Life and Nature of Asahara Shōkō

THE GURU AND THE TRUTH

During an intensive ascetic training period in the summer of 1987 Ōuchi Sanae described how she saw various emissions of light and sensed the awakening of her astral body.[1] She felt numerous channels of spiritual energy opening within her body and, in a moment of profound spiritual awakening, she realised that within her dwelt the power of the buddhas, and that 'the guru is the truth' (*guru wa shinri desu*).[2]

At that moment, she stated, a feeling of true belief in the guru permeated her mind. Inspired by this breakthrough she persisted with her practice until, over the following weeks, she attained enlightenment (*satori*) and liberation (*gedatsu*). In Aum *satori* and *gedatsu* were states of spiritual awareness in which one transcended the mundane world. *Satori* indicated the state of awakening to the ephemeral nature of the material world, in which one became indifferent to its ways and recognised that true happiness can only come from within one's own mind. *Gedatsu* referred to states of absolute freedom and happiness that could only come about after the realisation of *satori*.[3] The guru that Ōuchi was speaking about was, of course, Asahara Shōkō, while the truth, *shinri*, referred both to the concept of absolute truth and to the movement itself, Aum Shinrikyō (or, as it referred to itself in English, Aum Supreme Truth).

Just as the story of the death of Ochi Naoki, in which Ōuchi was deeply involved, served as a fitting introduction to the world of Aum, its thoughts and its violence (see Chapter 1 above), so does her revelation linking the guru and the truth provide an appropriate introduction to this chapter and the next, in which I examine the origins of Aum Shinrikyō, the background and personality of its founder, and the orientations and teachings of his movement. These topics are inextricably interwoven in Aum's belief system, as Ōuchi's revelation indicates: the truth, the guru and Aum itself were synonymous.

In its focus on its founder and leader as the source of authority and spiritual inspiration, Aum was not dissimilar to the Japanese new religions in general, which have frequently been centred around charismatic figures whose teachings and experiences formed the basis of their doctrinal structures, practices and attitudes, and whose personalities and spiritual powers have inspired devotion in the movements they founded.[4] However, in talking of the synonymity of the guru and the truth, and its belief that absolute, total devotion and obedience to the guru were prerequisites of spiritual liberation, Aum took this emphasis on the power of the leader to an extreme. Ōuchi's revelation was an expression of her total devotion, a necessary stage in her attainment of spiritual liberation in Aum's system, and an articulation of the basic, core principle in Aum Shinrikyō's world of doctrine, practice and belief.

Ōuchi's experience is clear evidence that any study of Aum Shinrikyō, its history, teachings and nature, needs to start with Asahara himself and with his experiences and life as they influenced the movement he created. This will be the focus of this chapter, along with an assessment of his personality, how he behaved towards and how he was seen by those around him, and how he saw himself and envisaged his role and mission in the world.

ASAHARA SHŌKŌ: PUBLIC IMAGES AND PROBLEMS OF INTERPRETATION

In dealing with Asahara's background and personality, I have relied on a number of sources, including interviews that I conducted with Aum members and ex-members, court testimonies by those who knew him, interviews that he has given with scholars and others prior to his arrest, and media reports and reminiscences of people who knew him prior to his emergence as leader of Aum. Besides these sources of information there are several thousand pages of published and unpublished material emanating from Aum which include the texts of his many sermons. These writings, especially in the years immediately prior to the subway attack, offer clear insights into Asahara's varying moods, feelings and characteristics. I have been unable to gain any closer access than this, for the obvious reason that Asahara is currently on trial for his life and inaccessible for interviews that could possibly elucidate his motives or the various factors that may have influenced him. Japanese laws greatly restrict access to prisoners being detained on serious charges (a point much criticised by reporters and members of the public following the case).[5] Moreover, it is highly unlikely that, at a time when he is on trial for his life and adopting an uncooperative attitude towards the court, Asahara would open up to outside interviews. As far as is known, no in-depth analyses of him have been carried out by psychiatrists: certainly, none has yet come to light. Hence I have not been able to supplement my readings of his personality with any publicly available expert analyses.[6]

There are further problems in studying Asahara. Although, in the aftermath of the subway attack, an immense amount of material has been presented about him in the mass media, this has generally been filtered through a lens of sensationalism and not all of it has been reliable. Asahara, as leader of the movement, has naturally become a figure of immense notoriety, portrayed in the media not simply as the main villain of the affair but as a personification of evil, a fraud and manipulator who beguiled idealistic young people into following him and into carrying out fanatical deeds on his behalf.

This image has been reinforced by the court testimonies of several Aum members, who have admitted participating in heinous crimes but who have sought to explain their actions by claiming that Asahara had 'brainwashed' and manipulated them, so that they were not wholly responsible for their actions. Such attempts by Aum followers on trial for their lives to shift the blame for their deeds are perfectly understandable. Although the concept of 'brainwashing' may not be regarded by scholars as a valid or adequate explanation of why followers acted as they did and why they readily contributed to Asahara's authority and helped reinforce his charismatic status,[7] it has been widely accepted and promulgated by the media and reinforces the sinister public image of Asahara.

Asahara's behaviour since his arrest has served to increase this profile. He has, for example, generally denied culpability and responsibility for the various crimes which he concedes were committed by Aum followers. He has asked his accusers how he, a blind man, could have committed any acts of violence, and has even claimed that his followers acted against his orders by attacking the subway system.[8] In the opening statement of his trial in April 1996, Asahara denied any wrongdoing at all, claiming that he had only, ever, sought to follow a religious path and to help people on a religious level, and that all his actions stemmed from this wish.[9] Whatever reasons might be behind these seeming evasions of responsibility, they do not go down well in Japan, where the legal system places great reliance on confessions and recognition of guilt from the accused. There is in Japan a culture in which senior officials and leaders are expected to accept responsibility for deeds carried out in their name. Asahara's denials have thus been seen by the general public as further evidence of a personality deemed evil and fraudulent, and have increased the anger felt against him.[10]

In the years since his arrest, as the court case has progressed and as some of his closest followers have turned on him and renounced their faith, he has exhibited signs (to outside observers at least) of some form of severe psychological disturbance and mental collapse. He has repeatedly behaved oddly in court, mumbling to himself, falling asleep, occasionally interrupting proceedings, on occasion speaking in broken and incomprehensible English, pleading with lawyers not to cross-examine witnesses, at times appearing extremely disturbed, and on one occasion even asking a former disciple to prove his faith by levitating in court.[11]

Such acts fit into a broader behavioural pattern with Asahara. The evasions and denials of responsibility could be seen not simply as signs of distancing himself from the realities of his situation, but as continuations of his tendency to deny fault in any situation. As will be seen later, Aum struggled to attain the requisite levels of support it aspired to, and Asahara consistently resorted to explanations of why his mission had failed in this respect. In doing this he constantly placed the blame for such problems on outside forces: there were conspiracies against Aum; the media had deliberately undermined his movement; his followers had been lazy and failed to proselytise adequately, and so on. There were never any hints that he might have been even partially responsible or at fault in any way. In other words, Asahara tended to externalise problems and project them on to others, rather than confront them and assume responsibility himself for them. Moreover, the signs of disturbance that come out in his court behaviour appear to fit with the signs of paranoia that reverberated through his later sermons in which he became obsessed with fantasies about future weaponry and imagined conspiracies against Aum, and in which he was repeatedly tormented by visions of hell and with the imminence and inevitability of death. Indeed, Asahara did not maintain a single, unchanging and clinical state of mind geared towards manipulation and the furtherance of evil throughout the affair. On the contrary, there is evidence of a continuing process of psychological disturbance that can be seen in his pronouncements in the years prior to the subway attack, and that has since been visible in his court behaviour.

Such interpretations, it should be emphasised, do not fit with public perceptions of Asahara's nature. Japanese public opinion, and the media in general, have generally taken his strange court behaviour as further proof of his evil and cunning character. In popular perception Asahara is not undergoing some form of mental collapse after seeing his aspirations and plans go hopelessly astray and his followers renounce him, but is simply acting mad in order to avoid the death penalty.

The sense of public outrage after the sarin attack, and subsequent public perceptions of Asahara as a deceptive manipulator, have conditioned what has been reported about him, and may well also have influenced the recollections of those who knew him before he attained notoriety. Put bluntly, in the aftermath of the subway attack what the media and the public wanted and needed was a focus for their opprobrium, and what the former wanted to report and the latter to hear, were stories that showed that Asahara was innately evil from the outset. It was thus unsurprising that after the subway attack the recollections and reminiscences of his school and childhood colleagues and teachers that appeared in the media were almost invariably negative, depicting Asahara from his childhood as a bully with overweening ambitions. Equally, media stories from ex-disciples and opponents relating to his period as a religious leader painted a picture of a self-serving and power-mad glutton and hedonist, with a penchant for money, food, young women and cruelty.

A former Aum member, for example, who had worked as Asahara's chauffeur, published a cartoon book entitled *Asahara wa tada no ossan da* [Asahara Is Just a Dirty Old Man] which depicted him as nothing but a manipulator, fraud, spendthrift, glutton and liar who deserved the death penalty.[12] Rumours that Asahara had sexual relations with some young female disciples (which were later confirmed when it emerged that he had fathered Ishii Hisako's children and had had other liaisons) became translated into inflated images of sexual excess.[13] Furthermore tales abounded to suggest that while his disciples were expected to obey rules of celibacy and to exist on a sparse vegetarian diet of 'Aum food' (*Oumu shoku*), Asahara continued to live with his wife and children, showered toys and other luxuries on them, and indulged in large and expensive meals.[14] In such contexts, his espousal of a path of religious leadership was portrayed as little more than a self-serving act designed to bring him money and power.

I mention these widely proliferated public images of Asahara, and the ways in which details about him and his life have been presented, primarily to illustrate how problematic it has been to develop a clear picture of Asahara the person, and how such images themselves create a plausible and publicly convenient 'interpretation' of the affair. The images of Asahara as a fraud, manipulator and hypocritical glutton with a penchant for sexual peccadilloes, provide a convenient means of 'explaining' Asahara, and hence the affair, in readily digestible forms for media consumption: he was always evil, hence the affair was a manifestation of evil. He was always a fraud, hence Aum was not a real religion.

Such simplistic pictures are not helpful in developing any serious analytical understanding of the affair, for they preclude serious discussion of the nature of Asahara as a religious leader. This, however, is an essential element that requires thorough analysis. Asahara certainly manifested deep flaws, but he also impressed many with his charismatic talents and spiritual capabilities, which proved to be a powerful source of attraction to his followers. These characteristics enabled him to establish a religious movement and to captivate a sizeable following, and many of those who came into contact with him spoke with awe of his spiritual powers, compassion and insights, and about the advice he gave them that spoke to their needs and helped them in their lives.

Although I thus warn against accepting at face-value these publicly produced one-dimensional images of Asahara, this does not mean that I wish to dismiss them simply as media-created fictions. The media accounts do contain some partial truths and represent partial illustrations of Asahara's nature. Some hints at this have already emerged: he did, for example, follow different rules than those imposed on his followers by having sexual relations with female followers such as Ishii. He lavished presents on his children and pampered his family in many ways,[15] and while such treatment might appear to be no more than that of any indulgent parent, it did contradict the ascetic orientations of his movement and of his own preaching against materialism. There were also various indications that despite having been a committed practitioner whose strict adherence to ascetic disciplines had won the admiration of his followers, he eventually departed from this rigorous practice and instead began to eat well and live an opulent lifestyle.[16] Moreover, there is evidence of fraudulent behaviour and violent outbursts in his life prior to becoming a religious leader, while his ambitions as outlined in the recollections of those who knew him at school are replicated in Asahara's own visions of his destiny as a religious leader.

My account of Asahara's life thus draws on and makes cautious use of media accounts. It seeks to flesh them out, however, by recognising that there are also other accounts and evidence that point to a rather different Asahara, and that indicate a more complex, multidimensional person, from that of public image. In the early 1990s, when Asahara went on something of a 'charm offensive' intended to win support and to counteract negative publicity about the movement that had emerged in the late 1980s, he was interviewed by various well-known media personalities and scholars, who appear to have been won over by his apparent warmth and friendly personality and impressed by his credentials as a religious leader.[17] Equally impressed were a number of prominent Buddhist leaders from different Buddhist traditions in Asia, including the Dalai Lama.[18] The warm and gentle side of Asahara experienced by many of those who met him is related in the many accounts given by his disciples who (admittedly in books and magazines published by Aum, and mostly before Aum became known for its criminal behaviour) have spoken extensively of how his teachings benefited them immensely and of his kindness and gentleness.[19] Aum members have also spoken of his prowess as an ascetic practitioner, and of how (in a movement which, as will be seen, emphasised and carried out severe austerities) he engaged in more extensive and more austere ascetic practices than anyone else in the movement.[20]

Aum publications, of course, have portrayed him in a wholly spiritual and compassionate light, but even ex-followers who have renounced their faith and been critical of Aum have painted a picture of Asahara that is far more sympathetic than his media image. Takahashi Hidetoshi, a former member who defected and denounced the movement shortly after the subway attack, spent several months in 1994 in close proximity to Asahara at Kamikuishiki, and paints a picture of Asahara that is not unsympathetic. He is portrayed as a man who lived simply in a similar manner to other commune members and who, while capable of immense anger and harshness towards close disciples who displeased him, displayed great empathy with and kindness to ordinary followers of the movement.[21]

There is, of course, a tension between these contradictory images of the empathetic guru and kind teacher living an austere life and the brutal and cruel manipulator who ordered murders and lived it up while his disciples toiled in penury. The tension is not, however, merely one resulting from two very different and contradictory media of production, the one created by Aum in the image of a sacred guru, the other by the mass media to satisfy the demands of public opinion, in which one is true and the other false. Rather, both these contrasting sets of images are partially true. They do not depict mutually exclusive personae so much as they illustrate (albeit to an extreme and through different means of presentation, each with its own particular and specific agenda) seemingly contradictory yet interlocking elements of his personality and of the experiences that shaped him. In these conflicting and polarised images one can discern some clues towards an understanding of Asahara's personality and his nature as the leader of Aum. It is to these elements of his personality that I now turn, to present a brief outline of his life up to his emergence as the leader of a religious movement in the 1980s in Japan.

'I HAVE REJECTED THAT NAME': MATSUMOTO CHIZUO, ASAHARA SHŌKŌ AND THE EARLY LIFE OF A GURU

Asahara Shōkō was born in Kumamoto in Kyushu on 2 March 1955. He was one of seven children in an extremely poor family and his father made *tatami* mats for a living. His name at birth was Matsumoto Chizuo, the name under which he is now charged in court but which he renounced in 1987 when he assumed the name Asahara Shōkō for religious purposes. Taking a new name is not uncommon in Japan, especially in Buddhist and ascetic contexts. It symbolises the shedding of attachments of the past in order to take on a new life dedicated to the pursuit of a spiritual path. Buddhist priests, for example, assume a new name when they become ordained, and it is not uncommon for the leaders of new religious movements to do likewise. For example, two of the most prominent leaders of new religious movements in the 1980s and 1990s, both of whom have some connections to the Aum story, have similarly changed their names. The founder of Agonshû, to which Asahara belonged for a time in the early 1980s, was born Tsutsumi Masao in 1921 but changed his name to Kiriyama Seiyû when he established Agonshû in 1978. Similarly Ōkawa Ryûhō, the founder and leader of Kōfuku no Kagaku (which developed in Tokyo in the mid-1980s at roughly the same time as Aum and with which Aum developed a bitter rivalry) was originally born Nakagawa Takashi in 1956, but assumed the new name when he left secular life to found his movement.[22]

Although such acts of renunciation may have a positive religious meaning tinged with the idealism of renouncing a way of life associated with the material and corrupt world, there also appears to be, in Asahara's case, another underlying and more negative dimension which demonstrated a strong rejection of his past. This came out during his first court appearance on 24 April 1996, when he was asked to state his name and he answered 'Asahara Shōkō'. Since the indictments use his legal family name, the chief judge asked him if he were called Matsumoto Chizuo, to which he replied simply that he had rejected that name.[23]

This rejection appears to be linked to feelings that developed when he was young, as a result of the impoverished situation of his family and his own physical state. He was born partially blind, having no sight in one eye and only 30 per cent vision in the other; other siblings also suffered from sight impairment. This disability, coupled with the poverty of his background, caused him to suffer discrimination at various stages in his life and marked him out as different from others. It appears also to have created in him a sense of injustice and resentment that set him at odds with society. Because of his disability (and because, apparently, his parents were too poor to be able to cater to his special needs) he was sent away to a special state boarding school for the blind at the age of six. This event had a huge impact on him: sent away by, and separated from, his parents, he experienced a deep sense of rejection and felt alone, frightened and isolated at the school.[24] The psychological scars left on him by this ordeal have been attested to by one of his closest followers, Hayashi Ikuo who, when questioned in court about Asahara's nature, spoke of how this experience of rejection had been a critical and damaging one. According to Hayashi, Asahara had often talked about his sense of loss, his feelings of betrayal by his parents, and his profound feeling of loneliness and fear at being alone in a strange place.[25]

While it is impossible to tell how far Asahara's feelings of rejection and alienation from his parents (he appears to have severed ties with his family after moving to Tokyo in 1977) impacted on the way he regarded familial relationships in general, it is worth noting that Aum developed into a movement that asked committed members to become *shukkesha* – people who leave their families behind to enter Aum's communal spiritual orders. In this way it emphasised a rejection of traditional family ties and values, an attitude that gave rise to some of the earliest problems Aum encountered in Japan. These problems centred on conflicts with the families of young people who had left the world, at times before they had reached the age of majority (which is 20 in Japan), to join Aum's communes. It is perhaps also worth noting that in the ensuing controversies Asahara appeared to be quite indifferent to the concerns of the parents, as if he had either no sympathy for them or no great understanding of familial relationships.[26]

Rejection was thus a prominent motif from early in Asahara's life: it became a recurrent theme later as well, not just in the nature of the world-renouncing movement he founded, but in his continued belief that his messages were being ignorantly rejected by the world at large. As I argued in my previous volume on Aum (Reader 1996), and will discuss further in later chapters, this sense of failure and rejection played a major part in arousing Aum's hostility to the outside world and in the development of the conspiracy theories that eventually gripped Aum and contributed to its espousal of violence.[27]

After being sent away from home, Asahara remained at the boarding school for the blind for approximately 14 years until graduation, during which time, according to his teachers, he displayed above-average academic abilities and was good at judo. He is reported to have been something of a bully towards younger children while at school. Some school colleagues also remembered him as having a short temper. This apparent tendency to violence and angry outbursts when things were not going his way led him into trouble soon after he had graduated from school, when he was arrested and fined on an assault charge after getting involved in an argument.[28] Such testimonies, as well as this particular assault incident, suggest a personality unable to handle opposition and prone to violent outbursts and responses when thwarted – traits that manifested themselves at later stages in his life as well.

This point was reiterated by the journalist Hiroiwa Chikahirō of the *Mainichi Shinbun* who interviewed Asahara in 1989. According to Hiroiwa, Asahara became confrontational and argumentative when pressurised and when things did not go his way.[29] The testimony of a former disciple, whom I shall call N-san and who left the movement in 1989, also confirms this impression. According to N-san, while Asahara was a good communicator, a serious seeker after truth and an active participant in Aum's ascetic training, he also had a harsh side and tended to become very angry if crossed.[30]

Along with this tendency towards anger and violent outbursts, Asahara appears to have had a predilection towards using violent actions as part of his ascetic programme. We have already seen how Aum meted out punishments to members, and later I shall discuss how Asahara used coercive means, including beatings, to make followers participate in austerities. This violent impulse was not only outwardly directed: he also engaged in bouts of self-flagellation as part of his ascetic activity, beating his legs with a bamboo stick in order to open up the channels of spiritual energy which, according to Aum's yoga-based beliefs, ran through the body. This practice was believed to eradicate the bad karma in his body.[31] One observer, Serizawa Shunsuke, has described Asahara's absorption in ascetic practices as 'masochistic'.[32] While such activities and uses of violence against the body are based in the belief that the body was a polluted entity that needed cleansing through austerities, they also illustrate that violence, both inwardly and outwardly directed, was deeply ingrained in Aum's thought and practices.

As will be shown in later chapters, virtually every act of violence committed by Aum was an aggressive response to people who had opposed Aum or who, Asahara believed, were working against the movement. In this Asahara displayed an inability to deal coherently or rationally when challenged, a character trait that has been described also by Takahashi Hidetoshi, who has written that Asahara could be very harsh towards and highly critical of those in the upper echelons of Aum when they did not act as he expected, and prone to outbursts of great violence, even throwing things at members who displeased him.[33]

Yet Takahashi, as was noted earlier, also paints a picture of Asahara as a kind teacher who cared deeply for his disciples. This recollection fits with the positive impressions that Asahara made on various interlocutors in the 1990s and with the memories of some of his former colleagues and teachers who remembered him as having a more amenable and generous side.[34] Testimonies from his many devotees, even while they have recognised his harsh side, affirm this warmer side as well, and many have paid fulsome tribute to his kindness and gentle nature. Kanai Ryōkō, for example, has written at length about Asahara's kindness and how impressed her father – who had been deeply opposed to her involvement in Aum at the outset – was with Aum when he was dying of cancer. He was cared for in an Aum facility and Kanai records how Asahara spent time by his bedside gently talking to him, praying for him and soothing him in his hour of need.[35]

These two apparently contradictory sides or traits – the harsh, volatile and aggressive Asahara, and the kind and compassionate one – fit together as parts of the whole. The cruel teacher who forces his disciples to perform austerities, or who beats them to this end, was (in Aum's view) acting compassionately, by helping them to eradicate the karma that otherwise would drag them down. Cruelty, in other words, can be a manifestation of compassion, a point Asahara made on a number of occasions when speaking of why he sometimes treated his disciples harshly.[36]

In my discussions with Aum members and ex-members about Asahara two words that occurred frequently were *kibishii* (harsh, strict) and *yasashii* (gentle, kind): they were often mentioned almost simultaneously.[37] The same member who could be treated with warmth and helped in moments of personal crisis could be berated for failing to do something or for neglecting his or her practice. In Aum publications disciples have described Asahara as *kibishii* in his insistence on austerities and because he constantly kept them on their toes. They have also recognised that embedded in this severity were signs of his kind (*yasashii*) nature as well: the guru who is kind and gentle has to be strict in order to push his followers and help them achieve greater spiritual heights.[38] Asahara has further commented on the necessity of being severe on his disciples, stating that without severity there can be no compassion: if he were to be lax with his disciples they would not do enough practice and hence would not eradicate their karma, and as a result would fall into the hells.[39]

These two faces of Asahara could emerge also in interviews that he gave to outsiders. Asahara sometimes came across as a compassionate and thoughtful teacher, clearly charming his interviewers in many ways. Yet, he could also display a remarkably callous and cruel side: for instance, in an interview with reporters from a regional newspaper in Kyūshū, in which he otherwise displayed similar charm, he was quite brutal about the plight of the villagers of Namino in Kyūshū, who opposed the building of an Aum commune in the area (see below Chapter 6). The Namino area had just suffered serious flooding, and Asahara told the reporters that this disaster was karmic retribution for the villagers' negative attitudes and behaviour towards Aum.[40] What is remarkable about this comment is that Aum was struggling, in the face of opposition, to establish its commune in the area and hence this was a time when a display of compassion and perhaps even offers of support in the face of the disaster might have been more diplomatic and might have helped Aum's case considerably. Instead, Asahara chose to blame the villagers for their suffering. His comments manifest a vindictive cruelty that illustrates his inability and unwillingness to consider any point of view other than his own, or any ability to make compromises, even when they might have served Aum's purposes better.

These contrasting traits – Asahara the kind and compassionate man who could charm disciples and others, and make them feel honoured, and the angry, tempestuous Asahara, capable of flaring up at any moment and unable to brook opposition or alternative views – operated in tandem and were important facets in enhancing his power and standing. Interviewers could be charmed by his warmth and impressed by his fierce adherence to strict austerities, while disciples often appeared to be terrified of him or of losing his favour and could find themselves on the receiving end of his temper, yet also be touched and won over by his gentleness and kindness. The anger that produced fear and made disciples eager to please him, and the warmth that could assuage anyone upset with him because of his anger, thus interacted to enhance his standing among his followers.

ACADEMIC AMBITIONS, FRUSTRATIONS, FAILURES AND MARRIAGE

As a youth Asahara was, according to those who were at school with him or taught him, extremely forceful, determined and ambitious, with desires to be a politician and prime minister.[41] Although it is perhaps hardly surprising that he, like many other young children, had great ambitions, there are enough indications from subsequent phases of his life to suggest that these recollections of Asahara as someone with a strong sense of mission and personal destiny, are not post facto manufactured memories. Humility was not one of his more striking attributes, for his self-image was suffused with a sense of grandeur and destiny, in which he claimed to have led illustrious past lives, stated that he was the only person in Japan to have achieved supreme spiritual liberation, and portrayed himself as a world saviour.

Whatever ambitions he had at school, however, appear to have been thwarted in various ways, in part because of his aforementioned disability and marginalised background. Making his way through the pressurised Japanese education system, with its emphasis on examination success and a college education to procure a good job, Asahara tried to enter the local university, Kumamoto University, to study medicine. However, he was refused because the university's medical faculty made no provision for sight-impaired people such as himself.[42] Coupled with the rejection he received in his family situation, this sense of discrimination appears to have fuelled in him a sense of injustice and estrangement from Japanese society.

Such sentiments may also have had an impact on other Aum members in a society whose discrimination against ethnic and minority groups is widely recognised. The dancer Kashima Tomoko, for example, who became a devotee of Aum and eventually was imprisoned on charges of helping to kidnap and coerce recalcitrant members, has described how, as the child of an American soldier and a Japanese woman who was subsequently adopted, she suffered abuse and discrimination at school. Indeed, she was bullied and insulted by other children because she was part-American, to such a degree that she felt discriminated against and alienated from Japanese society.[43] Perhaps unsurprisingly, she found solace and support in a movement that set itself apart from Japanese society and appeared to reject its social values.

Asahara's ambitions were blocked also by his own failures. Although denied the chance to study medicine, he did attempt to get into other university faculties, taking the entrance examinations first for Kumamoto University, and the next year for Tokyo University, albeit both times unsuccessfully. While studying for his examinations he also gravitated to an occupation traditionally favoured by the blind in Japan, that of healing, working first at an acupuncture clinic in Kumamoto, where he was regarded as a hard worker by his employer, and later becoming involved in the practices of acupuncture, moxibustion and herbal medicines in the Tokyo region to which he had moved in 1977 in order to try to gain entry into the nation's leading university, Tokyo University.[44]

While studying he met a young woman, Ishii Tomoko, who was aged 19. They married in 1978 and shortly afterwards had their first child. Matsumoto Tomoko, as she became at marriage (she has retained his family name), in all bore him six children and eventually herself became a prominent figure in Aum. After the birth of their first child it became impossible for Asahara to continue seeking entry to university, because of the need to provide for his new family. As a result he concentrated on his practice as a healer, establishing an acupuncture clinic, which later expanded into a herbal medicine business, in the town of Funabashi near Tokyo.[45]

THE RELIGIOUS INFLUENCES ON ASAHARA SHŌKŌ

In an interview in December 1991, Asahara told the Japanese scholar Yamaori Tetsuo that it was around the time that his ambitions in education had been frustrated that he began to take a serious interest in and to read books about religion, especially Buddhism, and to become involved in ascetic practices.[46] In his first book, originally published in 1986, he also stated that his turning to religion at this time came about because he felt frustrated at not being able to help his patients sufficiently through the cures he offered.[47] He told Yamaori that while he had had no real previous interest in religious matters, he had been conscious from childhood of the existence of other realms and that he had had deep fears about death from the age of around three, and felt as if he were being drawn to another world. This preoccupation with death recurs throughout his teachings, becoming, as we shall see in later chapters, a virtual obsession in the sermons he delivered in the two years prior to the subway attack. He told Yamaori that as a child he had had visions of a spirit world bathed in white (a vision, he stated, that had not changed throughout his life) and had sensations of his spirit being separated from his body.[48]

Like large numbers of Japanese, he had been brought up with a formal Buddhist affiliation. His parents were members of the Jōdo Shin or True Pure Land Buddhist sect and his family observed numerous seasonal customs and rituals at various shrines and temples. However, he found little spiritual satisfaction in these, judging them to be just 'custom' devoid of religious content.[49] Here and elsewhere Asahara manifested a disappointment and dissatisfaction with the established religious traditions of Japan, and especially Buddhism. He considered them as being formalistic, lacking in spiritual dynamism and – a criticism he made very frequently after having founded Aum – weak in ascetic practice and spiritual endeavour.[50] This perception was widely held among younger people in Japan and was a common theme among those attracted to Aum. While many of them were interested in Buddhist teachings and practices such as meditation, they were often disappointed with the established Buddhist orders in Japan, regarding its priests as (in the words of one Aum devotee) 'no different to ordinary lay people' (zokujin to kawaranai).[51]

While Asahara's involvement in herbal medicines and acupuncture may have come about in part because of his blindness, it also suggests an interest in the folk religious traditions of Japan and in traditional healing techniques. Spiritual healing techniques, concepts and practices are frequently emphasised in the Japanese new religions, serving as critical elements in their claims to religious efficacy and in the construction of their leaders' charisma and claims to spiritual power.[52] Aum was similar in this respect, claiming that its spiritual training techniques and especially its ascetic and yoga-related practices provided the means for overcoming all manner of ills and physical problems.[53]

Asahara also appears to have retained an interest in other areas of the Japanese folk tradition such as divination, fortune-telling and the ways and means to procure good luck and avoid misfortune. All of these influences surface in his later activities and teachings. In his account of life at Kamikuishiki in 1994–1995 Takahashi, for example, describes

46

how he was assigned to various research projects related to geomancy, divination and astrology that sought to predict the future.[54] Asahara also demonstrated his adherence to Japanese concepts of taboos and practices related to good and bad fortune, by changing his wife's holy name in 1992 because he felt that the name she had been given was bringing her bad luck and placing her in danger.[55]

THE 'NEW' NEW RELIGIONS AND THE RELIGIOUS ENVIRONMENT OF THE 1970S AND 1980S

Probably the greatest influence on Asahara's emergent religious world-view came from the popular Japanese religious culture of the 1980s as manifested by the 'new' new religions of Japan.[56] The 'new' new religions were perhaps the most visible manifestation of the religious culture that attracted many Japanese – and particularly the younger, well-educated urban population – from the late 1970s onwards. One of the underlying currents that these movements tapped into was a general dissatisfaction with and distrust of the modern scientific rationalism that forms the basis of the Japanese education and work systems. This reflects a more general antipathy to an ethic that places heavy emphasis on work, career and economic achievement; a system that has provided material wealth but affords its members little in the way of spiritual satisfaction or meaning in their daily lives. Scholars such as Nishiyama Shigeru have also commented that this unease at the rationalisation of daily and work life promoted or created a yearning for mystery and miracle as a counter-weight to, or form of escape from, the routine patterns of contemporary life.[57]

This has led to a search for new spiritual meanings and, because of the widespread belief that the older, established religions have become spiritually defunct or out of touch with modern needs, to a growing interest in yoga, meditation and alternative religious practices and to a fascination with seemingly exotic and esoteric religious forms. It is important to note that although the general perception was that Buddhism had become spiritually moribund, this did not entail a rejection of Buddhism *per se*. Rather, there was great interest in the spiritual dimensions of Buddhism and in the notion that some form of revival might occur which could produce a new and more dynamic Buddhism freed from the social ritualism of the established religions. This issue was widely promoted by new religions such as Agonshū, which talked of a revival of Buddhism, in which its spiritual values would be re-emphasised. This interest in Buddhism also included a fascination with esoteric, non-Japanese forms of Buddhism, especially Tibetan Buddhism, which provided a number of motifs that became important in Aum.

Along with this interest in spiritual techniques that offered the chance of spiritual transcendence, there was great interest in the potential acquisition of superhuman or psychic powers (*chōnōryoku*) such as divination, seeing the future, extra-sensory perception, enhanced energy levels and increased powers of thought. Other such powers included the ability to overcome the normal limitations on the human body, for example by acquiring the power to levitate. This interest in mystery, esotericism and psychic powers was one of Aum's early foundation points, but it had also been prevalent in many of the other and earlier new religious movements of the era, and most notably Agonshū. Indeed, its founder, Kiriyama Seiyū, first attracted widespread attention in Japan because of his pronouncements relating to the attainment of psychic powers. These were discussed in several of Kiriyama's books, but particularly in his *Henshi no genri* [The Principles of Transforming the Human Body], published in 1971, which discussed how, through following a path of spiritual practices laid down by Kiriyama and based on Agonshū's interpretations of esoteric Buddhism, one could attain various transcendent powers.[58]

This fascination with psychic powers was, in part, an expression of the desire for excitement: many people were drawn to such new movements because they held out the promise of extraordinary powers and appeared to offer a new means of stimulation. Moreover, such powers were portrayed in Agonshū and later in Aum as readily attainable: by contrast with the slower and more formalised ritual patterns of the established religions, they appeared to offer dramatic and speedy ways to attainment. This fitted in well with the ethos of an era and a generation accustomed to immediate gratification. It struck a chord too in an age in which there was a very deeply felt sense of apocalyptic urgency. This further contributed to the dynamic image that the 'new' new religions presented, which stood in sharp contrast to the seemingly ineffectual and moribund image of the older religions.

This interest in esoteric practices, mystery and psychic powers implied a rejection of and an alternative view to the overarching paradigms of the secularised, scientific, rationalist worldview that held sway in the spheres of public life, education, business and commerce. It was, in effect, suggesting that the human being, rather than being bound to the world and at the mercy of rationalised events and physical limitations, contained the potential for transcendence on spiritual and physical levels. While scientific rationalism might, in other words, hold sway in society, this did not mean that science was all-powerful, for humans could transcend the supposed limitations that were placed on them. Interestingly, alongside this apparent rejection of science and technology as the overarching gods of a modern, rational, secular and regimented society, there was a ready acceptance of modern technologies and scientific techniques in the service of religious ends. Many new religions such as Agonshū made great use of modern technologies such as computers, videos and the like as proselytisation tools. The people they appealed to were accustomed to using computers and videos, and were able to see these as tools offering people the potential to escape from the rationalisation processes of society. Aum operated in this way and, like Agonshū, became adept at incorporating scientific and technological motifs into its teachings and sought to align them with its religious orientations. While science as the guiding principle of a materialist society was thus criticised for being unable to answer basic spiritual questions, it was not rejected wholesale but adapted into a wider rubric in which, it was believed, it could serve the interests of the religion of the future rather than oppose it.[59]

Perhaps the most critical of all the religious currents that prevailed from the late 1970s through to the 1990s, centred around notions that the current materialistic era was drawing to a close and that society, by being so enmeshed in material pursuits, had come to the brink of chaos and disaster. In such a situation, what was needed was a major spiritual transformation in which the materialism of the present age would be jettisoned and a new, more spiritual age would begin. To a degree the new movements emerging in Japan in the 1980s thus paralleled the New Age movements in the West with their talk of a new spiritual age and the need for a turning point in human consciousness. While such ideas had positive dimensions, they also contained deeply pessimistic ones as well. As Charles B. Strozier has noted, New Age thoughts of spiritual renewal are frequently linked to apocalyptic images and to notions of end-times and imminent catastrophes.[60] This was certainly so in Japan in the 1980s and early 1990s, in which many religious movements were impelled by the notion that the world was on the brink of a crisis largely caused by human failings and scientific and technological excesses, and in which nuclear warfare and environmental destruction threatened to bring an end to life on earth.

Such concepts and expectations were by no means new in Japan: several of the new religions of Japan that developed in the nineteenth century such as Tenrikyō and Ōmoto had, especially earlier in their histories, quite urgent millennialist expectations of a change in the existing order.[61] These themes were also strongly felt among the wave of new religions that came to the fore in the latter part of the twentieth century. They have had a particular resonance at this time because of the calendrical millennium, and because of a widespread consciousness of environmental and other problems. The use of atomic weapons in 1945 has also naturally impacted greatly on Japanese thinking and made many people conscious of the potential for world destruction posed by the existence of nuclear and other high-technology weapons.

In Japan such apocalyptic scenarios were also fuelled by the writings of Nostradamus, the sixteenth-century French writer, whose prophecies suggesting that a terrifying series of events would spread destruction on earth in 1999 gained a remarkably large popular audience in Japan. They had been initially brought to public attention in Japan in 1973 through the writings of the New Age writer Gōtō Ben. As Robert Kisala has noted, this sparked a 'Nostradamus boom', which has led to the publication of dozens of books on his prophecies.[62] These have been supplemented and augmented by numerous equally dramatic end-time prophecies from various of the leaders of the 'new' new religions, which have helped to condition Japanese attitudes to the millennium and to heighten fears associated with its coming. A number of new religious leaders, including Kiriyama of Agonshū, Ōkawa Ryūhō of Kōfuku no Kagaku and Asahara himself, have published books about Nostradamus and have sought to unravel some of the mysteries of his obscure texts. Some leaders, including Asahara and Ōkawa, have even claimed to have travelled to higher spirit realms to speak with Nostradamus's spirit.[63] The prophecies were so important to Asahara that he and a number of disciples even travelled to France in 1991 to consult with scholars of Nostradamus because, by that time, Asahara had come to believe that the end of the world was at hand.

The impact of these apocalyptic prophecies could be seen widely in Japanese youth culture. Shimada Hiromi, for example, gives a fascinating illustration of how widely known Nostradamus's prophecies became, when he recounts how the prophecies even featured in one of the most popular television cartoon programmes of recent years, *Chibi Maruko-chan*. In an episode (set, as all the episodes are, in the 1970s) Chibi Maruko, a third-year female student in junior school, hears from a classmate about Nostradamus's prophecy: later she hears someone else making a similar prediction on television that the world would end in 1999. She bursts into tears because the second prediction seems to affirm that of Nostradamus, and next day at school all the pupils are in despair because they believe that the world will end and that they will die young. Some even announce that they will no longer study for tests as there is no point in continuing with their education since they are all going to die before long.[64]

Amusing as this story is, it reflects a mood that was highly relevant to younger Japanese. Serizawa Shunsuke has commented on this general sense of unease within contemporary Japanese society, which harboured not only worries about nuclear war and environmental problems, but also concerns about the economy and the rising tide of social disturbances, from the bullying in schools and growing crime rates, to concerns about the education system. According to Serizawa, this unease was an end-of-century phenomenon which expressed both an 'expectation of catastrophe' and a general receptivity to such ideas.[65] Such expectations of disaster were also widely reflected in the dystopic images that ran through such popular Japanese media forms as pop music, anime and cartoons in the latter part of the century, and which frequently focused on images of destruction and dark and frightening futuristic societies.[66] The former Aum member Takahashi Hidetoshi reiterates this point when he wrote that the images of doom and apocalypse prevalent in such popular cultural forms were not fantasies but represented the very real fears and concerns of young Japanese like himself.[67]

Many Japanese youths, in other words, expected some upheaval – a feeling that led them to look for new possibilities and changes at the end of the century. Thus these fears of apocalypse were fused with a sense of expectation: the belief in the possible coming of a new, spiritual age was interwoven with apocalyptic images, and some form of destruction was seen as a prerequisite for the establishment of a new spiritual order. For many this was not just an expectation but a hope, a wish that the materialistic society of the present would be swept away and destroyed, to be replaced by a simpler, more spiritual realm. This became a dominant motif in Aum, whose initially optimistic views of the millennium gave way to darker ones in which doom and destruction were not merely seen as inevitable, but were openly welcomed.

The threat of destruction was thus linked to the potential for salvation – and here again Nostradamus's writings had an impact. In his quatrains as they were translated into Japanese, reference was made to a saviour who would appear 'from the East' to lead the world to salvation, either averting the catastrophe through spiritual leadership, or by showing the way through the chaos and leading humanity into the new spiritual age. It is not surprising then that several of those who came to the fore as religious leaders of new movements in the 1970s and beyond, including Ōkawa, Kiriyama and Asahara, came to view themselves in this messiah-like role, assuming as they did so exalted and grandiose titles that signified their messianic mission. Ōkawa, for example, pronounced himself to be the Buddha Incarnate, while Asahara claimed he was the only person to have attained complete spiritual liberation, identifying himself at various times with Jesus and the Hindu deity Shiva.[68]

The mission of these cosmic leaders was to be accomplished with the assistance of their followers, who were to form the basis on which the new spiritual age would be built. They were, in other words, a newly emergent spiritual elite, the spiritual vanguard of the new era, capable of attaining superhuman powers and of achieving rapid spiritual breakthroughs. The promise that one could be part of such a spiritual crusade for world renewal proved highly attractive, especially since the religious leaders gave their followers exalted titles or epithets which appeared to mark them out as special members of a new spiritual elite. Ōkawa Ryūhō of Kōfuku no Kagaku, for example, referred to his followers as bodhisattvas and buddhas who would lead the world into the new spiritual age.[69] So too did Asahara, who also referred to his disciples as 'true victors' ready to take part in the fight to destroy evil and lead humanity forth to a new era of spiritual growth.[70] These assertions suggested that the followers of such religious groups were different from the rest of humanity, a notion that, as will be seen in subsequent chapters, became a dominant motif in Aum. It rapidly gave rise to a spiritual elitism that drove a wedge between Asahara's disciples and the rest of humanity, who came to be seen, in contrast to the spiritually advanced elite of Aum, as increasingly unworthy figures mired in the den of evil of this world.

One further point about these intersecting images of apocalypse and world salvation is the sense of urgency that the proximity of the date predicted by Nostradamus (viz. 1999), and the imminent end of the century infused into the situation. If the predicted apocalypse were to be avoided, and the chosen messiah(s) and his/their spiritual elites were to save the world through spiritual action, they had little time in which to do it. Several of the movements that emerged in this period were not only driven by a sense of mission but imbued with a sense of urgency, seeking success and rapid growth in order to fulfil that mission. Again, with Aum this proved to be an important factor in what ensued.

THE EMERGENCE OF A RELIGIOUS LEADER

Asahara was just one of the many young Japanese who were interested in the ideas being articulated in the popular religious culture of the

1970s and 1980s and especially in 'new' new religions such as Agonshû. It was Agonshû, with its criticisms of established Buddhism, its assertions that it was seeking to restore a more spiritually focused Buddhism, its warnings about the potential for global apocalypse in 1999, its uses of such practices as yoga and meditation along with esoteric Buddhist rituals, and its promises of psychic powers, that attracted Asahara. The exact nature of his relationship with the movement is obscure since, perhaps understandably in the light of subsequent events, Agonshû has been keen to downplay and for a time tried to deny any associations between it and Asahara. It does appear, however, that he was a member of Agonshû at least in the earlier part of the 1980s, and that he carried out some ascetic-type practices, including the *senzagyō*, an Agonshû practice involving reciting prayers each day for a period of 1,000 days.[71]

In June 1982 Asahara, who had continued to support his family through his activities in the fields of healing and alternative medicine, was arrested, convicted and fined for selling herbal medicines which he had manufactured without a licence and which he claimed could cure all manner of illnesses. This incident helped bankrupt his herbal medicine business and provoked a family crisis, with his wife finding it difficult to face the world afterwards for several months.[72] Asahara appears to have found solace in this predicament by focusing further on religious practices. He did not, however, stay much longer in Agonshū, leaving it in 1984 because he felt that, although it talked about yoga and meditation, there was not enough of an emphasis on these in practice, and that Agonshū did not offer the degree of spiritual experiences that he sought.[73] He had by this time begun to embark on severe austerities on his own and to devote himself to yoga practices.[74]

Asahara was clearly driven by a sense of mission and destiny and these impulses, along with his personal experiences during his practice,[75] seem to have been factors behind his decision to establish his own group in 1984, by which time he had attracted a small coterie of followers. By 1984, then, while still in his late twenties, Asahara Shōkō had imbibed much of the popular religious culture of the era, had engaged in religious practices and had become sufficiently confident of his own abilities and driven by a sense of his own religious destiny, to take on followers and to assume the role not merely of teacher but of guru. His engagement in this role was such that, from the early days of the movement in 1984, he was performing initiations in which he absorbed the bad karma of disciples and transferred his energies to them, and which were claimed to help such disciples attain higher levels of consciousness.[76]

I shall discuss in the next chapter the early years and nature of the movement Asahara set up. The point to emphasise here is the centrality of Asahara: it was because of his personal capabilities that people came to the group and because of what he appeared to offer that many of them stayed and became ardent devotees. It is clear, from the accounts of disciples and, in the aftermath of the affair also of ex-disciples, that from the outset Asahara displayed charismatic qualities and had the power to inspire – to such an extent, indeed, that those who were asked were prepared to kill on his orders. Some, too, even after their arrests, not having had any access to him for a number of years, and on trial for their lives, have declared that they are prepared to die for him and the faith he inspired.[77]

The members and former members whom I have interviewed have all emphasised that Asahara was charismatic. One ex-member, who had left the movement because of its activities and who was highly critical of Asahara's behaviour, continued to speak of his incredible personal power: Asahara was, he said, *sugoi* (powerful) and *kowai* (fearful) – an inspiringly awesome figure.[78] Another interviewee testified how he became a member of Aum in late 1992: he had gone to hear Asahara speak, and afterwards when he had got up to ask a question Asahara had responded directly to him. As he did so, my interviewee stated, he felt a tremendous sense of calm coming over him, which lasted for a week afterwards. He became a member almost immediately, and some months later, in March 1993, when he met Asahara again, he felt a powerful sensation which convinced him of Asahara's extraordinary power.[79] Aum produced many volumes outlining the experiences of its members, and in such testimonies the power of Asahara was a constant theme: he had superhuman powers of insight that enabled him to give advice to disciples on individual matters relating to their practice, phoning them up individually at the precise moment when they were experiencing difficulties, to help them out, or even calling them from hundreds of miles away to admonish them for listening to music rather than performing their austerities.[80]

A SACRED HERO WITH A MISSION

Asahara clearly sought an important role for himself. This was manifest in the images he had of himself, in the goals he aspired to as a religious leader, and in his belief that he had a sacred mission to lead the forces of good in an ultimate battle against those of evil. This vision of his role of world saviour in a grand cosmic struggle was an important part of his self-image and personality, fuelled by a series of visions and revelations he experienced after forming his movement and in which he was chosen or anointed by various deities. He saw himself as both saviour of the world and a warrior for truth – a phrase redolent with martial imagery – while his followers were 'true victors' in the cosmic war to come.[81]

In such self-perceptions, Asahara displayed a degree of grandeur and arrogance: he assumed epithets and titles such as guru, master and saviour, and spoke with a distinct lack of modesty about his own achievements. His comments about one of his own books give some hint of this:

> Tathagata Abdidhamma Book 1 has created a sensation. The reason for this is very clear: there has never been a book in Japan which elucidated the structure of the universe or the teachings of Buddha Sakyamuni as easily and yet as profoundly as this book.[82]

This sense of grandeur was reflected in his analyses of his past lives: Aum claimed that its practitioners could acquire the knowledge to discern one's past and future incarnations,[83] and perhaps unsurprisingly Asahara's past was one of unfettered achievements and exalted lives. He had, he informed Yamaori Tetsuo, been the creator of the pyramids, the king of various celestial realms, and an incarnation of the Buddha Maitreya in previous lives.[84] Such statements of course reflect Asahara's ambitious desires to be noticed and to attract attention, a theme that is par for the course for would-be world saviours.

The photographs and cartoons of Asahara that appeared in Aum publications provide further valuable clues to his personality and to the images that he and the movement wished to project. In such photographs he is invariably dressed in the robes of an Indian ascetic, at times meditating alone in the mountains. Such images are redolent with a sense of separation and, implicitly, of rejection: as I noted in my earlier book, the assumption of Indian dress can be seen as signifying a basic rejection of Japan and of Japanese modes of religious accoutrement.[85] The only exceptions to these images of separation are when Asahara is pictured with his children, in which case he may be cuddling them or holding their hands in the normal manner of a loving and doting parent, or when he is with devotees. In such cases he is always in a superior position, placing his hand on the head of meditating disciples to give them blessings or transfers of spiritual power, or giving sermons while ensconced on a huge cushion or armchair, with his followers seated at his feet. Otherwise he is standing alone in heroic or majestic postures, his hands raised to bestow a blessing or benediction on the world at large. The general tenor of these pictures and photographs is of a man apart: separation, of course, affirms power, and the photographs of Asahara used by Aum serve to emphasise this point time and again.

This imagery is repeated also in Aum cartoons and animated videos in which Asahara is depicted as larger than life, much bigger than his disciples, his beard, hair and body assuming massive proportions and dwarfing those around him. The parallel with Buddhist iconography and paintings, in which the Buddha is depicted in similar terms, far larger than his disciples, in a manner that emphasises his spiritual power and suggests that he is something more than just a human being, is striking. Given that Asahara and Aum were keen students of Buddhism and paid great interest to early Buddhism, establishing projects to translate Pali scriptures and visiting Indian Buddhist sites where such iconography is readily visible, the parallel was no doubt deliberate.

In spatial terms the photographs show evidence of a wish to create a realm of separation between himself and the rest of the world. This wish was apparent when he was arrested on 16 May 1995: according to media reports, he asked the arresting officers not to touch him, since he did not allow his followers to do so.[86] This emphasis on distance and separation comes out also in the hierarchic structure that Aum developed in which Asahara always occupied a status or rank two stages above even the most advanced of his followers. Moreover, as Takahashi Hidetoshi observed, Asahara appeared to create more and more hurdles to stop followers getting close to him: the gap between him and others was emphasised rather than played down, and he instituted more and more difficult practices, and established more and more levels of attainment that needed to be accomplished in the continuing path of upward spiritual mobility.[87]

While such distancing and separation on the one hand indicate Asahara's exalted self-image, they also hint at a fragility and insecurity, suggesting that he could not allow anyone to get close to him in terms of status lest they pose a challenge to him. Despite his stature as a world saviour, he displayed weaknesses and insecurities, and, as will be seen in later chapters, he frequently complained of sicknesses and of becoming exhausted as a result of carrying out large numbers of initiations.[88] While such recurrent declarations of weakness may well have served as a means of increasing his disciples' concern and care for him, they also suggest a recurrent fragility, which Asahara himself occasionally expressed by doubting whether he was capable of fully carrying out his mission. Even while expressing the importance of his mission to save humanity, he could simultaneously lament the hopelessness of the task and wonder if he could save more than a handful of those he aspired to reach and even stated that at times he felt 'powerless'.[89] The sense of persecution and paranoia that became a recurrent theme in Asahara's thought and sermons in the 1990s was a further indication of this fragility and concern about failure, while his response to problems and perceived challenges to his position was to increase his status, as if seeking constantly to shore up a massive yet fragile ego.

Even the famous image of Asahara that appeared on the cover of his two-volume series *Kirisuto sengen*[90] (later translated into English as *Declaring Myself the Christ*)[91] in which Asahara is depicted as Christ on the cross, his head bedecked with a crown of thorns, displays this nuance. While this image appears to reflect the heights of arrogance, with Asahara portraying himself as the Messiah and seemingly usurping the image of Jesus, it also betrays an element of self-doubt. Asahara was extremely conscious of the relative lack of success of his movement, and sought explanations for this apparent rejection of his message by the world at large. As he did so he turned increasingly to a discourse of persecution, in which he saw all around him the evidence of nefarious conspiracies designed to thwart his plans: these conspiracies became, as it were, explanations for the failure of his mission. They appear in full force in the *Kirisuto Sengen* books, in which Asahara is concerned also with the images of sacrifice: the dilemma as expressed there is between the roles of the messiah bringing world salvation through his actions on earth (i.e. the messiah as active agent, operating as a warrior to wipe out evil) and that of being a symbolic victim, the sacrificial lamb who loses his life for the sake of the world at large.

I shall examine these varying images of sacrifice, mission and persecution in more detail later. I have introduced them here in the context of Asahara's personality to show that while he constructed a self-image as a heroic saviour, this seemingly overarching image of grandeur and power had a reverse side of doubt and weakness, which itself played a part in the eventual construction of the persecution complex that became a critical element in Asahara and Aum's world in the 1990s.

CRAZY WISDOM AND RELIGIOUS LEADERS

In this chapter I have drawn attention to Asahara Shōkō's life up to the development of his movement, and to critical aspects of his personality. In emphasising the importance of Asahara's personality in the affair, I am not seeking to develop an analysis based solely on psychological grounds. Asahara's personality was certainly one of the most critical elements in the whole affair, especially in the light of his teachings that his followers should have absolute faith in him and should seek to become 'clones' of the guru. However, I would caution against the tendency to resort to a reductionist psychological interpretation of the affair, by simply portraying it as an externalised expression of Asahara's own inner demons and personality flaws played on a larger canvas.[92] As was shown in Chapter 1, a variety of complex factors played their part in the affair and need to be considered in any analysis of why Aum went down the path it did. One of the purposes of the ensuing chapters will be to illustrate and analyse these issues in greater detail. First, however, I would like to conclude this study of Asahara Shōkō the person by focusing on his emergence as the leader of a religious group, and in terms of the nature of religious leadership in general.

In the brief account of Asahara Shōkō's life and personality a number of traits have been highlighted, such as the seemingly conflicting sides of his nature, in which he displayed aggressive and harsh tendencies yet was capable of immense kindness and warmth. He manifested an almost overweening ambition which was transformed into a sense of destiny and mission, yet was also tormented by self-doubts. In the light of events in Aum, there have been suggestions in the Japanese media and elsewhere that the existence of such tendencies, and notably his aggressive and violent streak, as well as his apparent disregard of the law and use of fraud (as evidenced by his conviction for selling fake medicines), show that he could not have been a genuine religious leader or spiritual activist, but was a fake from start to finish.[93] However, this is a rather naïve perception of the nature of the charismatic religious leadership found widely in the Japanese new religions. Indeed, in his background, life and nature Asahara manifests many similarities with others who have been similarly driven to found religious movements in Japan and elsewhere.

His background alone displays similarities with other founders of new religions, many of whom have come from similarly marginalised and impoverished backgrounds, often with poor education, and who have sought to redress the imbalances and injustices they faced by preaching about spiritual change that would create a new and more just world. These themes are found, for example, in the lives and teachings of such religious founders as Deguchi Nao, who founded the new religion Ōmotokyō in the late nineteenth century, and Kitamura Sayo of Tenshō Kōtai Jingūkyō, which developed in the 1940s. Both these female leaders were confrontational, volatile and aggressive in nature: both were at times incarcerated because of their criticisms and denunciations of others and their messianic preaching about the need for world renewal.[94] Other figures of note in the new religions also displayed socially disruptive tendencies and extraordinary behaviour. Deguchi Onisaburō, for example, who was influential in the development of Ōmotokyō in the early decades of the twentieth century, manifested ambitions and pretensions of grandeur similar to Asahara's, unleashing a powerful barrage of criticism against the government and against materialism, experiencing ascents of the spirit into other realms and exhibiting a powerfully self-driven sense of mission as a saviour of the universe. He also had pretensions beyond spiritual leadership. By choosing to ride on a white horse (a symbol of imperial status, and hence an explicit challenge to the imperial order) and later mounting a failed expedition to establish a divine kingdom in Mongolia, Deguchi assumed poses not dissimilar to Asahara who, in 1994, established his own 'government' (see below, Chapter 7).[95]

In terms of Asahara's brushes with the law and his displays of violent behaviour, one finds parallels with other new religious leaders. Kiriyama Seiyū, the leader of Agonshū, also had a conviction for making and vending fraudulent substances, in Kiriyama's case, illicitly brewed alcohol, for which he went to prison for six months in 1953. This offence occurred at a time before Kiriyama had embarked on a religious path and was trying to make a living any way he could, and the misfortune itself served as a catalyst in his turn to religion.[96] Other founders of Japanese new religions have also been arrested and imprisoned for acts of violence while acting as religious leaders. Itō Shinjō, the founder of Shinnyoen, one of the larger and more socially conservative new religions, had, as Jay Sakashita has commented, 'a history of difficulty with anger management and was given to violent outbursts'.[97] In 1950 he was arraigned and spent 40 days in prison on being found guilty of a number of charges relating to beatings meted out to disciples suspected of infringements of the religion's rules. The disciples needed several days, or in two cases, a month, to recover from the beatings inflicted.

One could cite further examples to illustrate the point that, although Asahara exhibited a violent and at times cruel and harsh side, and although he was prone to aggressive behaviour and to disregard the laws of the land, this does not mark him out as unique among the charismatic figures who have established religious movements in Japan; nor does it disqualify him from religious leadership. His behaviour was not necessarily abnormal for someone in his position: no one who proclaims him or herself to be a mouthpiece of a god, an incarnation of Buddha or a messiah able to save humanity from apocalypse, is likely to conform too closely to the normative rules of society. Rather, one expects such people to display eccentricities and oddities and to manifest what Sandra Bell has identified as 'crazy wisdom' – the term she uses in her analysis of the Tibetan Buddhist guru Chogyam Trungpa. Trungpa established a major following in the USA in the 1970s and 1980s while seemingly flouting many of the religious conventions that normally are followed by Buddhist leaders; it appears that he behaved outrageously, liberally imbibing alcohol and engaging in numerous sexual affairs with female disciples.[98]

The enlightened guru who brings new revelations and truths operates in a different sphere from the everyday and normal: s/he is thus *expected* to be different to, and act in different ways from, others. Indeed, not only is eccentric or extraordinary behaviour such as licentiousness or fits of anger tolerated in such circumstances by followers: in a sense it serves as proof of the guru/leader's special nature. Trungpa's eccentric behaviour was seen by disciples as proof of his extraordinary powers as a spiritual leader who had transcended the normal boundaries of the universe. Similar themes can also be seen with Asahara and, indeed, with many other religious leaders whose movements have been surrounded by controversy. I shall return to this question of the leader who behaves abnormally in my concluding chapter and discuss how this fits into the understandings of disciples who not only accept and justify his or her seemingly odd and eccentric behaviour but actively appear to support and encourage it. Here the point I wish to make is simply that, although he clearly had numerous psychological faults, this did not prevent Asahara from being, at the same time, a religious leader who attracted a devoted following that was entranced by his charismatic power. This chapter has shown the elements in his personality that were influential in that process, and the themes that shaped his religious view of the world. In Chapter 3 the focus will shift to the movement he created, its basic themes and teachings.

超

3 Creation, Preservation and Destruction – The Development and Nature of the Religion of Supreme Truth

The name Asahara eventually chose for his religion was Aum Shinrikyō. He gave it this name in 1987, three years after he had laid its first foundations by setting up a yoga group in Tokyo. The name Aum Shinrikyō is significant and deserves some comment. The term *shinri*, as has already been stated, means truth, while *kyō*, meaning 'teaching', is a common suffix for religious groups. This emphasis on 'the teaching of truth' thus indicates an exclusivity central to Aum's worldview.

The term Aum (Japanese: *Oumu*) comes from Sanskrit. Commonly chanted as part of various esoteric Hindu and Buddhist mantras and prayers, it represents, in Hinduism, the interlocking powers of the universe, and the attributes of the sacred Hindu trilogy of Brahma, Vishnu and Shiva, the gods of creation, preservation and destruction. Asahara emphasised the link between his movement's name and the forces represented by these gods: 'A means creation, U means maintenance or continuation, and M is destruction.'[1] It should be noted that, in Hindu usage, the notion of destruction (and Shiva, the deity who most closely represents it in Hindu cosmology) does not signify *wanton* destruction of the phenomenal world or of life *per se*, but destruction of evil and of karmic hindrances to enlightenment. The term Aum in its basic meanings thus signifies the creation and preservation of good and the destruction of evil.

In Aum Shinrikyō, however, these nuances changed over the years. As will be seen in later chapters, while Aum Shinrikyō as the 'teaching of truth' originally commenced with the desire to erase evil, to create good, and to bring universal salvation, its impulses eventually turned towards destruction, whose images came to occupy an increasingly potent place in its leader's thinking and in its activities, supplanting its earlier mission of universal salvation. This shift and the tensions that it embraced were not, however, visible when Asahara established his yoga group in Shibuya in Tokyo. This group, which initially numbered around 15 members, was the nucleus around which his religion coalesced. Among its early members were several who later formed part of the elite group at the centre of Aum's activities. These members included Ishii Hisako, at the time an office lady working in a business concern in Tokyo, Iida Eriko, a work colleague of Ishii's, and Ōuchi Sanae, all of whom have since stood in the dock charged with various criminal activities related to the Aum affair.

In 1986 the group become formally established as a religious movement, taking the title Aum Shinsen no Kai (literally 'Aum Mountain Hermits' Society'). It was in this year also that Asahara began to publish books outlining his teachings, and that Aum started to acquire land in rural Japan, on which it planned to build communes, for example in the vicinity of Mount Fuji, which became its main centre of operations. In 1987 the movement changed its name to Aum Shinrikyō, under which, in 1989, it became legally registered in Japan as a religious organisation (shūkyō hōjin). It was in this same year, 1989, that the movement came to the attention of the wider public and became the focus of negative stories in the mass media, largely as a result of complaints made against it by disgruntled parents whose young offspring had given up their careers, education and university places to join Aum, often at the same time donating all their savings and possessions to the movement.

The negative image that Aum began to acquire at this time was intensified as a result of the disappearance of a lawyer, Sakamoto Tsutsumi, and his wife and young son in November 1989. At the time Sakamoto was representing a group of parents and others who had made complaints against Aum. Although the movement escaped close police scrutiny at the time, it was widely believed to have been involved in this incident (suspicions that were proved to be accurate several years later). It thus remained under a cloud, becoming a repeated target in the media and also attracting criticism from lawyers' associations who accused it of being involved in the disappearance of their colleague Sakamoto. By late 1989, then, Aum already had attracted a fair amount of criticism from parents, journalists and lawyers, and had gained a reputation as a controversial religious movement. In the years that followed Aum was rarely out of the news for long. In February 1990 it became a focus of controversy and public derision for establishing a political party and fighting an extraordinary and disastrous election campaign. Soon afterwards it became engaged in a series of long-running and bitter disputes with local residents in and around its communes in Yamanashi and Kumamoto prefectures.

Although scandal, controversy and conflict were thus cardinal elements in Aum's history, the movement grew over the years. It underwent a rapid expansion from around 35 members in early 1986 to 1,300 by July 1987,[2] to around 4,000 members by late 1989, and by 1995 it had approximately 10,000 members in Japan. However, it also lost members through defections. While this was not an uncommon problem faced by new religions in Japan, this was a recurrent source of concern to Asahara, since it hinted at a potential area of failure in the movement. Indeed, Aum had its share of failures, in particular in its attempts to expand overseas. From 1992 it had become active in Russia, attracting around 30,000 followers during its brief and turbulent history there, and had tried to establish overseas branches in Germany, the USA and Sri Lanka, albeit without much success.

Numerically, even at its apex, Aum was relatively small by the standards of many of the Japanese new religions which often have several hundreds of thousands or even millions of members. Indeed, its growth fell short of Asahara's own expectations and ambitions, and this failure was, in itself, a critical factor that influenced the ways Aum's teachings and the affair in general developed. Nevertheless, it is worth remembering that Aum's development, especially in the context of its short history up to 1995, was quite considerable both in terms of numbers (from 15 to 10,000 in a decade) and scope. In addition, around 10 per cent of its members had renounced the world, donated all their possessions to Aum and devoted themselves to it full-time. This was a unique achievement in the context of the new religions of Japan, which have invariably been lay-centred: Aum was the only sizeable new religion to emphasise world renunciation and to enthuse followers in such numbers to leave behind secular society and join a religious order. Especially in an era in which the established Buddhist sects were having difficulty in recruiting people to the priesthood, it was a striking achievement. This also demonstrates the levels of devotion and commitment that Asahara was able to engender in his followers. While the heavy emphasis on asceticism and the extreme demands Aum placed on its followers deterred the possibility of real mass growth, it still managed to develop an extremely dedicated and not inconsiderable following.

The movement developed enormously in other ways as well in the 11 years between its first beginnings and the subway attack which brought it world notoriety. By 1995 Aum had built a large commune with numerous buildings (including factories making illicit drugs and weapons, printing presses and many other enterprises) at its centres in Shizuoka and Yamanashi prefectures, and had established a network of commercial concerns including a publishing firm which produced and distributed Aum's books, as well as restaurants and a computer company, Mahapōsha, which was one of the largest vendors of personal computers in Japan. All of these were staffed by Aum members who worked tirelessly to generate income that could be channelled back into the movement, to support its communes, its *shukkesha* and its proselytisation campaigns – and also, it later became clear, its escalating illegal activities.

This 11 year period of Aum's history, from its formation as a small yoga group to its development as a highly centralised and hierarchic organisation overseeing various commercial enterprises and engaged in criminal atrocities on a large scale, was a tumultuous one. This was so not only in terms of the growth and activities of the movement, but also in terms of the various shifts it experienced in its orientations and views, and in the changing emphases it placed on various doctrines and ideas.

Such turbulence and change are by no means abnormal for new religious movements centred around inspired and driven charismatic founders. Being founded in the experiences, understandings and visions of such leaders, new religions such as Aum are almost inevitably subject to rapid changes and shifts in their doctrines, ideas and orientations, especially in their earlier years, as the experiences of their founders/ leaders develop and change. Charismatic founders, as was noted in the previous chapter, are not likely to be balanced individuals with over-whelming drives towards stability and tranquillity, so much as people driven by a special sense of mission. Hence it is unsurprising that the movements they create, especially in the earliest flushes of enthusiasm and dynamism, tend to be characterised more by upheavals, turbulence and shifts of focus as they adopt new ideas and directions with great rapidity, than they are by stability based on systematised doctrines. Rapid change is often one of the attractions of new movements, providing followers with the feeling of excitement and attracting new members because of the sense of dynamism generated.[3]

Such rapid, inspirational developments do not necessarily produce a coherent system of thought from the outset. Indeed, it is unrealistic to expect that they should do so: the systematisation of doctrines in religious groups is generally something that occurs incrementally over a considerable period of time. It may well occur after the demise of the founding figure – whose primary goal is more likely to be the creation of a faith-centred movement that will keep the flame of thought alive for posterity. This is important to note with regard to Aum because, at the time of the Tokyo attack, the movement was little more than a decade old and with its founder still active. Its teachings were still very much in flux and not yet fully systematised into a coherent doctrinal framework.

ECLECTIC FOUNDATIONS: AUM'S RELIGIOUS ORIENTATIONS

Aum was highly eclectic in nature, drawing on a number of religious sources and inspirations from Japanese popular religious culture and from various world religions. Such eclecticism is not uncommon among new religions, either in Japan or elsewhere. As Winston Davis has noted in outlining the derivation of ideas in another Japanese new religion, Mahikari, '[M]essiahs are seldom original thinkers'[4]: more commonly, their inspiration is based in personal charisma and in a deep belief in their own spiritual capacities, often related to such practical matters as their ability to heal, solve problems, divine the future and empower their followers.

Aum's religious background was of this type, involving the interweaving and juxtaposition of numerous ideas and practices taken from diverse religious traditions, but bound together through the person and authority of Asahara. In its widespread borrowing from different traditions, Aum also reflected a perception not uncommon among eclectic religious groups of the modern age, including the various groups that are loosely considered to constitute the New Age movement: that this is an era that requires not the religious divisions of competing traditions, but a merging of diverse religious themes within a new and encompassing movement. Often this type of thinking is linked to a fascination with other cultures, especially those of the distant past, which may be idealised as possessing ancient spiritual knowledge lost to the modern world but which could be recovered and used as a spiritual antidote to contemporary materialism and scientific rationalism. Such ideas have appeared in a variety of religious movements that have emerged in recent decades, from the Rajneesh movement with its extensive borrowings from Taoism, yoga, various forms of Buddhism, and Hinduism,[5] to the new spiritualist movements of Japan which, as Shimazono Susumu has shown, use a 'pick and mix' approach to their religious practices and structures, juxtaposing and combining numerous themes, ideas and practices from different sources and traditions.[6]

Aum operated in this manner, absorbing influences from a variety of traditions. Asahara was influenced by the folk and popular religious cultures of the age, and many of the ideas developed in Aum came from such sources. Aum's fascination with prophecy and its millennial perspectives, its interest in the workings and eradication of karma and in the acquisition of psychic powers and the practice of yoga, as well as its aspirations to develop a new, purer form of Buddhism, were drawn from this culture, and especially from Agonshū.[7] Aum also drew on the purported wisdom of ancient cultures, through its interest in what it idealised as original, pure Buddhism, and through a fascination with the culture of ancient Egypt. Asahara and his disciples visited the pyramids in order to meditate there and Asahara drew links between himself and the ancient wisdom of Egypt through his claims (mentioned in Chapter 2), to have been the architect of the pyramids in a prior existence.[8]

Aum also derived various ideas and doctrines from world religions such as Hinduism, Buddhism and, later in its development, Christianity. Its yoga practices and related concepts such as the awakening of the *kundalini* were drawn from Hinduism. India was a potent image and a popular religious destination in Aum. It was a holy land (*seichi*) which Asahara visited on many occasions and where he had some of his formative religious experiences. Hindu motifs were prevalent in the public images that he displayed to the world. In his clothing and appearance, for example, he took on the air of an Indian guru or ascetic, with long flowing hair and a beard and Indian-style robes. Moreover, as mentioned in the previous chapter, he often appeared in Aum publicity photographs in Indian settings, either meditating with Indian sadhus or posing against a Himalayan backdrop.[9]

Aum's most striking borrowing from Hinduism was that of the Hindu deity Shiva, who became Aum's main image of worship. Asahara felt an affinity for Shiva and regarded the deity as a personal guiding spirit.[10] The relationship was an enduring one, in which the messages imparted by Shiva served as guidelines for Asahara who, as an Aum magazine stated, 'always acts on Lord Shiva's suggestion', for example, by embarking in January 1986 on a visit to numerous sacred sites in India at Shiva's behest.[11] Over many years he claimed to have received revelations and messages from Shiva that confirmed his sense of mission.[12] One of the most important occurred while Asahara was in India in 1992, when Shiva told him that only he could save the world,[13] a revelation which was only retold to his followers in 1994. It was Shiva who, according to Asahara, provided the inspirational message that led to his choosing the name Aum Shinrikyō in 1987. Shiva had told him that there was no longer any truth in the world apart from in Asahara's movement (at that time called Aum Shinsen no Kai), and that Asahara should demonstrate this possession of the truth by giving it a new name, *Shinrikyō*, the teaching of truth.[14] Asahara's relationship with Shiva eventually moved from one of veneration and affinity, to one of identification: in 1991 Asahara even claimed to be a manifestation of Shiva.[15]

Shiva was important also to the movement's followers, who worshipped and made vows to him. On undertaking an ascetic retreat, for example, Ōuchi Sanae vowed to Shiva that she would 'cross the bridge of reincarnation with him and go to the feet of the guru'.[16] An Aum believer (writing under the pseudonym Nishiwaki Kei) has discussed the significance of Shiva in Aum's thought in an unpublished article that was given to me in 1997 by Aum officials who averred that it was an accurate representation of Aum's belief system. According to Nishiwaki, Shiva was a manifestation of the highest level of absolute consciousness and of pure, eternal truth, while spiritual practices related to the worship of Shiva (including yoga, meditation and the recitation of Shiva's mantra (Aum)) were means of transcending the polluted self, to attain the highest levels of consciousness and gain release from an endless and painful cycle of rebirth.[17]

However, it was Buddhism that formed Aum's primary frame of reference in terms of religious self-definition. Although he believed Japanese Buddhism to be spiritually deficient and incapable of providing the means for salvation, Buddhism remained an important feature in Asahara's spiritual landscape, providing the inspiration and basis for many of his most central teachings. While many of the ideas prominent in Aum (including karma and transmigration, as well as its meditation practices) are found in both Hinduism and Buddhism, Aum considered that its use of such concepts was based on Buddhist interpretations. Indeed, in an interesting spin on this issue, Nishiwaki has argued that Aum's veneration of Shiva was a sign of its Buddhist orientations. Shiva was, Nishiwaki stated, a symbol of the Indian, Hindu roots out of which Buddhism emerged: the historical Buddha Shakyamuni had grown up in this Hindu environment, and the Shakya clan from which he came venerated Hindu deities, including Shiva. Shiva was thus, Nishiwaki claimed, closely associated with the Buddha as an inspirational deity. Aum's veneration of Shiva was therefore not a contradiction to its focus on Buddhism: rather, Aum, in using yoga and meditation practices and reciting mantras associated with Shaivite Hinduism, had integrated these two traditions to form what he called *Shiva Bukkyō* (Shiva Buddhism). According to Nishiwaki, this view was expressed by Asahara during a sermon to disciples at the Indian Buddhist site of Sahet Mahet in November 1992.[18]

Buddhist ideas and teachings, though barely expressed in Asahara's very earliest teachings,[19] rapidly became predominant within its doctrinal system. In his second book, *Seishi o koeru* [Transcending Life and Death] published in 1986, Asahara emphasised the Buddha's teaching as the way to liberation and expressed Aum's understanding of karma and of the relationship of desire and suffering within a Buddhist framework.[20] Buddhist terminology began to appear increasingly in Aum publications: its journals bore Buddhist titles such as *Mahāyāna* and *Vajrayāna Sacca* (the successive titles of its regular monthly magazine), while the large majority of books that Asahara published contained Buddhist terms or nuances in their titles.[21] The holy names that members were given had Buddhist origins (see below), while Aum's conceptualisation of a structured path of spiritual attainment in which the practitioner rose through various different stages and levels leading eventually to ultimate liberation was based on Asahara's interpretations of Buddhist Abhidharma teachings.[22] Asahara and his disciples also made pilgrimages to Buddhist sites in India, and he often used such occasions to deliver sermons to them, and to emphasise the links he believed his movement had with early Buddhism.[23]

Besides its idealisation of early Indian Buddhism, Aum also developed a very strong fascination for Tibetan Buddhism. Asahara visited Tibetan centres in India, including Dharmsala, the headquarters of the Dalai Lama. He met the Dalai Lama there in 1987 and on a number of subsequent occasions, impressing him, according to comments made by the Dalai Lama and widely reported in the Japanese media, with his seriousness and spirituality. It was from Tibetan Buddhism that Aum absorbed a number of ideas (including the notion of *poa*) that played an important part in its development and in the evolving construction of its self-identity, and that provided Asahara with some of the ideas and images that he eventually used to construct a legitimating framework for the violence that developed in Aum.

Later in its development, too, Aum incorporated motifs from other religious traditions, particularly from Christianity. As will be seen in subsequent chapters, Aum's millennial beliefs became infused with Christian imagery drawn from the Book of Revelations of St John, while Christian images related to the concepts of suffering, persecution and sacrifice began to become manifest in Asahara's thought world in the early 1990s.

Aum, in other words, was highly eclectic although with a primary focus, in terms of self-identity, on Buddhism. This did not make it a Buddhist movement *per se*, and many of its uses and interpretations of teachings drawn from Buddhist sources (such as its use of the concept of *poa*) could, from a Buddhist perspective, be considered highly dubious.[24] However, it is important to recognise that Buddhism and Buddhist motifs were central to Aum's make-up and sense of self-identity, and that Aum's followers believed firmly that they were following a Buddhist path. This is a point that the various members and ex-members of Aum whom I interviewed have been uniformly clear about.

The main pillar of Aum Shinrikyō, of course, was its founder and leader, whose personality held the movement together. He provided it with its teachings and with a framework that unified the disparate and eclectic doctrinal strands. Asahara himself emphasised this when he stated that Aum possessed four pillars of truth: its teachings and doctrines, which represented eternal truth; its practices, which pointed the way to that truth; its attainers (i.e. members) who, through their practice and adherence to the doctrines, followed the path of truth; and its guru, who was the root and source of that truth.[25]

Asahara was not just the medium through which such teachings could be brought together, but its source and primary focus of veneration. While Shiva and the Buddha may have been exalted images of worship for members, it was Asahara, the guru whose mind was to be cloned, to whom disciples owed absolute obedience. In practical terms he was the dominant figure of worship in Aum. While Aum drew at various times on Hindu, Buddhist, Christian and Japanese folk religious themes, and while these various traditions (but notably Buddhism) were important in its self-definition, at root Aum Shinrikyō was, like many of the Japanese new religions, a charismatic religious movement framed around an inspired individual. As such, Aum Shinrikyō can best be described as 'Asaharan' religion and, as will be seen below, it was with his experiences and actions that the movement took shape and developed.

EARLY DAYS: ASCETICISM, PSYCHIC POWER, INITIATION AND ERADICATION OF KARMA

When Asahara established his yoga group in February 1984 it is unclear how qualified he was in formal terms as a teacher of yoga and meditation. He certainly had little formal training in these fields, and it appears that much of the yoga was learnt from books.[26] He was, in other words, a self-proclaimed religious teacher driven, it would appear, more by his frustration at the lack of ascetic practice and teaching in the established and the new religions, and by his sense of accomplishment and mission than by knowledge and skills acquired through formal religious training.

That he was able to attract members, albeit at first a very small number, retain their loyalty and build a considerable following in the years afterwards, indicates that, even if self-taught and self-proclaimed, he was more than capable in this respect. Indeed, for his followers he was an inspired teacher with great insights into his disciples' problems and a capability to advise them in the courses of practice that they should undertake. Serizawa, for example, cites a disciple who stated that Asahara was an excellent teacher who was highly skilled at ascertaining each follower's level of attainment and advising them accordingly as to the practices they should follow next.[27] Similar testimonies have emerged in the interviews that I and various colleagues have conducted with former and present members of the movement, and they form a recurrent theme also in the various publications of the movement.[28]

Asahara's lack of formal training in a spiritual tradition may not have been all that uncommon in the world of the new religions of Japan, which has a long tradition of self-proclaimed religious leaders. However, in the light of subsequent events it proved critical, for he at times displayed an inability to recognise the limits of physical endurance or capabilities with respect to some of the practices he instituted, or to know where to draw the boundaries or limit the demands he made on his followers. This failing was to have disastrous consequences for the movement. One cannot say for certain, of course, that such problems would have been avoided if he had undergone extensive training in an organised system and had been able to learn from the inherited knowledge of such traditions about the limits and dangers inherent in ascetic practices. However, there remains the possibility that if some scope for serious training in a formally established tradition had been available to him, it might have provided some safeguards against the pitfalls that Aum eventually encountered.

This is especially so given that the notions inherent in Aum's belief system about the polluted nature of the body and the need to purify it through physical austerities lent themselves to a focus on severe mortification and extreme practices. This orientation along with the lack of adherence to, or training in, a particular tradition manifested itself in Aum's readiness to experiment widely, trying out numerous means, including eventually the use of drugs, which, it was hoped, might lead to spiritual breakthroughs. Some of these experimental techniques had disastrous results, as in, for example, the 'Christ initiation' that claimed several fatalities inside Aum in 1994. As Takahashi Hidetoshi relates in his account of life inside Aum, when this practice was first instituted it involved, besides the ingestion of LSD, a series of ten immersions in extremely hot water. This number proved excessive and after one or more disciples who initially undertook this feat succumbed in the effort, the number of immersions was reduced to three.[29]

Of the various influences that Asahara had imbibed from the popular religious culture of the era, the ones that were most overtly expressed in the nascent group were an interest in the attainment of psychic powers (*chōnōryoku*) and an emphasis on eradicating karma. Both were closely linked to asceticism: the former was produced and the latter eradicated through it. The notion that the body was an impediment to the attainment of higher levels of consciousness, a polluted entity whose influences needed to be cast off so that the spirit could achieve liberation, was a cardinal tenet of Asahara's teaching. It was, he stated, due to one's love for and clinging attachment to the physical body, and through it to the realms of the senses, that one acquired the negative karma that pulled one down into the hells after death: liberation came from eradicating such attachments to the body via asceticism.[30] Severing this attachment to the physical body via ascetic disciplines and through the cessation of bodily activities (e.g. breathing) was equated with the cessation of desire and the attainment of enlightenment.

This doctrinal emphasis on the negative influences of desire was drawn from Buddhism and its view of suffering as a basic element in human existence, caused by desire and attachment to the things of this world, and its view that enlightenment is achieved through the cessation of desire. Aum thus concurred with the world-negating dimensions of Buddhism in its rejection of attachments and in its emphasis on suffering as a product of materialism and desire. It also believed that suffering was a spur to spiritual practice and a key to liberation, and Asahara frequently reminded his disciples that suffering was a major stimulus that encouraged them to engage in religious practices that could eradicate one's desires and attachments. As such one *needed* to suffer in order to achieve these ends and to develop one's faith. This was why, he argued, the harsh and painful ascetic practices Aum engaged in were necessary in order to attain liberation.[31]

Such a philosophy encouraged the use of extreme austerities which, from the outset, consumed a major part of the energies of Asahara and his followers. Hardship was thus an important element in the life of Aum followers, a means to improve their spiritual situation, increase their faith and eradicate their suffering. Asahara, indeed, created hardships for his disciples in the practices they were meant to follow, both as tests of their devotion and as a means of strengthening their resolve: the concept of struggle was thus intrinsic to Aum's path of practice.[32]

Asahara was the source of spiritual power within the movement, transferring his energies to his followers through rites of initiation that were intended to help them achieve spiritual breakthroughs. Ishii Hisako was the first disciple to receive such initiation when, in 1984, she received from Asahara the *shaktipat* initiation.[33] This was originally a Hindu initiation practice in which the guru places his/her thumb on the forehead of the person to be initiated and transfers positive energy to, while absorbing negative energy (karma) from, the receiver. Asahara's *shaktipat* was considered to be highly efficacious, as was evinced by its first use, in which Ishii was said to have experienced the awakening of *kundalini*.[34] Virtually from the beginning, then, Asahara's role as a source of spiritual energy and as a guru whose powers of initiation could move the disciple forward along the path of spiritual attainment was implanted in the movement's belief structures.

Initiation was both an affirmation of the power of the guru and an important element in disciples' progress up the ladder of spiritual attainment. While initiations eventually took a number of different rituals forms in Aum, the *shaktipat* initiation remained the most common, performed by Asahara on numerous occasions. It was, however, an extremely demanding practice that drained his energies and took its toll. According to various Aum sources, Asahara frequently became exhausted and ill as a result, and he often complained that absorbing negative energy and karma from disciples had severe effects on him.[35] Eventually, in 1988, he ceased performing *shaktipat* entirely and left this task to leading disciples such as Ishii and his wife Tomoko, who were considered to be spiritually advanced enough to act on his behalf.

Ascetic practices were also, it was believed, the gateway to the attainment of psychic powers (*chōnōryoku*). It was the possibility of acquiring such powers that initially attracted followers to the group and persuaded them to engage in arduous austerities. Amongst the powers that, it was claimed, disciples could acquire were levitation, the ability to divine the future, and the ability to attain high energy levels and extraordinary powers of perception. Levitation was perhaps the most widely sought and emphasised of these, and it was as a result of his claims in this area that Asahara first came to wider public notice. In February 1985 *Twilight Zone*, a Japanese magazine dealing with fringe religious issues and alternative therapies, carried a feature on Asahara in which he claimed to be able to levitate as a result of powers acquired through his ascetic practice. The magazine reproduced a photograph of Asahara, bare-chested, teeth gritted and with a look of great pain on his face, 'levitating' with his legs crossed in the Lotus position, several inches in the air.

The publicity that came from the *Twilight Zone* feature attracted a number of people in search of similar experiences. Asahara had doubtless learned from his days in Agonshû and through observing the activities of Kiriyama Seiyū that such uses of publicity could be beneficial in the development of a religious movement. Kiriyama was a consummate and highly skilled publicist who had made Agonshū widely known through the use of dramatic public events, skilfully managed mass rituals and widely disseminated books about the attainment of psychic power.[36] In the intensely competitive religious market of the 1980s, when numerous new movements and teachers were trying to catch the attention of potential members and spiritual seekers, Asahara clearly sought to emulate his former teacher. In later years, too, similarly dramatic public demonstrations of ascetic feats and attainments, including death-defying underwater and underground ascetic practices, were used by Aum to impress potential followers and draw attention to the movement.

As with many aspects of Asahara's life, the *Twilight Zone* photograph raised many questions and gave his later critics the chance to question his integrity and suggest that it was little more than a publicity gimmick. The pained look on his face, critics suggested, was because he was leaping rather than levitating, a point made with some venom by the lawyer and anti-Aum campaigner Takimoto Tarō, who had himself photographed leaping in a similar way, as if to suggest that Asahara's feat were merely a stratagem and fraud.[37] Asahara vehemently denied such accusations, claiming he had really levitated and that the pained look on his face was the result of the stress of having a photographer recording his practice.[38] Despite Takimoto's criticisms, levitation remained a widely publicised activity in Aum, seen as testimony to the efficacy of Aum practices and evidence of the powers that could be attained by joining the movement. Aum books continued to affirm the importance and validity of such experiences, conveying accounts not only of how various disciples had seen Asahara levitate, but of how they, too, had had similar experiences, and displaying numerous photographs to affirm this point.[39]

Whatever the truth about Asahara's levitation, its underlying message resonated with Aum's basic belief structures, and with the ethos of much of the popular culture of the age. Aum repudiated the scientific rationalism that, in its acceptance of physical laws, limited the human being to the physical, material realms. Hence, by striving to levitate, the practitioner was in effect demonstrating both his/her overcoming of the physical limitations of the body and of the material world that kept the body, as it were, firmly rooted to the ground. The body that could levitate was a body freed from spiritual pollution and from the attach-

73

ments of this world. Thus, while striving to demonstrate the powers of levitation might strike many observers as a rather risible form of publicity-seeking, there was a serious doctrinal point and meaning underlying such activities. It was a physical manifestation of Aum's teachings as well as of the powers that its practices could bring.

The acquisition of psychic powers was emphasised as a core theme in Asahara's first book *Chōnōryoku himitsu kaihatsuhō* [The Secret Method of Developing Psychic Power], which was originally published in March 1986. In it Asahara outlined his early religious experiences and gave instructions on the performance of yoga and other techniques that could facilitate the development of such powers. The volume was a seminal work for Aum that also contained various testimonies by members about their own psychic experiences, and established that the acquisition of such powers was a central aim within the movement.

Aum's thoughts on this subject developed further in later years. In a series of volumes published in the early 1990s under the general title of *Chōetsu jinriki*, Asahara jettisoned the term and concept of *chōnōryoku* (psychic powers), criticising it as being founded in egotistical desires and utilised by inferior religious groups. In its place he asserted that Aum could provide its followers with *chōetsu jinriki* (transcendent spiritual powers) which were the product of Buddhist spiritual practices that allowed one to gain release from and penetrate into one's real self.[40] *Chōetsu jinriki*, attained by Asahara and found through Aum's path of practice, were the spiritually transcendent powers of those who had gone beyond the realms of ego, such as Shakyamuni the Buddha.[41] In his extension of the concept of psychic powers, in other words, Asahara utilised Buddhist motifs to expand on the practices and notions initially expressed in *Chōnōryoku himitsu kaihatsuhō*. By denouncing psychic powers as egotistical he was also, implicitly, criticising rival religious groups such as Agonshū that claimed to be able to provide its followers with these powers.

There were six special powers that Asahara claimed to possess:

1. *jinsokutsū*: the powers of levitation, telepathy, and the ability to travel to other higher spiritual realms;
2. *tennitsū*: the power to hear the voices of the gods and very distant sounds;
3. *tajintsū*: the power to understand what goes on in other people's minds;
4. *shukumyōtsū*: the power to discern the previous lives of oneself and others;

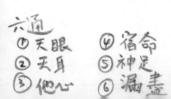

5. *tengentsū*: the power to discern one's and others' future lives and discern rebirths; and
6. *rōjintsū*: the attainment of the absolute wisdom of the gods.[42]

He could teach his disciples how to attain the first five of these abilities; however, the last, *rōjintsû*, was a special attainment and characteristic of the guru alone.[43] Disciples, in other words, could not attain the same levels as Asahara. Here is further evidence of the gap that Asahara assiduously placed between himself and his disciples. They might strive to achieve extraordinary levels of attainment, but they would always remain below the levels of attainment of the guru himself.

THE PSYCHIC POWER OF PROPHECY AND THE STRUCTURE OF THE UNIVERSE

Through his psychic powers Asahara claimed to able to prophesy and divine the future and to know the past and future lives of other people. In *Chōnōryoku himitsu kaihatsuhō* (Asahara 1993a) such powers of prophecy are mentioned, albeit somewhat in passing, with allusions to Nostradamus's prophecies about an end-of-century cataclysm and some claims about his own ability to foresee future events.[44] This nascent power steadily became a central element in his teachings as Asahara assumed the mantle of a prophet who could discern the future of humanity. Eventually such prophecies relating to a coming cataclysm appeared more and more frequently in his sermons, serving to shape Aum's development as a movement with a strong millennialist orientation.

Prediction and prophecy were not limited, however, to the macrocosmic arena of world destiny, but also applied to the lives of individuals. Asahara's prophetic powers were such, it was believed, that he could see the destinies of his followers and could design the correct and most appropriate path of spiritual practice for each of them in relation to that future.[45] This belief gave Asahara ultimate control over each member's practice and made them thoroughly dependent on him. This produced a highly individualised structure of practice in which members followed different personal paths of spiritual practice geared to their future needs, rather than following a co-ordinated system of practice common to all followers.

This is not to say that there were no common structures of practice in Aum at all, for the movement produced various manuals and texts which outlined the forms of practice members could follow.[46] However, individual members had their own individualised courses of practice, which meant that Aum centres often gave the impression of chaos and noise, with different people performing different actions. I realised just how pronounced this individualisation of practice was in Aum when I visited an Aum *dōjo* (training centre) in Yokohama in January 1998. Although there were relatively few people there (in all around ten people came in during the two hours I was there), each person seemed to have his or her own practice to follow. One, for example, sat at a small table reading an Aum text while making symbolic gestures (*mudras*) with his hands; another performed endless prostrations as she recited various prayers and chants; a third sat in silent meditation, swaying his body back and forth as he did so. Others came in and out, found an empty space on the *tatami*-matted floor of the small centre, and went about their practices. The overall impression was, even within what was a small room perhaps no more than 20 feet square, of a highly individualised system.

It was not only his devotees whose future he could foresee: Asahara also claimed the capacity to see the future lives of people outside the movement as well, paying particular attention to those who came into conflict with Aum. The claim that he could discern the future fates of others was central to the arguments that were subsequently used to legitimate the killings of opponents who, Asahara was to argue, would otherwise fall into the hells because of their actions. The prophetic dimensions of Asahara's teachings thus assumed a critical place in the movement's development, in his own status as a religious leader, and in the processes which led to and legitimated its crimes.

Asahara's claims of prophecy are important also for the insights they provide into Aum's view of the structure of the universe. It was this aspect of its thought world, that underpinned its beliefs in the validity and, indeed the certainty, of prophecy. According to Aum, the universe consists not only of the present, physical, material realm in which humans exist, but also of three further higher realms: the astral world, the causal world and, above these, the world of Maha Nirvana or the absolute, total extinction of cognition and experience, the realm of ultimate enlightenment.[47] Each of these worlds has a number of sub-divisions or realms within it, ranged in a hierarchic structure. Humans exist in the lowest world (the material realm, or the realm of desire) which is divided (as in Buddhist cosmology) into six levels, ranging from painful hells in which dwell the spirits of those who are suffering for their karmic sins in previous existences, through to the realm of human existence and to various higher spiritual realms. Above the material world or realm of desire is the realm of form, also known in Aum as the astral world, consisting of various celestial realms of sound and light. The spirit can ascend through these realms due to ascetic and meditative practices that enable it to shed all traces of the physical realms and body, and to enter into increasingly higher realms of consciousness. This upward path eventually leads to the causal world, which consists of various realms of light and infinite space. In this world the spirit has gone beyond all suffering, sadness and pleasure, to exist in a state of enlightenment;[48] beyond this is the world of Maha Nirvana.

In Aum's view, humans are normally mired in the material world of desire, condemned to slide down into the lower realms at death because of karmic impediments accrued in life. However, if they had been especially diligent in their behaviour, they could ascend into the higher realms of the world of desire. However, Aum offered them the potential to ascend further still and attain the ultimate heights of transcendence. This was not only after death, with the spirit having accumulated enough good karma to be reborn in higher realms, but in life. Through spiritual practice and initiations the practitioner could shed his or her links to the physical world and awaken his or her astral body, which would ascend to higher spiritual realms and engage in practice. Asahara, according to Aum, was able to travel spiritually to these higher realms in his meditation, and to act as a conduit between the astral, causal and material worlds. The sacred music that was played at Aum centres, used in its rituals and in some of its meditation practices, for example, was called 'Astral Music' and was 'made of pure melodies that Master Asahara has brought back from the higher Astral world through his deep meditation.'[49]

While he alone had attained the spiritual prowess to reach the very highest realms, other practitioners also could travel spiritually upwards. Ishii Hisako, for example, wrote a regular column in Aum magazines containing her messages from the astral world, to which she travelled in her meditations.[50] The experiences of Aum practitioners were generally interpreted in relation to these different realms of existence. It was common, for example, for practitioners to report that, during their various meditations and practices, they saw various forms of light and experienced various surges of energy or heard various celestial sounds: these were evidence, Asahara taught them, of their ascent through these various stages of being into the higher astral and causal realms.[51] The experience of Ōuchi Sanae reported in Chapter 2, in which she felt such surges of energy and emanation of light was, for example, seen as a sign of the awakening of her astral body, the spiritual form in which she existed in that world.[52] Clearly, this raises the question of the extent to which practitioners' experiences were shaped by their beliefs in what would occur when they engaged in meditation and other practices: whether they saw such emanations of light because, in the cosmological world to which they had subscribed, they expected and hoped to do so, is a moot question, albeit one that I am unable to answer. Certainly, there seems to be a close correlation between the expectation of what would result from an experience and the actual experience as it was later interpreted.

These different realms, while ranged hierarchically, were interconnected. This was at the root of Asahara's prophetic powers: events that occurred in the physical world were the result of impulses and spiritual vibrations from these higher, non-physical realms, which were the source of energy that gave life to the material world. The events of this world were the product of the laws and workings of karma, whose origins were in the spiritual resonance of past actions: such spiritual origins were formed in these higher realms and manifested as physical reality in the material world. Those who could penetrate into the astral and causal realms could thus 'see' the future events of the physical world as they were being formed. They could therefore divine the future. Such divinations were not, however, 'prophecies' so much as accurate and unerring statements of an emerging reality based on the clinical observations of an enlightened spiritual who was capable of entering the causal and astral realms.[53] While this power was a special characteristic of the guru, it could also be attained by those who ascended high in the spiritual hierarchy. Since Ishii Hisako could also ascend into higher realms, she too was able to see the future, and prophesy the future lives of those she encountered. Like Asahara, she often prophesied that those who came into conflict with her were destined for the hells after death.[54]

Asahara's stature as a prophet was thus based in Aum's beliefs about the workings of the universe and in his claims to be able to know the workings of karma by seeing into the astral and causal worlds. It was this, Aum asserted, that made his prophecies exact and infallible accounts of inevitable future events.[55] This claim had potentially dangerous implications. If his prophecies did not materialise as predicted, this would implicitly challenge the claims of spiritual transcendence on which his status as a guru, and hence Aum's as a movement, were based.

INDIA, ENLIGHTENMENT AND THE DEVELOPMENT OF BUDDHIST THEMES

In January 1986 Asahara visited India with the intention of finding a guru who could help him attain enlightenment. By this time, he stated, he had reached the highest states of yoga but this had not allowed him to achieve full liberation. Yoga, in other words, was not enough on its own, and he needed to find new or additional means of practice – such as advanced forms of asceticism – to produce such results.[56] However, although he met various sages, he was unable to find an appropriate spiritual guide who could assist him in his quest and instead practised alone for two months in the Himalayas. As a result of this he attained the liberation (*gedatsu*) he sought, an experience he described as the extinction of all suffering and a feeling of transcending life and death and entering into a state of absolute freedom and happiness.[57] He was later to embellish this by claiming to have become the first Japanese in history to have attained ultimate liberation (*saishū gedatsu*).[58]

This experience signalled a turning point in Asahara's career: likening the event to the Buddha's own 'turning of the wheel of the law', in which the Buddha, after his period of asceticism, meditation and enlightenment, returned to the world to start preaching the Buddhist doctrine, Asahara became convinced that it was now his mission to turn the wheel of law again.[59] Henceforth his teachings became more deeply suffused with Buddhist imagery and he began to speak of his movement primarily in Buddhist terms and to visualise himself and his followers as descendants of the Buddha and the earliest members of the Buddhist order, with a mission to restore 'original Buddhism' (*genshi Bukkyō*) to the world.

Several of the doctrinal themes mentioned in Chapter 1 began to manifest themselves in Aum in the years immediately after this. In a series of sermons and seminars between 1986 and 1988, Asahara emphasised and developed further the notions of karma and transmigration, and affirmed various aspects of basic Buddhist morality, invoking injunctions against killing, and affirming the importance of self-control, avoidance of inebriation, and not losing one's temper.[60] Other central elements in Aum's thought world which had Buddhist connotations or derivations also began to take clear shape, including an emphasis on the transient and ephemeral nature of this world as outlined in Aum's concepts of the relationship between the causal, astral and material realms, and its incorporation of rituals for the spirits of the dead. It was from this period after his return from India that Asahara began to emphasise the ability of the living to assist the dead through *poa* rituals, and to conduct *poa* seminars to train members in this practice.

Buddhist themes became prevalent also in the spiritual capacities to be cultivated through practice. He began to emphasise that spiritual practice and physical austerities should be engaged in not primarily (as had earlier been the case) to develop psychic powers and overcome the physical limitations of the body in this world, but to enable the spirit to go beyond the physical realms of desire altogether, to shed its attachment to the body and ascend into the astral and causal realms. To do this, members needed to cultivate a spirit of non-attachment to this world through following a path of practice based on the six *paramitas* or disciplines of Mahāyāna Buddhism: *fuse* (offerings), *jikai* (observance of Buddhist precepts), *ninniku* (patience and fortitude in practice), *shōjin* (devotion), *zenjō* (meditation) and *chie* (the cultivation of supreme wisdom).[61]

The first of these was especially emphasised as the gateway to further practice, a means by which to show one's devotion to and support of the movement. As in any religious movement, the donations of the faithful were essential for Aum's economic sustenance, and members were urged to give donations for the initiations they received and to donate their property and worldly possessions to Aum to further its cause and to demonstrate their lack of attachment to the mundane world. Large numbers of followers did this willingly, and all who renounced the world as *shukkesha* gave everything they owned to Aum. This did not necessarily involve large sums of money. Some of those who joined were poor students who hardly had anything to give the movement in material terms, a point made by one of my interviewees who said he had nothing to give the movement when he became a *shukkesha*, yet was able to take this step and be supported by the movement thereafter.[62] However, Aum's emphasis on the importance of *fuse* (donations or offerings) became highly controversial in the eyes of the outside world, and led to various allegations that the movement coerced followers to give it money – allegations which, as the case of Kariya Kiyoshi's sister, often had much substance, and which eventually led to many negative stories appearing about Aum in the mass media.

Of the various mental states to be cultivated through Aum's practices, perhaps the most important was that of detachment (*seimutonjaku*), being able to withdraw wholly from all emotions and attachments to this world and to be unaffected by any sense of pleasure or suffering.[63] True detachment was to be achieved by emptying one's mind of false and corrupt data and replacing it with correct data. This process of inserting correct data into the mind was to be accomplished by repeatedly stating the truth (i.e. Aum's teachings) and driving out untruths from one's mind. This, of course, is a reference to the concept of 'cloning the guru'. While Aum strove to accomplish this through repetitive practices such as the recitation of Asahara's teachings and the chanting of mantras, it also, eventually, turned to mechanically based techniques and means such as the electronic PSI units which members wore on their heads, and drugs such as LSD, both of which were widely used in Aum from 1994 onwards.

The cultivation of detachment, which was perceived as an expression of the highest levels of spiritual attainment, thus involved controlling one's own mind and transforming it into a copy of the guru's. It was here, Shimazono Susumu has suggested, that what he calls the 'peculiar imperturbability seen in certain Aum believers' might have its theoretical foundations.[64] What Shimazono is referring to was the much-commented fact that, in the immediate aftermath of the subway attack, many senior Aum figures were able to present a calm and unruffled face to the world at large, even while the police raids of spring 1995 were going on and while Aum was being besieged by the mass media. Leading Aum luminaries such as Murai Hideo, the head of Aum's science and technology section, and Jōyu Fumihiro were able to appear in television debates and face Aum critics with serene faces, as if they were innocent of all the charges against their movement. Murai, although with Asahara the most deeply involved of all of Aum's hierarchy in its sequence of crimes, was especially noted for his calm and detached manner.[65] This detachment, the former member Takahashi Hidetoshi has stated, was a characteristic of senior Aum figures, albeit one he found rather disturbing. Even as a devotee, Takahashi felt that members of Aum's senior hierarchy were indifferent to the feelings of their fellows, and behaved in a cold and machine-like way.[66] To outsiders and critics alike such detachment certainly came across not as a sign of spiritual prowess but as something highly negative, a sign of the move-ment's callousness, inhumanity and indifference to the sufferings of ordinary people. By contrast, in Aum it was seen as proof of the attainment of a higher state of consciousness and of detachment from the mundane world.

This state of detachment was also considered critical by those charged with carrying out Aum's crimes. The subway poisoners and those who killed other Aum victims such as the Sakamoto family did so in a state of detachment from the fates of their victims and from the horrors of their deeds. They were demonstrating their spiritual prowess and show-ing how far beyond the considerations of the corrupt material world they had gone. To have attained true detachment, Asahara taught, meant to be free of the karmic repercussions of one's actions.[67] If one could kill and remain detached, one was demonstrating one's spiritual superiority and transcendence of this world. The Buddhist spiritual virtue of detachment acquired through strict ascetic and spiritual practice was thus transformed into an element in Aum's evolving legitimation of violence.

RENUNCIATION, HOLY NAMES AND THE DEVELOPMENT OF THE *SANGHA*

In April 1986 the movement took the name Aum Shinsen no Kai and established its own magazine. This was initially entitled *Shambhala Newsletter*[68] but later its name was changed to *Mahāyāna* and, subsequently, to *Vajrayāna Sacca* and finally, in 1995, to *Anuttara Sacca*. Each of these name changes represented a shift in Aum's self-perceptions of its development as a Buddhist movement. In 1986 Aum also established its own printing and publishing firm, which enabled it to produce and sell its books without needing to attract a commercial publisher's interest.

The development of an organisational structure advanced further in September 1986 when Asahara took a step that, besides reflecting Aum's aspirations as a Buddhist movement, had immense long-term consequences for the movement and its relationship to the wider world. This was the formation of what Aum, using the traditional Buddhist word for a monastic community, described as its *sangha*, a community of practitioners and seekers who, in order to devote themselves fully to their practice and to be free of all attachments and worldly ways, renounced the world to follow a path of monastic discipline. From October 1986 members who so wished could join this *sangha* by 'leaving home' (*shukke*), severing all ties to their families and friends and donating all their belongings and wealth to Aum. Ultimately, *shukkesha* were also asked to sign papers declaring that it was their intention to seek liberation through ascetic practices, but absolving Aum from any blame should anything happen to them after they had joined its communes. They dedicated their lives to Aum and worked at its centres, communes and business enterprises, striving to spread its message to the world at large, and in return the movement undertook to support them and provide them with accommodation and sustenance, albeit at an extremely spartan level.

The origins of the system of renunciation are located in Aum's beliefs, drawn from Buddhism, of the need to become detached from the phenomenal world and to acquire a sense of liberation from it through spiritual practice. Withdrawing from the everyday world became an overarching ideal in Aum and was based on the practices of Buddhist monasticism: giving up one's worldly goods, changing one's identity by the adoption of a new name indicating one's dedication to the spiritual life, and taking up residence in, and being dependent on, a religious community.

At first the numbers who took this extreme step were, unsurprisingly, small. Amongst the first to do so were Ishii Hisako and Niimi Tomomitsu, the latter of whom had joined Aum in December 1985 and renounced the world in September 1986. In this first year of the *sangha* three people became *shukkesha*, while 23 more did so in 1987 and a further 87 in 1987.[69] After having renounced the world, the next stage in their progress was the acquisition of a 'holy name', granted by Asahara as a recognition of their spiritual achievements. These were generally Japanised versions of the Sanskrit names of the Buddha's disciples or of other figures associated with the development and history of Buddhism. The first person to acquire a holy name was Ishii Hisako who, in 1986, became known in Aum as Maha Khema Taishi (Taishi being Japanese for 'great teacher'); Niimi was later given the name Milarepa after the Tibetan guru. Among the other holy names so bestowed later were Maitreya (the future Buddha) given to Jōyu Fumihiro; Ananda, one the Buddha's closest disciples, to Inoue Yoshihiro; Tilopa (the name of another renowned Tibetan guru) to Hayakawa Kiyohide; Manjushri Mitra (after Manjushri the Buddha of Wisdom) to Murai Hideo; and Jivaka (an important disciple of the Buddha) to Endō Seiichi.

The use of holy names on one level represents Asahara's aspirations for his disciples who, like those of the Buddha, were to assist in turning the wheel of law. To an extent one can see, in the bestowal of holy names with their implicit meaning of future achievement, a mirroring of the scenes in the influential Buddhist text the Lotus Sutra, in which the Buddha makes predictions of future buddhahood for his close disciples.[70] Asahara, with his claims to discern the future of his disciples, was in effect drawing parallels with the incipient movement of that era, and implying that, just as the Buddha's disciples had a mission to spread the new faith and help turn the wheel of law for the first time, so had his.

This sense of aspiration, while it had clearly idealistic dimensions, also displays a pretentiousness and arrogance that typified many of Aum's actions and pronouncements over the years. Here was a self-proclaimed religious leader with a small following in Tokyo calling his disciples by the names of great Tibetan gurus and major figures in Buddhist cosmology, and here were followers with, at best, two or three years of yoga, meditation and ascetic training, quitting their jobs and assuming the names of buddhas and revered gurus and teachers. While the idealism of this is striking, the image produced by the seeming arrogance of such followers suggests a self-delusion that appears to have afflicted the movement's practitioners. Almost all those who willingly aspired to the names of buddhas and spiritual masters became involved in highly criminal acts which they carried out with a spirit of detachment, and all the above-named apart from Jōyu have been implicated in mass murder and conspiracies to murder or manufacture chemical weapons.[71]

Not all those who renounced the world received a holy name. To do so was a recognition of one's attainment and also of the guru's favour. Reporters from the Kumamoto Nichinichi newspaper who visited Aum's commune at Namino in the early 1990s and conducted numerous interviews there, noted that possession of a holy name was something that was much desired by those who did not have one.[72] In my interviews of Aum members who have remained faithful since the subway attack, one of the greatest regrets they appear to have is that, since Asahara is now incarcerated and unable to play a role in the movement, he no longer bestows holy names on followers. Hence those who at the time of Asahara's arrest in 1995 were not yet part of the elite hierarchy, have been unable to acquire a holy name.

The development of a *sangha* and a system of holy names drew Aum increasingly down a path of rejection and separation from the world. It contributed to Aum's development as a closed, introspective community primarily focused on the spiritual advancement of individual members. Renunciation also created a serious area of conflict for Aum. Those who joined its *sangha* and gave up their worldly goods were often young idealists, and some (such as Inoue Yoshihiro) were under the age of majority in Japan. As a result, disputes erupted and legal complaints were lodged against the movement because such people, still considered as minors in Japanese law, had taken this step without the consent of their parents. Since renunciation meant severing all ties – including social ones – with one's family, it was unsurprising that many concerned families and relatives began to voice complaints against Aum. This was to give rise to Aum's first serious external problems, sowing the seeds of future conflict and eventually contributing to some of Aum's earliest hostilities and criminal actions.

HIERARCHY, RANKS OF ATTAINMENT AND BUDDHIST PATHS

Along with the *sangha* and its holy names, Aum also developed a system of ranks related to each practitioner's levels of ascetic and spiritual attainment. Moving from one level to another in this hierarchic structure depended upon undertaking various levels and types of practice. Just as there was a hierarchy of ranks, so too was there a hierarchic ladder of practices representing (to use Aum's terms) stages (*sutēji*) that were to be challenged (*charenji suru*, *chōsen suru*) and overcome.[73] Along with various ascetic practices, courses in various forms of yoga and meditation and initiations, members also were expected to contribute to the movement by performing work (*wāku*) – a term that meant anything from working in one of its business operations to helping in the building projects at its communes.[74] Aum members were expected to show their dedication to the movement through this 'work'. Indeed, it was not uncommon for them to have to spend all their time on such work for quite long periods before they were allowed to undergo more severe ascetic practices or do meditation.[75]

The development of these various levels of practice, attainment and rank began around 1987. Scholars such as Shimazono Susumu and Robert Kisala have pointed out that as this happened Aum's training practices and the path to liberation became increasingly complex, with members' focus changing from the earlier, more direct attempts to attain psychic powers through their practice, to a search for more transcendent spiritual experiences and awakenings.[76]

One reason why this increasingly hierarchic and complex array of different stages and levels of practice developed was to maintain and reinforce Asahara's position as the guru who had reached higher levels than anyone else. Equally, it also afforded those close to Asahara a special status and gave them increasing positions of power in the movement. Another possible reason is suggested by Shimazono when he argues that 'the very promise of *gedatsu* [liberation] easily led to disappointment'.[77] Those who had joined and given up everything in the search for what they believed would be the rapidly attained experience of final liberation, found that this was not so readily experienced, and often members were unsure of whether or how far they had progressed in their spiritual search. The development of various stages and levels of practice was thus a way of providing a framework that enabled them to measure their progress. A further stimulus to the development of what became an extremely hierarchic and elitist structure was that gradually Aum's own visions of the potential for salvation and liberation themselves began to change in the light of the movement's own experiences. This point will be discussed further in Chapter 5 when I show how its visions changed from a universal to a selective form of salvation, in which only those from the spiritual elite would be saved. I would suggest here that the system also fulfilled the role of rewarding people for their service and devotion to Aum and for their commitment in recruiting new followers, and thus it encouraged them to work harder for the movement.[78]

The system developed into an extremely hierarchic one: by 1995 there were ten ranks among those who renounced the world and below them were the ordinary lay members of the movement. The term used to refer to those who had renounced the world and were on the first stages of the spiritual ladder was *samana*.[79] There were four categories of *samana*, each differentiated by its own style and colour of clothing. When one reached the third stage in the rank of *samana* one was given a holy name. Above that was the rank of *shiho* (assistant teacher). Those of this rank who underwent and succeeded in *kundalini* yoga training (which was usually done in an intensive session lasting several days or a number of weeks) would ascend to the more exalted echelons of *shi* (teacher) *seigoshi* (sacred awakened teacher) and, eventually, *seitaishi* (sacred grand teacher). These ranks wore coloured *kurta* (pyjama-like Indian clothing) to mark them out. There were two levels of practice and two ranks of attainment above those of the *seitaishi*, which no one had (as of 1995) attained in Aum. Above these was the stage of final liberation, achieved by Asahara alone.

The ranks, clothes and stages of attainment relating to each were (as of 1995) as shown in Table 1.[80]

The irony of this structure is that, in striving to give disciples a means of knowing how they were progressing in their practice, and in order to reward devotion and commitment, Aum ended by producing a system that was every bit as hierarchic and status-conscious as the Japanese society that its members had wanted to leave. As will be seen in later chapters, part of the dynamic behind this system was a growing spiritual elitism that developed within Aum. It was a system that naturally augmented Asahara's status and authority: he became a de facto Buddha-surrogate and his position at the apex of the movement became ever more unassailable.

The system also effectively divided Aum into three groups. Within the ranks of *shukkesha* those who had reached the higher levels (*shi* and above) formed an elite corps above the ordinary ranks of *samana*. The lay members of the movement formed a group that, in terms of status, ranked below the *samana*. As the movement came to focus increasingly on its communes and to emphasise the importance of world renunciation as an essential step for attaining salvation in the apocalypse to come, this lay group became increasingly marginal to Aum. As Takahashi comments, Asahara seemed eventually almost to disregard them as truly committed members of the movement, calling them 'guests' (*o-kyakusama*).[81]

This hierarchic elitism was also reflected in Aum's developing self-identity as a Buddhist movement. Asahara's teachings often referred to the widely held idea in East Asian Buddhism that there are three vehicles (*yāna*) or forms of Buddhism: the Hinayāna (literally 'small vehicle'),[82]

Table 1: The Ranks, Clothes and Stages of Attainment in the Aum Hierarchy

Rank or Status	Clothing and Symbols	Level of Practice Achieved*
Saishū gedatsusha (sonshi) (ultimate liberated master Asahara Shōkō)	Purple	Every stage and ultimate liberation
Causal yoga stage	None: No one (apart from Asahara) has succeeded at this level	Causal yoga
Astral yoga stage	As above	Astral yoga
Seitaishi (sacred grand teacher)	Green *kurta*	*Daijō* (*Mahāyāna*) yoga
Seigoshi (sacred awakened teacher)	Deep red *kurta*	Mahamudra
Shi (teacher)	White *kurta*	*Kundalini* yoga
Shiho (assistant teacher)	White *samana* robe	None specified
Samanachō (senior/ head *samana*)	White *samana* robe: holy name awarded at this level	None specified
Samana	White *samana* robe	None specified
Samana minarai (novice *samana*)	Orange *samana* robe	None specified

* The terms used in this column refer to types of practice, many of them based on yoga systems, as they were used in Aum. Most have names taken from Sanskrit and have roots in Hindu and Buddhist systems of practice as derived from India, although with variations that were placed on them by Aum.

Mahāyāna (great vehicle) and Vajrayāna (esoteric/diamond vehicle) paths. The first of these emphasises strict adherence to Buddhist precepts, and an austere path of individual discipline coupled with a focus on the search for personal improvement aimed at a higher rebirth on a long and difficult path to enlightenment. This path came to be seen in Aum as suitable for recruits in the earlier stages of their training, for those who were not ready to renounce the world and become *shukkesha* and also for *samana* in the initial period of their monastic training. However, it came to be seen as a transitory stage in the ascent of the hierachic ladder which mirrored the stages and spiritual realms of existence through which the spirit passed in the journey to ultimate liberation. In sermons from 1988 onwards, Asahara constantly emphasised this point and stated that the Hinayāna path was not one that could lead to final salvation.[83]

The second of these vehicles, the Mahāyāna, emphasises that individual liberation is attainable in this world, but also involves a commitment to assist all other sentient beings to attain liberation. The Mahāyāna practitioner thus had a mission to teach others and to lead them forward to liberation. This became important in Aum, and while it emphasised that the strict individual discipline of the Hinayāna path was useful in initial training, it believed that members should move beyond this and follow what it viewed as the idealistic Mahāyāna path of striving for universal salvation. In its earlier years, and especially from 1986 to 1988, its adherence to and identity with the Mahāyāna Buddhist path was a dominant force in Aum, as the movement expressed its commitment to striving for universal world salvation. From around 1988 onwards, however, Asahara began to emphasise the importance of what he referred to either as the Vajrayāna (or, as he also termed it, the Tantra-Vajrayāna) path of esoteric Buddhism.[84] This, he stated, was a path of intense spiritual advancement suited to a chosen elite who, through their absolute devotion to an enlightened teacher, were able to attain levels of spiritual awakening and ascendancy far beyond those of ordinary people.[85] I shall discuss in some detail what he saw as the main elements of this path, the reasons why this change came about, and the impact that it had on Aum, in Chapter 5. Here I just wish to note that this change towards what was portrayed as a more elitist form or level of Buddhism came about as Aum was developing the structure of ranks depicted above. In other words, relatively early in its history, and after having established its *sangha,* Aum Shinrikyō had begun to turn into an elitist movement in which those at its upper levels were accorded exalted spiritual status that placed them above their ordinary fellows.

MISSION AND SALVATION: THE PROPHET AND THE WAR TO COME

One of the most vital themes that emerged in Aum's early years between 1984 and 1988 was Asahara's sense of mission, in which he believed he had been charged with a special task of world salvation. This was closely linked to a further critical strand in Aum's thought: the emerging belief that a cataclysmic yet potentially salvific war was imminent. This war had the potential to engulf the world, destroying much of humanity but smashing the foundations of the present materialist system. It also heralded the possibility of a new spiritually oriented era. Asahara's claimed prophetic powers were naturally related to these two notions: he was both the prophet of cataclysm and the saviour who could prevent it, or who could use it to transform the world.

All these themes can be traced back to 1985 when Asahara first claimed to have foresight of future events. It was in this same year that he started to receive revelations from various deities. His mission of salvation – in which he was to assume the role of a sacred warrior or hero – was first revealed in a vision that occurred while he was performing austerities at Miura beach in Kanagawa prefecture during April and May 1985. As he did so a deity descended from the heavens, informed him of the coming battle between good and evil, and appointed him as Abiranoketsunomikoto,[86] who was 'the central figure of the war',[87] and 'the god who leads the armies of the gods'.[88]

In the same year another vision with prophetic and millennial undertones occurred when he visited Mount Goyō in Iwate prefecture in northern Japan. The visit was made apparently because of the mountain's association with the pre-war nationalist Sakai Katsutoki, who had predicted that Armageddon would come at the end of the century and that only a race of compassionate sages, whose leader would come from Japan, would survive.[89] According to a subsequent Aum account, at the mountain Asahara met an old man who had been with Sakai at the time of his vision, and who recounted it to Asahara: the people who would survive Armageddon would be the 'benevolent *shinsen* people'.[90] It was shortly after this vision that Asahara incorporated the term *shinsen* (hermit or mountain wizard) into the name of his movement by calling it Aum Shinsen no Kai. He thus identified himself and his followers with this apocalyptic vision.

In this period, also, Asahara began publicly to articulate the fears then prevalent in Japanese popular culture about the possibility of nuclear war or some form of cataclysm that could herald the end of the world. He claimed, for instance, that his spirit had left his body and travelled ahead in time to the year 2006, where it saw the aftermath of a nuclear holocaust. This vision further stimulated his belief that it was his mission to try to prevent this tragedy, and that the way to do this was by spreading his teachings across the world.[91]

His visit to India in early 1986 enhanced this sense of mission for he met a number of Indian sages and swamis who predicted to him that

Japan faced imminent destruction and that he alone could save it.[92] This visit was clearly an influential one: formerly a teacher of yoga and meditation capable of performing initiations and with a sense of future mission, he returned as a fully liberated being destined to fulfil a special role of salvation. He was no longer a seeker but a self-proclaimed spiritual leader with a mission to turn the wheel of law again to bring about a global spiritual transformation. Nor was he henceforth dependent on prophecies relayed to him by others for now, he claimed, his mastery of psychic powers was such that he could see into the future. He was a prophet who, from 1986 onwards, started to foretell what was going to transpire in the world in general and in the futures of his disciples. In May 1987, for instance, he gave a series of seminars in which he spoke openly for the first time about the possible outbreak of nuclear war: at the same time, however, he asserted that Aum could save the world from such a fate. At this stage his view was that growing political and economic tension between Japan and the rest of the world (but primarily the USA) would lead to conflicts, causing Japan to rearm, which would produce an inevitable nuclear war some time between 1999 and 2003. However, he asserted, Aum could prevent this happening if it had 'at least one or two branches in each country of the world by 1993': if it did not, however, then war was 'sure to break out'.[93]

Asahara saw nuclear cataclysm as the almost inevitable product of a corrupt materialistic society that existed in a spiritual void. Cataclysm and mass destruction were in effect the karmic repercussions of materialism. Nevertheless, his message of doom was framed in optimistic terms: karmic hindrances, even on such a vast scale, could be eradicated through positive spiritual action.[94] Aum could, he believed, prevent such a cataclysm through its mission to transform the world spiritually, thereby bringing about a new spiritual age. The expansion of his movement was critical to this salvation mission: Aum *had* to grow enough to create the positive spiritual energy necessary to overcome the world's bad karma. In this context Asahara set a number of targets or achievements that would be necessary to accomplish this task. Aum needed to open more centres around the world and create 30,000 spiritually enlightened practitioners who would renounce the world. This image proved an incentive to recruitment, attracting a number of people who were concerned with the state of the world but who felt that they could make a real difference by joining this spiritual crusade. One interviewee, for example, informed me that he had grave fears about the possibility of mass destruction, but when he heard Asahara preach on this subject and mention the need for 30,000 enlightened beings, he was inspired to see himself in such a role, and joined Aum as a result.[95]

Asahara's vision of the future was articulated through imagery derived from Tibetan Buddhism. Aum's plan was to construct Shambhala, a Buddhist paradise on earth, in Japan, whence its influence would spread across the globe. Ultimately the entire world would be transformed into the utopian paradise of Shambala.[96] The concept of Shambhala comes from Tibetan Buddhism and represents a popular form of Buddhist millennialism. In Tibetan Buddhist cosmology Shambhala was a hidden valley deep in the mountains from which it was prophesied that an enlightened sacred king would emerge to defeat the forces of evil and establish a new golden age of Buddhism. This imagery was expressed in the Buddhist text the *Kālacakra Tantra*, which foretold such a sacred battle between the forces of good led by this Buddhist king and those of evil. While the intent of the text is allegorical, depicting the struggle between enlightenment and ignorance in the guise of a war,[97] it clearly fitted into Asahara's own more militant visions of struggle and future conflict between good and evil. He was strongly influenced by the text and by the concept of Shambhala, which provided him with a Buddhist source for his visions of cosmic war and enabled him to frame his millennialist beliefs within a Buddhist nexus.[98]

As part of his 'Shambhala plan'[99] to transform the world into a utopian paradise, Aum began, in 1986, to acquire rural plots of land in Japan on which to build communes called 'Lotus Villages' which would be the basis of the future Shambala civilisation. At this stage the movement was clearly infused with missionary optimism. When in August 1986 Aum held an opening ceremony for its new headquarters near Mount Fuji, Ishii Hisako gave an inaugural speech which, as Shimazono Susumu has noted, was full of hope for the development of Shambhala.[100] At this stage, Shimazono comments, Aum was expressing ideas that are 'familiar to both observers and followers of the Japanese New Religions: the bright hopes of establishing a 'holy land' as a model of heaven on earth'.[101]

Initially, then, Aum's millennialism had an optimistic bent, under-pinned by its leader's belief in his salvation mission and infused with a vision of a utopia on earth. However, this optimism contained within it the seeds of potential failure. Asahara's ability to save the world from cataclysm appeared to be dependent on quantifiable levels of growth in his movement. If it did not manage to open two centres in every country of the world by 1993 or, alternatively, get 30,000 people to renounce the world, it would appear certain, judging from Asahara's comments in May 1987 and elsewhere, that the cataclysm would come.[102] Asahara was effectively setting the movement an extraordinarily steep task, given that at the time he set such targets in 1987, Aum had not yet opened any centres outside Japan and that little more than one hundred people had become *shukkesha*.

One can only assume that after having announced the need for Aum to expand and acquire a larger organisation Asahara expected there to be an extraordinary and exponential growth curve in the movement. Whether this expectation was simply over-optimistic, based in a remarkable degree of self-delusion founded in his own growing sense of grandeur, or perhaps was intended as a stratagem that would encourage large numbers of people to join the movement, is unclear. Whatever the case, his optimism was clearly misplaced. Though Aum experienced quite rapid growth in this period (by 1988 it had around 2,300 members) most of those who joined were lay members. Unsurprisingly the numbers of *shukkesha*, whose numerical growth was especially important for Asahara's salvation mission, were far less: by late 1989 they numbered about 380. Moreover, although Aum had started to make moves overseas by opening offices in the USA and Germany, it had yet to achieve any quantifiable success in these areas and was clearly a long way off its target of opening two centres in every country of the world by 1993.

Perhaps in the light of these figures, it is not surprising that Aum's initially optimistic millennialism gave way to a more pessimistic future vision. By early 1988 Asahara, in an interview in *Twilight Zone*, had begun to predict not only that a world war would certainly erupt between the USA and Russia in 1999 and that the world would be destroyed in 2003,[103] but also that Tokyo and much of the Japanese archipelago would sink and that 'something unusual' would occur around 1995 or 1996.[104] As 1988 wore on Aum's views of the millennium became increasingly catastrophic in tenor, until by the latter part of that year Asahara was openly stating that Armageddon was certain to occur and he seemed to have abandoned any hope that Aum could save the world from this fate. Between 1985 and 1988 Asahara's visions of the future thus shifted from an optimistic to an increasingly catastrophic form of millennialism.[105] This shift occurred at the time of Aum's change of self-image from being primarily a Mahāyāna Buddhist movement with a belief in the potential to save and strive for the benefit of all sentient beings, to the more exclusive Vajrayāna path. The reasons for this change will be one of the subjects of concern in Chapter 5, but clearly one important factor, as has been suggested here, was the relative lack of growth in the movement, which appeared to place Asahara's proclaimed mission of salvation at risk from quite early on. These issues will be discussed later, but first I shall conclude this general outline by discussing Aum's prominent characteristics as they had developed by the latter part of the 1980s.

THE NATURE OF AUM SHINRIKYŌ

By 1987, when Asahara changed its name to Aum Shinrikyō, the movement had begun to manifest a number of important characteristics that represented its basic orientations as a religious movement. It was a world-rejecting movement with a critical attitude to contemporary society and to materialism, which Asahara was to describe as being synonymous with the 'devil' (*akuma*).[106] It believed that only through turning one's back on the material world and seeking truth in an interior, spiritual world, could one attain liberation and salvation. What was important for practitioners, then, was what happened in their minds and in the realms of the spirit. Aum's criticisms of materialism were primarily directed at the Japanese society in which it grew, and there is much in Aum to suggest that one of its prime motivations emanated from a negative reaction to, and even hatred of, Japanese society.

However, it should be stressed that Aum's world-rejecting stance was not solely, or even primarily, directed at Japan *per se*, but at materialist society in general. After returning from India in 1986, Asahara had a mission to save Japan from destruction, and expressed this through his aspiration to transform Japan into Shambala. In fact, in subsequent years, as Asahara began to predict with greater emphasis the likelihood of a final catastrophic war and as he developed a list of enemies who, he believed, were conspiring against him and his movement, it became clear that his antipathies were more forcefully directed against the USA and other external groups than they were towards Japan. Indeed, in the very last book published by Aum and attributed to Asahara in summer 1995 after his arrest, he lamented the fate of Japan, which was going to be drawn into a war with America and ruined, and he expressed the hope that Japan would recover from that war and have a positive future.[107]

Aum was an ascetically-based movement, with an emphasis on withdrawal from the world and on austere practices as the means of attaining salvation and transcendence. In this process Aum had started to draw apart from the society in which it had developed, a distancing indicated in physical terms by moving from the urban environment to rural areas where it aimed to establish communes. In this way it began to create its own, separate and different moral universe – a tendency that developed quite rapidly in the next few years.

Although Aum constructed communes, it was not a communal movement in the sense that everyone was on a relatively equal basis within it.

Rather, it had become intensely hierarchical and based on a form of spiritual elitism that was manifest both between itself and other religious movements, in its claims to possess the supreme truth, and society at large, and even more strikingly within the confines of the movement itself. Aum had turned into a hierarchic religion with an extreme emphasis on the role and veneration of its founder and guru, in which Asahara was the central unifying figure holding the movement together, the supreme authority validating experiences. He had become the apex of its hierarchy and the gateway to all spiritual progress.

This was perhaps Aum's most seminal characteristic as a religious movement: it was, above all, a missionary religion with a dramatic and immediate millennial message. Asahara had been entrusted with a sacred mission to turn the wheel of law again, to save the world from disaster, and to bring about a universal spiritual transformation in the form of the Buddhist paradise of Shambhala. Much of what transpired in Aum, such as how it reacted to or interacted with the world at large, was framed by this sense of mission and by Asahara's visions of himself as world saviour.

The mission was of overriding importance, to be defended at all costs, and those who entered Aum's upper echelons pledged to strive with all their might to accomplish it. Conversely those who failed to honour it or who appeared to hinder it in any way became enemies of the truth and hence had to be resisted. Ultimately, too, the mission was so important that members had to fight and, if need be, kill for it. In this matrix Aum placed great emphasis on the concept of struggle, challenging and overcoming, and references to these terms (*chō, koeru*) appeared with great regularity in its publications and in the vocabulary it used. This can be seen, for example, in the title of one of Asahara's books *Seishi o koeru* [Transcending Birth and Death], or in the ideas of *chōnoryoku* psychic (or superhuman) powers or of *chōetsu jinriki*, transcendent spiritual powers. Members, as I previously noted, 'challenged' various stages of practice and sought to overcome them. This emphasis on struggle, challenge and victory was later to be expressed by Asahara when he began to refer to his faithful disciples as 'true victors' (*shinri shōsha*)[108] who were fighting with him on behalf of the truth. This image of the holy struggle became, along with its mission of salvation, one of the paramount and paradigmatic themes in the movement. It is to these 'devout warriors', the adherents of Aum Shinrikyō and particularly those who renounced the world and reached the higher echelons of Aum's spiritual ladder, that I shall turn next, in Chapter 4.

勝

4 The World of the True Victors – The Motivations, Experiences and Practices of Asahara's Followers

INTRODUCTION

Religious movements and charismatic leaders can only be effective if they can attract followers who help implement their goals through offering devotion and support. The purpose of this chapter is to examine the people who fulfilled this role in Aum by joining the movement, giving support to Asahara Shōkō and venerating him to the extent that they sought to transform their minds by cloning his mind to theirs. These were Asahara's 'true victors', his sacred warriors who were to aid him in his salvation plan and to fight with him in the cosmic battle to come. Their commitment to their guru and religion was such that they were prepared to renounce the world, families, wealth and careers and even, in some cases, to risk their lives in performing extreme acts of asceticism ordered by Asahara. Some of these disciples were also prepared to accept, accommodate and actively support violence or commit murders, manufacture biological and chemical weapons and try to use them against the general public. It was through such people that Asahara was able to build Aum Shinrikyō into a religious movement that was dedicated, hierarchic, closed, focused on extreme asceticism and committed to the concept of struggle.

This chapter will focus primarily on those followers who renounced the world, both because these were the people with the greatest dedication and commitment, and because it was from within their ranks that the active participants in Aum's crimes came. The chapter will engage with a number of questions and issues: it will look at how and why people joined Aum, what attractions Aum had for potential followers, what impulses and factors in their own lives led people to Aum, how they came into contact with Aum, and what they sought from it. It will also look at what was expected of them by the movement, including some of the practices they engaged in and what they gave to it.

THE MEMBERS OF AUM: SOME BASIC THEMES AND ASSUMPTIONS

Prior to the subway attack comparatively little academic study had been made of Aum. Apart from members' accounts published by the movement itself, a few general articles and a small number of books by journalists that touched on Aum or examined the disputes it was embroiled in, there was little material available to present an objective picture of the followers in the years before the attack. However, from the evidence available it is possible to make some reasonable assumptions or generalisations about Aum's membership. It appears to have been predominantly a movement of young people who, especially in its upper ranks, were highly educated, often qualifying for or graduating from leading universities in Japan.

The age profiles of those who become *shukkesha*, according to figures produced by the *Mainichi Shinbun*, illustrate that the large majority of

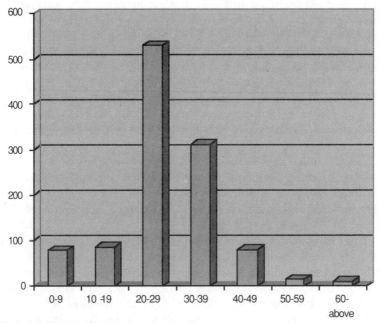

Figure 1: Age profiles of Aum **shukkesha**

ardent devotees were under 40, with almost half of all *shukkesha* aged between 20 and 29. In March 1995 there were 1,114 *shukkesha* according to figures obtained by the newspaper: this number included children whose parents had renounced the world and had brought their children with them to Aum's communes. Of the 1,114, a total of 79 were aged under 9; 86 were in the age range 10–19; 529 in the age range 20–29; 311 aged 30–39; 80 were in their forties; 15 in their fifties; and 11 were older than this, including one *shukkesha* over 80 years old (see Figure 1).[1]

This youth-dominated profile is borne out by the ages of the movement's senior figures. When, in June 1994, Aum formed its 'alternative government', the average age of its 22 'ministers' was a little over 30: Hayashi Ikuo at 48 was the oldest.[2] Many were still in their twenties when they reached the highest levels of the movement. Inoue Yoshihiro, for example, who was a 'minister' in Aum's 'government', was 25 at the time of the subway attack but had already been involved with Aum for eight years. Asahara himself was barely 40.

Many of those at the top of Aum's structure had succeeded in the competitive education market in Japan and gained entry to its elite institutions. Inoue, for example, had graduated from a prestigious private school and gained entrance to a leading university by the time he dropped out to join Aum. Many of his colleagues in Aum had graduated from elite universities and several had acquired postgraduate degrees or training, before going on to work in industry or joining Aum. Murai Hideo had graduated from Osaka University and had worked as a scientific researcher for Kōbe Steel, a leading industrial concern, prior to joining Aum, while Jōyu Fumihiro was a graduate of the prestigious Waseda University. Many were professionally qualified. Aoyama Yoshinobu, for example, had graduated from Kyoto University and passed the Japanese bar examinations to qualify as a lawyer, while Nakagawa Tomomasa and Hayashi Ikuo were qualified doctors, the latter being a cardiologist who had trained in the USA and held major positions in Japanese hospitals. They used their professional training inside Aum, Aoyama acting as Aum's chief lawyer and Nakagawa and Hayashi working at Aum's hospital in Tokyo. They also deployed their knowledge in other ways. Aoyama used his legal skills to block investigations into Aum and to help it purchase land in underhand ways, while Nakagawa and Hayashi were involved in several of Aum's crimes, using their medical knowledge to administer lethal injections to victims.

Because a number of senior Aum figures including Murai, Jōyu, Endō Seiichi and Tsuchiya Masami (the latter two of whom made Aum's chemical weapons) had graduated in scientific and technological subjects,

97

it has frequently been suggested in the media that Aum had specifically set out to recruit graduates in these fields, as part of a co-ordinated strategy aimed at furthering its militaristic schemes. The reality appears to be a little more mundane, at least as regards the more senior Aum figures. These appear not to have been directly recruited because of their scientific backgrounds but, rather, to have come to Aum of their own accord, often after having read Asahara's books, which they found addressed their concerns and provided them with a sense of spiritual meaning. Murai Hideo and Hayashi Ikuo are examples of this process; both first encountered Aum while browsing for books on spirituality and picking up copies of Asahara's books.

It is likely that young people with scientific and technological backgrounds who felt uneasy about the impact of scientific rationalism and technological change might have been attracted to Aum's apparent belief that science could be incorporated into the religion of the new era and to Aum's readiness to use new technologies. Aum's emphasis on science and technology (or rather on a fantasy version of science and technology) grew greatly over later years, and especially from around 1992. It is possible that this development may have come about because of the prominence of people such as Murai, Jōyu and Endō, who had ascended to the apex of the movement. It is possible, too, that their scientific and technological orientations led them, in later years, to a more active recruitment of people with similar backgrounds. It was not, however, a prominent element in Aum's early search for followers and there appears little or no evidence to suggest that the movement went out actively to recruit scientists from the outset.

It is not clear whether the pattern seen among Aum's senior hierarchy, of attaining success in the education system, was replicated among the ranks of Aum's membership as a whole. Those occupying what I would term the middle ranks in Aum's hierarchy – the ordinary *shukkesha* at the level of *samana* or just above – were not necessarily such high-fliers, although many of them appear to have had a university education. The Aum members and former members whom I interviewed were all articulate and intelligent, and the three whose histories I recount later in this chapter had graduated from university: one was in his forties, the others in their twenties. They, too, had given up careers – one as a schoolteacher, another as a postgraduate student – to join Aum.

This does not mean that all Aum's devout followers were young or highly educated professionals. In their study of the dispute surrounding Aum's Namino commune, journalists from the *Kumamoto Nichinichi* newspaper talked to several Aum devotees who had come from rather different backgrounds. One of these was the 61-year-old wife of a Jōdo Shin (Pure Land) Buddhist priest, who felt, despite her family connections to established Buddhism, that it had failed to answer her questions or provide her with spiritual solace, with the result that she began searching elsewhere and was drawn to Asahara's teaching. Another was a middle-aged former owner of a restaurant and bar in the Gion quarter of Kyoto, who had enjoyed a materially pleasant life until he became ill with heart disease. After this he had begun to seek out alternative therapies and religions. Eventually, after unsuccessful encounters with such new religions as Agonshū, he came across Aum, received a *shaktipat* from Asahara which, he stated, did him the world of good, and then decided, with his wife, to renounce the world and devote himself thereafter to the movement.[3]

However, the general evidence available indicates that Aum, like other 'new' new religions of the era, was a movement that appealed primarily to the young and well educated. It attracted young, ambitious people who were capable of, or indeed had found, success in society – but who also had come to believe that the system in which they had succeeded failed to offer them satisfaction other than on a material level. These young people were interested in directing their ambitions towards other ends, such as the acquisition of psychic powers. Especially for those who were ambitious and highly motivated and capable, yet so dissatisfied with the careerism and spiritual vacuity of modern society that they were prepared to reject it, Aum offered an alternative avenue for them to express and focus their drive and energies.

Those who succeeded in Aum's hierarchic structure, which was built on a process of attainment and achievement and of challenging and overcoming various stages, were by and large people who had previously succeeded in the hierarchic and competitive world of Japanese education. One might suggest that, in such terms, Aum offered them a world that was both different – an alternative, because of its spiritual emphases, to the world they rejected – and yet somehow familiar and reassuring, based as it was on a series of stages, challenges and attainments that led to prestige and recognition. They were zealous and often fired with youthful idealism and energy, and in Aum they found a way of expressing their ambitions and energies, and a way of acquiring prestige and merits in the alternative universe that Aum, in its communes and through its system of spiritual ranks, offered. They could strive to become sacred teachers, bodhisattvas and buddhas. Moreover their path up this hierarchy was not restricted, as is often the case in Japanese society in general, by questions of age, seniority or, indeed, gender. Female devotees such as Ishii and Ōuchi, who had worked as 'Office Ladies' in Japanese companies and whose careers would doubtless have involved, in the normal pattern of things, little chance of advancement, found that Aum offered them not just the hope of spiritual development and salvation, but the possibility of enhancing their positions and acquiring some degree of control and power in their lives.

I am not suggesting that people such as Ishii, Murai and Hayashi joined Aum *because* it offered them such opportunities. They (as is shown by the testimonies of Aum believers given below) were clearly engaged in a spiritual search in which Asahara's teachings struck a chord. However, their ambition to attain the highest levels of spiritual development and to acquire psychic powers gave them the impetus to ascend Aum's spiritual ladder, and in so doing, placed within their grasp various possibilities of power and influence that might have been denied them within mainstream Japanese life.

That Aum attracted such people, and that it developed a predominantly youthful profile, is unsurprising since it had emerged from the popular religious culture of the age which appealed especially to younger, well-educated Japanese. Aum's message, with its critique of contemporary materialism, its predictions of potential cataclysm at the end of the century, and its emphasis on spiritual matters and practices, and on the attainment of psychic powers, fitted with that culture and appealed to the spiritual ambitions of its participants. It developed originally in Tokyo, a city with a high concentration of universities and a large population of students and young graduates, and gained much of its early publicity through the alternative religious magazines such as *Twilight Zone* that were popular among this sector of society. Aum had a large number of young, highly educated members, one might say, because they were its natural constituency.

Moreover, like its 'new' new religious rivals such as Kōfuku no Kagaku, the ways in which it proselytised and recruited brought it directly into contact with such a constituency. Many of Aum's proselytising campaigns were focused on universities: Asahara gave numerous talks on university campuses (including a campaign in autumn 1992 when he spoke at a number of university festivals) which were organised by Aum supporters in the student body. Hearing Asahara speak, and coming into contact with his leading disciples at such occasions, caused a number of people to join the movement, for he was by all accounts a persuasive and engaging speaker who captivated audiences with both his message, which many found put across direct and accessible teachings in a forthright manner, and his personal charm.[4]

Asahara was not the only person in the movement with the charisma that could attract followers. Takahashi Hidetoshi's account of his conversion to Aum shows how various of Asahara's leading disciples impressed potential followers with their charismatic qualities. Takahashi found Inoue, who had a powerful reputation in Aum as a meditator, and Murai to be particularly charismatic, calm and self-assured, and it was to a great degree because of them that he was drawn to and later remained in the movement.[5] My interviewees reiterated this point: Ishii Hisako, Murai Hideo and Inoue Yoshihiro were particularly mentioned in this respect. As one informant told me, when he encountered these figures he immediately felt that they exuded a sense of spiritual power, tranquillity and confidence that served as a good advertisement for Aum. If, he reasoned, Aum could produce people like this, it must be efficacious, and he hoped it could do the same for him.

The written word was another important medium for recruitment. There is a very large and active Japanese religious book publishing market, and most bookstores in city areas have 'spiritual corners' or sections given over to books about spirituality, the occult, psychic powers, and esoteric and alternative religious issues and ideas, which cater to the needs and interests of the spiritually dissatisfied and curious. Like many others of the 'new' new religious movements, Aum ran its own publishing company, which marketed its publications zealously, and its books and magazines could be found on the shelves of most bookshops in Tokyo and other cities in Japan prior to the subway attack.[6] Many of Aum's devotees first encountered Asahara's teachings in this way. One of my interviewees whose story is given later, for example, was looking around for spiritual inspiration and for a spiritual teacher in this way when he came across an Aum magazine featuring Asahara, which led him to contact the movement. This was also the route through which Murai Hideo and Hayashi Ikuo first came to Aum.[7]

THE ATTRACTIONS OF AUM

While the followers who were drawn to Aum were attracted by the various promises it appeared to offer them in spiritual terms, they were also, in joining a world-rejecting movement with a severe critique of materialism, expressing their dissatisfaction with the society in which they had been raised. They were unhappy with the pressurised education system and the demands of work and the rat-race, and were disaffected with scientific rationalism and the modern emphasis on economic progress and technology.

The comments of one Aum devotee made to a journalist in 1992 illustrate this point well: N.F-san[8] was aged 28, and had a good, well-paid job in a company. He was materially well provided for, and was about to engage in the Japanese *o-miai* process of seeking a marriage partner. On the surface all was going well with him, yet he found little satisfaction in his situation. His job offered no scope for self-fulfilment and he felt he was just a replaceable cog in the company machine: if he quit someone else would come in and take his place. Searching for meaning in his life, he began to read books on spiritual matters and in so doing came across one of Asahara's books. Within six months he had quit his job and joined Aum. Now, he said, he felt fulfilled: he was in command of his own experiences and through Aum he had been able to find his real self.[9]

This sense of feeling unfulfilled or alienated was a constant refrain in the testimonies of Aum followers. Such alienation and dissatisfaction did not, however, result from material disadvantages. Indeed, as the *Kumamoto Nichinichi* reporters have commented, the *shukkesha* they talked to appeared to have come from generally well-off and comfortable backgrounds and, on the surface, often appeared to be archetypal examples of the modern Japanese success story. They had been good, obedient children who had gone along with and fulfilled their parents' wishes and aspirations by working hard at school, getting into good universities and embarking on good careers. There was none of the poverty and deprivation that, the reporters felt, might have explained their interviewees' conversion to a religious movement.[10]

However, as they looked further into matters, the reporters found a recurrent theme of deprivation and alienation, not at the material but the emotional and spiritual levels. They found that the aspirations of the devotees' parents were often so heavily focused on success in quantifiable terms (pushing their children in educational terms so that they could get into leading universities and pressurising them to take up a particular type of career) that they had given their offspring little emotional support or nourishment. The reporters uncovered stories of fathers who had ordered their offspring to follow a certain profession or go to a certain type of college, or who spent so much time at work pursuing their own careers that they had little or no time for their children, and of mothers so concerned with pushing their children forward academically that they stifled them emotionally, and set store only by their material achievements. Many of those who joined, in other words, had been emotionally deprived and placed under enormous pressures to succeed materially. It was perhaps understandable that, having succeeded in such terms and graduated from good universities, and having found that such success did not satisfy them emotionally and spiritually, they felt an attraction for a religion that appeared to offer spiritual solace and to reject materialism.[11]

Aum's emphasis on renouncing the world and leaving one's family was therefore understandably appealing to these young people and provided them with the ultimate means of rejecting their parents and their parents' values. The reporters relate an incident that illustrates what many of the *shukkesha* were reacting against. A group of parents and families of Aum devotees had gathered outside the gate of Aum's Namino commune in November 1990 and were calling, through a microphone, to their offspring who were staying there. In trying to persuade their offspring to leave Aum and return to the family home, however, they frequently transmitted messages that demonstrated how little they understood the motivations of those they claimed to love. One parent, for example, called out to his son that if he returned to his home town there were all sorts of jobs available, and that they had enlarged his room at home and got him a computer, video and television set.[12] It is perhaps unsurprising that such appeals were in vain. Having rejected materialism and the career treadmill by joining Aum, commune members were hardly likely to be captivated by inducements of jobs and videos.

People did not, of course, join Aum simply as an escape from a materialistic world; the movement offered them numerous attractions, hopes and possibilities that they could not find in their everyday lives. As we saw with the cases of NF-san, the priest's wife and the former restaurant owner, Aum offered them answers to questions about their lives, gave them a sense of meaning and enabled them to come to terms with personal problems. It held out the hope of acquiring psychic powers and attaining spiritual liberation. It was these facets of its teaching that proved particularly attractive in its earlier days. Moreover Aum attracted people (like Asahara himself) who were frustrated with the weak levels of commitment to ascetic practice found in Japanese Buddhism and in the other new religions, and offered them some real opportunities to test themselves to the limits and engage in arduous ascetic practices.

Aum also offered its followers the hope of salvation after death and solace in the face of the final war which, it was prophesied, would engulf the world. Such hopes of salvation were extremely important in an era when this fear was very real for many young Japanese. This topic surfaced frequently in the interviews that Takimoto and Nagaoka conducted with former followers who had left Aum (and who, in their view, had broken free from Asahara's 'mind control'): the fear of falling into the miserable realms at death was a very strong force drawing followers to Aum and it caused them immense distress in their deliberations about whether to leave it as well. Takimoto and Nagaoka cite the case of a woman who eventually left Aum in 1994 on her fifth attempt. Despite feeling threatened and repelled by the atmosphere that had developed inside Aum by this time, and despite running away from the commune, she had gone back four times because she was terrified that by renouncing Aum she was incurring bad karma and would fall into the hells at death. It was only on the fifth occasion that she felt able to break free from the movement.[13]

Egawa Shōko, in her interviews with Aum disciples in the early 1990s, also discovered that a similarly powerful fear of the hells influenced some members. One *shukkesha*, for example, when asked whether he feared falling into hell, responded 'of course'. He also proceeded to tell her that she would suffer endless torments in the hells because of her attacks on Aum. In Egawa's view such concepts of hell and of the resultant need to use this life to attain a rebirth in a higher world were uppermost in the minds of Aum members.[14] The reporters from the *Kumamoto Nichinichi* newspaper also interviewed members who had been beset by worries about death and the afterlife but who, since renouncing the world in Aum, had ceased to have any such fears.[15]

DEVOTEES AND EXPERIENCES: PERSONAL TESTIMONIES OF AUM MEMBERS

Having discussed in more general terms the membership of Aum and the reasons for joining the movement, I now turn to some more specific accounts of disciples, which illustrate in greater detail the points made above. I shall outline the experiences of five followers or former followers who were, at the time of the subway attack, loyal members. The first three accounts come from interviews I conducted in October 1997; all three were *shukkesha* at the time of the 22 March raids on Aum, and two were still in the movement at the time I met them. The third left soon after the attack, shocked at what he had come to learn about the movement. He still, however, retains something of a sense of awe for Asahara, and an empathy for Aum's teaching. The other two accounts I shall cite are of prominent Aum leaders whose experiences were recounted in Aum publications in the early 1990s. Both had climbed to the apex of Aum's hierarchy and were deeply involved in Aum's crimes, but both have since recanted their faith. Since my main interest here is in the attitudes and feelings of Aum members at the time that they were actively involved in the movement, I shall focus on the period when they had ascended its spiritual ladder and were prominent and devout followers of Asahara, rather than on their later recantations of faith.

A-san: A Current Member

I met A-san[16] a number of times in October 1997 and January 1998. He was 29 years old at the time, and struck me as a self-conscious, thoughtful and quiet person. He had joined Aum in autumn 1992 and renounced the world in 1994. He remains a member of Aum, currently engaged in helping run its Internet site and playing a part in liaising between members in different parts of Japan. While he recognises that Aum was involved in carrying out criminal acts ordered by Asahara, he remains deeply committed to its religious message and considers that the real reasons for the subway attack and Aum's manufacture of weapons have not yet been fully revealed. In an extended series of conversations with him (including an initial four-hour interview) we talked about his background, his reasons for joining Aum, his experiences in the movement, and his views of what would happen to Aum in the era after the sarin attack. I shall refer in other parts of this book also to other aspects of our conversations and interviews; here I focus primarily on his reasons for joining Aum and his experiences in the movement.

In autumn 1992 A-san was a postgraduate student studying literature at Kyoto University. He had no interest in religion and regarded himself as a 'normal Japanese person'. In autumn 1992 Asahara came to the university to deliver a sermon[17] and A-san, out of curiosity, went along to listen. He was immediately struck by its contents – particularly the emphasis placed by Asahara on the necessity of attaining enlightenment (*satori*) and liberation (*gedatsu*) – and by Asahara himself who seemed to have a powerful personality. Interestingly, although the text of Asahara's sermon dealt at some length with his predictions of a coming war and of Aum's plans to survive this,[18] A-san barely noticed this point. What caught his interest was that Asahara talked of the importance of spiritual practice and of striving to raise one's consciousness: here, A-san felt, was a teacher who could speak in direct and straightforward terms and who, in emphasising the importance of maintaining strict practices, was very different from other religious leaders in Japan.

A-san was the interviewee cited in Chapter 2, who asked Asahara a question after the talk and who was deeply affected by the sense of Asahara's charismatic power when Asahara replied to him. It was this that led him to visit Aum's centre in Kyoto shortly afterwards. He was aware that Aum had a bad public image because of various conflicts and incidents, as well as rumours connecting it to the disappearance of the

Sakamoto family, but this did not put him off. Indeed, when he met the Aum devotees at the centre he felt that they were dedicated and sincere, and hardly likely to be involved in a movement that engaged in the sorts of activities alleged by the media. He quickly joined Aum as a lay member, a status he held for around 18 months, performing various Aum practices and studying its teachings.

A few months after joining Aum he met Asahara directly for the first time in March 1993, and received an initiation from him. Asahara, again, struck him as an immensely powerful and spiritual person. Indeed, A-san was constantly at pains to emphasise that, no matter what Asahara might have done (and he recognises that he was involved in Aum's crimes), he was nevertheless a remarkable and insightful religious leader and an excellent spiritual guide.

Under Asahara's guidance A-san studied what he termed 'esoteric meditation' and, as he did so, he felt his evil passions (*bonnō*) quieten down and disappear.[19] He increasingly felt a sense of estrangement from the everyday world and from a society whose values he had come to feel were meaningless in comparison with what now interested him: enlightenment and spiritual awakening. In this process, too, he became estranged from his family, and decided to sever contact with them. This process of distancing oneself from the world was a common pattern among those who joined the movement. Takimoto and Nagaoka also cite examples of members who, having become involved and absorbed in their practice, felt the wish to break off contact with people who were not members of Aum because they 'knew' that such people were wrong and that only Aum was correct.[20] Those who wanted to renounce the world, in other words, had already begun the process of withdrawing and distancing themselves from their families and friends prior to becoming *shukkesha*. It appears then that Aum's insistence that its followers should sever all contacts with their families when they renounced the world often simply mirrored wishes and inclinations that were already present in the minds and hearts of its novice members.

In May 1994 A-san decided to leave the world and sought entry into the ranks of *shukkesha*. He had very little money, but this did not appear to matter as his request was accepted. Although he went to live at Aum's commune at Kamikuishiki, he remained in close contact with his colleagues at the Kyoto centre. He was assigned to work for Aum's publishing section, which meant that he travelled a lot, often journeying between the commune and Aum's offices throughout Japan. However, he especially liked being at Kamikuishiki where he felt a powerful sense of community and shared purpose, and where everyone got on with their work and practices. It was a strict life with little food, but since he was interested in ascetic practice this suited his purposes well.

His primary concerns as a *shukkesha* were the same as those that attracted him to Aum in the first place: asceticism and the hope of spiritual awakening. The most important thing was his own practice and this, he averred, was central to all those who renounced the world. It was what happened inside one's mind that was important: focusing on one's own individual practice was the very essence of Aum's teaching. It was by developing one's individual practice and improving one's own mind, that one could affect and improve society at large. Critical to this was the relationship between the guru and disciple, which was highly individual. The link he had with Asahara was secret and direct, his alone, and essential to his path to enlightenment. Because of this relationship and his experiences of and faith in Asahara's spiritual power, he had found the concept of 'cloning the guru' to be highly attractive. While humans were normally tainted by the ways of the world and by the corrupt data that was fed to them, the guru was a perfect being who could transmit pure data to his disciples. He had worn the PSI headgear and found it highly beneficial, for it gave him a sense of calm that informed him of the exalted state of the guru's mind – a feeling and experience that other Aum devotees also reported to me.

By contrast, other of Aum's teachings, including those relating to Armageddon and to the 'conspiracies' against Aum, were of relatively little importance to him. He accepted that Japan was in imminent danger, and that some form of apocalyptic scenario was under way (a feeling he continues to adhere to even after the events of 1995), but felt that if anyone could save the situation it was Asahara. Even so, Asahara's sermons on weapons and destruction made comparatively little impact on him. He was too involved with his own practice and too busy with his work to worry about such things as the end of the world. He felt the same about the concept of Shambhala, which he considered rather vague and idealised. It was of little concrete relevance to him, for what he saw as ultimately real and important were the states of consciousness that developed in his mind, the freedom and happiness that came from such practices, and the spiritual salvation which would come when all his evil passions had been eradicated and his spirit had become able to ascend to a higher spiritual world.

A-san admitted he had been worried about aspects of Asahara's personality and nature. He knew that Asahara was engaging in sexual liaisons with female followers and that his eating activities were – compared to the lifestyles of his followers – lavish. However, he also was aware that gurus were special people who could behave in different ways from ordinary mortals (because they were enlightened and operated in a different realm of being). This was something he had learned through reading stories from the Tibetan Buddhist tradition of how gurus trained their disciples and how, in so doing, they would often depart from the rules of conventional morality for the sake of pushing their disciples to higher realms of consciousness. He thus appeared to accept that Asahara's behaviour represented a form of 'crazy wisdom' and despite the guru's apparent faults, he still remained faithful to him and relied on his individual spiritual guidance. He remains highly critical of the material world, and believes that,whatever problems may have occurred in Aum, its basic message about the corrupt nature of materialism was accurate and remains so.

For A-san, then, entry into Aum came as a direct result of attending an Asahara sermon, being struck by his message about asceticism and enlightenment, and being drawn in by his powerful charisma. Though it was not prominent initially, as a result of his joining he developed a growing sense of antipathy to, and espoused a deep-seated rejection of, the values of the present material world. These elements conditioned his subsequent experiences of Aum and remain central to his continuing faith. For A-san, external realities appeared almost inconsequential compared to his relationship with the guru, with his practice and with the states of mind that developed as a result. This was why he joined Aum, and although he can no longer have access to his guru, he can continue to maintain his practice which, he believes, remains his only hope of salvation and the only path to enlightenment and liberation. He certainly does not believe that rejoining the mainstream of Japanese society, getting a career and doing all the things that 'normal' people are supposed to do would be of any value. For him Aum provided meaning to a life which was otherwise meaningless, so to leave Aum now, even after all it had done, would be to return to a futile existence.

H-san: A Former Member

By contrast with A-san, H-san has left Aum as a result of the evidence that emerged in summer 1995. He had been a member of Aum for almost seven years at that point, and a *shukkesha* for almost six of these years. He was in his late twenties or early thirties when I met him in October 1997. Compared to A-san, who had expressed little interest in spiritual matters before curiosity led to his attending an Asahara lecture and rapid conversion thereafter, H-san had long had been interested in such questions prior to encountering Aum. These interests had developed in his early youth, probably as a result of the death of his elder brother, then aged 17, when he himself was only 14. He began to read *manga* (cartoon books) with futuristic, religious and science-fiction themes, and became interested in a variety of religious and spiritual matters ranging from Buddhism and Theosophy, to the Tarot, the spirit world and occultism. Amongst the writers that attracted his interest was Motoyama Hiroshi, a popular author of books about the occult, yoga and the spirit world.[21] He also became worried, during the 1980s, about the imminence of Armageddon: he was, in short, deeply interested in many of the themes prevalent in Japanese popular religious culture at the time.

He was frustrated with everyday life and was sure that he did not want to have a run-of-the-mill existence as an ordinary Japanese office worker or company employee. He wanted his life to mean something special, and he wanted to do something extraordinary for the sake of the world and its inhabitants. In such a frame of mind he had come across Asahara's book *Seishi o koeru* in 1987. It made a profound impression on him: just reading it gave him a feeling of great relaxation. He started to attend Aum meetings, although he did not formally join for another year, by which time he had read numerous other books on Buddhism which convinced him he was on the right path. He also was deeply impressed by Asahara's personal power, and in December 1988 he joined Aum.

As a lay member he went once a week to the *dōjō* to take part in voluntary work and to study yoga. He was, however, inspired to deepen his commitment after hearing Asahara state in a sermon that the world could be saved from destruction if Aum could produce 30,000 enlightened people. This, he realised, was what he had been looking for. It dealt with one of his main worries, the threat of a final war that would erupt some time at the end of the century, and gave him the opportunity for which he yearned, to do something special. It was his mission in life to be one of these 30,000, and in June 1989 he renounced the world and dedicated his life to Aum. He was, he said, also inspired by other senior figures in Aum, such as Ishii, Murai and Jōyu and wanted to be like them.

After becoming a *shukkesha* he worked in Aum's publications department and, although it was a demanding life, lacking in creature comforts and involving much hard work, he was happy and found it to be spiritually rewarding. He did, however, feel unhappy at how Aum was projecting itself outside the movement, and was especially perturbed by the decision to run for election in 1990. This, he felt, was wrong. Armageddon was at hand and he felt that Aum's energies could have been channelled into dealing with this issue and the spiritual problems confronting the world, rather than being wasted on such engagements with the corrupt material world of politics. He was, at the same time, also angry at what he saw as the unfair and unreasonable assaults on Aum by the media, and felt that these reaffirmed Aum's view that the media was a pernicious source of moral decay.

In his view the election of February 1990 marked a watershed in Aum's history. After this event a barrier descended between Aum and the outside world, although this hardly affected him. His life as a *shukkesha* remained peaceful as he dedicated himself to his work for Aum (which was primarily involved with making animation films to spread its message) and with his ascetic practice. Like A-san he was so absorbed in his own internal state of mind and practices that he had little time for what went on in the outside world – a world that he, like A-san, essentially regarded as superficial and illusory compared with the 'real' world of his own practice.

His underlying calm, however, began to be disturbed from 1994 onwards. He felt that Asahara had become remote and was too closely surrounded by a group of highly placed disciples such as Murai, who reinforced Asahara's ego and kept him isolated and out of touch. In addition he found the contents of Asahara's sermons to be increasingly disturbing, because they had begun to express violent images relating to Asahara's legitimations of violence (which were based in part on the concept of *poa*) and were focusing increasingly on images of death and destruction. He was shocked also by the ready acquiescence and even joy with which, he felt, other members had received Asahara's teaching that the righteous practitioner had the right to kill those who were destined for the hells. Although he was deeply enough involved in his work and meditations to remain somewhat detached from these changes, it was clear to him that something was amiss in the movement, a point that became starkly clear to him on 22 March 1995 when the police raids occurred. It was after this that he really began to understand the horrors of Aum – horrors that he had managed to ignore in part by having focused so strongly on his internal states of being. He had, in effect, drawn a curtain across the world of everyday reality. He left the movement in summer 1995.

Since then he has sought to come to terms with himself and his in-volvement with Aum. Although he personally committed no crimes, he was clearly disturbed by his support of and adherence to a movement that did commit them, and feels a deep sense of shame that in his pursuit of what he termed an 'idealised freedom' (*risōteki na jiyū*) he had ignored what was going on around him. He remains shocked at what Aum did, and feels that he was somehow complicit in the affair because of his involvement in and unquestioning support for Asahara and Aum. Unlike A-san, who came across as calm, at ease with himself and sure of the life path he has followed, H-san is clearly uneasy and unsettled. Although he has left Aum, he is still struggling to adjust to life after it, and to come to terms with his departure from a movement that has provided him with many deep experiences, both relating to his own spiritual development and in terms of relationships and the sense of community he had derived within it. H-san clearly feels, on some level, a sense of loss, compounded by the fact that his primary dissatisfaction with Japanese society at large (which lay behind his original decision to join Aum), remains as strong as ever.

I-san: A Seeker and Committed Member

I-san was aged 40 when I interviewed him in October 1997. He had been in Aum since April 1988 and remained a committed member who doubted much of what had been revealed in the press about Aum. He was by no means convinced that Aum had really committed all the crimes attributed to it, or that it had been the primary agent involved in them. Reiterating the conspiracy theories that had been prevalent in Aum prior to and immediately after the subway attack, he suggested to me that various *agents provocateurs* (probably, he thought, from rival religious movements) had infiltrated the movement and played a part in the affair. Even compared to A-san, who voiced some concerns and doubts about Aum and Asahara's activities, I-san's faith remained unquestioning and undiminished.

Although I-san had not been implicated in any of its crimes, he had been highly placed in Aum, a senior official who met Asahara regularly in the course of his work in the movement. His chosen career was as a teacher, but he had spent much of his time outside of work delving into philosophical and religious issues, and in this context had either read about or examined at some length a variety of religious ideas and traditions. As a student he had read books on Buddhism and on Western philosophy, been interested in Christianity and briefly involved with the Unification Church. After graduation he continued his spiritual search, practising Zen meditation for a time before abandoning it since he felt that it was too focused on the self and lacked concern about others. He then turned to Shingon Buddhism, and acquired an interest in its Japanese founder, Kūkai, the great eighth-century Buddhist teacher who had established esoteric Buddhism in Japan. He felt that he needed to find someone who was as ardent a practitioner and skilled a teacher as Kūkai had been, and with this in mind had visited various Shingon Buddhist teachers and joined the Buddhist group run by a one of these teachers. This had not, however, answered all his questions or resolved his doubts, and he continued in his spiritual search. In 1988 his interest was piqued by Asahara when he came across a copy of the Aum magazine *Mahāyāna*. As a result he went to listen to him speak, and found the sermon direct, easy to understand and relevant to his needs. He began to visit Aum centres and within a month had joined and started doing ascetic training. Soon after he received a *shaktipat* initiation from Ishii Hisako, which proved to be a powerful experience. In the days afterwards he experienced a fever and high temperatures as, he said, his body began to expel the various pollutants that, he believed, were in his body. He underwent a second initiation a month later.

When I asked him how he felt about paying large sums of money for such initiations, he laughed and said he did not have any problems with this: we buy all sorts of things with our money, mostly what he regarded as transient and ephemeral material goods which were of no value in terms of providing spiritual happiness. Money was merely a materialistic device to which people became attached, and that hindered them from attaining true salvation. In giving *fuse* (alms) to Aum he was receiving what he described as true merit and spiritual awareness – these were lasting, enduring things, unlike the transient material things on which most people spend their money.

His primary motive for joining Aum was to attain enlightenment and advanced states of consciousness: he was not especially interested in psychic powers. In spring 1990 he faced a severe crisis. He was still working as a teacher when Aum held an important seminar at Ishigaki in Okinawa – a seminar that all Aum devotees were urged to attend. He could not go because of his work commitments: in the conflict between his inner spiritual inclinations and his position in Japanese society he had chosen the latter. It did not, however, feel right, and within a few months, in July 1990, he quit his job and become a *shukkesha*.

He spent much of the next few years doing construction work at Aum's communes and remembers this as a period of intense hard work in which everyone would rise at 6 a.m. for meetings before starting work at 8 a.m. Work would continue until 8 p.m., when everyone would do their own spiritual practices (in his case for around four hours until midnight). They were encouraged by sermons from Asahara and stimulated by a form of frontier spirit, as they engaged together in building the foundations of a new era.

From this period on, I-san's life revolved around the communes at Kamikuishiki and Namino, where he also worked as a teacher looking after the children of Aum followers. He readily agreed that what they were taught and the regime they followed (with sparse diets and the like) were very different from those experienced by Japanese schoolchildren in general: they were mostly taught about Buddhism and about Asahara's teachings. He also engaged in various spiritual retreats when the opportunity arose. In autumn 1992, for example, he underwent a three-month ascetic retreat in which he did not lie down to sleep. What sleep he had was while seated in the Lotus posture, and he spent all his time chanting, meditating, listening to Aum tapes, and singing Aum songs. He had to stop this practice eventually in December 1992 because new buildings were being erected at Kamikuishiki and all able-bodied people in the movement were ordered to assist. Like A-san his main focus was on his own practice and hence he had been reluctant to stop his retreat, but had done so for the sake of the movement. Afterwards he continued to work at Kamikuishiki, and to be involved in a number of the movement's projects, while continuing to pursue his own practice whenever possible. He remembers the last years at Kamikuishiki as a period fraught with worry as (in his view) Aum was beset by opponents and surrounded by spies and possible infiltrators. It was in this atmosphere that the police raids occurred, in March 1995, while he was at Kamikuishiki, and despite the evidence that has since been brought forth by the authorities, I-san remains sceptical that the deeds attributed to Aum were solely carried out by the movement.

I-san was a spiritual seeker who, prior to encountering Asahara, had looked for, and failed to find, full spiritual satisfaction in a number of movements and groups. Asahara's teachings and Aum's practices had struck a special chord in him, and answered questions others had failed to answer. His main interest and focus was, like A-san's, on his own practice (hence his reluctant termination of his retreat in December 1992) which remained the most important thing in his life. Like in the case of A-san, too, it was the internal states of mind that developed from this practice that were paramount and it was for these that he willingly yielded up his money. He could also, it would appear, dissociate himself from any consideration of Aum's possible guilt in criminal activities. For him what mattered above all was what it had provided for him in terms of spiritual development, and whatever had occurred in the external, material world, appeared of less relevance.

In many respects, although I-san reacted to the police raids and the public declarations of Aum's involvement in criminal activities in somewhat different ways from A-san and H-san, there is much in his testimony and experiences that accords with theirs. All three had been self-absorbed and focused on their work and practice to the extent that they had not been aware of what their leaders were doing. In their voluntary isolation from the events of external reality and in their emphasis on the primary importance of their own practice, they had all, in effect, eschewed any particular interest in what went on in the everyday world and had relegated it to a secondary importance compared with the 'real' world that existed in their minds and through their practices.

THE EXPERIENCES OF THE ELITE: TESTIMONIES OF SENIOR AUM MEMBERS

The three disciples whose accounts I have related could be seen to be representatives of the general *shukkesha* of Aum. They were not amongst those who rose to the highest levels of the movement or who became actively involved in the commission of crimes. In this section I shall look at two such people, both of whom rose to the very top of Aum and who became confidants and highly valued disciples of Asahara, entrusted with important missions and tasks. Both these testimonies are taken from Aum publications from the early 1990s and were written at a time when they were deeply committed disciples. They make interesting reading since both the people concerned, Hayashi Ikuo and Inoue Yoshihiro, have subsequently renounced their faith in Asahara (in Hayashi's case claiming to have been somehow manipulated and misled by Asahara) and have admitted that they had been grievously wrong in the paths they followed. These testimonies, however, illustrate a rather different picture of the two when they were devout followers. They are presented here as examples of the life trajectories and paths of faith of two of the most elite members of the Aum organisation – two members who were so deeply involved in Aum and so committed to its cause that they conspired to commit murder on the Tokyo subway in its name.[22] Their accounts show us, in a sense, what was expected of the most devoted Aum disciples, and how they could ascend Aum's spiritual ladder and become part of its elite.

Elite Doctor and Subway Poisoner: The Experiences of Hayashi Ikuo

In January 1998 Hayashi Ikuo wept profusely in court as he apologised to the families of those his actions had killed, and told them that it had not been the 'real' Hayashi Ikuo who done these deeds but another person, whom he referred to as Krishnananda (Hayashi's holy name in Aum). In his court statement Hayashi suggested he had been a true spiritual seeker who had, under the malign influence of Asahara Shōkō, taken a wrong path, departed from his true self and become involved in acts of which he later felt deeply ashamed. Hayashi's professions of repentance were widely seen as genuine and were accepted as such by the families of those he had helped kill and by the court, which sentenced him to life imprisonment rather than death.

It is, however, Hayashi (or, in his terms, Krishnananda) who will form the focus of my analysis here. I base my account on Hayashi's own story as he recounted it in a 1991 Aum publication.[23] The testimony is interesting not so much because of the contrast that it presents with the subsequently penitent Hayashi (for I have no problems in accepting that, after a period of reflection in prison away from the movement, Hayashi along with other participants in the crimes could have come to a new and more sanguine recognition of their behaviour) but because it illustrates the type of mind-set of someone who had given up a flourishing career to pursue his spiritual goals and who had been successful enough in his new life course to ascend to the top of Aum.

Hayashi had made a successful career as a doctor specialising in heart problems. He graduated from the elite Keiō University's medical school and studied and trained in the USA before assuming a senior position at a state hospital in Japan. Despite such success, however, he remained troubled. He felt emotionally stifled and was unable to find any true sense of freedom or happiness in the material world in which he had gained his career success.[24] He had always, he stated, had an interest in religion but had found Japanese Buddhism to be spiritually unsatisfying, feeling that it had a 'dark image' because of its focus on funerals. Equally, while he admired Christ, he had negative views of Christianity because of the damage he considered it had done in the world, through wars and colonial activities. [25]

Hayashi read widely on spiritual matters, and eventually found what he felt was a good religion in Japan, one which, in its emphasis on spiritual transcendence and on the restoration of original Buddhism, appeared to offer him real hope of liberation. This was the Kannon Jikeikai, the movement founded by Kiriyama Seiyū which later became known as Agonshû. Hayashi was a member of the Kannon Jikeikai and of Agonshû for over 10 years, but was unable to attain the sense of spiritual liberation he sought. Indeed, just like Asahara, he felt disappointed that, despite Agonshū's claim to focus on meditation and yoga, it had, in reality, become more and more like an older, established religion in its emphasis on the procurement of worldly benefits for its followers and its avoidance of the sorts of ascetic practice he deemed necessary if one were to overcome one's passions. Despite his original faith in Kiriyama, he felt unable to advance spiritually and gradually became disenchanted with Agonshū.[26]

It was at this time that he came across Asahara's book *Chōnōryoku himitsu kaihatsuhō*. It immediately struck a chord in him, appealing to the interest he had developed through Agonshū in Tibetan Buddhism, in the guru–disciple relationship and in the practice of initiation. His interest increased as he read the experiences of Asahara's disciples who had received the *shaktipat* initiation and had undergone extraordinary experiences as a result. The photographs he saw of Asahara also proved inspirational, with Hayashi sensing that this really was a liberated being (*gedatsusha*) whom he wanted to meet.[27] He next read two more of Asahara's books[28] and, impressed by their teachings on karmic causation, was infused with a sense of great joy. Thereafter he quit Agonshū and joined Aum.[29] Within a year he had renounced the world. In November 1989 he informed Asahara of his desire to become a monk, resigned from his position at the hospital and – despite the pleas of his employers, family and friends – became a *shukkesha*. It was a decision, Hayashi said, that had effectively been made the first time he met Asahara.[30]

Hayashi stated that he was dissatisfied with what he felt were the limitations of his job as a doctor. The doctor's mission was to save lives but, Hayashi said, he aspired to something more than this. He wanted to save not just physical lives but *souls* by helping people get rid of their karma.[31] Here again, in Hayashi's frustration with the limits of his profession in the field of medicine, and his sense that spiritual actions could achieve more profound accomplishments, there is a resonance with Asahara's own thoughts and frustrations with the limits of alternative medicine.

Hayashi devoted himself to Aum's severe ascetic practices and in January 1991, after an intensive five-month period of austerities, achieved the sort of spiritual breakthrough to which he had long aspired, and which had driven his religious quest. This was the awakening of the *kundalini* as a result of his dedicated and intensive ascetic practice. He was awarded the holy name Krishnananda and entered into the elite ranks of Aum, being placed in charge of Aum's medical facilities and its hospital in Tokyo, which used its own special blend of healing, with its melding of Western medical practice with Eastern healing techniques.[32] Hayashi was clearly proud of his role in Aum and in what he believed it and his guru could offer the world. He believed that Asahara could save all souls on a spiritual level and possessed teachings that could bring absolute truth to the world. This was a path of world salvation, and it was one that Hayashi, too, aspired to follow. He was striving with all his might to eradicate all his evil passions and succeed in the higher levels of practice that he was engaged in, to this end.[33]

Hayashi's account was given in 1991. In the years afterwards he not only remained a prominent member of Aum's elite but ascended further in its ranks, eventually being named 'Minister of Health' in the quasi-government Aum established in 1994 and being entrusted to participate in various of its crimes. Although Hayashi has subsequently recognised the wrongs he has committed, he was a dedicated and ardent member of Aum's inner elite until May 1995, when he first confessed to investigators that he had participated in the subway attack and began the process of reflection that led to repentance. He had rapidly made the transition from being one of the elite of mainstream Japanese society – a highly qualified heart doctor who had graduated from a top institution, studied abroad and then assumed a major position in the Japanese healthcare system – to one of Aum's spiritual elite. That conversion had come about because of his spiritual unease with the mores and nature of the modern, materialist society in which he had achieved economic and career success, but which had failed to deliver any solace on other levels; moreover the other religions that operated in Japan at the time had also failed to provide an adequate alternative for him. He had been drawn to Aum through books, and subsequently because of Asahara's charisma. In Aum he believed he had found something that had been lacking elsewhere: a dedicated path of ascetic and spiritual practice capable of leading him and others to high levels of spiritual awareness. It was because of his dedication to this cause and his deep belief in its efficacy and power of Asahara Shōkō that he pledged total obedience to the movement and to Asahara and was ready to carry out the actions which he subsequently came to regret.

Dedicated Ascetic, Charismatic Practitioner and Ruthless Enforcer: Inoue Yoshihiro

Inoue Yoshihiro was the youngest of Aum's leading lights. He joined the movement at the age of 17 and when he was arrested in May 1995 and charged with multiple offences, he was just 25 years old. By that time he had earned a reputation in the media as a ruthless enforcer of Asahara's dictates, ready to kidnap, torture, elicit information and kill for his guru.[34] However, he was also known for his abilities as a charismatic practitioner and gifted recruiter for the movement, serving as a source of inspiration for those who joined. It was, for example, Inoue's personal example and charismatic presence that first drew Takahashi Hidetoshi to and kept him interested in Aum.[35] Inoue was widely regarded as a very gifted practitioner of yoga and asceticism, and praised highly by Asahara himself for his abilities in this area.[36]

Inoue had felt uneasy as a child and at school, even though he did well in the education system, attending a private high school and being accepted into a highly regarded university to study law. [37] Like many others of his fellow Aum members, he had doubts early on about the nature of Japanese society and the contradictions and the egotistical influences that he felt were inherent within it. His doubts were resolved when he came across books by Asahara, particularly when he came across Asahara's assertions that the world was evil and that the truth was to be found within oneself. He began to do ascetic practices on his own and then joined Aum, attending its summer and winter training seminars and receiving a *shaktipat* initiation from Asahara.[38] He made great progress in his meditation practices, had a number of mystical experiences and, he claimed, acquired the ability to levitate. He recorded how energy rose through his body and how his body began to rise and float before then gradually settling down.[39]

It was at this point that he began to experience doubts, and to be gripped by a sense of fear and impermanence. However, Asahara's teaching about the nature of suffering helped him through the crisis and inspired him to deepen his practice. He devoted five hours a day to austerities at home, making further rapid progress which was recognised by Asahara who gave him further encouragement. As a result, Inoue decided, while still only 17, to become a monk – a decision strongly opposed by his parents who wanted him to go to university. He partially accepted their wishes, sitting and passing the university entrance examinations. At this point, however, he rebelled and took the decision to become a *shukkesha* rather than continue with his studies.[40]

Asahara pushed him further along the path of asceticism, ordering him to undergo retreats and to succeed in *kundalini* yoga. This proved an arduous and painful task, and Inoue records that he had a difficult struggle to deal with his passions. He was also afflicted by immense bodily pains during the austerities. Again, he was wracked by self-doubt, but his faith in and the support of Asahara enable him to overcome these. Recognising that the real basis of ascetic practice is faith in one's guru, he extended his practices further and further until he was performing meditation for 24 hours a day in a darkened room. At this point he saw a bright light descending from on high. This, Asahara informed him, was a sign of spiritual breakthrough and of the successful attainment of the stage of *kundalini* yoga. It was a rapid breakthrough, taking him only 12 days, rather than the two weeks predicted by Asahara, and he was rewarded for his success with the bestowal of his holy name, Ananda.[41] After this, Inoue reports, he began to be able to discern the auras of others and to acquire various other extraordinary powers, including *tennitsû* (the divine hearing of gods).[42] However, Inoue stated, he felt that the highest merit of Aum's ascetic practice was not the acquisition of such powers, but the ability to understand karmic law (*karuma no hōsoku*). This was what he had achieved, for he could now *see* the suffering and karma of others, and as such could work to save them from their fate.[43] For Inoue, the keys to such salvation were ascetic practice and absolute faith in the guru.[44]

Inoue was one of Asahara's most devout disciples and was certainly also one of his favourites. Indeed, it was Inoue's appearance in court to testify against Asahara that seems to have disturbed Asahara more than anything else, causing him to become highly emotional, to interrupt the court, to plead with his own lawyers not to cross-examine Inoue and even to ask Inoue to levitate in court.[45] Following his arrest Inoue, like Hayashi, had publicly acknowledged his responsibility in the affair and the error of the path Aum had taken. Beforehand, however, he had been an utterly dedicated follower of Asahara, finding in his teachings and guidance the answers he sought to his fears and concerns about the world. His readiness, at the age of 17, to renounce the world and a privileged career path, and to fling himself into arduous austerities is indicative of the zealous nature of those who entered Aum's inner circle, and of how far they were ready to go to in their desire to find meaning in a world they considered evil. It also shows how Asahara was able to discern, in some disciples, an inner fire, determination and despair that meant they would be prepared to go to great extremes in order to achieve their goals and to attain spiritual breakthroughs, and illustrates how he was able to work on that fire and determination to push them harder and harder in this quest.

PRACTICES AND CHALLENGES: GIVING ONE'S ALL FOR AUM

Aum was very much a unique case among the new religions of Japan in its focus on extreme asceticism as a means of liberation and also by its use of such practices to demonstrate its efficacy. Moreover, while the new religions in general naturally make some demands in terms of time, financial support and practice on their followers, none has quite gone to the extremes that Aum did.

Those who joined Aum had to be highly motivated, zealous and dedicated, prepared to cast off their former selves through leaving behind their families and careers and yielding up their worldly goods. The first stage of this path was the giving of alms (*fuse*), a practice that was vital for *shukkesha* who donated all their worldly belongings and money to Aum. It was also a mark of commitment for lay followers.

These monetary donations have been widely seen by Aum's critics (and by many disaffected former members) as examples of Aum's manipulative and acquisitive nature. The sums demanded for initiations were large, and a considerable amount of the complaints that were directed against Aum related to this matter, of disgruntled former followers who had paid hundreds of thousands of yen for initiations that, they felt, had not benefited them. Yet many followers (and not a few former followers) saw matters a little differently. I-san's view that money was merely a transient product of a corrupt and material world, valueless in comparison with spiritual development and liberation, has been reiterated in interviews conducted by various reporters who spoke to Aum devotees in the years prior to the subway attack. The *Kumamoto Nichinichi* newspaper reporters found commune members at Namino who had donated everything to Aum without regret: a 60-year-old woman who had become a *shukkesha* along with her son commented that money was of no use when one was dead, while others who had given large sums of money for various initiations, made comparisons with the sorts of expenditure people in society make on what they saw as meaningless material goods such as cars and the like.[46]

One might note that for those who rejected the values of the ordinary world – and of course, this was the basic orientation of those inclined to become *shukkesha* in Aum – and who sought spiritual liberation, money fell into the same category as families and careers: something that could be readily jettisoned in pursuit of a higher, more lasting value system and state of being. Moreover, especially for young people reacting against and rejecting the values of their parents, donating all their (and doubtless some of their parents') possessions and money to a communal religious movement was an ultimate demonstration of contempt for such value systems.

The demands placed on disciples could be even more extreme, especially for those who, like Inoue and Hayashi, were driven to pursue the path of liberation to its extreme ends. Aum used public demonstrations of ascetic prowess as a means of displaying to the world the 'truth' of its path, and such demonstrations came to be seen both as an extreme test of the faith of its disciples and as a means of achieving higher states of consciousness. Some of these practices sought to challenge normal conceptions of what was physically possible by placing the practitioner in death-defying situations. In March 1988, for example, Asahara and Ishii Hisako underwent an extended underwater immersion (known in Aum as the 'underwater *samadhi*') to demonstrate that they had acquired the ability to suspend their normal breathing patterns, had gone beyond any attachment to the body and desire, and had entered into the realms of *samadhi* or enlightenment.

A further extension of this practice, the 'underground *samadhi*', in which disciples were buried in an airtight box for extended periods that would be impossible to survive if one maintained normal breathing patterns, was also considered in Aum to be a death challenging (*hesshi chōsen*) practice.[47] This practice was also adopted by Aum in the early 1990s. Understandably, given their extreme nature, these two forms of practice were not widely undertaken in Aum. They were, however, considered as important challenges to be overcome by aspirants to the highest realms of consciousness, and their successful completion was a sign that marked such practitioners out from the ordinary ranks of followers. Amongst those who undertook the underground *samadhi* practice was a disciple named Ueda Tatsuya, who rose to the rank of *seishi* ('sacred teacher') as a result.

Risking One's Life in Pursuit of the Truth: The Story of Ueda Tatsuya

Ueda's story was published by the movement in 1992, at which time he was 27 years old and known under his holy name Anupama.[48] He had previously been a company worker who had become interested in spiritual matters. He also reports that he had been tormented from his childhood by a sense of impermanence because of various deaths in his family. During his search for ways to overcome this feeling and to attain happiness he came across Asahara's book *Metsubō no hi*. This volume, published in 1989, was the first book in which the theme of apocalypse which was to dominate later Aum thought, was openly expressed. It had an immense impact on him and shortly after reading it he joined Aum, deciding almost immediately to become a *shukkesha*.[49] As a result of his austerities he had various mystical experiences, seeing visions of shining light and feeling energy rising in him and making the crown of his head tingle. He succeeded in *kundalini* yoga which he saw as the first step to the goal of transcending impermanence and achieving absolute happiness. To achieve this success he had followed a severe ascetic schedule at Aum's commune at Namino, during which he had various mystical experiences in which he felt sweet nectar flowing down from the top of his head. He devoted all of his time to various forms of spiritual practice, including *kinhin* (walking meditation), a slow meditative walking practice used also in Zen temples, which he performed virtually non-stop. As he did so, he began to feel his 'polluted data' being gradually purified and his evil passions becoming subdued.[50]

Further ascetic and mystical experiences followed, at which point he was told by Asahara to undertake Aum's underground *samadhi* practice. This, Ueda explained, involved a five-day meditation retreat with no food or water in an underground airtight chamber about 3 metres square. If one breathed normally in such a confined chamber one would run out of oxygen and die. To survive one had to enter *samadhi*, which meant one had to cease breathing and 'die' to one's normal bodily functions. According to Ueda, by succeeding in this practice and surviving this retreat, the ascetic 'proved' that s/he had entered the state of enlightenment.[51]

Since he was aware of the potential dangers involved in the practice, the order initially took Ueda aback. However, he immediately prepared to follow his guru's command – testament, one might note, to the faith Asahara inspired in his disciples. If he ordered them to perform a practice, they would do so, considering that if it was something he believed they could attain, they would be able to succeed. His faith in them, in other words, inspired them to believe in their capacity to overcome the normal limitations of the body. Before he entered the chamber Ueda received an initiation from Asahara to give him power and strength during the days to come. A phone link was also placed in the enclosed compartment to enable Asahara to keep in touch and give him guidance.

Ueda records that during the five-day retreat he controlled his breath and saw various forms of light which signified the different realms or levels of being he was passing through during his meditations. The third day of the retreat was especially difficult, and he was tormented by such feelings of immense pain that he could not continue meditating. At this point of extreme distress the telephone rang: it was Asahara, telling him that the pain he was undergoing came from winds rising in his body because his energy channels had become narrow and confined. If, however, he could remain mentally focused the pains would drop away. This communication inspired Ueda to overcome his pain, and he notes that it proved to him the powers of the guru, who had a direct spiritual link to his disciples. It was a further example, in his view, of Asahara's depths of spiritual insight.

Subsequently Ueda felt all his various fears and desires disappearing: first, his fears of death, and then his worldly desires and evil passions, as well as his wish for food, dropped away. As they did, on his fourth day underground, however, a new desire arose: the wish to do more ascetic practice, to strive for the salvation of all beings and to spread the word of truth in the world. As he felt this awakening he gave thanks to his guru, to Shiva and to all of Aum's 'true victors'. At this stage, he records, his breath stopped completely: on the next day the underground retreat came to an end, and he left the chamber, to be greeted by Asahara with the pronouncement that he had achieved *samadhi* and attained the rank of *seishi*.[52]

After his successful completion of the practice, Ueda stated that he had really deep feelings of power and spiritual calm. He had, he claimed, lived like the gods in the higher spiritual realms, existing only on spiritual sustenance. In his new state as a *seishi* he had gone beyond the realms of ordinary humanity, shedding his worldly passions and acquiring the power to see into the nature of others. He emphasised how much he owed to Asahara for enabling him to achieve such states of being and urged all others to follow this path of action: via asceticism, he asserted, anyone could enter *samadhi* and attain the highest spiritual realms.[53]

Ueda was by no means the only person to perform this extreme and demanding feat of asceticism or to be declared, on successful completion, to have attained higher levels of consciousness. Indeed, the underground *samadhi* appears to have been practised by many of those who reached Aum's highest ranks, including Murai, Jōyu, Ishii and Ashara's wife Tomoko.[54] Like Ueda they were prepared to go to great extremes in the pursuit of their goals and to follow Asahara's commands, even to the point of risking their lives.

Not all devotees, of course, were keen to go to such lengths and these extreme practices were only undertaken by a select few. Such extreme austerities, in fact, reinforced Aum's stratified hierarchic system and served to create divisions within the movement. When Jōyu Fumhiro was due to emerge from a five-day underground retreat in November 1991 (this was the first time that the practice had been attempted) the occasion was transformed into a festive event in which Asahara and his followers celebrated Jōyu's successful emergence, which, they believed, would show to the wider world how effective Aum's practices were in leading its followers to higher levels of consciousness, and how devotees could transcend and overcome the physical state. Yet, as Takahashi Hidetoshi has commented, the mood among many of the faithful waiting for Jōyu to emerge was anything but festive. While some feared that Jōyu might not come out alive – which would be a public relations disaster – there was an even greater fear among the disciples that if he emerged successful, they might all be made to do the practice.[55] The fear was under-standable given Aum's central tenet of unquestioning obedience to its guru.

These fears did not materialise. Jōyu came out alive, but the practice did not become standard for all *shukkesha*. Indeed, it served as a form of barrier and gateway to higher ranks and states of attainment, and one that reinforced the hierarchic nature of Aum that had begun to develop since the inception of the *sangha* system. By the time Ueda, Jōyu and others were undertaking such practices in the 1990s, Aum had developed a spiritual elite, entry into which depended on the willingness to display extreme forms of devotion such as these death-defying ascetic practices.

A Demanding Religion with Extreme Followers

Asahara Shōkō's teachings proved attractive to people dissatisfied with contemporary society, appearing to answer their fears about the future and to offer ways through which to acquire higher states of consciousness and psychic powers. Asahara's own charisma drew people to his movement and inspired their devotion, while the abilities and charismatic qualities of his senior disciples demonstrated in a practical way the efficacy of Aum's methods of practice. As the testimonies in this chapter have shown, Aum appeared to deliver what followers sought: extraordinary spiritual experiences and a spiritual home where they could take refuge from the corrupt material world. Aum also offered them the hope of salvation from the forces of karma and from the apocalypse they feared might engulf the world, and gave them an active role, as sacred warriors, in this process.

In return, however, Asahara made enormous demands on his followers, asking them to give up their money, jobs, careers, family ties and identities and, in its use of extreme techniques, asked them to put those lives on the line. These extreme demands, offset by the high rewards of becoming a sacred warrior on a mission of world salvation and a bodhisattva with a holy name, encouraged the emergence of a zealous elite who, driven by the will to succeed, were determined to ascend Aum's hierarchic ladder.

Aum's system and structure thus led to the emergence of a zealous elite cadre around Asahara who displayed extremes of devotion and detachment, and who were prepared to undertake potentially life-threatening austerities or carry out extreme orders for their guru. The extent of their devotion and zeal is shown by the comments of senior disciples such as Tsuchiya Masami and Niimi Tomomitsu who, on trial for their lives, have declared their willingness to die for Asahara. It is shown also by the comments of one of the subway attackers, Hirose Ken'ichi, during his own trial. Hirose told the court that he joined Aum with the hope of acquiring psychic powers and had spent 12 hours a day on ascetic practices in order to attain salvation. He believed he had made immense progress in this respect and his zeal was such that he could not have envisaged leaving the movement. Indeed, if he even contemplated such a thought he would have wanted to be killed by Aum (*poa saretakatta*).[56] That way he would have had a chance of salvation, rather than suffering the fate of all who were not members of Aum and falling into the hells. Even though he now recognised the terrible crimes committed by Aum, Hirose continued to have some empathy for the movement and to assert that, despite all that had transpired, he liked Aum and clearly still yearned for the experiences he had had in it.[57]

Hirose's comments are further evidence of the extraordinary bonds of commitment that Aum forged with its most ardent members, and the extremes they were prepared to go to for their guru and movement. Eventually those extremes involved not just severe austerities but the commission of criminal acts and the taking of lives in the name of their sacred mission. Within a very few years of its formation, Aum Shinrikyō turned to violence and murder, and it is to this issue that I shall turn next.

ポア

5 Losing the Struggle – From World Salvation to World Destruction, 1988–1990

THE DEVELOPMENT OF TENSION

In August 1988 Aum opened its commune at Kamikuishiki. This signalled a further step in its apparent transition from a small yoga group into a successful religious movement financially sound enough to buy tracts of land for religious development and capable of establishing religious communities at the centre of its mission for world salvation. However, despite this semblance of success, there were already problematic signs indicating a much less positive side to Aum. Its earlier optimism had started to give way to a darker and more pessimistic vision in which catastrophe and war came to be seen as inevitable, universal salvation as impossible, and only selective individual salvation for the faithful and devout practitioners of Aum as feasible. As this shift occurred, Asahara's thoughts turned from the possibility of universal salvation to the inevitability and eventually the *desirability* of mass destruction.

This turn to a catastrophic millennialist vision was paralleled by changes in Aum's primary focus of religious self-identification, with its move from Mahāyāna path dedicated to the liberation of all souls, to the more exclusive Vajrayāna path of esoteric Buddhism centred on elite practitioners who were prepared to renounce the world, express absolute devotion and obedience to their guru, and undertake severe austerities. These changes in doctrinal perspective added to the grow- ing divisions and hierarchic impulses within Aum, widening the gap be- tween the lay and monastic sections of the movement. They also heightened the tensions that existed between Aum (as a movement with world-rejecting inclinations) and the world it regarded as corrupt and materialistic.

In the period between August 1988 and spring of 1990 these tensions grew virtually to breaking point as Aum entered into repeated conflicts with interest groups ranging from the parents of young people who had joined Aum, to the mass media, to legal authorities, to the civil authorities and villagers in the areas where it built its communes. While these conflicts were not necessarily or always of its own making, they were widely provoked or exacerbated by Aum's hostile and intolerant attitude to the world at large – an attitude that was founded in its self-created sense of spiritual superiority and special mission.

In this period Aum also experienced massive public rejection and humiliation because of its ill-fated attempt to establish a political platform; moreover it attracted widespread public criticism for its practices, and came to the attention of law enforcement agencies and legal authorities as suspicions grew that it had engaged in illegal activities. It was also in this period, starting, it would appear, from late summer or early autumn 1988, that Aum first resorted to violence, at first inside the movement but subsequently outside. This violence was initially linked to Aum's focus on asceticism as a means to liberation, and to its assertions about the absolute authority of the guru, but it developed into a means of dealing with those who appeared to oppose or undermine the movement, and eventually became a means of articulating its concept of struggle against the forces of evil with which it was destined to do battle. This escalation of violence occurred quite rapidly. In autumn 1988 coercion within Aum caused the accidental death of a follower. By November 1989 senior members of the movement had committed four murders in Aum's name and in the spring of 1990 Aum had started to experiment with weapons of mass destruction and made a first (unsuccessful) attempt to bring about indiscriminate mass destruction through the use of biological weapons in Tokyo. All of these actions were legitimated in doctrinal terms by Asahara in the sermons he preached to the *shukkesha*.

Why and how this happened will be the subject of this chapter, which examines Aum's history and development from the summer of 1988 to late spring 1990. This period was probably the most critical in Aum's history in the context of its development of a culture of religiously motivated and legitimated violence. It was the era when Aum first crossed the borders into illegality and began to regard violence as a legitimate means of action in the furtherance and protection of its mission.

THE VAJRAYĀNA PATH: ABSOLUTE DEVOTION AND THE EXALTED GURU

In August 1988 Asahara delivered a sermon in which he announced that henceforth Aum would primarily follow what he called the Tantra-

Vajrayāna, or more succinctly the Vajrayāna, path of esoteric Buddhism.[1] The sermon was the first in a series of 57 that were eventually collated into a xeroxed text with the title *Vajrayāna kōsu kyōgaku shisutemu kyōhon.* [The Vajrayāna Course Teaching System Textbook] – hereafter referred to as the Vajrayāna sermons. The first of these 57 sermons was delivered on 5 August 1988, and the last on 30 April 1994. They were not the only teachings or sermons that Asahara gave during this six-year period, and many of the 57 were published elsewhere in collections of Asahara's talks and sermons. However, it was the Vajrayāna sermons and the issues on which they centred that were considered inside Aum (and indeed by various scholars who have studied the movement)[2] to be at the very heart of Asahara's teaching. The sermons were never published together as a publicly available course of teaching, and access to them was restricted to committed members who had renounced the world, for whom they were essential reading.[3] The text is thus an important means of gaining insights into Asahara's frame of mind from August 1988 onwards and into the teachings that were being imbibed by Aum's advanced practitioners. It also serves as a historical source (the sermons are reproduced in the text in calendrical order) showing the development of Asahara's thought and his mental state between 1988 and 1994.

It is perhaps understandable that the sermons as a coherent body of teaching were not made available outside of Aum's inner sanctum since, taken as a whole, they demonstrate some alarming doctrinal developments and attitudes. It was in these sermons that Asahara expanded on the concepts of *poa* and karma, using them as elements in the construction and development of a doctrine that ultimately legitimated and justified violence, killing and mass destruction. The sermons – and especially the later ones, in autumn 1993 and spring 1994 when Aum's plans of making chemical weapons were in full flow – were infused with extremely pessimistic thoughts about the negative effects of karma, and spoke repeatedly and in often highly emotive tones about the inevitability of death and the likelihood of falling into the hells. They were also obsessed with apocalyptic images and with the means of mass destruction. Other major themes that permeate them are Asahara's prophecies of a coming war that will be fought with futuristic weaponry and his recurrent concerns about the conspiratorial forces that he believed were striving for world domination and were seeking to persecute and destroy his movement.[4] In this dramatic scenario Aum was increasingly portrayed as the sole force capable of resisting this evil conspiracy, whose participants included the US government (which was seen as the epicentre of evil and the ultimate symbol of corrupt materialism) and various other groups that frequently crop up in 'conspiracy' theories, such as the Jews and the Freemasons. This theme of conspiracy against and persecution of Aum was not overtly present in the earliest of the Vajrayāna sermons but by spring 1990 it had become one of the defining elements of Aum thought.

Asahara commenced, in the first Vajrayāna sermon, by asserting the superiority of the Vajrayāna path: it was the shortest and most efficacious route to liberation, absolute freedom and happiness. However, it was also an extremely hard path requiring intense ascetic practice, absolute devotion to the guru, and absolute faith in the unity of the guru, truth and Shiva. Because of the extreme demands of faith, obedience and asceticism it made of practitioners, it was not a path suited to everyone, and Asahara admonished those who were unable to endure such levels of practice to continue to follow the Hinayāna or Mahāyāna paths of Buddhism instead. While neither abandoning nor denigrating these forms of Buddhism, Asahara made it clear that they were only stages in the development of the true practitioner whose real aspirations were to get to the Vajrayāna level which was the *only* path that true spiritual seekers could choose, as it was the only one that led to complete liberation. At its heart was the relationship of the guru and the disciple: it was only through this relationship, which was the highest possible human relationship, 'higher than the parent–child relationship, or that relationship of lovers, or of husbands and wives',[5] that liberation could be achieved. Implicitly, then, anyone who chose *not* to follow this path was displaying a lack of absolute faith in the guru, a lack of commitment to the goals and ends of the movement, and a lack of true desire to achieve liberation. Those who did not follow this path were implicitly declaring themselves to be weak and unable to attain liberation.

This was clearly how the disciples present at the sermon viewed matters, and they enthusiastically embraced this new path. By so doing they were no longer aspirant buddhas and bodhisattvas striving for the liberation of all, but a chosen elite, the select few who could attain liberation. They had transcended the realms of the ordinary world: soon, as the next Vajrayāna sermon was to show, they could be free of its moral strictures as well.

Asahara asked his disciples which path they wished to follow, directing the question initially to Endō Seiichi, a zealous disciple who later was one of the chief architects of Aum's weapon-making schemes. When Endō affirmed his desire to follow the Vajrayāna route, Asahara told him that he was not doing enough ascetic practice: he, and all other aspirants, had to do more. He then posed the same question to the rest of the audience: which path do you wish to follow? Unsurprisingly all responded in unison that they, too, would henceforth follow the Vajrayāna.[6] It was a typical Asahara sermonising performance in which his rhetorical powers were given full play.

In the second Vajrayāna sermon, in October 1988, Asahara outlined two further themes that were crucial to the Vajrayāna path. The first was his assertion that it transcended conventional morality and was beyond good and evil.[7] This assertion, which was developed further in subsequent sermons, indicates the first overt step taken by Asahara to place his movement and its actions beyond the realms of moral criticism: the claim that practitioners of the Vajrayāna had gone beyond the confines of normative morality freed them of the need to adhere to it or indeed to the laws of society. In effect this meant, Asahara explained, that what might be considered wrong from the perspective of conventional Buddhist morality could, from the perspectives of Tantric and Vajrayāna Buddhism, be seen as good if it furthered the spreading of truth or if it removed hindrances and opposition to the mission of spreading the truth.[8] Of course, what Asahara meant by the 'truth' was synonymous with his own actions and with the interests of his movement and teaching. It was a view that was subsequently used to legitimate attacks on and murders of various of Aum's opponents.

A second major theme of this sermon was that of 'cloning the guru' as a necessary step on the path to liberation and as a means of ridding oneself of the corrupt data of the material world. While Asahara and his followers had previously talked of the need of the disciple to 'copy' the guru (a term that implied following in his footsteps, performing the same practices and striving to be like him) this, as far as I have been able to tell, was the first occasion he spoke of 'cloning'.[9] It was an interesting shift of nuance: the use of the term 'clone' is especially noteworthy also because it occurred at a time when the pattern of Aum initiations was changing. This was a period in which there had been a relatively sharp increase in the number of disciples, which meant that the demand for direct, person-to-person initiation had increased greatly.[10] This in turn had placed an immense stress on Asahara which eventually caused him to cease performing *shaktipat* initiations because they were having an extremely draining effect on him physically. Instead he delegated this task to a number of highly placed disciples such as Ishii Hisako and eventually also his wife Tomoko. This change occurred at about the time that he began the Vajrayāna sermons in August 1988.

Nevertheless, Asahara remained the primary focus of initiations and the sole source of power in Aum. Initiations continued to focus on his person by making use of his body and its traces as a source of psychic power and spiritual energy. The concept of cloning the guru thus extended to absorbing his power through ingesting elements of his physical body: phials of his blood that followers drank in the 'Blood Initiation' rite, glasses of his bath water in the 'Miracle Pond Initiation', and a liquid that, it was stated, had been manufactured by Aum's scientists to replicate Asahara's DNA structure and which was imbibed in the 'DNA Initiation' instituted in January 1989.[11]

These initiations were underpinned by the belief that by imbibing Asahara's bodily traces, followers would achieve some form of spiritual transformation: Asahara's charisma, in other words, had a physical, bodily dimension. Later in its history Aum was to institute numerous other forms of initiation that were based on the ingestion of substances that were believed capable of altering the mind and consciousness, including, from mid-1994 onwards, hallucinogenic drugs such as LSD.[12]

Some of these types of practice can be found in other religious cultures. The practice of ingesting the traces of holy persons so as to absorb their sanctity is found in various guises. In her seminal study of pollution, taboo and power, for example, Mary Douglas cites the case of South Indian villagers drinking the water that had been used to wash the feet of an Indian holy man, as a mark of respect for his sanctity and so as to partake of his spiritual power.[13] The physical traces of holy persons and saints have – as the cults of relics found in religious traditions such as Buddhism and Christianity – long been regarded as living corporeal sources of power capable of transforming or healing those that touch or worship them.[14] Ingesting hallucinogenic drugs as a means of attaining changes in consciousness, too, is not unknown in religious terms or in initiation rituals in various parts of the world. However, in the modern Japanese context, the use of such practices (and particularly those relating to the body) was, at the very least, rare, and when reports of such initiations began to appear in the media, they contributed to the perception that Aum was a strange movement that engaged in bizarre practices.

The media also raised suspicions that its guru made extortionate demands on his followers and was using his authority to acquire large sums of money from them. This belief was reinforced by the fact that followers were asked to pay large sums of money for such initiations: in the case of the 'Blood Initiation', for example, the sum was ¥300,000.[15] These sums were considered as 'donations' (*fuse*) and were necessary elements in the path of practice and journey to liberation Aum offered. Many followers gave willingly, finding such initiations valuable and testifying to the uplifting experiences they had had, or claiming that they had received cures or relief from pain as a result of such initiations.[16]

However, the impression gleaned by the mass media and public (and especially the families of those who had joined Aum and given it substantial donations), was invariably more negative. Complaints also began to be heard from some former members who had paid out large sums for initiations and who had complained of not receiving any spiritual advancement as a result. Since, with the shift to the Vajrayana, so much emphasis had been placed on the centrality of the guru as a gateway to liberation, suspicions were aroused in many quarters that in purveying such costly initiations, Asahara was effectively manipulating his followers and extorting money from them. Egawa Shōko, reviewing the variety of initiations that Aum members were encouraged to undergo – and of course pay for – expressed the feeling that 'everything was money, money, money'.[17] As she also notes, advancement in the movement had become quite dependent on the extent to which followers demonstrated their faith and their renunciation of the material world by making such donations.[18]

Aum had claimed, when publicising its Blood Initiation and its DNA Initiation, that Asahara's blood had been analysed by Kyoto University's medical laboratories and found to contain a unique form of DNA structure, and that this was one source of his spiritual power. By imbibing this special DNA, followers could acquire some of this power, thereby expanding their consciousness.[19] It was Endō Seiichi, apparently, who had conceived this idea and who had claimed he had been able to 'verify' this through his own experiments.[20] The claim that the blood had been tested in a university laboratory, however, was false – a case, perhaps, of Aum's tendencies towards extravagant claims and gestures allowing it to fall into a trap of its own making – and Aum's lawyer Aoyama Yoshinobu later had to amend it by claiming that the blood had been tested by an Aum disciple who had been a graduate student at the university.[21] This falsehood was subsequently to have grave repercussions for the movement. It also further contributed to the image of a leader who ceaselessly promoted himself in order to acquire funds from his followers. While Asahara and his cohorts were clearly in great need of money to finance their various projects, communes, proselytisation efforts and much else besides, it was evident that they paid little regard to issues of legality and had few scruples about how they got their money. In a sense they were thereby demonstrating not so much their belief, founded in their perceptions of the Vajrayāna path, that they had gone beyond the limitations of conventional morality, but their apparent contempt and disregard for it altogether.

TENSIONS AND THE GROWTH OF A PESSIMISTIC WORLDVIEW

Changes also occurred in another area of Asahara's teaching at this time. His earlier optimistic views on world salvation had begun to give way to the feeling that this was not achievable. The pessimistic shift of focus that had begun to manifest itself in January 1988 when Asahara made the predictions reported in *Twilight Zone*. By late 1988, these forebodings had escalated to such an extent that Asahara was predicting mass destruction and cataclysm, ceasing to suggest that he could save the world, and stating that henceforth his and Aum's energies could only be directed towards saving the movement's own members.[22]

There are few overt indications in the teachings of this period to explain why these images of cataclysm and a more narrow vision of salvation occurred. However, it is striking that this was a period when other crucial developments and changes were taking place in the movement's belief structures, activities and orientations – notably the development of Aum's posture as a Vajrayāna movement, the increasing demands of obedience that were made on its followers, and the cessation by Asahara of some forms of initiation and the development of others that centred on his body. There was, I would contend, a correlation between all these changes, and here I will suggest why Asahara's prophecies took on a more pessimistic slant, and why he needed to emphasise a more elitist path in his movement, and to boost his own status accordingly at this time.

I have previously touched on one of the most critical factors in this process: that of Aum's size. Asahara's predictions of salvation had been tied to the attainment of quantifiable levels of growth and success in a relatively short period of time: six years for Aum to open two centres in every country of the world so as to stave off a prophesied nuclear war; 30,000 people to renounce the world and be led to enlightenment within little more than a decade. Even by early 1988, it could be argued, the problem of so closely tying the mission of universal salvation to Aum's visible growth would have been apparent. Changing the orientations of the movement and turning it away from universal salvation was, in a sense, a way of evading the questions that would have come from the failure to achieve the previously stated goals of his mission. Asahara's increasing pessimism about the world at large, as well as his narrowing of the gate of salvation through his espousal of the Vajrayāna path, should be seen in this light. Since the world at large was not heeding his messages, he turned against and began to distance himself and his movement from it: rather than viewing it as the focus of his salvation efforts, he began to consider it as not meriting the salvation he could offer.

By shifting his emphasis from universal salvation through mass spiritual action (an ambition that was clearly not going to succeed in the terms that he had previously framed) to a more narrow salvation only for the chosen few, and by accepting or preaching that mass destruction was virtually certain, Asahara was able to continue with his self-created vision as a messiah while providing himself with an answer for the relative failure of Aum's proselytisation efforts. It was the fault of those who had not heeded his messages and had ignored the teachings of truth – not his failure to spread the word correctly – that world salvation was not going to be possible and that disaster and destruction would come instead. If they had listened and joined his movement, the global disasters and cataclysms that were about to engulf them would not occur. It was *their* fault that they could not be saved. This was a typical Asahara interpretation, an example of how he repeatedly and consistently shifted the focus of blame for Aum's problems and failures away from himself and his followers. It was always someone else's fault, either the mass media who were blamed for conspiring against Aum and hindering its efforts to spread the word, or politicians and civil authorities, accused of conspiring against Aum to subvert its mission, or the general public, who simply disregarded the truth and remained in ignorance, following the false gods of materialism. The emphasis on prophecies of coming cataclysms thus served as a message to the wider world about the fates it would meet – and *deserve* to meet – for disregarding or impeding Aum's sacred mission. It was also a pledge to Aum's faithful who were reassured that they had chosen the path of righteousness.

The espousal of the Vajrayāna path, besides providing a way out of the unachievable commitment of saving all of humanity, thus nurtured Aum's innate elitism and further elevated Asahara's status in the process. It also served, I would suggest, to compensate him for not achieving the status of a religious leader with a large movement and a mission that was proclaimed world-wide, by increasing his power, status and degree of reverence within the movement.

The escalation of dramatic prophecies might, at the same time, have also been a stratagem designed to attract greater attention and a more receptive audience. Asahara was, after all, by no means the only voice in Japan prophesying visions of possible destruction and potential salvation in Japan. In the late 1980s and early 1990s the prophetic utterances of

134

several other religious leaders had assumed an extremely catastrophic air that reflected and shaped the ethos of the time. They had also attracted many new followers. Kiriyama Seiyū's discussions of the prophecies of Nostradamus and his emphasis on the potential for world cataclysm in 1999 had attracted much attention,[23] as had those of Ōkawa Ryūhō, whose movement Kōfuku no Kagaku grew rapidly in the latter part of the 1980s and early 1990s. Ōkawa's prophecies in particular had assumed an extremely dramatic tone, with mass destruction and wars seen as inevitable elements in the future landscape, leading to the collapse of contemporary civilisation and the dawning of a new era around the turn of the century.[24] It is thus likely that in this competitive religious market, Asahara felt compelled to make increasingly dramatic and catastrophic prophecies in order to capture public attention and compete with and mark himself out from his rivals, and particularly from Ōkawa, whom he perceived as a special rival.[25]

The development of Aum's *sangha*, and its system of world renunciation, also played a role in the development of these pessimistic millennial messages, for it had sowed the seeds of tension and confrontation with the world at large. From an early stage the families of those who joined the *sangha* had registered complaints against Aum with the authorities and voiced criticism of a movement that (as they saw it) took their sons and daughters (and often their money) away and caused them to sever all family ties. The parents of Ishii Hisako, for example, reacted with anger to her decision to renounce the world in 1986, and began a vociferous campaign against Aum, striving for years afterwards to get her to quit the movement.[26] Such confrontations, which grew in scope and numbers over the years, were perhaps the earliest indications of the hostility that Asahara's religious ideas and his movement's activities would provoke.

There were tensions also between two dynamics which, while both reflecting Asahara's aspirations for his movement, effectively stood in contradiction to each other. One related to his wish to build a large-scale movement capable of the world-wide expansion that he deemed necessary for salvation, and that would have thus satisfied his ambitions as a saviour and world religious leader. The other was his continual desire to maintain close and tight control over his disciples, to be the sole guru overseeing their spiritual progress. This wish to retain absolute control over his disciples' progress, while of course reflecting Asahara's interests in and desires for power and control, also showed his basic insecurities. By insisting on direct and close control, and one-to-one, individualised relationships, Asahara was precluding the possible emergence of independent and alternative sources of religious authority in the movement and thus avoiding the potential for challenges to his authority.[27]

However, this stress on the importance of direct interaction between guru and disciple, in which the guru guided and kept track of each individual's needs and path of practice while providing personal initiations and transfers of power, sat very uneasily with the movement's emergence as a mass movement. Even though the growth of Aum was relatively modest in numerical terms, its exponential leap from a mere handful of followers to around 1,300 by 1987 placed serious strains on Asahara. It was simply not possible to maintain close guru–disciple relationships with so many people. Such growth therefore necessitated changes in the way the movement operated. The intimate nature of contacts between guru and disciples that could operate easily in a small group gave way to the formation of an increasingly rigid structure and system of rules of the sort necessary in larger organisations. As it did so, the turn to the Vajrayāna effectively, by insisting on extremely rigorous and severe levels of commitment, limited the numbers who could become close disciples. For the larger numbers of followers who had not made the ultimate commitment of renunciation, the path to the guru's power was to lie increasingly in their ingestion of his charismatic powers through the physical substances and traces of his body in initiation rituals. To enter the higher realms and gain closer access to their guru, followers had to first demonstrate increasing commitment and faith through their donations and sacrifices for the movement.

According to Serizawa Shunsuke, while Aum's expansion meant that Asahara could no longer see all his disciples on a one-to-one basis, he nevertheless continued to take on an enormous amount of the work needed to deal with the training of their growing numbers. This severely restricted the time he had previously been able to devote to his own practices and, Serizawa states, at some time in 1988 Asahara ceased performing the intensive austerities to which he had hitherto devoted much of his energy.[28] Asahara's own words corroborate this, for he later stated that he had had to give up his practice of meditation in the latter part of 1988 due to exhaustion.[29] It is possible that this cessation of austerities may also have been connected to his increasingly exalted role of supreme guru. Having attained the ultimate spiritual heights that required absolute devotion from others, he may have felt that it was no longer necessary to perform austerities which were intended to lead to a state and level of attainment that he claimed to have already achieved.

Serizawa considers that Asahara himself underwent something of a transformation at this point, changing from the disciplined ascetic of earlier Aum (a persona that Serizawa interestingly refers to as the 'real Asahara') into the hedonistic figure of later years.[30] His emphasis on the narrow and difficult Vajrayāna path and on the need for absolute obedience certainly suggests an attempt to bolster by other means the status that he had earlier attained because of his ascetic prowess. The emphasis on the guru's transcendence of the ordinary boundaries of morality also provided a legitimating mechanism for his cessation of ascetic practices and his enjoyment of more hedonistic impulses.[31] It is, of course, impossible to tell for certain whether, or to what extent, Asahara's cessation of austerities affected the way he viewed the world. However it is not beyond the bounds of possibility that the progressively dark images that came to colour his teachings in the years that followed were influenced in this way and perhaps also by his own awareness that he had fallen from the path of dedicated asceticism which he had for so long affirmed as an ideal.

BEATING THE DISCIPLES: THE EMERGENCE AND JUSTIFICATION OF VIOLENCE IN AUM

In this same period, in late summer 1988, another important development occurred: Asahara started using violence by beating disciples who displeased him, who challenged his authority or appeared, in his view, to be slacking in their ascetic practices. He also began to legitimate such actions and explain why it was necessary to use violence in such circumstances. He was especially severe on those close to him, whom he regarded as his chosen disciples. While it is by no means clear when this coercive violence first occurred in Aum, the first case I have come across was in September 1988, and it concerned Asahara's wife Tomoko.

She had previously displayed little interest in her husband's religion, but in September 1988 she was ordered by her husband to take part in ascetic practices which would enable her to attain liberation, and to become a committed member of the movement. She initially refused, at which point force was used to make her comply. Tomoko later stated in interviews that because of her refusal she was beaten 50 times with a cane until she yielded, and was made to spend time in isolation, meditating. Prior to 1995 Tomoko had mentioned this coercion in a rather positive context, telling interviewers that she had become a devout member, performing numerous austerities and attaining some spiritual peace and satisfaction as a result, and she implied that, although the experience was painful at the time, it had pushed her into doing something that was good for her. She had thus accepted the 'logic' of Asahara's Vajrayāna teachings, in which actions that appeared on the surface to be bad, from other perspectives could have positive results.[32] Subsequently, after being arrested in the wake of the police raids and charged in connection with the killing of Ochida Kōtarō, a dissident follower, in 1994 – an act at which she was present – Tomoko has pleaded in mitigation that she was forced into participating in Aum activities by her husband and has put a much more negative spin on this coercion.[33]

It is perhaps significant that Asahara turned to violence at this time. While he possessed an aggressive streak that had in earlier times been expressed in violent outbursts, there appear to have been no incidents of violent behaviour from the time when he had been arrested soon after leaving school until September 1988. Yet, at about the same time that he ceased his own ascetic practice and began to emphasise the importance of absolute obedience to the guru, this side of his nature appears to have come to the fore. Tomoko's initial refusal was a direct challenge to his authority, and this may well have conditioned his violent response. It is also possible that his aggressive tendencies had previously been held in check by what Serizawa has described as his masochistic absorption in ascetic practice,[34] and that once this had ceased, these impulses began to surface again and be directed outwards. The growing belief that salvation was no longer universally achievable, and was available only to the advanced practitioners of the Vajrayāna way, also provided an impulse towards such coercion. Since ascetic practice was a vital key to liberation, those who would not do it voluntarily had to be forced to do so for their own good. Tomoko, in other words, was beaten so that she could be saved, and because her continuing refusal to practice was an overt challenge to the authority of her husband.

She was not, however, the only person to be coerced or beaten, for references to beatings and to the need to use physical force on his disciples began to appear in Asahara's sermons. He was quite open about this, as Egawa Shōko noted: in interviews in Aum magazines he spoke of how he often bullied or beat disciples in order to drive away their bad karma.[35] This painful eradication of bad karma fitted with his belief that suffering and hardship were necessary elements in the struggle for liberation. In various Vajrayāna sermons he pointed to the same rationale behind the beatings including an account of how, through such means, he had induced his teenage daughter to learn to sit in the Lotus position and meditate properly.[36]

Such brutality and harshness were not, he argued, sadistic but rather manifestations of his compassion in striving by any means possible to save his disciples from falling into the hells. Indeed, the use of such seeming brutality and violence was a sign of the spiritual transcendence of the guru who had gone beyond moral constraints and beyond the bounds of good and evil, a line of argument that was developed in several sermons. In August 1989, for example, he spoke of how, if one person beat another, this would normally cause bad karma to accrue to the perpetrator of violence. However, if the beating were done by a higher spiritual being in order to force the other person to improve that person's spiritual endeavours, and thus to save him or her from falling into the hells after death, then it would be justified. Indeed, Asahara claimed, this was the *only* way a guru could act in such circumstances.[37] This argument was later extended (in conjunction with the concept of *poa*) to justify not just beatings but murder, as discussed below.

To Asahara this was how a guru should act. Moreover, it is clear that he had imbibed this idea from his understandings and interpretations of esoteric Tibetan Buddhism, with its emphasis on obedience to the guru and its stories of how great Tibetan gurus such as Marpa and Milarepa demanded absolute obedience from their disciples and pushed them to the limits in order to assist them in their path to enlightenment. Asahara in particular seemed transfixed by the story of how Marpa had seemingly behaved in a cruel and brutal way towards Milarepa when the latter sought his teaching. While Marpa had set Milarepa various harsh tasks that caused him immense suffering, they had been designed to fortify his spirit, to instil the appropriate sense of discipline and obedience in him, and had helped Milarepa attain enlightenment.[38]

Although it was from the world of Tibetan Buddhism that Asahara drew his inspiration and legitimations of violence, there were readily available sources within the Japanese religious and cultural arenas that also served as a legitimating cultural background to his use of violence. For example, the use of ritualised beating, through the use of the *kyōsaku* or 'waking stick', is legitimated and practised widely in Japanese Zen Buddhism as a means of assisting the disciple to achieve awakening and to keep him/her alert during meditation. This use of ritualised violence is frequently portrayed and indeed glamorised in the mass media and in the publications of Zen sects in Japan as a symbol of the strictness and austerity of the Zen tradition.[39] In Japanese folk and shamanic healing practices, too, the use of physical force to purify, exorcise or drive spiritual pollutions and spirits from the body is by no means unknown. Indeed, in July 1995, only a few months after the subway attack, a case came to light (although it passed with surprisingly little comment) in Fukushima in northern Japan, in which six bodies were found at the home of a shamanic healer. All had apparently succumbed as a result of beatings administered during exorcisms and purification rites designed, according to the shamaness concerned, to drive evil spirits out of their bodies.[40]

The use of violence as a means of strengthening character and spiritual resolve can be found in other areas of Japanese life and cultural history as well. The pre-war Japanese military tradition, for example, demanded absolute obedience of its men, and, as a former soldier speaking in a recent television documentary aired on British television put it, used frequent beatings and violence as a means of forging the strength of its soldiers.[41] Even if the military tradition may have been publicly discredited in the post-war era, elements of its systematised brutality, a residue also of the samurai tradition and warrior culture of Japan, linger on in the culture of martial arts and sports clubs, in which similarly ritualised uses of coercion and violence surface as a means of disciplining and training members. Such patterns of behaviour have been utilised also by protest and extremist political movements in Japan. In the case of the Rengō Sekigun (Japanese Red Army), the extremist left-wing militant faction that engaged in guerrilla war against society in the late 1960s and early 1970s and ultimately descended into an orgy of internal violence and killings in 1972, beatings were administered and legitimated as a means of enhancing the movement's revolutionary purity and forcing members to face their own weaknesses.[42]

The point is that, shocking as Asahara's espousal and legitimation of violence against his close disciples might appear, and surprising as their acquiescence and participation in this process (Asahara's orders wrere readily carried out and there appears to have been little resistance when members were ordered to give or take beatings) might seem to be, there was a shared cultural background which legitimated and facilitated the use and *acceptance* of such systematised violence. This is a point that has been made by Patricia G. Steinhoff in her study of the Rengō Sekigun which, as she notes, used violent rhetoric and martial imagery in its political struggle and, as such, failed to give its followers any guidance on when to avoid the use of violence.[43] The same was true of Aum, whose rhetoric and imagery was framed around the concepts of struggle and of holy wars conducted by sacred warriors. Those who ascended to Aum's upper ranks had accepted and embraced these concepts and the violent imagery within which they were expressed, and had thereby an implicit and essential empathy towards the use of violence in the name of their faith. Having, as adepts of the Vajrayāna, accepted the absolute authority of their guru and of a path that they knew was harsh and severe, they were prepared for the acceptance of and acquiescence in the spread of violence that began to engulf the movement.

DOOMSDAY, PROPHECY AND THE EXPECTATION OF VIOLENCE

In February 1989 Asahara published a book entitled *Metsubō no hi* (subtitled with the English word 'Doomsday'), which had been compiled in autumn 1988. It was an important book in Aum's development for in it the underlying dark images of potential destruction that had begun to surface in Asahara's prophecies had their clearest public expression so far. In *Metsubō no hi* Asahara abandoned any hope that war (which at this point, prior to the collapse of communism, he saw as likely to be a nuclear one involving the USA and the USSR) and world destruction could be avoided and he foresaw a general unleashing of apocalyptic forces such as pestilence, earthquakes and volcanic eruptions. In this doomsday scenario all he and his followers could do was to concentrate their energies on saving themselves: everyone else was doomed.

In *Metsubō no hi* Asahara added to Aum's eclecticism by using Christian themes and images, in particular those with apocalyptic dimensions. The initial impulse for this absorption of Christian images came, Asahara stated, in autumn 1988 when he collapsed in a state of exhaustion after having done too many *shaktipat* initiations. As a consequence he was unable to teach his disciples properly or do any meditation. At this time Shiva told him to rest, and while he was doing so, a follower interested in the study of prophecy introduced Asahara to the Bible and especially to its Book of Revelations of St John.[44]

The prophecies of Revelations and its scenario of a final war gelled with and reinforced many of Asahara's own ideas. It also provided him with the word that would henceforth be used in Aum's apocalyptic pronouncements to describe this war: Armageddon. In sum, it reinforced his sense of mission as a messiah. In Revelations attention is drawn to a text (a book or scroll) bound by seven seals which, if opened, would set forth the train of events prophesied in the text, leading to the 'climax of history and the end of the world'.[45] The person who can bring about God's will by breaking open the seven seals is described in Revelations as the 'Lamb', and while this would appear to be a reference to Jesus (and hence to the Christian concept of a second coming), there have been various prophets through the ages who have claimed this role for themselves. Perhaps the best known in modern times has been David Koresh, the leader of the Branch Davidians, who met his death along with 73 of his followers in the fire that engulfed his movement's com-

141

pound in Waco, Texas, on 19 April 1993. Koresh had identified himself with the messiah of the second coming, and he was engaged in this process of opening, or interpreting, the seven seals when that siege ended in tragedy.[46]

Almost five years before David Koresh came to world attention, Asahara Shōkō had, on encountering the Book of Revelations, similarly identified himself with the 'Lamb' who was to open the seven seals. Indeed, in a superb example of Aum's eclecticism, he stated that the message informing him that he was the person to open and explain these seals, thereby setting in motion Aum's salvation plan, had come from Shiva.[47] These biblical images of revelation and prophecy further affirmed Asahara's belief in a coming end-of-history scenario, and added new dimensions to his already grandiose sense of mission: he was now also the Lamb, the messiah prophesied in Revelations. His interest in Christianity and its messianic images also later led Asahara to identify himself with Jesus, particularly with the image of Jesus on the Cross, and to thereby incorporate into his movement Christian images of sacrifice, salvation and persecution.

In Revelations Asahara encountered the image of the devil, Satan, the graphic embodiment and personification of evil. It was an image that affirmed Asahara's view of the world as polarised between the forces of good and evil, and he was to argue that modern society was governed by the devil, and to equate the devil with materialism.[48] In *Metsubō no hi* he expressed the fear that Satan was a corrupting force capable of infiltrating the minds of his practitioners and undermining his followers. It was here that some of the earliest indications of Asahara's suspicious and paranoid mentality (from which grew the conspiracy theories that dominated his later sermons) can be seen. Even high-level practitioners could be at the mercy of Satan and he worried about the extent of their resolve for, he announced, Aum was beset by spies, including some with allegiances to rival religious groups, who had infiltrated the movement. Because of such spying he had had to expel some followers from the movement.[49]

Thus in autumn 1988 Asahara harboured various doubts about those around him: they were vulnerable to the machinations of Satan or they were perhaps spies seeking to undermine his movement. These early indications of suspicion and paranoia illustrate again the fragile aspects of his nature. Because of his deep insecurities he needed to demand absolute obedience from his followers, yet he still harboured doubts about the real extent of their devotion and feared that they would lose their faith or be lured away by the evils of materialism, and he suspected them of spying on and secretly working against him. They therefore had to demonstrate their faith constantly and to reassure him of their devotion.

CRIMINAL TRANSGRESSIONS: THE DEATHS OF MAJIMA TERAYUKI AND TAGUCHI SHŪJI

There were also more tangible reasons why Asahara would have had grave fears about spies and the possibility of Aum's secrets leaking out to the world at large at this time for, in late September 1988, an Aum devotee named Majima Terayuki, had died unexpectedly and accidentally at Aum's Mount Fuji centre.[50] He had been undergoing an extended ascetic retreat when he started shouting loudly and displaying signs of mental disturbance, as a result of which Asahara ordered Murai Hideo and others present to douse him repeatedly with cold water in order to calm him down. When they did, however, Majima suddenly dropped dead, apparently of shock.[51]

The incident caused consternation among Aum's senior hierarchy and had major repercussions on their thinking. The death of a follower in this way, if it became publicly known, would have had grave consequences for the movement at a time when it was beginning to face criticism from the families of young *shukkesha*. Aum had widely proclaimed how its members performed severe austerities and how its guru could determine which particular practices its members should undertake in order to attain liberation, and these issues were major reasons why ardent and idealistic young seekers came to Aum. If news got out of this death, it could have called Asahara's judgement into question and would have severely undermined his reputation as an omniscient guru able to foresee the future of each of his disciples. It would have suggested that, instead, Asahara was inexperienced as a teacher and unaware of the repercussions or dangers of the practices he instigated. A further factor in this dilemma was that Aum was in the process of applying for legal recognition as a registered religious organisation – a step that would have great advantages for the movement – and news of such an event would have been fatal to that aspiration.

In short, Majima's death, if it became publicly known, had the potential to ruin Aum and Asahara, and to threaten his mission. As a result Asahara and a number senior members of the *kanbu*, including Hayakawa Kiyohide, Murai Hideo, Asahara's wife Tomoko and Okazaki Kazuaki, took the decision that the death had to be covered up.[52] Majima became the first Aum member to be considered disposable, and his body was secretly burnt and the ashes disposed of in a nearby lake. Since the illegal disposal of a corpse was a criminal offence, the cover-up itself represented a serious breach of the law, to say nothing of normal standards of behaviour and morality. The senior figures who took this decision to flout the law and cover up the death were in effect articulating – although perhaps not in a way they would have wished – the views expressed in Asahara's Vajrayāna sermons. As practitioners of the Vajrayāna way they were not bound by conventional laws or morality, but could act in seemingly immoral ways in order to further or defend their movement's mission. The action joined together those who took and carried out this decision in a bond of criminality. It also established a pattern of disregarding the law of the land that Aum was to follow on future occasions when it faced challenges or encountered what it perceived as threats to its mission.

It is little wonder that the apparently paranoid worries about spying that appeared in *Metsubō no hi* surfaced at this time, or that Asahara was worried about possible weaknesses among his followers. With the death and disposal of Majima, Aum had very grave secrets to hide and much to fear from close scrutiny. It is unlikely, too, that the temporal correlation between Asahara's need to rest, the shift towards a more overtly apocalyptic and prophetic orientation, the incorporation of messianic and sacrificial imagery, and the Majima incident, is coincidental. What I mean to suggest by this is that the shock of Majima's death and the implicit challenge that it posed to Asahara's claims as a supreme guru were factors in Asahara's illness in autumn 1988 and in his increasingly dramatic apocalyptic perspective. Having, as it were, led a follower not to liberation but death through the practices he ordered, Aum had to produce new interpretations of doctrine and of the future in order to incorporate this new event into Aum's belief structure. Once Asahara had failed to save Majima, a message of universal salvation became impossible to sustain. Henceforth it became necessary to emphasise that Aum could not save everyone and to instead find reasons why some people could not be saved or were not worthy of being saved.

In fact Majima's death precipitated an even greater breach of moral and criminal law, for the very thing that Asahara most feared, in his concerns about spies and the weakness of his disciples, transpired. In February 1989 Taguchi Shūji, a disciple who was present at Majima's death and knew of the cover-up, decided to leave the movement. His faith in the guru had been shattered because of the incident and there were grave fears that he might disclose details of it if he left. Asahara ordered that he be detained, interrogated and forced to do austerities that would purify him of such thoughts. However, since Taguchi remained adamant that he would quit and make the incident known, Asahara ordered that he be killed, telling his aides that there was no choice but to 'poa' him because of the dangers he posed to the movement.[53] The killing was carried out by Hayakawa Kiyohide, Niimi Tomomitsu and Okazaki Kazuaki, and the body was incinerated.

The killing of Taguchi created a stronger bond – and a darker secret – within Aum's upper echelons, making it more fearful of investigation. Basically he had been killed to cover up an earlier death and to protect the guru's reputation. However, a clear doctrinal explanation was needed for this incident. Whereas Majima's death had been accidental, Taguchi's was cold-blooded murder, and his killers needed to find a way to legitimate such an act. The concept of poa with its meanings of transforming the spirit after death fitted this purpose and, in the period after Taguchi's death, Asahara turned to further discussions of this concept, developing it so that it no longer merely referred to interceding after death to assist the spirit of the dead, but came to take on the meaning of killing for salvation.

In a Vajrayāna sermon not long after Taguchi's murder on 7 April 1989, Asahara raised the question of what should be done if someone were engaging in bad deeds and piling up negative karma that would cause them to fall into the hells after death. In such cases it might be necessary to 'transform' them spiritually so as to prevent further accumulation of bad karma. This act of transformation, which would enable them to attain a good rebirth, was the true Vajrayāna way, and it was for such purposes, he said, that the Vajrayāna path emphasised the concept of poa.[54] The disciples who had killed Taguchi could be in no doubt about his meaning: Taguchi, by threatening Aum's mission, was about to bring on himself an enormous amount of bad karma. Taguchi had thus been killed both to protect the movement's mission, which was more important than the life of a single follower, and to save him from falling into the hells, which would have been the inevitable karmic result of his going public on Majima's death and thereby damaging Aum's mission. His spirit had been transformed through the murder, and this, Asahara appeared to be saying, was the true Vajrayāna way. Just as Tomoko had been beaten to save her in this life, so Taguchi had been killed in order to save him in the next.

Asahara spoke again about such issues in subsequent Vajrayāna sermons during 1989. It was on 20 August 1989 that he delivered a strong affirmation of the right of the guru to beat disciples in order to encourage their practice and save them from falling into the hells. On

24 September 1989 he turned again to the subject of *poa*, using the hypothetical example of someone who, having led a decent life and accumulated good karma, became slack and started accruing bad karma that would inevitably lead him/her to the hells. If, however, the person died or were killed before s/he could accumulate such bad karma, s/he would attain a good rebirth. Hence a spiritually advanced person who, seeing the direction the person was headed in, interceded to kill the person before they could accumulate bad karma, would thus be performing an act of salvation and a meritorious act of transformation. It would be, as Asahara described it, a 'splendid *poa*' (*rippana powa*), that saved people from contemporary evils, gave them new hope and led them to salvation.[55]

Murder, in other words, was legitimate if it were carried out by spiritually advanced practitioners such as himself or Aum's 'true victors', who had gone beyond the confines of normal morality and were able to see into the future of others. They could determine whether someone 'needed' to be killed in order to attain salvation. Aum's elite had crossed the final border in terms of illegality. They had committed and sanctioned murder, and in so doing had adapted their doctrines accordingly to make this a meritorious and justifiable action. The killing, in retrospect, proved their spiritual status as people who had the right to kill if the situation demanded it. It also strengthened the bonds between them, while the dynamic impelling them towards further violence became more powerful as any reservations they might have had about killing were swept aside.

REJECTION AND RECOGNITION: THE CAMPAIGN FOR LEGAL STATUS

In April 1989, two months after Taguchi Shûji's murder, Aum presented the case it had been preparing for legal recognition under the Religious Corporations Law (*shūkyō hōjinhō*) to the Tokyo prefectural government. Registration under this Act gives religious organisations numerous advantages, from tax breaks to legal protection from state interference. This law, passed in 1952, was designed to help safeguard the religious freedoms which had been abused in pre-war Japan, and one of its basic premises was, as Mark R. Mullins has put it, that 'registered religious organisations contribute to the public good (*kōeki*) and for this reason should be permitted to engage in economic activities to support their religious work and public welfare activities (*kōeki jigyō*)'.[56]

To qualify for registration at that time a religious organisation had to have been in existence for three years, to have its own facilities, and to be able to demonstrate that it behaved in a tolerant and law-abiding way, allowing people freely to join or leave as they wished. It is a process that most religious organisations undergo when they have been in existence for more than three years, and Aum (which had initially been established as a formal religious movement in 1986 with the founding of the Aum Shinsen no Kai) did likewise. In its case, however, the application was turned down because of objections from concerned parents who complained that their offspring had severed all ties with them, joined Aum and given it all their money, and that all attempts to make contacts with them had been blocked by Aum.

Asahara reacted angrily, appealing against the decision, filing lawsuits, complaining of 'religious persecution' and holding protest demonstrations in front of the prefectural government offices. In a sermon to his followers shortly after the rebuff, he spoke of the conflict that had arisen between Aum and the civil authorities. This was an attack on the truth which left Aum's followers with three choices: to fight for Aum, to turn away from the struggle and yield to the authorities, or to leave Aum entirely and return to the mundane world. His disciples called in unison that they would fight for Aum, and Asahara responded with the exhortation that, if someone degraded 'the truth', one had to strike back and fight for that truth.[57] Through such sermons and because of the militant campaign that was launched to challenge the government's decision, Aum's concept of a struggle between the forces of truth and evil moved from the symbolic and cosmic to the practical level of actual confrontation as the movement challenged and took on the public authorities that had denied it recognition under the Religious Corporations Law.

In August 1989 its appeal was successful and Aum became officially registered as a legally constituted religious body, a status that was subsequently revoked in October 1995 because of the movement's misdeeds. The dispute had, however, shown Asahara the value of assuming a militant posture and of fighting and making loud and vehement protests. Its campaign had won Aum much publicity and had caused the authorities to back down. It also, however, further convinced Asahara that hostile forces were ranged against his movement and that somehow Aum needed to develop a firmer base for itself – including a political presence – in order to protect itself and to wage its campaign for the truth more effectively.

AN EXERCISE IN COMPASSION: THE MURDER OF THE SAKAMOTO FAMILY

Even though Aum had just won official status under the Religious Corporations Law, fears and doubts continued to exist within the movement's upper echelons. The deaths of Majima and Taguchi remained dangerous secrets that threatened to undermine the existence of the movement and the freedom of its leaders at any moment. Asahara was clearly troubled by these events and appeared, in autumn 1989, to be extremely pessimistic about the future. He complained that no one listened to his messages of truth, preferring instead to wallow in hedonism and to choose (as he saw it) the path to hell, and he fretted about the possible collapse of his movement. A number of quite senior *shukkesha*, he announced, had recently 'fallen' from grace and left the movement: they would, for these karmic sins, inevitably fall into the lowest hells as result of their defections. The defections disturbed him because they suggested that Aum's support was ebbing away and he feared that Aum itself would collapse unless he took steps to increase support and raise its profile.[58] It was for such reasons, he informed disciples, that he had taken the decision to enter the political arena and contest the parliamentary elections of February 1990.

Before the election, however, other serious problems arose. In October 1989 the *Sunday Mainichi*, a weekly magazine published by the Mainichi newspaper group, began a series of seven articles that were highly critical of Aum. Aum was accused, amongst other things, of exploiting its followers through the use of expensive and strange initiation rituals, and of breaking up families by refusing to allow those with relatives or offspring inside Aum to have any communication with them, while Asahara was portrayed as an exploitative and manipulative leader with an overbearing ego. While the tone of the articles was sensationalist, they were not out of the ordinary in Japan, where the mass media have made a habit of dirt-digging and running 'scandal' stories about religious movements in general and the new, and very new, religions in particular. However, the contents of the articles caused grave offence to Aum and, coming not long after the initial rejection of its application for legal religious recognition and the defections of a number of close followers, added fuel to Asahara's fear that hostile forces were working against Aum. A former member I interviewed in 1997 told me that Asahara had been extremely angry at this time because of the magazine articles.[59] Asahara went on the attack again, filing lawsuits against the magazine and making verbal assaults on its editor, Maki Tarō.

The articles produced a widespread response from the public. The magazine received well over 200 communications from people with complaints against Aum, including former members who said they had paid for costly initiations that failed to give them any spiritual benefits. These various complainants were put in touch with one another by the magazine, and a protest group called the *Oumu Shinrikyō higaisha no kai* [Aum Shinrikyō Victims' Society] was established. A lawyer based in Yokohama, Sakamoto Tsutsumi, who was experienced in civil rights issues, was retained as its legal representative.[60]

Sakamoto began to examine Aum, and this raised serious problems for Asahara and his aides. He publicly criticised Aum for its activities, and found that the claims Aum had made about Asahara's DNA were false: it had not been tested at Kyoto University nor found to be unique. To Sakamoto this was a case of fraud that indicated serious problems with the way Aum was operating, and he arranged a meeting with Aum's legal representatives to discuss the matter. The meeting, which took place on 31 October 1989, was rancorous. The chief lawyer representing Aum, Aoyama Yoshinobu, was a highly placed devotee in the movement, and he angrily rejected Sakamoto's arguments and questions, complaining instead that Sakamoto's campaign against Aum had infringed its rights and represented an assault on religious freedom.

While Sakamoto realised that Aum's leaders were uncompromising and unlikely to discuss matters reasonably, the meeting also brought it home to Aum's leaders that Sakamoto was a determined opponent who was committed to pursuing the case. Hence he posed a serious threat to them. This was not simply because of the fear that he might take his investigations further and uncover even more damaging material against the movement, but because Sakamoto was about to air his grievances and charges against Aum in public. He spoke out against Aum in a television programme being made by the Tokyo Broadcasting System (TBS) in autumn 1989. Before airing the programme, however, TBS representatives, fearful that the movement might take offence and start a lawsuit against them, showed it to senior figures in Aum. They objected strenuously, as a result of which the programme was never aired.[61] The movement, however, had been made aware that Sakamoto was prepared to speak publicly against the movement, and this clearly made him a greater threat than ever.

Asahara had already once ordered a murder to protect his mission, and it was perhaps easier to do so a second time. Whatever qualms or moral restraints he might have had previously on this score had been swept away with the killing of Taguchi and by the construction of doctrines that legitimated this act. In a statement in late 1995 Asahara admitted that Sakamoto had caused immense problems for Aum at a delicate time, shortly after the campaign for religious recognition and prior to its planned election campaign. The attacks by the *Sunday Mainichi* magazine had hurt the movement and further criticisms, often prompted by Sakamoto, were being made in the mass media about Aum. The lawyer was thus an obstacle to Aum's plans and a threat to its mission and so, as a result, Asahara stated, there was 'no choice but to *poa* him' (*poa suru shika nai*).[62]

He gave this order to Murai Hideo, Hayakawa Kiyohide and other senior disciples who readily accepted the reasons why Sakamoto had to be killed and set about carrying it out. As Hayakawa told a court in January 1998, Aum was suffering as a result of Sakamoto's activities and the killing was thus carried out to silence this threat and protect Aum's mission: it was a 'salvation activity' (*kyûsai katsudō*).[63] In all six members of Aum went to Sakamoto's apartment in early November 1989 to commit the act. Among them was Nakagawa Tomomasa, a young doctor who had quit his ordinary job soon after graduation because of his interest in Aum and who had renounced the world in September 1989, just two months before the murder. He was chosen for the task because, as a doctor, he could administer the injection with which Sakamoto was to be killed. In a statement after his arrest, Nakagawa gave a chilling yet vivid insight into the mind-set of Aum's elite: rather than feeling horror and repulsion at being asked to commit murder, he experienced a sense of 'elation and pride'.[64] Being asked to kill for his guru was a sign that he had entered the inner elite of Aum and that his devotion and zeal had been recognised. It was evidence, too, of his spiritual attainment as a practitioner who had transcended the boundaries of conventional morality and achieved the necessary powers of detachment to kill yet be karmically unmoved by such acts.[65]

Since Sakamoto's wife and 14-month-old son were also present when the murderers arrived, they too were killed along with the lawyer. The baby had clearly done nothing to hinder Aum's mission and had not yet had the chance of accumulating bad karma, and, as such, could hardly be seen as someone, in Aum's doctrinal formulations, meriting 'transformation'. His murder was clearly simply a pragmatic action.[66] However, his death, too, needed an explanation that could fit it into Aum's logic of murder and salvation, and transform it from what it looked like on the surface – a vicious and barbaric act – into what Aum needed it to be, namely a compassionate act of salvation. Asahara accomplished this by stating that killing the baby boy was a means of allowing him to attain salvation. If he had remained in the world brought up by his parents he would surely have acquired so much bad karma that he would have fallen to hell. If he had been spared when his parents were killed, he would have had a pitiable existence, growing up alone in the world as he himself had. He was referring, of course, to his own sense of loneliness and isolation when he was sent away to school and – so he felt – virtually abandoned by his parents when he was six.[67] Elsewhere he referred to the 'good karmic deed' of killing the mother and baby because it saved them from accruing the bad karma of being associated with a person (Sakamoto) who was engaged in attacking the truth.[68]

After the killings the bodies were taken far from Tokyo into central Japan, where they were buried separately in the mountains in three different prefectures – a deed that was designed to make any investigations (which would thus involve several different prefectural police forces) more complex, should the bodies ever be found. It was also an act that, when it came to light in September 1995, after confessions from some of those involved had finally enabled the police to locate the remains, caused immense public revulsion. Comments made to me by friends in Japan summed up the extent of public sentiment in this incident. It was especially abhorrent in a culture where it is customary to have family graves and family altars so that spirits of family members can be together in death. The outrage was not just that they had killed a baby, but they had even deprived the family of being together and had left the poor Sakamoto child alone in death.[69]

The brutal Sakamoto killings represented a further escalation of Aum's violence. They were its first acts of violence outside the movement, but were at the same time part of the cycle of violence and criminality precipitated by the unforeseen death of Majima. That, in turn, had resulted from the growth of coercion inside Aum that began with the guru's 'right' to beat his disciples and the advocacy of the Vajrayāna path. The killing of Taguchi and Sakamoto had been carried out because of the threat they posed to the movement. In committing these crimes, Aum transformed its vision of a sacred struggle against the forces of evil into a fight against *anyone* who threatened Aum's continued well-being and who therefore was deemed to be an enemy. These crimes had been accompanied by the pragmatic development of doctrines that placed them within a spiritual framework showing that they were necessary.

The Sakamoto murders also set a new benchmark of faith in the guru: absolute faith meant being ready to kill for him if so ordered. As Nakagawa Tomomasa showed in his enthusiastic participation in the crime, it was a benchmark of faith that the elite, and those who aspired to be part of it, readily embraced. Since absolute obedience to and faith in the guru was a prerequisite for liberation, according to Aum's Vajrayāna path, it thus followed that anyone who wished to attain spiritual liberation had to be prepared to kill for it. Actions that in conventional terms would have been seen as sins became transformed through the processes of doctrinal 'logic' into a form of empowerment in which the murdered were guilty and in need of salvation, and the murderers were noble, compassionate and kind. After the killings of the Sakamoto family there were no restraints on what they might do – or what they were entitled to do in order to defend their movement.

SUSPICION AND OPPROBRIUM: REACTIONS TO THE DISAPPEARANCE OF THE SAKAMOTOS

The disappearance of the Sakamoto family caused concern among Sakamoto's relatives and colleagues, and led to a police investigation. Because of Sakamoto's ongoing disputes with Aum, the movement came under immediate suspicion, especially since an Aum badge along with traces of blood had been found at the family apartment. It later transpired that the badge had been dropped by Nakagawa Tomomasa during the struggle to kill the family. However Asahara denied that his movement had any connection with the incident, suggesting that someone had tried to set Aum up by abducting the family and leaving an Aum badge at the scene. There appears to have been relatively little investigation of the movement by the police, who hardly pursued any possible Aum links in the matter. The police have rightly attracted much criticism in Japan as a result of their failure to examine Aum properly, whether in the Sakamoto case or in others that transpired later. It could, indeed, be argued that Aum was able to progress as far as it did in its activities because of police inaction.[70]

For years afterwards relatives of the Sakamotos and colleagues of his in the worlds of the law and journalism pressed for a fuller investigation of Aum and tried to link the movement with the disappearance of the family. In fact, by eliminating a troublesome enemy, Aum had provoked greater opposition than ever. Friends and colleagues of Sakamoto, such as the journalist Egawa Shōko and the lawyer Takimoto Tarō, took up the struggle against Aum. Egawa began a thorough journalistic investigation of the movement, writing articles and a book in which she focused on what she (rightly, as it turned out) considered to be the dangers and the socially disruptive aspects of Aum and of Asahara's ambitions as a religious leader, while Takimoto came to represent the Aum Victims' Society and became heavily involved in campaigns to persuade members of Aum to leave the movement.[71]

Despite the police inactivity there was widespread suspicion of Aum's guilt which was transmitted through items in the mass media.[72] By killing Sakamoto, Aum gained new enemies, while its public reputation became increasingly unsavoury. All of this served to increase paranoia and the bunker mentality that had developed among the movement's leaders as a result of their increasing separation from the mundane world and their complicity in a shared and secret bond of murder. The Sakamoto murders, rather than simply ridding Aum of an enemy and safe-guarding its mission, had instead increased the external threats it faced, and had placed its mission in greater jeopardy than before.

THE PARTY OF SUPREME TRUTH AND THE ELECTION OF FEBRUARY 1990

In July 1989 at a meeting of Aum's senior officials, Asahara put forward a plan to establish a political party, the Shinritō or Party of Supreme Truth, to contest the Lower House elections of the Japanese parliament that were forthcoming in February 1990. The idea was adopted, although not without some opposition. The decision caused great unease among the rank and file of the movement, who had joined Aum because of its radical opposition to the practices and mores of conventional, material-istic society. A former follower whom I interviewed stated that he had felt very uneasy at the decision and that a strong anti-election faction developed inside Aum.[73]

Asahara explained his decision to his followers in September 1989, telling them that it had been necessary to enter politics because of the pressures of time. A final war was imminent and in this end-time scenario speed was essential: religion alone could not enact Aum's plans of salvation quickly enough. Hence it needed to develop a political base and authority as well through which it could advance its Shambhala project.[74] The election campaign was also a means of reaching out to more people and of alerting the Japanese public to the coming disasters that Asahara predicted.

The establishment of a political party was nothing new in the world of the Japanese new religions. The largest of all the new religions, Sōka Gakkai, had established a political party, the Kōmeitō, in 1964 to advance its religious-political agenda, and while the two now are officially separate, it is a matter of common assumption in Japan that the agenda of the political party mirrors closely that of its religious creator and mentor. Asahara was no doubt mindful of Sōka Gakkai's success in this respect, for the Kōmeitō had become one of the largest political parties and a major player in the Japanese political arena.

Aum's establishment of a political party and its engagement in a political campaign in which it put up 25 candidates (including Asahara and many of the senior members of its hierarchy) for parliamentary seats in the Tokyo region, however, were of a different order from that of Sōka Gakkai and Kōmeitō. For a start, Aum was numerically extremely small, and hence could not count on the mass block vote of members that enabled Kōmeitō to secure a political footing. More pertinently, it was the manner of Aum's campaigning that set it apart. Unlike Kōmeitō which, while having a religious underpinning to its platform, assumed a conventional political face, the Shinritō made no attempt to look like a standard Japanese political party. Its candidates all ran for office under their holy names and dressed in white, while they and their supporters donned either elephant masks representing the Hindu deity Ganesh (in Hindu lore the offspring of Shiva) or masks of Asahara, and they paraded the streets chanting songs in praise of their guru and putting on song and dance performances relating their religious messages and warning of the coming apocalypse.

It was a performance that bemused the general public and contributed further to the movement's already problematic image. The campaign itself showed the vast gulf that had opened up between Aum on the one hand and the Japanese public on the other, while it and the decision to enter politics illustrated the extent to which Asahara and his cohorts had lost their sense of reality. At a time when the movement had become beleaguered because of parental complaints and disputes over its application under the Religious Corporations Law and when it had had been unable to develop a mass following, it would have seemed improbable, to a dispassionate analyst, that Aum could have entered an election and gained any success. After the problems of autumn 1989, when Aum's image had been severely tarnished by the *Sunday Mainichi* articles and Sakamoto affair, the possibility of success was even more remote. It was made even more so by the strangeness of the campaign itself, which appears to have been, at the very least, an exercise in massive self-delusion.

Despite Asahara's confident predictions of victory, the election was a disaster for Aum. The voters, when selecting the candidates they wished to represent their political interests, clearly felt the wish for something more than apocalypticism, elephant masks, songs repeating Asahara's name, and young candidates who, while running under strange and unpronounceable Buddhist holy names, were suspected of involvement in the disappearance of the Sakamoto family and who, by all accounts, drank the blood of their guru. Every Aum candidate lost heavily, and none more so than Asahara, who received only 1,783 votes out of the half million cast in his constituency. The blow to Asahara was even greater because he was not even the most popular Shinritō candidate:

Jōyu Fumihiro, standing in the same constituency, got more votes than he did.[75]

Asahara appears to have been shocked when the election results came through, merely observing that it had been a complete defeat for Aum.[76] Indeed, it appears that he even contemplated, if only briefly, standing down from the movement, and that he circulated a taped message to the *shukkesha* saying as much.[77] Quite why he was surprised is hard to fathom, save that he had become so enveloped in his aura as a sacred master surrounded by devoted and obsequious acolytes and so totally captivated by his belief in his ability to see the future, that he had simply become incapable of recognising reality and had failed to see how ludicrous his campaign had been.

The Shinritō's brief life (it went out of existence immediately after the election) was an unmitigated disaster for Aum. The campaign was extremely costly, posing a serious threat to its financial stability in the short term.[78] Moreover, one follower (Okazaki Kazuaki, one of the murderers of the Sakamotos) decamped with a large amount of money from Aum's election funds.[79] He apparently negotiated a deal with Aum to keep a proportion of this in return for his silence over the Sakamoto affair. Furthermore, doubts were cast about Aum's tactics, and accusations were made that it had illegally changed the residential registrations of a large number of Aum members so that they could vote in Asahara's constituency.

The political campaign had a severe impact on Aum's membership and its public image. According to a number of reports, Aum suffered defections as a result of the campaign and the new direction that Aum appeared to be taking.[80] Many who remained had been very unhappy at the ways in which Aum campaigned and the affair thus caused some internal dissent and unease in the movement. One ex-member, for example, informed me that the election posters that Aum used and the holy names under which the candidates ran were 'stupid' (*baka*) and embarrassing, while the campaign made him fear that Aum had lost its direction and was heading for disaster.[81]

It should be noted that not all Aum members saw things in this way. I-san told me he believed that there was a deliberate element of parody in the campaign. Japanese elections are not renowned for their political subtleties, and much campaigning consists of candidates travelling around accompanied by glamorous young ladies who wave enticingly from cars at the public while the candidate bellows imprecations to the electorate through loudspeakers. In that respect Aum's campaign, the faithful disciple argued, was a parody of the political process, and he took delight in the feeling that the movement had scored a subtle point against society.[82]

This perspective was not widely shared in the public domain. Aum's behaviour appeared to confirm the alien images conveyed in the media about Aum. The mass media lost no chance to alert the public to the farcical nature of Aum's campaign or the scale of its defeat, while constantly reminding them of previous scandals associated with Aum, such as the disappearance of the Sakamoto family. Indeed, such scorn was poured on the movement that at least one scholar admitted that he almost felt sorry for Aum: commenting that the media's 'Aum-bashing' had developed into 'almost a national pastime' he asked why, after Aum's 'abject defeat', did it have to have its nose rubbed in the dirt?[83]

REACTING TO THE DEFEAT: THE CONSPIRACY AGAINST AUM AND THE HELLS TO COME

Perhaps predictably, Asahara had his excuses for the defeat, claiming at first that the ballots had been rigged against him.[84] He used the occasion, however, to restate the truth of his way and the falsity of all others. In sermons delivered shortly after the election he reaffirmed that the Vajrayāna path was the only one to follow but warned his followers that it was beyond the capacity of many people for whom Aum was therefore a 'threatening religion'.[85] He then explained why the defeat had occurred: because of the threat Aum posed, the media and authorities had sought to undermine it. A campaign of religious persecution, which he called 'Aum-bashing', had started with the *Sunday Mainichi* articles of October 1989, and Aum had been victimised and fraudulently portrayed in ways that prevented people from seeing its true nature as a religion intent on salvation.[86]

It was in the aftermath of the election defeat that the conspiracy theories that dominated later Aum thought were first openly expressed. In his Vajrayāna sermon of 11 March 1990 Asahara referred to a dark conspiracy that was aimed at world domination and at suppressing Aum, which, as a religion with a mission of truth, stood in its way. It was not just the Japanese authorities who were involved, for the conspiracy had truly international dimensions. For the first time he mentioned the Jews and Freemasons as groups that were implicated in this process.[87]

By invoking this conspiracy at the time of Aum's greatest public humiliation, Asahara had produced an explanation for that failure that fitted in with Aum's visions of struggle and of sacred war. Aum had lost because it was being persecuted and conspired against by various dark forces that secretly controlled society. It was an accusation that was used increasingly to excuse or explain Aum's failures and problems. Aum was thus a victim of persecution – a frame of reference which of course inflamed the movement's anger, fuelled its resentment and demonstrated that it had to fight in order to preserve its mission and defeat the forces ranged against it. It also elevated the movement's status at a time of apparent defeat and humiliation. Rather than being a small and insignificant movement that had been rejected totally by the electorate, it was transformed into one so important that it required a huge international conspiracy to block its development.

In the same period Asahara also revealed a fearful truth that he had previously not spoken about, but which followers needed to know about. This was the actual (rather than figurative) existence of the three miserable realms or hells (*sanakushu*) into which all who incurred karmic demerits would fall.[88] He revealed this new truth on 13 March 1990, two days after speaking for the first time about the conspiracy against Aum, in a sermon shot through with violent images, with the legitimation of violence in the furtherance of truth, and with visions of death and hell which became recurrent themes in his sermons thereafter. He had, he asserted, descended into the hells during his meditations and had seen and experienced the awful terrors in these realms, such as fires and sharp needles upon which the tormented souls of the dead were forced to walk: for Asahara the hells were real, awful, painful and frightening places of unendurable agony. Without the removal of the bad karma that accrued to all who live in this world, people would inevitably fall into these three evil realms, and it was for this reason – in order to drive their bad karma away and to make them perform the austerities that could eradicate this karma – that he had to beat his disciples. This was his mission, and this, he stated, was the difference between a guru and his followers. The latter would, he suggested, be merciful and gentle in their treatment of others, while the guru would have no mercy and would continually beat and coerce them in order to get rid of their negative karma. His violence and severity were thus expressions of his 'cruel compassion'.[89]

In the spring and early summer of 1990 Asahara's tone was often angry. He was a guru who had been slighted and rejected by the public, and the pain and anger of that experience was evident in his post-election sermons. So, too, was his malevolence towards those who had rejected him: those who were not devotees in Aum could not be saved and would inevitably fall into the hells at death.[90]

These post-election sermons stressed the imminence of Armageddon and the impossibility of saving anyone outside of Aum, while also dwelling on the measures to be taken to guarantee Aum's survival and to prepare for the war to come.[91] In May 1990, for example, he announced his intention to have a nuclear shelter constructed at Aum's centre at Fujisawa near Mount Fuji region as part of his Shambhala plan.[92] By this time the Shambhala plan was not infused with any hopes or aspirations to save the world at large: what concerned Asahara in the period after the election was the fate of his disciples. The rest of the world had rejected him and in so doing had lost its chance of being saved in the apocalypse to come.

BREAKING POINT: THE ISHIGAKI SEMINAR AND THE MANUFACTURE OF BIOLOGICAL WEAPONS

Asahara's reactions to the public rejection of Aum involved accusations of conspiracies, an escalation of his prophecies about death and Armageddon, an abandonment of any commitment to save anyone except members of Aum, a re-articulation of the legitimacy of using violence, and a call for Aum to fight for its survival. All these themes were reaffirmed by Asahara in an intensive three-day seminar held on the island of Ishigaki in Okinawa in April 1990. Asahara had announced that this was to be a very important training seminar and that all who could possibly do so should attend. He combined this injunction with a prediction that a major disaster was about to engulf Japan, either a comet that was about to crash into the earth, destroying Japan, or a major earthquake or a volcanic eruption. Whatever the disaster, followers would be safe if they decamped immediately for Ishigaki.[93]

Although costs were high, and travel arrangements and accommodation on the island were either sparse or non-existent, the seminar attracted a large number of Aum's faithful. Around 1,000 in all attended the seminar, a sizeable proportion of whom used the occasion to renounce the world and become *shukkesha*.[94] There was also a massive media presence at Ishigaki, with numerous journalists descending on the island to cover the event. There was apparently even some speculation that Aum would, in the aftermath of its election disaster, use the seminar to carry out a mass suicide.[95]

The Ishigaki seminar appears to have had a positive effect on Aum. The spirits of the faithful were lifted and the numbers of *shukkesha* were boosted. Aum was able to generate a large sum of money from seminar fees and donations from those who renounced the world, which helped restore its finances. The readiness of followers to commit all to Aum even at a time when the movement appeared to be at its lowest ebb, suspected of murder and publicly ridiculed, testified to the extent to which members were already alienated from Japanese society and hence not prepared to accept what the media said about their movement. It showed, too, that Aum's teachings had a continuing potency and could still reach some disaffected members of society, and it illustrated the extent to which Asahara continued, despite the setbacks Aum had experienced, to inspire devotion.

The increase in the number of *shukkesha* necessitated the acquisition of more communal facilities, and in May 1990 Aum purchased land at Namino in Asō district in Kumamoto prefecture, on the island of Kyûshû, for this purpose. The purchase and development of the Namino commune, however, proved to be yet another area in which Aum became embroiled in conflict and controversy. For the next four years it was to be a major new flash-point in Aum's hostile relationship with Japanese society.

Unknown to the public, or to Aum's rank and file at the time, another deeply sinister event had happened at the time of the Ishigaki seminar. Following Asahara's orders, and under the supervision of Murai Hideo, Endō Seiichi and a group of his associates had set up a secret laboratory for the manufacture of biological weapons and they had made a quantity of one of the world's most dangerous poisons, botulism toxin, along with a device with which to spray the toxin. Indeed, it has been widely suggested that the real intent of the Ishigaki seminar was to get as many of the Aum faithful as possible away from the mainland of Japan, for the intention of the leadership was to use the toxin to cause mass destruction in Tokyo. This is, in fact, what they tried to do: Endō and his associates drove around Tokyo spraying clouds of botulism toxin into the air. Nothing happened: the attempt failed, as indeed did subsequent Aum endeavours to utilise biological weapons.[96] Its scientists may have been adept at making such substances but they proved con-stantly incapable of finding an effective means of delivering for them – a failing that recurred on other occasions in the years that followed.[97]

This was Aum's first attempt at making or using weapons of mass destruction: five years before the subway attack it had already signalled its willingness to sow death and destruction on the public at large. The decision to make biological weapons appears to have been taken in the aftermath of the election debacle and in the light also of Asahara's growing obsession with a 'conspiracy' hostile to Aum. The need to con-front such forces meant that Aum had to acquire the weapons to fight, and in order to do this effectively it had turned to what is commonly known as the 'poor man's nuclear bomb' – biological and chemical weapons, which can be as deadly as more conventional and nuclear weapons, but which are easier and cheaper to make.

The attempted botulism attack can probably be best viewed as Aum's hostile response to the electorate that had humiliated it, and as an attempt to vent karmic retribution on it for its rejection of the truth. It may also have had the intention of 'proving' the validity of Asahara's prophecies relating to Armageddon and apocalypse, and hence of strengthening the resolve of the Aum faithful and bringing more followers to the movement. It was also a further development in the process that has been outlined in this chapter: as events in Aum's history from this period show, and as Asahara's sermons demonstrate, Aum had moved from a philosophy and mission centred on world salvation, to one that emphasised hell, destruction and death, and in which those who were not with Aum were its enemies or were complicit in a massive conspiracy aimed at destroying the truth.

The attempted botulism attack of April 1990 was the first sign that Aum was prepared to engage with its 'enemies' on a grand scale and it thus marked a radical change in Aum's activities. Where it had previously used violence in a directed sense against individuals, it now had turned, through seeking to produce and use biological weapons that could potentially wipe out vast numbers of people, to the possibility of indiscriminate mass murder. Its potential victims were not just particular foes who had taken on Aum directly and posed a threat against it, such as Sakamoto, but members of the ordinary public who had become, after the election of February 1990, complicit, in Asahara's eyes, in a conspiratorial war against Aum. The polarisation of its worldview was complete: all those not in Aum were henceforth enemies of the truth. They were not merely unworthy of salvation. Rather, in Aum's view, they could – and indeed, *should* – be killed for the sake of their own salvation and so that the mission of truth could be protected.

LOSING THE STRUGGLE: THE INTERNAL PRODUCTION OF VIOLENCE

The period between August 1988 and April 1990 was a critical one for Aum in which it committed a variety of crimes, from the beating of followers and the concealment of an accidental death, to killings to silence internal and external threats, to the attempt to murder on a vast scale. It had engaged in conflicts with the legal system, with the parents of its disciples, and with lawyers and journalists, and fought with and against all who appeared to challenge it. In the process it had developed a series of doctrines that had been modified in relation to circumstances but that were based on ideas that had been present from early in its existence, and that justified its violence and enabled it to kill while maintaining its sense of spiritual superiority.

It is important to note that Aum's initial turn to violence had not come about because of external pressures placed on Aum. When violence first was used in the movement, with the beating of disciples, and when Aum first broke the law with the concealment of Majima's death and then the murder of Taguchi Shūji, it had experienced little external pressure. There had been some complaints from parents when followers left their homes to enter Aum's communes, but there is no evidence of any major or concerted campaign against Aum until the spring of 1989, when Aum applied for legal registration. This was after it had committed its first murder. It was not until after Aum had turned to violence and criminality that any serious opposition emerged to challenge the movement, or that any extensive pressures built up on the movement in the shape of negative media stories and the like.

These external pressures, when they appeared, certainly exacerbated the inner tensions in the movement and heightened its readiness to use violence against its enemies, but they did not create those tendencies. Violent images of sacred and heroic struggle were intrinsic to Aum's worldview from its earliest days. In the period between the death of Majima and the murders of the Sakamotos, these images and practices had become deeply embedded in Aum, and placed within a framework of doctrinal legitimation that made further violence more likely. Aum's visions of the future had begun to shift accordingly. The potential for mass salvation through Aum's triumphant expansion had receded, the world was increasingly damned as evil and in need of purification, and Aum's visions of the future became increasingly bleak and infused with destructive images.

In this period, Aum produced a culture of violence from within its own dynamic, sanctioned by its leader and his teachings and readily supported and carried out by its senior members. The movement's internal dynamics, teachings, attitudes and behaviour also played a major part in creating the external problems (the disputes and conflicts) that it faced in this period. They also contributed spectacularly to the move-ment's humiliating election loss, which signified the extent to which Aum had, during this period, lost what John Hall and Philip Schuyler have termed the 'struggle over cultural legitimacy' in Japan.[98] This humiliation provoked an escalation in Aum's use of violence, marking the point where it embraced violence and destruction on a mass scale and visualised itself as surrounded by enemies and beset by a vast conspiracy against which it had to fight. In the years after 1990 these tendencies were to intensify and develop further, and it is to these issues that I turn next, in Chapter 6.

悪魔

6 *Perpetual Conflict, Foreign Excursions and Cosmic Wars – Conspiracies, Retribution and the Right to Kill*

INTRODUCTION

Once Aum had crossed the boundaries into illegality, placed its interests above the laws of the land, created a doctrinal framework to justify its actions and become fired with the vision of a real fight between itself and the forces of evil as a result of the events of 1988–1990, there was little to hold its proclivities towards violence and conflict in check. In a real sense the dramatic, violent events that occurred in later years were the product of and generated by the patterns of behaviour that developed in this period. The negative reputation that Aum acquired meant that those it encountered in subsequent years invariably regarded the movement with suspicion and hostility, and this in turn led to further confrontations and problems. In the ensuing years, Aum's world-renouncing stance hardened and Asahara's prophecies and millennialist visions became increasingly catastrophic and violent in form. From this period onwards the dates which Asahara ascribed to Armageddon moved increasingly closer to the present. These interactions between a violent, catastrophic vision of the future, the violent and militant religious imagery of a sacred struggle to confront evil and to defend Aum's mission, and actual prepara- tions for and uses of violence were central to the history of Aum in the five years between the Ishigaki seminar and Aum's first attempts to use weapons of mass destruction, and the Tokyo subway attack of 1995. This and the following chapter will examine this period in the light of these elements. This particular chapter will focus more particularly on the ways in which Aum's teachings and its relations with the outside world developed, while the following chapter will look more specifically at its violent activities especially in the two years prior to the subway attack.

In the first three years of this period, between late spring 1990 and spring 1993, there were, as far as is known, no further murders committed by the movement. None of the charges brought against Asahara or other senior figures in Aum criminal activities relates to this period, although it appears that Endō and Tsuchiya continued unsuccessfully with their experiments into biological weapons. The earliest dates cited in the indictments against Asahara relating to the manufacture of illegal weapons refer to late 1992 and the early spring of 1993, when Aum's unsuccessful plan to manufacture guns is alleged to have started.[1] It was, according to the prosecution's case against Asahara, at this juncture also that he first ordered Tsuchiya and Endō to manufacture chemical weapons, and it was at this time that Aum began to construct a chemical plant for this purpose under the guidance of Murai Hideo.

In the two years thereafter, from spring 1993, its criminal activities escalated dramatically. Besides attempting to manufacture guns and chemical weapons such as sarin and VX gas, it also produced hallucinogenic drugs such as LSD and mescaline, forcibly detained and punished recalcitrant members including Ochi Naoki, accused other members of spying on it and on occasion killed them as a result. It also attacked and on occasion murdered people outside the movement whom it viewed as enemies, used its chemical weapons on the general public, and marshalled its forces for a future confrontation or battle with the authorities.

A TROUBLESOME NEIGHBOUR: COMMUNES AND RECURRENT CONFLICTS

Although most of these crimes occurred in the two years dating from spring 1993, this does not mean that the earlier period, from 1990 until 1993, was one of tranquillity followed by a rapid escalation of conflict and violence. Besides its ongoing involvement in attempts to make biological weapons, the movement continued on a turbulent and confrontational path, remaining under a cloud of suspicion because of the disappearance of the Sakamotos, and subject to continuing criticisms from the parents and families of its members. It also became embroiled in drawn-out disputes and court cases with the civil authorities and its neighbours in the places where it constructed its communes and centres. Because of its reputation as a problematic religious group, Aum invariably encountered resistance and hostility from the people living near its communes and centres. It often provoked or added to that hostility by its own actions, for Aum proved not to be a good neighbour, displaying a habit of riding roughshod over the concerns of local residents and treating them with disdain.

Aum's practice of concealing its identity through dummy companies when purchasing land (a stratagem based on the fear that vendors, were they to know the true identity of the purchaser, would balk at selling to Aum) further exacerbated tensions when Aum's identity was revealed. Disputes flared around its two communes at Namino in Kyūshū and Kamikuishiki in Yamanashi, as well as around various of its centres in different towns and cities in Japan. Aum experienced, for example, repeated conflicts with the residents who lived close to its centre at Kameido in Tokyo, and with the local populace, civil authorities and courts in relation to the centre which it built in 1992 in the town of Matsumoto. This latter location was one where Aum had concealed its identity when purchasing the land, and this provoked another series of conflicts and a court case. It was in Matsumoto, and in connection with this dispute, that Aum first used chemical weapons in June 1994.

Such disputes, in which Aum displayed an arrogant inability to compromise in any way with its neighbours, and in which its rural neighbours reacted with hostility to the controversial religious movement that had moved into their midst, fuelled further Aum's belief that the world was conspiring against it and gave the movement no respite from controversy. They also strengthened Aum's conviction that it had to fight for its truth by defending its mission at all costs and by combating vigorously all who stood in its way.

The conflicts and hostilities were particularly intense around the commune which Aum established at Namino in May 1990. This move did not bring Aum the peace or provide it with the sanctuary it sought so that its members could pursue their meditation and disengage from society at large. Aum was not the first religious movement to find that rural conservative farming communities do not always welcome as neighbours radical new communal movements that espouse different lifestyles. This is especially so when such movements come with an established reputation for being problematic or controversial. Such troubles are also likely to increase when the newcomers have the potential, through sheer weight of numbers, to outvote the locals at the ballot box and hence wrest control of local community governing bodies.

Such a situation can be seen, for example, with the Rajneesh movement led by the Indian guru Bhagwan Shree Rajneesh and largely consisting of Western acolytes, which moved from its centre at Poona in India to establish a commune at Antelope in a sparsely populated farming area in Oregon, USA in the 1980s. The Rajneesh movement had, while in India, acquired some notoriety for its sexual liberalism and, although this was displaced by a more austere attitude to sexual relations after its move, the group's reputation caused concern among the rural Oregon populace. Equally, the Rajneesh devotees' dress and behavioural codes (which included dressing in red or orange Indian-style clothing and adopting Indian names signifying their new identities as spiritual seekers), and their devotion to an Indian guru, did not fit well with the attitudes of the local populace. It was not, however, just their intrinsic opposition to a group whose lifestyle appeared to be highly contradictory to its own that caused concern, for local residents feared that the commune members would outnumber them and would, as a result, be able to gain democratic control of the local political structure. While the local populace was thus immediately suspicious of and inimical to the new community, the commune members appeared to confirm their worst fears by attempting to manipulate the electoral process to their own advantage and by treating the locals with disdainful arrogance.[2] I have already discussed the parallels between the activities of and dynamics in the Rajneesh movement in my earlier volume on Aum. There I noted how it, like Aum, was infused with apocalyptic visions and engaged in criminal acts including attempts to manufacture and use toxins against its opponents,[3] and I will refer again later to such parallels. Here I will note that the experiences and behaviour of Aum at Namino and Kamikuishiki, and the reactions and opposition of its neighbours, also show many similarities to that of the Rajneesh experience in Oregon.

The land at Namino was originally bought through dummy companies that concealed Aum's identity. The local populace (and indeed the vendor of the land) were thus deeply unhappy when they discovered that their new neighbours were members of the religious movement that had so recently been the focus of attention because of the *Sunday Mainichi* exposés, the Sakamoto affair and its peculiar election campaign. It was especially the suspicions relating to the disappearance of the Sakamoto family that concerned the villagers. The fear that their new neighbours might have been involved in a murder case hardly encouraged them to establish good relations and was a primary reason, the villagers later argued, why they took every step possible to thwart the development of the commune.[4]

The civil authorities, too, were less than happy because Aum had acquired 5.9 hectares of woodland at Namino and had begun to clear it in order to build its commune. However, under Japanese law, special permission is required for any woodland development of over one hectare, and Aum had not sought this. This was another example of Aum privileging its own self-interests and disregarding, or considering itself as not bound by, conventional laws. Even in matters relating to the environment and the uses of rural land, it refused to consider interests apart from its own.

The prefectural government decided Aum had infringed the law and sought to block the work it was doing. The movement responded aggressively, claiming that the land was moor rather than woodland and hence not subject to this regulation, issuing writs against the government and accusing it of religious persecution. Local opposition grew accordingly, and numerous protests were mounted against the movement, which responded likewise. Especially in the months immediately after the establishment of the commune there were a number of clashes between commune members and local residents which erupted into violence and mass fights between the opposing parties.[5]

In October 1990 three Aum officials including Ishii Hisako, who was in charge of the movement's finances, and Aoyama Yoshinobu, its lawyer, were arrested, incarcerated and charged with infringing the laws relating to the purchase of rural land in Japan. This was the first time any senior figure in Aum had been arrested or charged with a crime, and the movement reacted with its typical aggression. Ishii unleashed a vituperative stream of insults at the public prosecutor who interviewed her, describing him as a frog and as little more than an insect or a tapeworm. Although subsequently an Aum spokesman attempted to justify this outburst by stating that Ishii, as a highly trained spiritual practitioner, had the ability to 'see' the past lives of those she met, and thus 'knew' that the prosecutor in question had had some such previous incarnation, the outburst appeared, to onlookers, to typify the arrogant and hostile demeanour of Aum's senior officials and their contempt for the law.[6]

Aum continued, however, to insist that it was being persecuted. Ishii spent 50 days in prison for her part in the affair, during which time she wrote a series of articles for Aum magazines stating that 'dire persecutions' were being inflicted on the truth in Namino and that Aum's persecutors would suffer torments in hell because of their 'crimes', while those who were persecuted would 'accumulate the great good deeds of protecting the truth'.[7] Aoyama, although a trained lawyer and hence fully aware of the legal issues that had led to his and Ishii's arrests, also reacted in similar terms, claiming that the media, the government, local officials and the Namino villagers had joined together in an orgy of religious persecution against Aum that was, he claimed, on a par with that used against Christianity in Japan in the seventeenth century.[8] Ishii's and Aoyama's responses to their arrests typified the attitude of Aum's elite. They were holy figures, superior to ordinary beings who, living in the world of delusion, simply did not merit the same consideration as themselves. Any action that impinged on their right to do as they wished in furtherance of their religion's aims was seen as an act of persecution – even if it involved implementing the law of the land when it had been contravened.

While Aum made no attempts to engage in harmonious relations with its neighbours, the latter, also acted with hostility and violated various laws in their desire to keep Aum out. The residence applications of Aum members at Namino were rejected by the village authorities so as to prevent the commune residents from being able to vote locally. This action was later declared illegal by the courts. Aum's access to such standard services as telephone lines, piped water and proper sewerage facilities was blocked because the local authorities refused permission for telephone poles or water and sewage pipelines to be built along the roads leading to the commune. Local shops refused to sell food or other goods to the commune, which meant that materials had to be trucked in from some distance, causing the movement additional financial strain. The children of Aum members were refused entry to local schools, a rejection based on the fact that the parents were not registered as residents of the district; they were not registered, of course, because their applications had been illegally rejected by the local authorities.[9]

The Kamikuishiki commune was also surrounded by tensions and conflicts. Takeuchi Seiichi, a resident of Kamikuishiki who was heavily involved in a campaign against Aum's presence in the area, has painted a picture of Aum as aggressive and hostile from the moment it began to build the commune, making little attempt to win friends or to come to terms with the villagers and their different attitudes. While Takeuchi's account is biased due to his bitter opposition to Aum,[10] it nonetheless tallies with the reports of Aum's behaviour in Namino and elsewhere where it built its centres. Takeuchi also shows that Aum's entry into the area was met with strong local resistance, and that the movement was never really given a chance to establish good relations with its neighbours. The villagers objected to Aum's frenetic building activities because the movement constructed numerous buildings on its land without, it appeared, paying much heed to building regulations, and they objected to the noise and turmoil created by the constant flow of cement lorries that accompanied such building work. They responded with dubious measures of their own, erecting hostile posters and billboards attacking Aum, putting up concrete pillars by the roadsides to prevent trucks using certain roads, and hindering (although not to the same extent as at Namino) the residence applications of commune members. They also worked together with the Namino residents to co-ordinate campaigns against the movement, including sending joint delegations to Tokyo to lobby the government and ask it to revoke Aum's status as a religious organisation.[11]

Such external pressures and conflicts exacerbated Aum's inherent tendency to engage in conflict with anyone who appeared to stand in its way and to strengthen its belief in the importance of confronting its opponents. The conflicts at Namino and Kamikuishiki played into Aum's polarisation of the world into good and evil, its fixation on enemies, its readiness to complain of persecution and its belief that it was facing a vast conspiracy intent on destroying it. By opposing the religion of truth, the villagers appeared (from the movement's perspective) to affirm Asahara's views about the deluded and evil nature of people living in the ordinary world and further illustrated the necessity of fighting those forces. The neighbourhood conflicts also kept the movement in a permanent state of hostility with the outside world at large, while further legitimating that struggle within a framework of karmic righteousness – an attitude typified by the comments made by Asahara about how the villagers at Namino had suffered from floods because of their opposition to Aum, and by Ishii's prophecies of retribution against those who arrested her.

The Kamikuishiki commune remained a source of conflict and tension until the latter part of 1995 when, after the arrests of many of its leaders, the defection of large numbers of its members, and court rulings that ordered Aum to pay compensation to various victims of its crimes, the movement had to abandon the commune. The Namino commune closed earlier, in 1994, after a court-ordered compromise was reached by Aum and the villagers. The refusal of the local authorities to allow Aum members to register as residents had come to the attention of civil liberties groups in Kyūshū because it appeared to be a clear breach of the right under Japanese law for citizens to choose the place in which they wish to reside. Their unhappiness at this seeming breach of human rights, which they felt was rooted in a hostility to alternative lifestyles and in religious intolerance, led to various civil rights campaigners giving their support to Aum, not in religious terms but in the context of civil liberties.[12] The courts also supported Aum, ruling that the Namino authorities had acted illegally and suggesting that some compromise should be reached between the warring parties. As a result, a settlement was reached in which the village paid Aum ¥920,000,000 (US$7–8 million) for the land if Aum moved out. The settlement was far in excess of the sum Aum had paid for the land, and it placed a huge financial burden on every household in the district. Although Aum thus received a welcome cash boost, the loss of its commune was still a serious blow for its morale, giving it one less place where its members could live and accordingly increasing the pressure on its Kamikuishiki commune.

SACRIFICE, SALVATION AND PERSECUTION: THE SUFFERINGS OF A MESSIAH

In 1991, in the midst of this turmoil, Asahara published two volumes entitled *Kirisuto sengen* Numbers 1 and 2, which were later translated by Aum members and published in a single English volume with the title *Declaring Myself the Christ*.[13] The covers of all these books bore the same image, a drawing of Asahara as Jesus on the Cross, wearing a crown of thorns. The image, the book titles and their contents, in which Asahara 'read' the New Testament in terms of prophecies that demonstrated that he was the Christ or messiah come to save the world, represent Aum's most pronounced appropriation of Christian imagery. They also illustrate the extent of Asahara's arrogance and megalomania in his assumption of the Christ role. The contents of these volumes also illustrate how his sense of persecution coupled with his belief that salvation was no longer a universal possibility but one restricted to true believers, had developed since the election disaster of 1990.

In these volumes, which I shall henceforth refer to as the 'Christ books', Asahara developed further the interest in biblical Christian motifs first manifest with his adoption of the term Armageddon in late 1988. In the 'Christ books' what particularly interested him were biblical references to the restricted path of salvation, and the interwoven images of the Christ as messiah, as saviour and as sacrificial victim. The first of these he found in the Gospel of St Matthew (7:13–14), which appeared to confirm his belief that only a chosen few would be saved:

> [F]or wide is the gate and broad is the road that leads to destruction, and many enter through it. But small is the gate and narrow the road that leads to life, and only a few find it.[14]

Arguing that Christianity had provided a 'wide gate' which could no longer lead to salvation, he asserted that his teachings represented the narrow gate prophesied in Matthew and that he was the messiah prophesied in the Bible come to lead the select few to salvation. However, following him was a hard and difficult path, and those who followed it would face hatred and persecution – as, indeed, had Aum.[15] Asahara's biblical 'interpretations' were closely related to Aum's basic teachings. The passage in Matthew relating to the narrow gate leading to salvation and the wide gate leading to destruction, for example, was portrayed as an expression of the laws of karma and a recognition of the forces that lead people to the lower realms at death.[16] In espousing the notion of the narrow gate, Asahara also found further confirmation of his belief that the world was essentially polarised into good and evil, for Jesus, according to Asahara, taught that there were two kinds of souls: on the one hand the majority, who were destined to fall into the hells, and on the other hand the select few, who would ascend upwards and return to God.[17]

The images of Jesus as a messiah who was crucified and of the Lamb of God, who, through being sacrificed, takes away the sins of the world, appealed to Asahara, speaking as they did to his beliefs in a mission of salvation and his focus on persecution. They also provided a way of dealing with the dilemma of a messiah whose proclaimed mission of salvation does not reach the mass audience he sought and who, in response, has had to narrow the gates of salvation to a select few and to claim that his mission was being thwarted by hostile forces. Asahara utilised Christian arguments that Jesus's death on the cross was a symbol of ultimate triumph to explain the movement's own tribulations: just as Jesus had been crucified so, too, had he been persecuted and 'crucified' in Japan. Just as Jesus had triumphed because the religion he had founded had outlasted his persecutors and spread across the world, so too would he triumph in the end.[18] He equated himself and Aum's followers, persecuted at Namino, with the sacrificial lamb. He was destined, like Christ, to save others and to take on to himself their illnesses and impurities. His earlier cessation of *shaktipat* initiations was placed in this context: in taking on to himself the illnesses of others through these initiations he had suffered total blindness, various cancers and liver diseases, and had come close to death.[19]

The 'Christ books' thus also emphasised the concept of the suffering guru who had become ill and sacrificed his health and possibly life in the service of the movement. While these books were not the first occasion on which Asahara referred to illnesses he had acquired while ministering to this followers, they brought the possibility of his imminent death very much to the fore, and this subject was to recur with some frequency in his later sermons and publications. In 1994, for example, he accused various 'enemies' of having poisoned him and his close followers with chemical weapons and claimed that he had become seriously ill and was close to death as a result.[20] Whether Asahara was seriously unwell at such times is uncertain: followers and former followers confirmed that he frequently appeared to be ill in 1994 and that when he spoke his voice seemed to be husky.[21] When he was arrested in May 1995 he was, by all accounts, overweight and in poor condition, and at that time there were many rumours that he was dying of liver failure or some such ailment. However, after he had been incarcerated, he appeared to regain his health and to become trimmer, and in the years afterwards reporters observing him in court have commented that he had begun to look well again.[22] Clearly, whatever ailments he might have had beforehand, they did not – despite the comments he made in various sermons and volumes such as the 'Christ books' – include terminal cancers.

It is unclear whether these sicknesses were wholly imagined (the products, as it were, of the paranoia that Asahara manifested in his beliefs that Aum was surrounded by malevolent conspiracies), wholly invented as part of a broader process of deception, or somewhere in between.[23] My own inclination is that they were the product of a number of factors: a combination of physical debility caused in part by exhaustion and part by the indulgences that appear to have followed from his disengagement in ascetic practices; his growing paranoia which, coupled with his obsession with death which I have commented upon earlier, enabled him to imagine that he was gravely ill; his belief in the importance of suffering for the truth; and, critically, the power that being ill – or being believed to be ill – gave him over his followers, increasing their dependency on him and strengthening his control over them.

This theme of the sick or dying guru or charismatic leader has presented itself in a number of the religious movements that have, in recent times, been associated with outbursts of violence and/or group suicides. As James S. Gordon has shown, Bhagwan Shree Rajneesh was believed to be seriously ill after the move to Oregon, and disciples were constantly told that he might not be with them for much longer. Although there were various grounds for disquiet at the commune at the time (including Rajneesh's erratic behaviour, the increasing pressures on followers to donate money to the cause, and the hardship of life at the commune), the impact of this belief in their guru's illness was to strengthen his position in the movement and deflect or eliminate any possible criticism that might otherwise have emerged. Since disciples feared that they would soon lose their ailing guru, they were reluctant to say anything against him, and instead offered him more devotion and regarded him with greater concern and warmth than ever.[24]

Other leaders have manifested similar tendencies. Jim Jones, leader of the Peoples Temple movement, had deteriorated mentally and physically – apparently because of drug abuse, including taking massive doses of the tranquillizer pentobarbital – in the period prior to the group's mass suicide in Guyana in 1978. Jones had become overweight and, according to close associates, was a physical wreck. Moreover, he had become infused with paranoid thoughts about his condition, claiming that he was seriously ill with cancer, fevers and heart problems, although a subsequent autopsy showed that he had had none of these maladies. Again, as with Rajneesh, one of the effects of these perceived illnesses was to increase his stature as a leader who had given so much to his movement that he had sacrificed his health in the process.[25]

Other such cases include Joseph Di Mambro of the Order of the Solar Temple and Marshall Applewhite of Heaven's Gate. Applewhite apparently had come to believe, prior to the collective suicide of 39 members of Heaven's Gate in California in 1997, that he had terminal cancer: subsequent autopsy reports disproved this contention. In the period prior to the collective suicide and murder in 1994 of over 50 members of his movement in Canada and Switzerland, Di Mambro had health problems that appeared to undermine his charismatic authority and his position as leader of the movement, and that were a factor in his paranoid responses to police investigations of his movement and to the subsequent murders and suicides that occurred.[26]

The imminent (real or imagined) death of the guru could also serve as a potential trigger to violence or suicide, either by the leader deciding to take his followers with him or by infusing in them a sense that time was running out for their mission on earth. At times, too, the actual death of a leader can operate in similar ways, as was the case with the small Japanese religious group Michi no Tomo, seven of whose female members committed suicide together in Wakayama in November 1986 in order to 'follow' their leader, Miyamoto Seiji, who had died the previous month of natural causes.[27]

In circumstances where the death of the leader/guru is foretold or feared rather than actual, his[28] illness can serve as a trope increasing his authority and the ways in which his followers regard him, while also contributing to a heightened sense of urgency and concern within their movements. In Aum's case, the emphasis on the suffering guru, which appeared not long after the tribulations caused by the election defeat and thus at a period when his position might otherwise have been open to question, operated as a means of re-emphasising Asahara's importance and reminding his disciples of their dependence on him for spiritual advancement. It also instilled a renewed sense of urgency into the movement. Since the guru was the truth and the gateway to liberation, his possible departure from this realm served also as a stimulus to encourage more intense practices. The end-time scenarios that formed in Aum were thus given an added impetus by the end-time scenario surrounding its guru's life.

While such suggestions of illness and impending death served to increase the guru's control and encourage his disciples' practice, one should be cautious about regarding such illnesses (even when, as in at least some of the cases mentioned here, they did not physically exist) solely as devices dreamt up by cunning leaders in order to bolster their authority and to further their aims. In three of the cases mentioned above (Jones, Di Mambro and Applewhite) the suffering guru/leader committed suicide and took many of his followers with him. While the illness might have been imagined, it does not appear in these cases to have been simply dreamt up in order to heighten the leader's authority or status. Being terminally ill (even if only in the imagination) was, in effect, a means of escape from the problems facing these figures (who all were, in one way or another, aware that their messages had not reached the audiences they sought and whose own rhetoric showed that their missions were coming to an end). Death was thus a solution or way out of a personal dilemma. The imagined illnesses of Jones and Applewhite, and the physical deterioration of Di Mambro, appear to have been, at least in part, a product of the paranoia that gripped them. Rajneesh's and Asahara's claims of illness could certainly have been devices intended to reinforce their charisma, intensify the devotion of their followers and deflect any potential criticism that might otherwise have emerged inside their movements. Given the extent to which both these gurus manifested paranoid concerns in other areas, one cannot rule out the possibility that these 'illnesses', too, might have been products of their own minds. In Asahara's case, the re-petitive emphases on illness that are found in the later Vajrayāna sermons, and their often paranoid contents, indicate a seriously disturbed state of mind, and this, coupled with the comments of his disciples about apparent ill-health, suggest that physical frailty and mental disturbance also played their part in this process.

IMPROVING THE IMAGE? NEW ATTEMPTS AT SPREADING THE WORD

Despite the pessimistic themes and images of sacrifice, sickness and persecution in the 'Christ' books, some more positive impulses emerged in Aum in 1991–1992. The troubles that Aum had experienced around its communes, especially at Namino, had, as I have already indicated, brought Aum some support from civil liberties groups. In the early 1990s Aum also became involved in bitter disputes with Kōfuku no Kagaku about the claims both movements made regarding their orientations as Buddhist movements and about the predictions their leaders made regarding the future: it was a dispute that in some ways helped Aum's image in Japan. The arguments themselves were aired during a live television show involving representatives of the two movements. Commentators generally agreed that Aum had won the debate, since its spokespeople, including Asahara, displayed a deeper grasp of Buddhism than their rivals.[29] At least one scholar, Shimada Hiromi, felt more favourably inclined towards Aum, with its focus on asceticism, than to Kōfuku no Kagaku which, while speaking about its orientations as a Buddhist movement, appeared to place far less emphasis on basic Buddhist practices such as meditation than did Aum.[30]

Aum probably also benefited from the fact that Kōfuku no Kagaku, which had grown appreciably in size in the early 1990s, appeared to have taken over from Aum as the main focus of media opprobium among the 'new' new religions. This was because Kōfuku no Kagaku, like Aum, had assumed an extremely abrasive attitude to any criticisms of the movement, and had resorted on a number of occasions to law suits when negative articles appeared about it in the press. In 1991 Kōfuku no Kagaku attacked one of Japan's main publishers, Kōdansha, for having published an article which it considered to be insulting to its leader, and its members waged a concerted attack on the publishing group, mounting protests at its offices and flooding it with fax and telephone calls which effectively jammed its lines of communication for days on end.[31] This assault on (and, in the media's eyes, attempt to censor the reporting of) a major publishing corporation transformed Kōfuku no Kagaku into the *bête noire* of the Japanese media, and temporarily at least deflected attention away from Aum.

During 1991 and 1992 Asahara made use of such favourable circumstances by appearing on a number of television talk shows and making himself available for interviews with a number of academics, including Shimada, and celebrities. In these he was able to present a favourable impression, coming across as a warm and engaging person, and clearly charming many of his interlocutors.[32] Asahara clearly had hopes that such activities might create a groundswell of public sympathy and boost Aum's membership. In February 1991 he appeared to be particularly optimistic, announcing that 1991 was going to be a year of great development for Aum. Asahara claimed that the movement had gained 260 members in January and that this was a great achievement in a period of adversity, one that affirmed Aum's role as a 'keystone organization of world salvation'.[33]

In November 1991 when Jōyu Fumihiro successfully completed his five-day 'underground *samadhi*' austerity, to be followed shortly afterwards by Asahara's wife Tomoko, Asahara was delighted, claiming that this showed that his disciples were able to transcend the human realms and enter those of the gods. Such successful ascetic activities were proof of the miraculous nature of Aum, and were part of his plans to construct a religion for the coming century that would provide its followers with the spiritual powers they would need in the new age.[34]

Despite this new wave of optimism, Asahara continued to regard Armageddon as inevitable, and in a sermon on 26 January 1992, announced that it would come not at the very end of the century as previously had been suggested, but during 1997, and that this would lead to vast changes in the world in the following years.[35] However, there was an optimistic side to this, for he believed that its imminence would stimulate spiritual practice and make people realise the importance of overcoming their spiritual pollution. Certainly he believed that he could still get his message on these issues across to the Japanese people at this stage, and he mentioned a number of projects, including one to translate basic Theravada Buddhist teachings from Pali into Japanese.[36]

Throughout 1991 and 1992 immense efforts and resources were poured into attracting new members. Besides its widely publicised demonstrations of ascetic prowess and Asahara's various public interviews, sermons and television appearances, Aum produced numerous videos, magazines and books aimed at getting its message across to as many people as possible. At times during this period the movement was publishing a book or more per week: a glance at the Aum references cited at the end of this book will show just how active Aum was in these years.

FOREIGN EXCURSIONS: AUM IN RUSSIA, SRI LANKA AND ZAIRE

Aum also expended energy and money in efforts to develop overseas. Besides setting up offices in the USA and Germany it sought to build a centre in Sri Lanka in 1991. Using contacts in the Buddhist world, Asahara managed to schedule a meeting with the Sri Lankan President Premdasa, which fell through at the last minute because, apparently, urgent political matters caused the President's schedule to change. Later, Asahara was to cite this 'snub' as 'proof' of Premdasa's participation in a conspiracy against Aum, and to claim that Aum had failed to develop in Sri Lanka because of the hostility of its President who had maliciously deployed his forces against the movement. Indeed, when Premdasa was assassinated in 1993 by Tamil separatists, Asahara asserted his death was a karmic retribution for his evil deeds against Aum.[37]

Aum's most important overseas development, however, and its only successful one, was in Russia. In the turbulent period following the collapse of communism and of the dominant ideology that had framed that society for several decades, the region experienced a tremendous upsurge in interest in religious movements – a veritable 'rush hour of the gods' as Yulia Mikhailova (borrowing a memorable phrase used to describe the rapid rise of new religions in post-war Japan) has termed it.[38] Aum was one of many movements that took advantage of this growing religious market, gaining entry there in 1992, and its teachings quickly attracted an audience in a society beset by unease.[39]

Aum's entry into Russia appears to have been facilitated by Oleg Lobov, then Secretary of the Security Council in Russia and a close associate of President Yeltsin. Lobov was involved in promoting the Russo-Japanese University, a facility for developing business contacts between the countries and for promoting Japanese investments in the region. He was first introduced to Aum while on a visit to Japan. It appears that Lobov felt that Aum could be useful in supporting the university, and so assisted the movement in setting up links with Russia. This pattern of entry, Mikhailova notes, was not special to Aum: other religions entering the region did so by first establishing contacts with the country's bureaucrats.[40]

Asahara's teachings were translated into Russian, and Aum began to proselytise, establishing centres in a number of regions and gaining access to the mass media by setting up its own radio and television stations. Certainly in comparison with its other overseas ventures, which brought it almost no recruits, Aum in Russia was successful, recruiting around 30,000–40,000 followers in a short time, including several hundred who became *shukkesha*.[41] Its attractions were similar to those it offered in Japan, appealing to people who were interested in mysticism, yoga and Buddhism. However, it also proved to be fascinating to many people because of its very exoticism as a Japanese movement using esoteric terminology and practices. It may well also have attracted some followers (amongst whom, Mikhailova suggests, were a considerable number of people who had lost their jobs in the economic upheavals of the period or who were unemployed postgraduates)[42] because it was Japanese and hence associated in people's minds with the potential for economic advancement.

Despite a rapid period of growth soon after entering the Russian religious market, Aum's success there was short-lived. Like in Japan, it ran into trouble as the families of those who renounced the world to join it formed a pressure group aimed at opposing Aum. They enlisted the help of an organisation known as the Committee for the Protection of Youth from Totalitarian Religions, which had campaigned against other new religious movements in Russia. This organisation voiced its opposition to Aum and brought law suits against it relating to converts who had left their families. Eventually the Committee's campaign gained success in the courts and Aum's registration as a religious organisation was revoked in August 1994. Later, too, penal suits were lodged against Aum claiming damages on behalf of families whose relatives had joined it, and by March 1995 – just before the sarin attack in Tokyo – it had become clear that Aum's activities in Russia had come to an end. According to Mikhailova, 'it looked like the civil court was about to rule against Aum. On 15 March police arrived and confiscated the property in one of Aum's Moscow centres with the purpose of reimbursing damages'.[43]

Aum's brief history in Russia, in other words, was a troubled one in which the movement was beset by legal problems and in which, despite its initial smooth entry aided by bureaucrats and officials, it fell foul of the courts and official bodies. Again, the patterns of conflict paralleled those it had faced in Japan and centred on its demanding system of world renunciation and severing ties with one's family.

The success that Aum had initially encountered in Russia, however, cast its relative lack of success in Japan in a harsh light. As his sermons in autumn 1993 indicated, Asahara was very much aware of this contrast, which contributed further to his sense of being a prophet spurned in his own country. Aum had grown in Russia, he stated, because it had not had to face a hostile media, unlike in Japan, and it would have been far larger in Japan if it had been treated fairly rather than being persecuted by the press. He also turned his wrath on his disciples in Japan for this lack of growth and accused them of having been deficient in their campaigns, compared to the disciples he had sent to Russia.[44]

When Aum began to run into problems in Russia as well, the 'obvious' explanation was that there, too, it had fallen prey to vicious conspiracies aimed at impeding the spread of truth. By the spring of 1994, by which time its Russian mission was in serious difficulties and Aum in Japan had become enveloped in conspiracy theories, Asahara was complaining openly that Aum had been impeded in Russia by 'conspiracies' aimed at preventing its message reaching the Russian people. The conspirators he named included those common bedfellows the CIA and the Vatican.[45]

Aum's Russian expansion thus brought additional strains and problems and created another arena of conflict for the movement. It also had a further and perhaps more significant dimension, for in Russia Aum encountered the possibilities of gaining access to military weapons and arms. The collapse of values and the extremes of a free and unregulated market meant that those with money could have access to whatever they wanted, including military equipment, chemicals and other such materials. Whether Aum was keen to enter Russia because of this potential, or whether, on entering what appeared to be a religious market with vast opportunities, it found itself in a situation where such technologies and materials could be acquired, is unclear. My feeling is that, since its initial entry into that country came during a period of general (attempted) expansion, Aum's move into Russia was originally based on a desire to expand its religious base rather than to acquire weapons. Other scholars such as Mikhailova, however, feel that the hidden agenda was the procurement of weapons.[46]

Whatever the case, it is clear that in Russia Aum found that it could acquire weapons and other materials, and its leaders, having already engaged in violent activities and displayed an interest in manufacturing biological weapons in 1990, certainly possessed the mind-set necessary to follow up with interest any opportunities to acquire military technologies that presented themselves. It was at some point during autumn 1992 or perhaps early 1993 that, according to the prosecution's indictments, a plan was hatched to manufacture guns at Kamikuishiki. In February 1993 Murai Hideo, having made contact with arms dealers in Russia, smuggled a Russian A-74 rifle into Japan for this purpose.[47] Russia became a source of materials, equipment and machinery for the movement. Eventually Aum also acquired a former military helicopter there, and perhaps much more besides including, it has been alleged, blueprints for the manufacture of nerve gases such as sarin.[48]

In autumn 1992 Aum made a further overseas excursion, when Asahara and a large group of followers, including doctors, nurses and chemists, visited Zaire on what was loudly proclaimed by Aum to be part of its programme of world salvation. It was a mercy mission intended to help eradicate diseases such as malaria in the region.[49] This appears to have been a one-off mission with no further attempts to engage in missionary or other work there. The venture might have been a gesture aimed at gaining Aum publicity and helping improve its image in Japan, and it is possible that Aum sought to follow in the footsteps of other Japanese new religions that have engaged in social welfare missions overseas. Agonshû, for example, had conducted missions in Africa in which it supported medical facilities and sponsored drives to improve living conditions, and these had helped its public image. However, more sinister suggestions have been made about this trip: that Aum's real purpose was to try to isolate the Ebola virus then raging in the region, in order to utilise it as a biological weapon.[50]

THE VIVID IMAGERY OF ARMAGEDDON: A RENEWED
EMPHASIS ON VIOLENCE

While media reports that the real purpose of the Zaire mission was to acquire the Ebola virus have not been fully substantiated, it is easy to accept them because of Aum's earlier attempts to make biological weapons. The timing of the mission is worthy of note also because it coincided with a change of tenor in Asahara's sermons and Aum's publications. The more optimistic and expansionist nature that had been manifest in Aum's proselytisation activities of 1991 and the first half of 1992 gave way in the latter part of 1992 to a more decidedly stark vision of the future, while the images of Armageddon portrayed in Aum literature became increasingly violent and vivid in nature. As they did so, Asahara's rhetoric became more focused on what he saw as conspiratorial forces that were massing against Aum and on the necessity for Aum to fight against these forces of evil for the sake of truth. The sacred war of good and evil that had been foreseen in his visions dating back to the mid-1980s was thus materialising as a real conflict, and as it did so Aum's attention began to turn to visions of what this cosmic conflict would be like, who would be involved in it, and how Aum should prepare itself for this event. The acquisition of arms from Russia that began in late 1992 or early 1993 was one step in this process, and it is likely that the visit to Zaire was another.

I shall shortly outline why these changes appeared during the latter part of 1992, but will first briefly illustrate some of the violent images of conflict that came to dominate Aum's publications from this period on. In *Risō shakai: Shambala* [The Ideal Society: Shambala] published in August 1992, for example, emphasis is placed not only on the inevitability of Armageddon, but on the weapons and methods of destruction that it would involve. Whereas, in earlier publications such as *Metsubō no hi*, the images of apocalypse are often biblical in nature, featuring angels, devils and quasi-medieval scenes of suffering, along with some focus on the conventional weaponry of war such as guns, soldiers and bayonets, the images in *Risō shakai: Shambala* are high-tech, full of pictures of nuclear mushroom clouds, Gulf War images of rockets and missiles, and increasingly dire comments about the scale of destruction and the types of weaponry that would be used in the coming war.[51]

These images became increasingly pronounced in subsequent Aum publications and in the Vajrayāna sermons, which speculated frequently about the futuristic weapons of destruction that would be used at Armageddon. As the images of and fascination with the means of destruction became progressively more graphic, Armageddon came closer at hand.

In sermons during autumn 1992 Asahara spoke of an inevitable nuclear war, of visions in which he had seen the world bathed in radiation,[52] of cataclysmic disasters beginning in 1996 that would hasten the end, and of the coming of imminent death and doom to most of humanity.[53] He also prophesied that the weapons used would not only be nuclear or high-tech, but would also include biological and chemical weapons.[54]

In the following spring there came further assertions about the inevitable occurrence and imminence of a final war which would result from the evil karma inherent in this world. The emphasis on the mechanics and the futuristic technologies of destruction found in his autumn sermons reappeared in ever more intense forms as Asahara spoke of plasma weapons that could atomise human bodies, large mirrors several kilometres across that floated in space and were capable of reflecting the sun's rays so that they destroyed all life in the process, and vast laser-guns and other such imaginative means of destruction developed by the superpowers, notably by the USA.[55]

In his sermons in spring 1993 he also emphasised repeatedly that a final war was at hand, and he announced (based, he claimed, on his disciples' study and reinterpretation of the writings of Nostradamus) that it would occur in 1997.[56] Elsewhere at this time he prophesied that this war would specifically bring disaster for Japan which, by 1998, would flow with blood.[57] Although in different sermons his predictions about the precise timing of this final cataclysmic war varied slightly, the general focus was always of a disaster that was about to happen in the very near future, and of time that was running out. This urgency and immediacy reached its apogee in January 1995 when Asahara stated that Armageddon was at hand and that the Hanshin earthquake that devastated the Japanese city of Kōbe on 17 January 1995 was the first blow in this final war, triggered by earthquake machines that had been developed, he hinted, by the USA.[58]

These graphic images of destruction and of the coming apocalyptic war were accompanied by allegations of a conspiracy against Aum that grew in scope between autumn 1992 and spring 1995 until it appeared to involve almost everyone outside of Aum, ranging from people it had come into conflict with, to various imagined foes and conspirators who were working to undermine the movement. With this change came a further escalation of violence as plans were initiated to acquire the technologies that could produce various weapons of destruction, including poison gases and guns. Let me now attempt to account for this escalation of violence from early autumn 1992 onwards.

FACTORS IN THE INCREASE IN VIOLENT IMAGES AND CONSPIRACY THEORIES

Japanese scholars have suggested a number of reasons for the manifestation of more technologically based and vivid images of violence in Aum's teaching from around autumn 1992.[59] One was the impact that the Gulf War of 1991 had on the movement and on much of popular culture in general in Japan. The war, with its uses of advanced technology and its images of the formation of a 'new world order' spearheaded by the USA, was, according to Asahara, a 'trial war' for the forthcoming apocalyptic world war in which the USA and its partners would claim world domination.[60] Another element in the process might have been simply because, in expanding in Russia, Aum became aware of the availability of weapons and thus had begun to acquire the capacity to fight. Another factor was the closeness of the end of the century, when Aum expected something dramatic and catastrophic to happen.

A further possible factor that has been suggested relates to the illnesses that Asahara complained of at this time and that, according to his sermons, threatened to end his life. While these illnesses appear in part to have been a means of reinforcing internal loyalty, one cannot discount the possibility that they were also a product of Asahara's paranoid imagination. Just as the real or imagined incapacity of leaders such as Di Mambro of the Solar Temple and Applewhite of Heaven's Gate may have played their part in the suicides of their groups, so Asahara's (imagined) illnesses may have played a role in the hastening process of violence in Aum.

Shimazono Susumu suggests that, besides the above, there was a further, more critical factor at work. He states that defections had increased from Aum's communes in 1991–1992, while there was a lack of new members to fill their places. This raised the spectre of internal collapse and threatened the movement's stability. Shimazono believes that Asahara turned to extreme apocalyptic prophecies as a means of restoring the movement's sense of direction and of rekindling faith.[61]

Such an interpretation accords with the patterns that can be discerned in other of the religious movements that have been mentioned in this book in the context of religious violence, such as the Peoples Temple, the Rajneesh movement and Order of the Solar Temple. As Mary Maaga has demonstrated, the possibility of group suicide had been present in the consciousness of Jim Jones, the founder of the Peoples Temple movement, for some years prior to the mass suicide of 1978, as a response to the defections of members. When members defected, this threatened the solidarity and continuity of a movement that was earnestly seeking to implement its ideal of creating a model socialist community. As problems arose within the movement after its establishment of a commune in the jungles of Guyana and as complaints grew about the harshness of life there, the potential for defections grew. This, coupled with mounting external pressure on the movement from relatives of commune members and backed by their political representatives in the USA, sparked a crisis at Jonestown. The commune leaders became concerned with the potential for disloyalty among its members and became increasingly vigilant against those they saw as possible traitors.

When a number of quite senior figures began to defect in the autumn of 1978, thereby further threatening the solidarity and perhaps even the existence of the movement, the impetus towards group suicide began to gain momentum. Then, in November 1978, a US Congressman, Leo Ryan, arrived at Jonestown with an entourage of relatives of commune members and media representatives in order to persuade those commune members who wished to leave, to return to the USA with him. A further group of commune members did so, and their defections were the spark that set off the mass suicide of the movement and its leaders that had been evident in the movement's consciousness for some time previously. As Maaga demonstrates, the potential fragmenting of the movement due to defections, along with the internal problems that arose because of the stress of life in the Guyanan jungle, and the sense that the movement's dream of creating an ideal socialist community was failing proved a potent mixture. Ryan and his entourage were gunned down as they tried to leave, after which the mass suicide took place. Maaga shows that the Jonestown community turned to mass suicide as a way of remaining loyal to the cause and enabling the movement 'to succeed as a symbol where it had failed as a model'.[62]

Gordon's account of the Rajneesh movement shows similarly how, as tensions developed around the Oregon commune and defections began to occur, its leaders began to fear that the movement might collapse. This caused an increase in intimidation and violence inside the movement, exacerbated by Rajneesh's growing use of apocalyptic images and visions that foretold a coming cataclysmic war, along with various suggestions about conspiracies surrounding the commune. These perceived external threats to the group served to shore up and strengthen the movement internally, imposing a bond of common purpose on members. As a result, the movement's leaders began to gather arms in order to 'protect' the commune and to prepare itself for a confrontation with its 'enemies'.[63]

The fears of defection and an impending sense of failure were elements also in what Jean-François Mayer terms the Order of the Solar Temple's slide from survivalism to suicide. Until the early 1990s, Mayer shows, the movement had an apocalyptic vision infused with a will to survive the cataclysms that were ahead.[64] However, as it began to suffer defections, notably in early 1993 and again in early 1994, its leaders began to talk not of survival but 'departure', of abandoning the world and travelling to another dimension: in other words, suicide.[65] Mayer also shows that Di Mambro and his close associates inclined towards their plan to leave this world as they became more and more conscious of the Solar Temple's failure to get its message across to the numbers of people it had hoped to attract. Di Mambro and his cohorts were effectively saying that, if the world was not interested in them, they were no longer interested in the world.[66]

All of these movements were relatively small and close-knit with strong lines of demarcation between themselves and society at large. In each case, defections thus proved to be a catalyst for the ensuring violence (largely internally directed in two cases, and in Rajneesh's externally at its 'enemies'). Defections were a catalyst because they challenged the movements where they were most vulnerable: in their claims to truth and righteousness that could not be found in the wider world and in their sense of unity and cohesion in the face of a hostile and evil world. When formerly loyal members no longer found the 'truths' and the lifestyle offered within the movement palatable, and instead returned to mainstream society, it caused their leaders to strengthen the boundaries and barriers between themselves and the outside world, and to increase the perception of external threats so as to reinforce a sense of internal cohesion in the group.

This dynamic was also present in Aum. Although Aum was considerably larger in total than the other movements mentioned here, at its core it was not that much bigger. The core, consisting of its *shukkesha* who dwelt at Aum's communes, numbered around 1,100 people in all (not appreciably more than were at Jonestown, for example). It was this inner core that were of primary concern to Asahara. Defections from amongst these ranks, along with the feeling that its message was not being properly received, were recurrent concerns for Aum. Asahara had earlier questioned whether his movement could continue because of defections, and his sense that his mission was in some senses failing or, rather, as with the Solar Temple, that his message was not being listened to, had been a major factor in Aum's hostile attitude towards society at large.

In 1991 and 1992, only 43 people became *shukkesha* in Aum.[67] Despite its attempts, outlined above, to increase its following through extensive proselytisation activities during this period, the movement appears not to have gained any exponential growth. Certainly Asahara's frequent outbursts of anger vented both at the various forces (the media and various opponents) who had – as he saw it – deliberately stultified Aum's growth through their persecutions and conspiratorial campaigns, and occasionally at his own disciples for not having been as active in spreading the word as they should have, indicate his frustration in this manner. In Vajrayāna sermons in spring 1993 Asahara repeatedly suggested that Japan would suffer various ills and retribution for not having listened to him or for having, as he saw it, persecuted him.[68]

The failure to attract large numbers of followers, even though Aum had engaged in an intensive campaign to this effect, clearly angered Asahara considerably, especially since other new religious movements that he saw as rivals such as Kōfuku no Kagaku (which had similarly engaged in a major proselytisation campaign from around 1991),[69] appeared to enjoy considerable success and growth in the early 1990s. Indeed, Asahara's anger on this score turned into bitter resentment and attacks against religious leaders who appeared to be more successful than he, eventually leading to failed Aum attempts on the lives of two such leaders (Ōkawa Ryūhō of Kōfuku no Kagaku and Ikeda Daisaku of Sōka Gakkai).

Aum's failure to achieve such mass audiences, coupled with the dangers posed to the movement because of defections that threatened its internal stability and challenged its emphasis on obedience and loyalty to the guru, were therefore precipitate factors in the intensification of violent images, apocalyptic messages and allegations of conspiracy and persecution that characterised Aum from late summer 1992 onwards. Indeed, it appears in many respects that, after late 1992, Aum virtually ceased mass proselytisation. Compared to the large number of books that were published in 1991 and 1992, from 1993 the movement's publishing activities were rather sparse, a point reiterated by an interviewee who worked in Aum's publication department and who told me that by 1993 the pressures on that department to maintain its previous levels of publication, and the resources that were available for this work, had dwindled considerably. By 1993, he felt, Aum had ceased to put any real energy into further expansion. He also concurred with my suggestion that perhaps at this stage it had started to divert its resources elsewhere, into purchasing equipment and making chemical and other weapons.[70] What publications did emerge in this latter period were, like the Vajrayāna sermons themselves, full of apocalyptic images and assertions that Aum was being persecuted. They appeared to be geared not towards attracting new followers but towards preventing defections by warning existing members of the dangers that existed in the outside world

Asahara had virtually given up hope of getting his messages across to the Japanese public. Attempts to recruit never completely ceased, but from this period on that Aum became more focused on retaining the disciples it already had and on trying to make them increase their commitment. Pressure was put on lay members to enter its communes and donate their possessions to Aum, while Aum strove to strengthen its inner core by emphasising that only those who renounced the world could achieve salvation.

SHIFTING POWER AND SCIENTIFIC FANTASIES

The increasingly technological nature of Aum's apocalyptic images may also in part have been due to the increase in influence, inside Aum, of a group of senior figures who, coming from scientific or technological backgrounds, had a major fascination with such worlds. Prominent among these was Murai Hideo, who was promoted to the highest rank in the movement (*seitaishi*) in 1994. He had already become perhaps Asahara's closest confidant, advising him on scientific matters and the development of new technologies, striving to implement and adhere to every idea and whim of his guru, and wielding great influence in the movement.[71] Others who acquired influence in this area included Endō Seiichi, whose ideas about the special nature of Asahara's DNA had won Asahara's confidence (and no doubt flattered his ego).

The emerging influence of this 'science lobby' occurred as that of Ishii Hisako appeared to wane. As Murai rose to become Asahara's right-hand man, Ishii appears, according to Arita Yoshifu, to have lost her position as Aum's de facto second-in-command. This power shift occurred sometime after the 1990 election defeat and her subsequent imprisonment because of the Namino affair in late 1990.[72] Quite possibly, also, her influence waned because, as a result of giving birth to Asahara's children in 1991-92, she had become preoccupied with matters beyond the immediate internal affairs of the movement.[73]

The influence of people such as Murai, who had the ear of Asahara and who came from scientific and technological backgrounds and retained a fascination with those worlds, was a major factor in Aum's interest in futuristic weapons and technologies as displayed in its visions of Armageddon and its attempts to further incorporate modern technology into its practices. From around 1992, Aum's publications emphasised this point frequently, claiming that spiritual experiences could be verified, explained, tested and proved scientifically.[74] Aum displayed a huge interest in measuring, classifying and quantifying what its practitioners did. For example, it conducted experiments to measure the effects of its practices such as meditation, by wiring up members to machines so as to record their brain waves, heartbeats, breath and so on while they performed this practice.[75]

Aum also demonstrated great faith in the powers of science and technology to produce means through which humans (who, in Aum's view, were somewhat akin to machines, conditioned and programmed by the data they had ingested and capable therefore of being transformed through having that data removed) could be reshaped and spiritually cleansed. Projects such as the creation of an astral teleporter, 'an electronic device to clean one's astral dimension',[76] had been established earlier in Aum's short history, but from around the earlier 1990s such activities developed apace. Resources were invested in attempts to produce machines and technical innovations to improve the spiritual health of practitioners and advance their path to liberation. The PSI headgear, designed to transmit Asahara's brainwaves to his disciples and thereby replace their impure data, was one of the results of such endeavours. Prophecy and divination – already considered by the movement to be an exact science because of the karmic interactions between the causal, astral and material realms – were also the focus for research and investment, with projects set up during 1994 into astrological divination and the prediction of earthquakes.[77]

In reality, this turn to 'science' and to images of futuristic technology was a journey into the world of fantasy, in which Asahara – as the increasingly paranoid contents of his sermons illustrated – and his close associates became enveloped not just in a persecution complex with its images of conspiracies against Aum but a world of imaginative fantasy and technological madness – almost a science-fiction virtual world that was divorced from reality. The extraordinary fascination that developed with futuristic and fantasy means of destruction was also replicated by similarly far-fetched schemes that Aum announced in order to enable the movement to survive the apocalypse. I shall discuss the question of surviving the apocalypse shortly, but here simply mention one of the schemes, which Asahara proudly announced to his disciples in autumn 1992: the creation of underwater cities.[78]

It is important to stress that the emergence of a group of influential figures around Asahara who, from their backgrounds in science and technology and their religious impulses, created a quasi-scientific fantasy world of underwater cities, prophecy machines, astral teleporters and the like, did not in and of itself lead to Aum's violence. These impulses were already well established in Aum and in its doctrines prior to the shift in the balance of power from Ishii to Murai. However, it was with the growth in influence of what I term the 'science lobby' that Aum's apocalyptic visions began to be framed in such vividly destructive forms and that a consciousness of advanced and destructive forms of weaponry became instilled in the upper echelons of the movement. It was these people, such as Murai and Endō, who devised and implemented Aum's schemes to create such weapons of destruction.

THE COMING WAR AND THE NEED TO FIGHT

By the spring of 1993 Asahara was focusing on the USA as the main force of evil in the coming apocalypse.[79] Initially Asahara believed that Japan would be its victim, that America's plans for world domination involved the military subjugation of Japan and that Japan needed to take steps to prepare for a fight.[80] Might and strength, he asserted, were necessary in this age in order to confront the forces of evil: if Japan were to survive it had to wake up and fight, and to acquire the military strength to do so. This involved acquiring the appropriate technologies relevant to the age. Claiming that Japan's previous defeat by American forces in 1945 had come about because the Japanese had been 'an ignorant people who tried to fight atomic weapons with bamboo spears',[81] he argued that the country needed to seek alternative means of arming itself in the face of America's continuing military and technological supremacy. He hinted that biological weapons were a possibility but that these tended to be ineffective (a point underlined by Aum's previous failed attempts in this area), before arguing that the answer was chemical weapons such as sarin, the Nazi-invented nerve gas, which the Japanese should make forthwith.[82]

It was in a sermon delivered in April 1993 that Asahara first mentioned this substance, which was to become a recurrent theme in subsequent Aum discourse as well, of course, as in practice. It was from around spring 1993, also, that Aum began acquiring the materials and equipment that were used to construct laboratories and to manufacture this toxic weapon. Why Asahara chose to draw attention to sarin, and hence to the movement, at a time when his disciples were engaging in the illegal production of this poison, remains unclear. Two possibilities, admittedly both highly speculative, come to mind. One is that since his frequent subsequent references to the nerve gas played their part in identifying

Aum as the possible culprit when sarin was used in the town of Matsu-moto in June 1994, he might have been deliberately drawing attention to himself and his movement on this score, in the way that murderers and other criminals occasionally do after their crimes, as a form of attention-seeking. A second is that, since he knew that Endō and Tsuchiya were preparing to make sarin and was probably aware of the dangers inherent in this process, he was deliberately bringing the issue of sarin as a weapon to the attention of his disciples in case anything went wrong with their experiments. This did, in fact, happen, and Asahara was later to claim that the various forces conspiring to destroy Aum were using chemical weapons against the movement. He used as 'proof' of this the allegation that some of those close to him had suffered injuries consistent with exposure to sarin.[83] Sarin, in other words, became part of Aum's paranoia, and evidence of the conspiracy against it as well as becoming a weapon in the sacred struggle.[84]

While one cannot be sure why references to sarin or other chemical weapons began to appear in Asahara's sermons, the fact that they were so mentioned can be seen as a further example – along with the emphasis on futuristic weapons and technologies of survival – of a distancing from reality, as indeed were his pleas for Japan to manufacture chemical weapons and his apparent belief that anyone outside Aum would listen to him on this score.

It was not long before Asahara abandoned any further hope of influencing Japan. It had not responded to his pleas to make itself strong, and so was bound to be subjugated by the USA. Indeed, it had already become little more than a puppet of the USA, and its government part of the conspiracy to achieve world domination.[85] From this juncture onwards, the focus of the coming war shifted again, from a more traditional geopolitical confrontation between different countries such as the USA and Russia (as predicted in *Metsubō no hi*) or the USA and Japan (as in the Vajrayāna sermons of spring 1993) to a final confrontation in which Aum took centre stage and would stand alone in defence of the truth. It was time to fight: the cosmic struggle and the sacred war of Asahara's visions in the mid-1980s was materialising as a real war.

CONSPIRACIES AGAINST AUM: THEMES AND MEANINGS

Aum had resorted to complaints of persecution whenever it encountered difficulties or opposition to its activities. The initial refusal to grant it recognition under the Religious Corporations Law, the media exposés of the movement, the rejection of Aum at the polls, the arrests of Aum officials for law violations in Namino, and the hostility of villagers near its communes were all examples of such 'persecution'. In various sermons Asahara claimed that he and his disciples had been subjected to attacks by forces intent on destroying Aum because, he stated, it was the sole force left capable of saving the world from chaos, resisting the forces of evil and preventing the conspiratorial forces from taking over the world and instigating a reign of evil.[86]

The 'conspirators' against Aum had become the vague and ill-defined enemy and the 'other' against which the sacred struggle was to be fought. They included the USA, by now fixed in Aum's rhetoric as the primary element in the conspiracy, along with numerous other forces, from the Japanese government and various Japanese religious movements, such as Sōka Gakkai, to various vaguely defined groups such as the Jews and the Freemasons. Other conspirators at various stages included the Vatican, and numerous individuals, including the Japanese Crown Princess Masako (who, having been educated in the USA, was especially suspect and who, Asahara alleged, was America's secret agent in the Imperial household),[87] the Japanese head of the United Nations Refugee agency, Ōgata Sadako, assorted Japanese politicians, and various popular entertainers living in Japan.[88]

Amongst the evil deeds purportedly carried out by the conspiracy were the disappearance of the Sakamoto family in 1989, which had been engineered so as to cast aspersions on Aum,[89] and countless attacks using poisonous gases against Asahara, his family and close disciples, which had been going on, Asahara claimed at various times, since 1988 or 1989.[90] As a result, he stated, Aum had had to take preventative measures, importing gas detectors from Russia and doing research on poisonous gases in order to protect themselves against their effects.[91] The movement also, in various publications, accused the Americans of conducting continual military overflights of the Kamikuishiki commune[92] and of dropping poisons on it.[93] After the subway attack in March 1995 Aum also initially claimed that the attack had been carried out by its enemies in order to blacken its image and to justify a massive crackdown on the movement.[94]

Though Aum's conspiracy theories were obviously ludicrous fictions, they were by no means unique. The Rajneesh movement in Oregon exhibited a set of similarly fanciful conspiracy theories, supposedly orchestrated by the US government, whose planes flew over Rajneesh's commune just as they did over Aum's.[95] The Order of the Solar Temple also exhibited beliefs in the probable imminent destruction of the planet.[96] Moreover, in the period immediately before its collective suicide in 1994, it was gripped by paranoid delusions in which its leaders claimed that the police forces of the world were concentrating their resources on harassing the movement, spying on its members wherever they went.[97] Similar themes of vast conspiracies are found in various right-wing survivalist groups in the USA, which claim that their President is some form of anti-Christ or foreign agent and that their own government is in league with various other forces, notably the UN, but also those other favourites of conspiracy theorists, the Freemasons, the Jews and various esoteric groups such as the Illuminati (who also surface on more than one occasion in Aum's conspiracy theories)[98] and even, at times, members of the British Royal Family, in a satanically inspired plot to destroy the freedoms of the USA and hand control of the country over to foreign powers.[99]

Aum's allegations of conspiracies form, with its other fantasies, a pattern of deceit, delusion and paranoia in which Asahara and his cohorts persuaded their followers (and quite possibly also themselves) that they were being subjected to attack, and hence that they needed to fight back and resist such oppression. These paranoid theories fulfilled a number of important functions in Aum, as indeed they did in the other movements mentioned above, in forging the movement's self-identity and uniting members spiritually against a common enemy.

Especially when linked with prophecies of a coming disaster or end-of-the-world scenario, they reaffirmed the polarisation that existed between Aum and the corrupt, evil world beyond, and thus intensified the pressure on members to remain faithful to the movement and to devote themselves more than ever to their practices to ensure their liberation. The manufacture of weapons of mass destruction, although never explicitly mentioned in his sermons, thus came to be sanctioned within the parameters of the movement's own belief system.

The notion of conspiracy, as with persecution, also served as a pretext for the movement's failure to achieve its salvation mission. It served as a means of answering the otherwise puzzling (for Aum) questions: why was Asahara, the liberated spiritual master, messiah and prophet of truth, not attracting large numbers of followers? And why did he and his movement suffer rejections and encounter opposition in their attempts to spread the truth?

Within the movement, then, the talk of conspiracies helped to deflect any suggestion of blame for its problems or failures, away from the movement and its founder. Viewed through the lens of conspiracy and persecution, it was not Asahara's, or Aum's, fault that it lost so badly in the election, or that its officials were arrested in Namino. Conversely, such conspiracies, rather than simply explaining the movement's lack of success, also demonstrated just how *important* the group was. The 'fact' that some of the world's leading economic and military powers, as well as leading religious organisations and other groups intent on world domination, felt the need to gang up on Aum, and that the USA needed to deploy its military resources to attack the movement, showed this clearly. Rather than being, as it appeared on the surface, a small and marginalised religious group, it was a key to world salvation, the heroic force of good and absolute truth against which the USA and its cohorts felt compelled to act.

The same dynamic operated in the Order of the Solar Temple. As Mayer has suggested, Joseph Di Mambro and his associates, in talking of a world-wide conspiracy intent on harassing and destroying them, created a myth of importance around what was in reality a numerically insignificant movement. In such ways, Mayer argues, the Solar Temple enhanced the egos of its leader and of those who, through their 'transit' from this earth, saw themselves as celestial spiritual voyagers akin to gods who received messages from other worlds, and who were spiritually superior to the humanity they were leaving behind on this planet.[100]

SURVIVAL, DEATH AND THE WORLD TO COME

As Aum became focused on apocalypse and conspiracy, it became important for Asahara to articulate some concept of Aum's future and of the ways in which the movement could deal with the imminence of mass death and destruction. As with much else in this period, his thoughts appeared to be less than clear as he wavered between the importance of surviving the apocalypse (so that Aum's chosen elite could enter and enjoy a paradisal new world) and apparently welcoming death and leaving this life behind.

Unlike movements such as the Order of the Solar Temple and the Peoples Temple, which ultimately, in the face of their problems and fearful of disintegration, determined to terminate their association with this world through group suicides (coupled in both cases by the killing of reluctant suicides), Aum ultimately appears to have rejected the possibility of collective suicide as a way out of the situation it had got into. Nevertheless it was considered as an option and Asahara on occasion did mention, in his Vajrayāna sermons, the possibility of group suicide as a way of dealing with the critical state Aum was in, surrounded as it was by enemies and with an inevitable apocalypse to hand.[101] Some observers of Aum became worried, particularly in the latter part of 1994 (a time when the movement was under suspicion for the sarin gas attack in Matsumoto and showing clear signs of internal chaos), that the movement would attempt such an action, and Takimoto Tarō issued a warning to the authorities to this effect.[102] However, this would have been an unlikely scenario: if the movement were to respond to the situation in any violent way, it was always less likely that this would be directed inwardly, in terms of collective suicide, than externally in terms of a confrontation with and acts of violence against those it saw as its enemies. This was partly because Aum's rhetoric of struggle and its visions of sacred war meant that it should fight against its enemies rather than (as was the case with the Solar Temple) departing from this realm and abandoning the unworthy remainder of humanity who would therefore lose the chance of salvation that the Solar Temple had offered. It was also because Aum's teachings about liberation, karma and rebirth meant that this present realm was where one accrued the merit that would enable one to achieve a better rebirth. Aum's followers may have considered this world to be polluted and transient but this did not cause them to think of their own lives in it as valueless. Rather, they believed in the importance of surviving so they could perform ascetic practices, shed their bad karma and attain a better rebirth. In other words, Aum's doctrines created a dynamic of survivalism in the movement.

This became a critical theme from around spring 1993 onwards as Aum's plans changed from the idea of constructing sacred locations which would be the focus of a new utopia, to building defences and constructing the means to survive the holocaust in some form. One of the ways in which this was done was via the development and stockpiling of weapons – a common theme among survivalist groups preparing for Armageddon[103] – which could be used to defend the faith. Another was withdrawal to remote locations where the movement could feel protected from the effects of war: in 1993 Aum acquired a tract of land in the Australian Outback where it is believed to have tested chemical weapons but which may also have been considered as a possible survival refuge.[104]

Some of its survivalist ideas were more in accord with the quasi-technological fantasies that it had developed about future weapons, as with Asahara's repeated statements that Aum planned to construct under-water cities fortified to repel gamma rays and other such destructive forces that might be directed at them and to allow them to survive the coming apocalypse.[105] He also suggested that the body could be trained to withstand the plasma weapons that would be used at Armageddon and claimed that through spiritual practice the body could be transformed or even cast off in such ways that it could withstand weapons of destruction.[106]

Generally, however, it was through this body and through spiritual practices that the main hopes of surviving and transcending the apocalypse were to be found, for only those who purified their minds and spirits through ascetic practices could survive the apocalypse.[107] For such people Asahara occasionally offered hopeful post-millennial visions: those who survived the apocalypse would enter into a utopia in which life would be virtually immortal, extending for one hundred thousand years.[108] Aum could in such ways realise the 'millennial kingdom' (*sennen ōkoku*) but this was a highly selective process, and those who wished to enter this realm first had to face the judgement of the gods, and only those who had completely purified their spirits would be allowed to enter.[109]

While concepts of survival and the possible attainment of an idealised, post-millennial world existed in Aum, Asahara remained preoccupied by the inevitability of death, and frequently appeared to see it and what would follow it, as the primary issue facing his followers. Frequently he stated that the way to deal with the imminent apocalypse was to accept the inevitability of death and train the mind for this event. Indeed, he was to state on occasion, death was a desirable and welcome event through which one could overcome the trials of this world, be freed from these animal-like realms of existence and ascend to higher realms.[110] The imminence of death became an overarching concern in the Vajrayāna sermons in autumn 1993 and spring 1994, with Asahara speaking at times of how the 'blessings of the light of death' (*shi no hikari no shufuku*) were close at hand.[111]

'TO *POA* ALL OF HUMANITY WOULD BE A GOOD THING': KARMIC RETRIBUTION, RIGHTEOUS KILLING AND THE VALUELESSNESS OF ORDINARY LIFE

As Asahara became obsessed by thoughts of conspiracies and by the need to fight against its opponents, the emphasis on *poa* and karma became increasingly prevalent in his sermons. Those who had persecuted Aum were creating bad karma for themselves and would suffer the consequences of their actions. All who had dared to insult the truth through their ignorant attacks on Aum or their participation in anti-Aum conspiracies, would suffer karmic retribution for their evil deeds, and while such retribution might be in their next lives and in the hells, it could as easily be in this life.[112] Indeed, he claimed that many of those who had attacked Aum had suffered karmic retribution: the villagers at

Namino, punished by floods for their opposition to Aum, and the Sri Lanka President Premdasa, blown to bits by a terrorist bomb for having conspired against Aum. Another example was the editor of the *Sunday Mainichi*, Maki Tarō, whose exposé of Aum caused it such problems in 1989 and who had later suffered a stroke; this, Asahara told his disciples, was the immediate consequence of his evil attacks on the truth.[113]

Besides preaching that his immediate opponents would suffer illness and death for their sins, Asahara also emphasised and developed his earlier pronouncements about the downward pull of karma, the need to save people from falling into the hells at death and the spiritual value of killing for salvation. People who lived in the contemporary material world were, he told his disciples, abhorrent: they were greedy, ignorant and driven by base desires, and they clung on to life without realising where the karma they had acquired was going to take them.[114] Therefore they could not expect salvation and did not deserve to survive the apocalypse.[115] They were, in short, unnecessary to Aum's salvation plan, in which only select souls – those of advanced practitioners – would be able to enter the new post-apocalyptic world. In articulating these views, Asahara asked an audience of devoted followers whether they felt it was good to be propagators of a faith that sought to *poa* all spirits and send them to higher realms. With one voice they exclaimed 'yes!'[116]

Responses such as this affirm the comments made by H-san that Aum's *shukkesha* did not simply condone the concept of killing for salvation but actively and happily embraced it. They responded favourably when Asahara affirmed that the path of the *shukkesha* was the shortest and quickest route to salvation and that their role was to transform themselves into incarnations of the guru, and to 'crush the karma of all people in order to save them',[117] and when he told them that for those who had acquired bad karma, *poa* was the only way to salvation.[118] They readily embraced, also, his declarations that there was no parity in value of souls, for a true victor's was worth 1,000 or 10,000 times or even a million times that of an ordinary person's.[119] Acceptance of such a premise would lead quite logically to the acceptance of Asahara's resounding injunctions about the moral obligations of the advanced spiritual practitioner to kill ordinary people in order to save them spiritually. Repeating his assertions that anyone living in this world was accumulating bad karma and would therefore fall into the hells at death (unless, of course, they had joined Aum), Asahara told his devotees that, for every ten years someone lived in the world like this they would have to endure 1,000 million years of suffering in the hells. Therefore the quicker they left this current life (i.e. the sooner they were killed) the better it would be for them, and the less bad karma they would accumulate.[120]

In spring 1994 (the period in which the final Vajrayāna sermons were delivered) Asahara not only embellished on these themes of the need to kill (or, as he phrased it, to *poa*) all of humanity for their own good, but returned with a vengeance to the concomitant theme of karmic retribution and to the necessity of bringing death to all who oppressed Aum. Aum was being attacked by conspirators who wanted to kill him so as to remove the truth from the world and to further their plans of world domination. However, these conspirators would reap karmic retribution for their deeds. They had attacked Aum with poison gases, and these evil deeds would rebound on them, causing them to be '*poa*-ed'.[121] Since, ultimately, all who were not in Aum were parts of or complicit in the conspiracy against it, it was clear that Asahara both willed the death of all of humanity and believed that everyone in it deserved to die.

In March 1994 Asahara told his disciples that he had received a message from Shiva, informing him that the time for war had come, and that only he (Asahara) could purify this polluted world.[122] This was his mission and that of his true victors: to confront the polluted world and eradicate its evils. Fired by their karmic righteousness and spiritual superiority, Asahara and his disciples had become like the protagonists of medieval European millennialist movements described by Norman Cohn, who followed self-proclaimed charismatic messiahs who preached of apocalyptic destruction that would bring about a new and pure spiritual world. As Cohn shows, these medieval millennialists believed that they were righteously engaged in a war against the forces of evil (most commonly represented by the established churches) and, as such, considered themselves to be free from all restraints, able to kill and steal with impunity.[123]

Aum's ardent protagonists were similarly driven. Having purified their bodies and minds of the inherent pollutions of the material world through physical austerities and through taking on the mind of their guru, they could now purify humanity and eradicate the pollutions inherent in the world at large. Aum's sacred war against evil became a real one. The means with which it was to conduct this war and purify the world were the weapons that its scientists had been striving to make. It is to this final stage in Aum's violence, in which it moved from talking about sarin to using it, and to the period of chaos that ensued as Aum struck out against its (imagined) enemies and confronted the world at large, that I turn next.

戦

7 The Violence of the Lambs – Murder, Chaos, Vengeance, Power and Immortality

INTRODUCTION

As Aum became obsessed with conspiracy theories, persecution and spies, and as it developed its programme of chemical and other weapons, it issued a number of videos outlining the dilemma the movement faced. One such video reiterated the conspiracy themes outlined in Chapter 6, complaining of constant attacks on Aum using poisonous gases and of a co-ordinated campaign by the USA and its co-conspirators to subjugate Japan and to strike at Aum. It also accused the media of complicity in a vicious campaign to 'brainwash' the general public so as to allow the massive conspiracy for world government to achieve its ends. The title of the video asked whether it was time for Aum to 'fight or be destroyed'.[1] In January 1995, the mass media had hinted that Aum Shinrikyō was manufacturing sarin and that it was the culprit behind the June 1994 attack in Matsumoto. In response the movement had mounted a ferocious counter-offensive in which it complained of conspiracies against it and stated that its enemies were making 'attacks' on it using poison gases. The video Aum released at this time played on the 'lamb' imagery derived from Christianity that had previously featured in Aum's rhetoric of sacrifice, mission and persecution, by describing Aum's followers as 'slaughtered lambs' (*hofurareta kohistuji* – the title of the video itself).[2]

Despite the sacrificial imagery and complaints of persecution, however, the reality was rather different. If the 'slaughtered lambs' of the video – Aum's commune members and true victors – were being afflicted by sarin or other poisonous gases, it was because a core group of activists supervised by Murai Hideo were experimenting with and making such weapons at a secret laboratory at Kamikuishiki and because on occasion, it would appear, accidents had led to escapes of toxic substances. Rather than being 'slaughtered' by fiendish conspirators, it was the lambs themselves – or at least a dedicated number of them close to Asahara – who were at the heart of the violence surrounding Aum, and who were arming themselves with the means of mass destruction and using such weapons on their enemies, both real and imagined.

PURIFYING THE WORLD, PURIFYING THE MIND: THE CHEMICAL SOLUTION

Between spring 1993 and the subway attack two years later Aum embarked on an extraordinary campaign to arm itself and to get its hands on advanced technologies for this purpose. Its primary drive was towards chemical weapons, and it established or acquired various business companies for this purpose, using them to purchase the materials required for building laboratories and making chemical weapons. The materials were brought to Kamikuishiuki where Endō Seiichi and Tsuchiya Masami experimented and manufactured various chemical weapons, including sarin, VX gas, which was later used against a number of individual targets, and also, it would appear, cyanide and mustard gas. In addition, attempts were made to steal the blueprints for other weapons from one of Japan's leading defence contractors (Mitsubishi Heavy Industries in Hiroshima) in December 1994 and to carry out research into various other advanced weapons, including some, such as machines that could produce earthquakes, that clearly fitted with its technological and science fiction fantasies of underwater cities and astral teleporters.[3]

From spring 1994 Aum also became heavily involved in the manufacture of drugs, including amphetamines (which were used in some initiation rituals but also marketed using underworld connections to raise funds for the movement), mescaline and LSD. The latter two have been widely used by people and religious groups in the pursuit of spiritual experiences, as they were also in Aum, which turned to mescaline and LSD in its initiation rituals, as a means of opening the 'doors of perception'.[4] Their usage reflects a further step in Aum's continuing drive for new experiences and for breaking through new barriers. While many commentators regard Aum's use of drugs as indications of a concerted attempt to manipulate and control the minds of its followers,[5] it could also be seen as an indication of the desperation that had gripped Aum in the face of the approaching apocalypse, and as a further problematic extension of its belief that the mind could be liberated through overcoming the constraints of the body. Aum had, after all, experimented with, and adopted, numerous techniques that it thought could help in the pursuit of total liberation. The process of producing fully liberated beings continued to be slow, however, leading to a continuous search for new ways of breaking through to full emancipation. Aum was not the first religious group to feel that hallucinogenic drugs offered the possibility of a short-cut in this process. As with other of Aum's activities, its use of such drugs was experimental and proved costly to human life, as with, for example, the deaths that resulted from the 'Christ Initiation' in 1994.

Aum's manufacture and use of hallucinogenic drugs should also be considered, in conjunction with its manufacture of chemical weapons, as a manifestation of its interrelated views of the body and world. LSD and other such drugs that had a direct effect on the mind were utilised to provide a rapid but artificial means of attaining liberation where physical austerities and other spiritual techniques had not fully succeeded. The use of drugs to enlighten the faithful was therefore a chemical means of purification aimed at liberating the mind and overcoming the constraints of the physical world. As such it mirrored the manufacture of chemical weapons that could be used to purify the world and 'enlighten' and liberate non-believers from their delusions and transform them to another plane. The difference of course was that while the drugs were intended to enlighten and liberate the faithful *in* this body and life, chemical weapons were intended to take non-believers to higher spiritual realms by liberating them *from* their bodies.

'THE TIME HAS COME': THE NEW STATE AND THE MIND-SET FOR WAR

The work that went on at Aum's facilities, and especially at Kamikuishiki, had to be kept secret not only from the authorities but also from the Aum faithful, lest details slip out and become public knowledge. Certain areas – notably Satian 7, the building with the secret laboratory where Endō and Tsuchiya worked – were made off-limits to the ordinary *shukkesha* and to all but a select few. Those who were engaged in this 'secret work' were told to keep silent about it, and were frequently kept in the dark as to exactly what it was leading to.[6]

During this period of apparent preparation for war, contacts between Asahara and the majority of his followers decreased. He seems not to have appeared in public to give sermons to his disciples as frequently as he had done prior to spring 1994: there were, for example, no more Vajrayāna sermons after this time. Takahashi Hidetoshi has commented on the 'closed society' of the Satians, the buildings in which Asahara and the senior members of the movement lived and worked.[7] One interviewee spoke to me of how, from some point in 1994, an in-group had developed around Asahara, and of how only a small, select group of people were able to enter Satian 2 where Asahara spent most of his time. The people who did so were members of what I have previously termed Aum's 'science lobby', such as Murai and Toyoda Tōru, a young man who had studied physics at Tokyo University and who later took part in the Matsumoto and Tokyo sarin attacks.[8]

It would appear, in other words, that Asahara had surrounded himself with (or had become surrounded by) a small coterie of extremely loyal devotees who effectively ran the movement's day to day activities and schemes, and that he had become somewhat remote from his ordinary followers. This appears to be a fairly common pattern in the development of charismatic religious groups, where access to the leader empowers and elevates those who have such access, and can lead to the emergence of an elite controlling group which becomes the guru's means of communication with the movement at large.

This was the case in the Rajneesh movement, where access to Bhagwan Shree Rajneesh once the movement settled in the USA, became controlled by a small and dedicated group of senior disciples. Rajneesh was unable to speak publicly to his followers in the USA because of the status under which he had entered the USA,[9] and hence needed such disciples as intermediaries. Those who fulfilled this role, including his chief assistant Ma Anand Sheela, in turn became a dominant force in the movement, either with Rajneesh's acquiescence or perhaps, as he later alleged, by sidelining him and ruling in his name.[10]

In the Peoples Temple, too, after the move to Guyana, Jim Jones was surrounded by a powerful group of followers who constituted the de facto ruling group in the movement and who controlled access to Jones. In part this was a protective measure: due to Jones's personal debilitation because of his drug abuse, one of the motivations of the leadership circle around him was to stop him discrediting himself in front of the wider Jonestown community.[11]

In the cases of Rajneesh and Jones, the leader himself had lost a degree of power through different means – Rajneesh initially because of being unable to reach out directly to his followers, Jones due to physical and mental deterioration – and hence power passed to those around him, who, by restricting access to the guru/leader, elevated his status and hence, in effect, their own. It is unclear to what extent this happened in Aum, although the indications, from testimonies of followers at Kamikuishiki, are that from at least 1994 onwards there were similar undertones to Asahara's relationship with the small group of powerful disciples around him.

By the time Asahara had delivered his last Vajrayāna sermon in April 1994, there was clearly a sense of expectation in Aum, with ardent devotees readying themselves for the confrontation that they believed was inevitable with the authorities and the world at large. Takahashi illustrates how this sense of expectation and the mind-set for confrontation was fostered in Aum at this time, with his description of the *Vajrayāna ketsui*, a text he was told to recite repeatedly when he became a *shukkesha* in 1994. The term *ketsui* means 'resolution or determination', and in Aum it referred to texts or tapes that were recited out loud or listened to again and again in order to focus the mind on a particular vow or course of action – or, as Takahashi has subsequently claimed, to 'control the mind' of the practitioner. The *Vajrayāna ketsui* Takahashi was given to chant affirmed the determination of the practitioner to ascend to higher spiritual realms, and pledged his/her commitment to '*poa*' the forces of evil and to follow the Vajrayāna path. It also affirmed that Armageddon, as prophesied in the Bible, was close at hand and that in this final war the practitioner would without fail join the sacred army and *poa* all evil. The chant ended with the words 'to *poa* in itself is an act of salvation: to *poa* in itself is the highest virtue. And to *poa* is in itself the way to lead oneself to the highest realms'.[12]

Killing, in other words, was the means of liberation both for the killed and the killers. The recitation of such *ketsui* texts further instilled this message into the minds of the faithful, and aroused in them expectations and hopes of the approaching battle when they would be able to fulfil their salvation mission by fighting for the truth and killing the forces of evil.

Although Aum's rupture with mainstream society had effectively come several years earlier, when it had placed itself and its mission above the law by disposing of the body of Majima, it was in June 1994 that Aum took an important symbolic step which signified its final break with Japanese society. It announced that it was setting up its own government in order to prepare for Armageddon and protect itself against the attacks it faced from conspiratorial forces. With this 'alternative government', which had 22 ministries and placed Asahara at its apex with the title of 'sacred master/emperor' (*shinsei hōō*), Aum was declaring itself to be a separate entity that existed independent of the Japanese state and society. It was a state within a state, subject only to its own laws, and it had seceded from and existed in open opposition to that of Japan.

This pattern of withdrawal from the remit of the secular state or of creating a de facto independent entity that is set apart from the society and state within which it is located, has occurred amongst other of the religious movements mentioned in this book. As John R. Hall has commented, Jim Jones of the Peoples Temple and David Koresh of the Branch Davidians at Waco had each established 'what amounted to a state within a state', in the one case that of Jonestown, the community Jones developed in the remote jungle of Guyana, in the other of Mount Carmel, Koresh's 'tiny principality' (as Hall termed it) in Texas.[13] In developing these seemingly independent entities, Koresh's and Jones's movements, according to Hall, displayed a refusal to submit to external authority which, they believed, was intent on destroying them, and both prepared for 'militant armed struggle' with those forces.[14]

While similar motifs are visible in Aum's rejection of external authority and its preparations for an armed struggle, Aum was perhaps unique in its overt declaration of such a 'government' complete with formal titles (which, as I have stated elsewhere, further reflected the grandiosity of Asahara and his disciples).[15] What also marked out Aum's declaration of its own government was what accompanied it: the Matsumoto sarin gas attack of 27 June 1994 which has been described as the 'new nation's first act of war'[16] in which the movement made a murderous attack on the general public and on officials (three judges who were officiating in a case involving Aum) of the Japanese state. The heightened sense of expectation and of imminent confrontation that followed the formation of its government and the Matsumoto attack, appears to have been reflected in the comment that Murai Hideo made to Takahashi Hidetoshi shortly after, in August 1994, when he told Takahashi that the time for confrontation with the police was at hand.[17]

DEATH AND DESPAIR: THE GURU IN TURMOIL

The implication as outlined above and in the previous chapter is that Aum was thoroughly geared up for a final confrontation and that it was marching in a direct and co-ordinated way towards the millennium and the expected triumph of good over evil and of the sacred hero/master and his true victors over the corrupt world. Certainly some of Aum's activities – the schemes to acquire chemicals, the singular manner in which disciples' minds were turned towards the inevitability of conflict and final war, and even the organisational structure of its 'alternative government' – hint at this, and also give the impression of efficient organisation. This image has been developed also by some of the more sensational accounts of the affair, in which the participants in Aum's weapons' schemes have been depicted as brilliant scientists and dark geniuses capable of destroying the world and making all manner of extraordinarily high-tech weapons.[18]

While such a portrayal, especially when coupled with the image of the sacred master/evil genius guiding the enterprise, makes a good story, heightening the terror and danger that the movement posed, it is not, however, particularly accurate. The reality is that, at the time when his movement was taking the steps to arm itself for war and confrontation, Asahara appeared – at least insofar as the contents of the later Vajrayāna sermons indicate – to have become increasingly disjointed in his thoughts, displaying a more and more tenuous grasp on external realities, and being ever more obsessed with conspiracy theories, death, destruction and despair. Moreover, the movement itself and the commune at Kamikuishiki were in a state of some chaos, with evidence of large-scale disorganisation, decisions made and changed at whim, of resources thrown into projects that failed to work, and of incompetently run experiments which caused poisonous gases to escape and injure the faithful. This organisational chaos was mirrored by growing internal paranoia as the movement as a whole became convinced that it was being attacked and that a final war was at hand, and by a reign of fear in which Aum sought out the 'spies' that it believed were in its midst. At the same time, the chaos and the internal violence that erupted within the movement from around summer 1993 onwards, when those who wanted to quit were forced to remain members, and when anyone who did leave was forcibly 'rescued' and brought back to Kamikuishiki, also provoked many others into wanting to escape the confines of a movement that they could clearly see was disintegrating. It led also to warnings from people inside the movement and from outside observers that Aum was spinning out of control.[19]

The contents of Asahara's later sermons indicate a desperate and destructive mood rather than the focused calculations of an evil genius plotting to take over the world. His recurrent references to exhaustion and illness, and his uncertainty about whether Aum's spiritually gifted practitioners could or would survive the cataclysm, indicate rather different priorities and concerns. In the final few Vajrayāna sermons in March and April 1994 the images of death, destruction and gloom are paramount, as Asahara turned to Hindu notions relating to the final age. We are living, he declared, in the *Kali Yuga*, the final era in Hindu thought, in which evil karma abounds and in which all who dwell in this world are dragged spiritually downwards. The despair that this thought brings is evident in the final words of the final Vajrayāna sermon:

People die. They die without fail. One cannot escape death. And I think that our approach to death is in itself the highest challenge to us as living human beings and indeed is the highest way of living our lives. I pray that you, while living in this world, do not breathe in the poisons of the *Kali yuga* and do not fall into the three evil hells.[20]

These, one should emphasise, are the concluding words of Asahara's most central and seminal teachings that were required reading for his most devout disciples. Here one finds none of his earlier assertions that through practice the elite will transcend the boundaries of this world, avoid death at Armageddon and enter higher realms. At this stage, it appears, there is no real message of potential salvation: all Asahara appears able to offer is the hope that his disciples will not fall into the hells. The inevitability of doom and destruction, of the downward pull of karma and the hells, the desperate yearnings for survival manifest in his fantasy schemes, and the feeling that at some stage Aum must fight against the authorities, appear to be all that was left in this escalating sense of doom and darkness. This bleakness, accompanied as it was by fantasies and speculations about weapons and the nature and means of destruction, by Asahara's allegations of attacks on and conspiracies against Aum, and by his growing paranoia about spies in Aum's midst, is indicative, in my view, of a process of mental disturbance and instability, and of a slide towards despair.

CHAOS, PARANOIA AND FEAR: ACCIDENTS, INCOMPETENCE AND VIOLENCE IN A MOVEMENT AT WAR

Asahara's later pessimistic sermons do not appear to illustrate the workings of a calculating mind with a plan to take over Japan. Nor do the actions of Aum in this period suggest that it was capable of anything remotely approaching a coup. My account of the earlier stages of Aum's development – from the amateurish failure to produce delivery systems for its biological weapons, to the signs left at the scenes of its crimes (such as Nakagawa's dropped badge at the Sakamoto abduction site) – does not indicate any degree of professionalism in Aum's activities. The signs are that matters had become more chaotic still as Aum engaged in making chemical weapons.

All the evidence suggests that on a number of occasions its experiments went wrong. An incident at Aum's centre in Kameido in Tokyo, in July 1993, when foul-smelling odours emitted from the building, arousing grave suspicions among the local populace, appears to be one such example, as was the escape of poisonous gases at Kamikuishiki in July 1994, shortly after Aum had carried out the sarin attack at Matsumoto. Asahara's complaints in various sermons about being attacked by sarin, and his reporting of how followers had died at Aum centres as a result, appear to be stories designed to cover up actual gas escapes that probably resulted from incompetently run experiments.[21]

Aum's scientists and technological experts proved inept not only in their experiments but in the mechanisms they developed in order to deliver the weapons they had made. All the various spraying devices bar one that they made, starting with the attempted botulism attack of spring 1990, failed to work properly. The only such system that appears to have met with any success was that used in Matsumoto, which required the customisation of a refrigerated truck, and this produced numerous problems and did not work exactly as planned.[22] Eventually, unable to produce a functioning delivery system, Aum had to resort to sharpened umbrellas and plastic bags of liquid sarin when it carried out the subway attack.

Takahashi Hidetoshi, who in 1994 was assigned to work under the direction of Murai Hideo in Aum's Science and Technology section, draws a picture of chaotic disorganisation in the commune, of resources being poured with little seeming logic into particular projects that were then rapidly abandoned in favour of other, newer (and often more extraordinary) ones. He also felt that the facilities in which people were working were dirty and badly organised, and proposed to Murai that things would be more efficient if some steps at reorganisation were to be taken. Murai, however, declined, stating that Aum was besieged by enemies and spies and that any attempt to co-ordinate the organisation better would allow such spies to gather their data more easily.[23]

If disorganisation and chaos were characteristics of Aum in the period from 1993 to 1995, so were paranoia and internal violence. Takahashi's account depicts a movement enveloped in the paranoia of conspiracy: the main talk at the commune by 1994, he reports, was of the conspiracy against Aum, and the hostile intentions of the US Army, the Freemasons and their agents.[24] Kashima Tomoko's account, too, shows similar feelings, and indicates that her belief in the conspiracy was very real.[25]

In this climate of fear and suspicion, violence began to be used against suspect followers at the commune, who were accused of spying or who, because they either indicated that they wanted to leave or took steps to do so, became immediately suspect. The movement was unable to let them go, partly because it feared internal collapse as a result of mass defections, partly because it needed to 'rescue' such dissidents from the terrible fates that awaited them if they bowed to their folly and left the truth, and partly because of fears that they would pass on negative information about Aum to the outside world. As we saw with Ochi Naoki and the 'spy' who were mentioned in Chapter 1, such suspicions could lead to punishment and death. Takahashi, like other commune members, was well aware of what was going on: spy checks became the norm in the summer of 1994, and these increased a lack of trust between the commune members, who suspected each other of perhaps being a spy planted by Aum's enemies. Takahashi shows, too, that he and the other *shukkesha* at Kamikuishiki knew full well that dissident members who had been caught trying to leave were incarcerated in cargo containers at the commune as a punishment.[26] Former members have testified to this culture of violence and to the punishments they received in such circumstances: for example, Murakami Eiko, a 30-year-old *shukkesha*, has given a witness statement of how she was shut inside a container, forced to fast and then to endure upside-down suspension and beating with a stick as punishment for leaving the commune.[27]

Although coercion and internal violence had been part of Aum's dynamic at earlier stages, a rapid escalation of aggression and punishment took place in mid-1993 (when Ochi was killed) which soon developed into a culture of physical intimidation at the commune. Such internalised violence in closed religious communities that are at odds with the world at large was not unique to Aum; indeed, it became a feature of life at the Rajneesh commune in Oregon as it became embroiled in tensions and external conflicts. Similarly, as Rebecca Moore has demonstrated, violence within the movement was an important element in the life of the Peoples Temple at Jonestown, especially in the period leading up to the mass suicide. As pressures increased on the commune, dissent mounted: so too did repression and internally directed violence. Dissidents were sent to Jonestown's 'Special Care Unit' where they were locked up, sedated, shackled with chains, and confined in coffin-like containers. Beatings and public humiliation sessions were also used regularly against potentially dissident members, who were also threatened in private. Moore shows that, while in the Peoples Temple violence operated as a means of social control, it also created and strengthened bonds within the movement. The shared suffering of the community, while it led to some followers becoming alienated and wanting to leave, in general drew the movement closer together. As Moore puts it, violence in the Peoples Temple (which included not only beatings and other disciplinary actions but participation in the movement's common rituals such as the suicide drills the movement conducted) was part of the glue that held the community together.[28]

The increase in internal violence appears, in all these groups (Rajneesh, Aum and the Peoples Temple) to be a response to (perceived) external threats to the group and to fears of internal collapse. Such fears increased the doubts of the leaders about the 'purity' of their followers' thoughts and led them to suspect them and demand greater displays of loyalty from them. By participating or passively acquiescing in the violence being meted out to colleagues, group members demonstrated their faith and their commitment to the cause. In Aum the defectors and 'spies' were seen as being complicit in the conspiracies against Aum, hence they *needed* to be punished for their sins. It appears that the *shukkesha* at Kamikuishiki who knew that recalcitrant members were being locked up in containers or severely punished, were able to go along with these punishments not so much because they feared what would happen if they opposed it, but because it appeared, within the confines of a group under (so they believed) immense external pressure, to be the correct thing to do.

EXTERNAL VIOLENCE: ATTACKING THE ENEMIES OF TRUTH

Aum's violence, held in check for a number of years since the murder of the Sakamoto family and the failed botulism attack of 1990, manifested itself also in a series of externally directed attacks in this period. While the victims inside the movement were those suspected of having weak faith (a crime which implicitly suggested a challenge to the guru's authority and a lack of absolute obedience), those who were attacked outside the movement were people who made complaints or campaigned against Aum, or who had displeased Asahara in some way and posed apparent threats to his status and authority. Amongst those on the receiving end of such attacks was Takimoto Tarō, whose campaigns against Aum have been mentioned in earlier chapters and who had, in 1993, begun a counselling service for defecting members of Aum. He was poisoned (but survived) when sarin was placed in his car by an Aum devotee in May 1994 after Asahara and his advisors decided that he was a problem that had to be removed.[29] Hamaguchi Takahito, a man in his late twenties who had visited Aum centres and was suspected of being a spy, was murdered by Niimi using VX gas in Osaka in December 1994,[30] while Nagaoka Hiroyuki of the Aum Victims' Society survived a similar attack a month later in January 1995. Others against whom attacks were planned or carried out unsuccessfully included the anti-Aum journalist Egawa Shōko, and two religious leaders Ōkawa Ryûhō of Kōfuku no Kagaku and Ikeda Daisaku of Sōka Gakkai.

That Aum planned to assassinate Ōkawa and Ikeda[31] says much about Asahara's state of mind and attitudes. Ōkawa and Ikeda both represented something that Asahara clearly wanted but had not managed to attain: they were leaders of religious movements that were large and more successful than Aum, and whose teachings and aims appeared to challenge Asahara and Aum in terms of their self-projected images as Buddhist movements.

While Asahara proclaimed his movement as encapsulating the spirit of true Buddhism and portrayed himself as the only wholly enlightened and liberated being in Japan, Ōkawa not only publicly criticised Asahara and Aum but declared himself to be the 'eternal Buddha'.[32] Kōfuku no Kagaku and Aum had a history of hostility and rivalry which came about because, although they were very different in terms of membership structures and practices, both had emerged from a similar cultural milieu and appeared to be competing for a similar type of follower among the educated young urban elite. Although very different in ambience – with Aum's world-rejecting stance and focus on withdrawal and asceticism contrasting with Kōfuku's far more world-affirming focus on living in society and its lack of emphasis on asceticism – there were numerous similarities in the teachings, particularly in such areas as their conceptions of different spiritual realms and rebirths and their emphases on their leader as a saviour figure and their followers as a new spiritual elite for a new age. Both had similarly dramatic millennial visions and apocalyptic themes in their teachings and had produced their own interpretations of the prophecies of Nostradamus.

It was perhaps unsurprising, then, that rivalry and conflict would develop between two movements each proclaiming themselves as holding the key to salvation and their leader as the coming saviour. It was also perhaps unsurprising that the less successful of the two should become consumed with resentment towards the other. In contrast to Aum, Kōfuku no Kagaku had experienced large-scale growth in the early 1990s, at a time when both movements had mounted campaigns to gather new followers.[33] It appears that Ōkawa's status as a seemingly more successful rival (and one who, in Aum's eyes, committed such unpardonable heresies as making claims that contradicted Asahara's standing as the only en-lightened being in Japan) made him not simply the focus of immense animosity on Asahara's part but also a potential target for assassination.

Asahara's resentment of Ikeda Daisaku culminated in an assassination plan in December 1993. Even more than Ōkawa, Ikeda represented what Asahara aspired to be. He was the leader of the biggest new religion in Japan, which published Japan's third largest newspaper, ran a university, and had established a successful political party which had become the third largest in Japan. Moreover, the orientations of his movement were almost diametrically opposite to those of Aum. Like Aum, Sōka Gakkai argued that all other religions were false and claimed it alone possessed the truth. In contrast to Aum, however, Sōka Gakkai had a strong world-affirming ethic, emphasising the importance of lay life, and its members regarded their personal development and success in the world as products of their religious practice. Originally a lay branch of the Nichiren Shōshū Buddhist sect, it had seceded in the early 1990s and, when it did so, launched a campaign to develop what it viewed as a new, lay-centred Buddhism for the modern age. As such it posited itself as being the future face of Japanese Buddhism. Sōka Gakkai, then, appeared to be another rival to Aum's claims of leadership in the development of a new age of Buddhism in Japan.[34]

It was, however, when Kōmeitō, the political party originally established by Sōka Gakkai, became a coalition partner in the Japanese government after elections in 1993 – a success that put Aum's catastrophic political failure into stark relief – that Asahara became unable to refrain from expressing his sentiments in public. In the Vajrayāna sermons from autumn 1993 onwards he denounced Sōka Gakkai and Ikeda repeatedly as pernicious influences on the Japanese government.[35] Asahara appeared so angry at Sōka Gakkai's success at this time that he even visualised a special hell for members of Sōka Gakkai, which he termed the Lotus Hell (after the Lotus Sutra, the text which the movement regarded as the supreme teaching of Buddhism and as the embodiment of truth) into which Sōka Gakkai followers would fall because of their karmic sins and where they would endure suffering and torment because of their heretical faith.[36] He also added Sōka Gakkai and Ikeda to the list of conspirators working against Aum.[37]

This feeling of anger and resentment towards more successful rivals who, Asahara believed, had used duplicitous means to captivate followers with untruths, tells us much about Asahara. Incapable of accepting that other religious leaders with other points of view could attract followers, he clearly saw their success as a slight on himself. Moreover, as peddlers of falsehoods (as he saw it) they deserved to be punished, just as the deluded faithful of Sōka Gakkai merited the hells for which they were destined. Consequently Ōkawa and Ikeda were included in Aum's growing list of enemies and became the target of its murderous plans.

MATSUMOTO, 27 JUNE 1994

Aum also extended its murderous activities beyond attacks on individuals. On the evening of 27 June 1994 a group of devotees including Murai, Nakagawa Tomomasa and Toyoda Tōru, drove a specially converted refrigerated truck to the town of Matsumoto in central Japan, where they released a quantity of sarin. This attack – the first use of chemical weapons on a population by a non-state organisation – marked a radical shift from individual and directed acts of violence and terror, to more indiscriminate ones in which Aum was prepared to use the weapons at its disposal against the general public.

The immediate aims of the attack were related to a court case involving Aum. The case itself was typical, involving Aum's acquisition of land on which it intended to build a centre. As at Namino it had kept its name secret when it originally acquired the land, purchasing it through one of its dummy companies, ostensibly to build a food plant. When it transpired that the purchaser was Aum and that it was building a meditation and religious centre on the land, the vendor went to court, seeking to have the sale annulled. There was immense opposition to the centre also from the local civil authorities and the populace in general, and it became yet another focus of contention between Aum and the wider world.

The judges in the ensuing court case were about to pass judgment, and Asahara had been informed by Aum's lawyers that the verdict was likely to be unfavourable, resulting in the loss of the Matsumoto training centre. The attack was therefore ordered as a means of stopping this happening by incapacitating the judges and preventing them from delivering their verdict. In this Aum were at least temporarily successful. The van was parked near the place where the judges were staying and a cloud of sarin pumped out, eventually killing seven people and injuring hundreds more, including the judges who, as a result, were unable to attend court and deliver their verdict.

Besides the immediate aim of neutralising the judges, one further reason has been put forward for the Matsumoto attack. One chemical warfare specialist speculated that it looked like a trial run for a much bigger operation such as an attack on Tokyo.[38] There was, however, a further reason for the attack, and one that had a similar resonance to the attacks on various individuals outlined above: besides the pragmatic aim of blocking a court verdict, the attack also sought to defend the veracity of Asahara's prophecies, to defend his reputation against the apparent challenge that would occur if the judges returned an unfavourable verdict, and to punish the judges and the citizens of Matsumoto for having opposed Aum.

The clues that point to these motives can be found in the text of a sermon that Asahara delivered at the recently opened Matsumoto centre on 18 December 1992. Many of the themes in this sermon reiterated other such sermons in this period, such as the imminence of war and the conspiratorial manipulations of groups such as the Freemasons and the Jews. However, this particular sermon had a different tenor to it in that Asahara appeared relatively optimistic about the future. He returned to a theme that he had not articulated for some years, by claiming that Aum could achieve universal salvation. Although he complained about the oppression and harassment it suffered, he declared that Aum was committed to its task and that it was on the verge of making a dramatic breakthrough and attaining immense growth in the coming year, 1993.

He linked this prediction of future success directly to the new centre in Matsumoto, which he elevated into a symbol of Aum's status and success in its mission. The original plan, he stated, had been to make the centre three times larger than it was. However, due to the duplicitous activities of the landowner, the courts and the local Matsumoto author-ities, who had lied, refused to provide proper water supplies and so on, this plan had been blocked. Nevertheless, the centre had been built, and this showed that, no matter what obstacles Aum faced, they would be overcome and that Aum would triumph in the end and accomplish its mission. Its completion was a validation of Aum's truth and of the eventual triumph of Aum's teaching, and from the centre Aum's truths and teachings would spread throughout the region and lead many people to salvation. In making this prophecy of eventual triumph, Asahara thus drew a direct symbolic link between the success of the Matsumoto branch of Aum and that of Aum itself.[39]

The fact that Aum's ownership of the land was going to be brought into question by the judges in the case fitted with another of the themes in this sermon. Nostradamus, Asahara stated, had prophesied that in the final age the judiciary would get out of control and be unable to distinguish between right and wrong.[40] In a sense, then, the judgement that was about to be delivered, since it was reportedly going to go against Aum, could be seen as a sign that the judiciary had got out of control and had become unable to see right from wrong: in Asahara's logic, of course, the right decision would naturally have favoured Aum. It was a sign, in other words, that the prophesied end-time was at hand.

Asahara's affirmations of a bright future for Aum and for the Matsu-moto centre had, by mid-1994, come to look distinctly problematic. The predicted rapid growth had not materialised, while the very symbol that indicated why Aum would triumph, the Matsumoto centre, was under threat from a judiciary that was clearly incapable, in this current age, of seeing right from wrong. Thus, I would suggest, the judges at Matsumoto had to be silenced in order to block a judgment that would have invalidated Asahara's prophecies. In his sermon in 1992 Asahara had invested immense symbolic capital in the continuing existence of the Matsumoto centre. The judges had to be neutralised not just because their judgment would have hampered Aum on the practical level of depriving it of a training centre but also, and perhaps more significantly, it would have been a direct challenge to Asahara's spiritual authority and his powers of prophetic vision.

FROM MATSUMOTO TO KASUMIGASEKI AND X-DAY

The general details of the period from the Matsumoto attack to 20 March 1995 and the attack on the Tokyo subway, through to what became known in Japan as 'X-Day', 16 May, when Asahara was finally arrested, have been widely recounted in the media and elsewhere, and so I shall just run through them briefly here. At first the local police in Matsumoto appeared incapable of understanding what had happened: a chemical weapons attack in a relatively small and quiet Japanese town known as a historic and tourist centre in the Japanese Alps with one of the finest castles in Japan seemed beyond the bounds of comprehension. The police appeared incapable of even conceptualising the event as a deliberate act of terrorism or mass murder, and their first step was to blame a local man, Kōno Yoshiyuki, whose wife was severely injured in the attack and near whose house the gas cloud had first appeared. According to the police, Kōno had accidentally created the poisonous gases while mixing fertilisers in his garden. Many in the press leapt upon this allegation and ran stories about Kōno's guilt, and he was not officially exonerated until after Aum members had confessed in summer 1995 to the attack. Nor did he receive any apology from the police or press for their disgraceful and incompetent behaviour until well afterwards.

A number of journalists, however, were sceptical of this 'accidental' explanation and realised that a poison such as sarin could not have been made by mistake. Various writers with scientific knowledge spoke out about what they saw as an erroneous police judgment. Shimosato Masaaki, for example, argued that Kōno did not have the means or the chemicals to manufacture sarin, and that the attack had to have been deliberate, carried out by an organisation with adequate resources to develop a chemical weapons programme and a sufficient motive and mind-set to carry it out.[41]

Aum's obsession with sarin, its link to Matsumoto through the court case and the controversy surrounding its centre, its rhetoric of fighting

211

and its reputation as a movement widely believed to have committed previous illegal acts, made it an obvious suspect for those who were not convinced by the accusation against Kōno. Because of the complaints that had been made against Aum in connection with the noxious fumes that had emanated from its facilities in Tokyo and Kamikuishiki, it clearly ought to have been a potential suspect in the case, a point further emphasised when on 9 July 1994, two weeks after the attack, villagers at Kamikuishiki saw a number of people in laboratory clothing and wearing gas-masks, fleeing from a building at the commune. At the same time they detected a foul smell in the air, and shortly afterwards noticed that the surrounding vegetation had been damaged and showed signs of having been affected by poisonous chemicals.

When confronted by the villagers and members of the media, Aum's spokespeople claimed that the damage had been caused by sarin dropped on to its commune by its opponents – a defence that hardly sounded convincing to any save the members of the commune who believed in Asahara's prophecies and his conspiracy theories. The direct link between Aum and Matsumoto was verified in November 1994 when police analysis of the samples taken from around Aum's compound showed the presence of sarin.

However, the police remained extremely reluctant to move on the matter. No clear reason has emerged as to why the police continued to display such reluctance to investigate a movement that appeared to have done everything it possibly could to make itself a prime suspect in the affair. The most likely possibility was that, since Aum was a registered religious organisation with extremely militant tendencies that readily complained of persecution and resorted to lawsuits whenever challenged, the police were fearful of making mistakes or leaving themselves open to the charge of interfering with religious freedoms – a delicate subject given the ways in which religious liberties had been trampled on in 1930s and early 1940s, when the police served as instruments of the fascist state in investigating potentially deviant organisations such as religious movements.

The story, however, soon entered the public domain. On 1 January 1995 the *Yomiuri Shinbun*, Japan's biggest newspaper, carried a story stating that the substance that had damaged vegetation at Kamikuishiki in July 1994 had been sarin, the substance used in the Matsumoto poisonings, and that the police were looking at possible links between the two incidents. For those who did not make the immediate connection with Aum, another national newspaper, the *Asahi Shinbun*, followed up with an article stating that Kamikuishiki, where the gas traces that were linked to the Matsumoto attack had been found, was where the controversial religious movement Aum Shinrikyō had a commune.

Aum responded in typical style: besides issuing writs for libel against the *Asahi Shinbun,* it claimed that a local factory (which had been the focus of some local complaints about environmental pollution) had been the source of the sarin and accused its owner of using it against Aum. The sarin which the movement had stockpiled was disposed of (although a small quantity was hidden for later use), its equipment removed, and Satian 7 was rapidly transformed into a temple complete with a large statue of Shiva. The academic Shimada Hiromi, who had spoken up on behalf of Aum previously, was invited to the new temple, and he supported the movement in its denials. According to Shimada, Satian 7 was not a plant for making sarin and Aum was not responsible for the Matsumoto attack. Rather, it had been set up by someone else to take the blame for this and other incidents. Shimada's folly, which came about because he did not investigate the new temple properly and because he had naïvely trusted his informants in Aum, was to cause him much trouble later, as he was publicly castigated after the subway attack by the mass media and by many critics, including academic colleagues, and was eventually forced to resign from his position at his university.[42]

Despite Aum's attempted cover-up, there was a widespread assumption that before long the police would begin a proper investigation of the movement. The novelist Murakami Haruki, who had only recently returned to Japan after a long period overseas, records that in early spring 1995 Aum's activities were widely discussed among the people he knew in Japan and that their general assumption was that the movement had been involved in nefarious activities.[43] The journalist Shimosato Masaaki has also stated that there was a general expectation from the beginning of January 1995 that police raids on Aum were inevitable and imminent.[44]

Despite being under such suspicion and despite the obvious need to maintain the façade of innocence, Aum was incapable of maintaining a low profile or eschewing its aggressive activities for long. On the day (4 January 1995) when it launched its defence against the articles linking it to the Matsumoto attack, Niimi Tomomitsu attacked the head of the Aum Victims' Society, Nagaoka Hiroyuki, in Osaka using VX gas. Nagaoka was injured but survived. On 28 February 1995 Aum conducted an even more brazen crime, seizing and abducting Kariya Kiyoshi, a 68-year-old public notary, from a street in Tokyo in broad daylight. Kariya clearly feared such an attack because he had previously left a message for his son saying if anything happened to him Aum would be to blame. It had been his dispute with Aum concerning the whereabouts of his wealthy sister – an Aum devotee who had left the movement and gone into hiding because of the financial demands the movement made on her – which had prompted this fear. Aum's leaders saw the sister as a continuing source of money that could help finance their costly activities, and they wanted her back. They had abducted Kariya because they thought he knew where she was, and he died as a result of the maltreatment he received when Hayashi Ikuo and Nakagawa Tomomasa attempted to extract this information from him.

This particular atrocity, at a time when so much suspicion was already directed at Aum, shows that the movement had lost all semblance of control over its actions. The Kariya abduction was the catalyst that brought the forces of law down upon Aum. The kidnapping on a city street had been seen by members of the public, and a witness had taken the number-plate of the van that was used, which was traced to the Aum follower who had rented it. The mass media widely reported the kidnap and informed the public that Kariya had been in dispute with a religious organisation at the time of the abduction. In case the general public had not understood which organisation this was, members of Kōfuku no Kagaku held public rallies demanding that Aum Shinrikyō release Kariya.[45]

The police could hardly hold off any longer, and it is clear that, by the middle of March 1995, preparations for a massive raid were under way as the police acquired various items of equipment, including gas-masks, for this task. The news leaked out that a raid would occur on or around 20 March: the kidnap of Kariya was the reason given, and the warrant was ostensibly to search for his whereabouts. The leaking of the news about the raid was probably the fault of the police, who appear to have briefed various news agencies so as to gain media coverage when they moved in on Aum.[46]

On Saturday 18 March, it appears that Aum's leaders found out about the raid and immediately prepared to head it off by a pre-emptive strike.[47] Although Asahara ordered the attack, the general assumption among the perpetrators is that Murai Hideo was the primary force in its planning.[48] Endō was ordered to make a new batch of sarin, which he did using the materials hidden in January 1995. The plan was to attack the subway in the rush-hour of Monday morning, 20 March, by releasing sarin on trains converging on Kasumigaseki station, the nerve-centre serving numerous government and public offices including the National Police Agency's headquarters. Endō had 36 hours to refine the sarin, which he was unable to do, managing to get it to only 30 per cent pure. The liquid sarin was then sealed in a number of plastic bags and wrapped in newspapers.

The inability of Aum's technologists to produce a reliable mechanism capable of spraying sarin effectively meant that a crude and simple means was chosen on this occasion. Inoue Yoshihiro, who helped co-ordinate the operation, purchased a number of cheap umbrellas and had their metal points sharpened. Five Aum disciples each carrying an antidote to the sarin in case of accidents, took the bags of sarin and an umbrella and boarded different trains that were all timed to converge at or around Kasumigaseki at approximately 8.30 a.m. Each placed their bags of sarin on the floor of their respective trains and, at approximately the same time, stabbed them with their umbrellas, releasing the poisonous liquid which vaporised into gases that wreaked havoc through the trains and subway system. The attackers themselves alighted before the effects could be felt and made their escape.

Twelve people died and thousands were injured. The media were quickly on the scene, transmitting pictures of the horror that had been caused. Images of the survivors emerging from the subway gasping and choking, and of victims being stretchered away, were broadcast across the world. Aum came under immediate suspicion, especially when hospital reports on the victims quickly identified sarin as the cause of their sickness.

Within hours the attack was unofficially attributed to Aum and by the early morning of 22 March, when massive numbers of police carrying batons and wearing gas-masks, and some carrying canaries in cages, marched under media spotlights into the commune at Kamikuishiki and other Aum premises throughout the country, everyone in Japan, apart from Aum's own members, was certain who was responsible. Asahara himself went into hiding, while his followers strenuously denied any wrongdoing and complained about police intrusion and persecution. Murai Hideo and Jōyu Fumihiro led the Aum response, handling questions from the media calmly and maintaining a blanket denial of culpability, while Aum rushed out magazines and leaflets claiming that the subway attack and the raids were parts of the fiendish conspiracy against Aum.[49]

Gradually the façade of denial cracked. The raids uncovered a great deal of evidence linking Aum to the production of chemical weapons, while gradually Aum followers who had been taken into police detention began to confess to various illegal activities. The news in the spring and early summer of 1995 was dominated by the affair. This was not only because of the numerous stories and rumours that emerged out of the police investigations but also because, after the subway attack, a number of other violent incidents took place that seem to have been carried out by Aum followers such as Inoue Yoshihiro who had evaded arrest. There were a number of unsuccessful attempts to release poisonous gases on other commuter trains in the Tokyo region, and an attempt that was only just foiled to release cyanide gas into the ventilation system at Shinjuku station, the busiest in the Tokyo area, on 5 May 1995.[50] In addition, Kunimatsu Takaji, the head of the National Police Agency, was shot, although not killed, outside his apartment on 30 March in an attack reputedly linked to Aum. On 23 April 1995, Murai Hideo, who had remained free although clearly a target of the police investigations, was stabbed to death in public as he made his way through a crowd of journalists outside Aum's main Tokyo office. The murder occurred in front of television cameras which continued recording as Murai fell dying, and his very public death, broadcast across the country on television news programmes, became another visible sign of the cycle of violence surrounding Aum.

The killer was a Korean resident of Japan who belonged to a *yakuza* (gangster) organisation and who has subsequently been given a 12 year prison sentence for the murder. Although no definitive motive has been deduced for this killing, the rumours that abounded afterwards suggested Murai had been killed either in an Aum-sponsored hit because he knew so much about Aum's crimes and other leaders feared that he was about to confess everything to the police, or that it was a murder ordered by the *yakuza* to cover up its dealings with Aum, from whom it had bought drugs.

During the late spring of 1995 perhaps the biggest question in the media was the whereabouts of Asahara himself, and there was much speculation about when 'X-Day' – the term given by the media to the day when the police would finally discover and arrest Asahara – would happen. It was clear in retrospect that the police were aware that Asahara was at Kamikuishiki and that they were waiting until enough evidence existed to arrest him on charges of murder that would stand up in court. In addition, there were fears that close disciples such as Inoue and Nakagawa, who were still unaccounted for, might attempt something desperate if their guru were arrested. Inoue was finally captured on 15 May and the next day the police conducted further raids at Kamikuishiki. They knew where to look, entering Satian 6, where they found Asahara in a concealed room. He was arrested and charged with murder and conspiracy to commit murder, and brought to Tokyo in a convoy of vehicles, amidst massive media coverage. On the same day a letter bomb posted to the Tokyo Governor's office exploded, injuring an aide. It appeared to be virtually the last of the acts of violence conducted by members of Aum.

INTENTIONS, SCHEMES AND PATTERNS OF VIOLENCE

It is generally accepted that the 20 March subway attack was an ad hoc action intended to prevent or disrupt the impending police raids on Aum. Although the attack was thus carried out in 'defence' of Aum's mission – a motive that underpinned many of its earlier atrocities such as the murders of Taguchi and the Sakamotos – it was readily assumed in Japan that it was also a stage in a wider scheme. Combining Asahara's recurrent sermons about Armageddon and conflict, his formation of an alternative government and the obvious ambitions that were reflected in his earlier election campaign and assumption of a quasi-imperial title, it was widely rumoured that Aum's ultimate plans were for a coup d'état. Hayakawa Kiyohide was in possession of notebooks which contained jottings in which he had mused or fantasised about the possibility of acquiring nuclear warheads in Russia, and about carrying out a coup in November 1995 in which Aum would attack Tokyo with sarin and assault troops.[51] Media reports in 1995, too, spoke of a plot to drop sarin on the city from a helicopter Aum had acquired from Russia.[52] When, in a court statement in October 1995, Inoue Yoshihiro referred to the willingness of disciples to sacrifice themselves so that Asahara's plan of salvation could be realised and Japan awakened to the truth, he appeared to confirm a grand co-ordinated design of some sort in which Aum saw the use of violence as a way of carrying out its mission to produce a new spiritual age or to seize control of society.[53]

Much, if not all, of this was fanciful thinking. Hayakawa's journal musings appear to be little more than further extensions of the techno-logical and science fiction fantasy world in which Aum's senior ranks appeared to live. Aum – as the descriptions of its incompetence and organisational chaos outlined earlier in this chapter illustrate – can hardly be considered to have had either the ability or the capacity to engineer anything approaching these scenarios. One can hardly envisage coups or similar actions being carried out with sharpened umbrellas and plastic bags of poison. Even the helicopter that was supposedly going to drop the sarin on Tokyo was in such poor condition that it could not fly, and hence the purported sarin attack of November 1995 would have been impossible.

Nevertheless, such was Aum's reputation in summer 1995 that stories like this were readily believed. Certainly the underlying justifications and the doctrinal stance for such a course of action existed in Aum, and had been expressed by Asahara and readily embraced by his close disciples. Asahara had told them that the mass of humanity was unworthy of salvation and deserved to die, while an apocalypse was inevitable and to be desired. Doctrinal stances centred on the notions of karma and *poa*, which had initially provided the justification for violence on an individual level, had become extended to society as a whole. Asahara's accusations about the massive conspiracy that was intent on destroying Aum and subjugating the world had further developed this doctrinal position, and had created a 'logic' for the manufacture of weapons capable of destroying vast numbers of people and fighting a sacred war.

However, although Asahara willed some form of massive destruction, there is little evidence of a co-ordinated or coherent plan of such a sort. Nor were there any indications that the subway attack was part of a strategy to spread turmoil so as to make it appear that Asahara's prophecies were coming true, or in order to precipitate the final war and the millennial scenario that was, in his prophetic view, 'inevitable'. Suggestions along these lines have been made by several commentators in the aftermath of the affair, and in my earlier book on Aum I also came to that conclusion.[54]

It is, however, a line of analysis with which I no longer feel comfortable. Although there was a continuing dynamic of violence in Aum, it was neither co-ordinated nor focused in any way that indicated long-term goals or strategic aims. Indeed, rather than any form of coherent strategy of violence, what is apparent in the period leading up to the subway attack is that Aum's crimes were all ad hoc and *reactive* outbursts of violence directed against individual enemies, often with the underlying aim of settling scores with those who had proved to be hostile to Aum and to have attacked Asahara in any way, or against groups and communities who had done similarly. All the cases of externalised violence against individuals that occurred in this period (such the attacks on Egawa, Takimoto, and Nagaoka) fall into this category – as indeed, did the earlier killings committed by Aum, such as the murder of the Sakamotos. The attacks on communities and the general public, whether at Matsumoto or the Tokyo subway, were also acts carried out in order to prevent something happening, and were responses with punitive dimensions to specific situations – as indeed, was Aum's earlier attempted botulism attack of 1990, which was a reactive and angry response to a city and people who had resoundingly rejected and insulted Asahara at the ballot-box.

There was, of course, an underlying pattern to all these separate incidents of violence. All were woven together within the matrix of a world polarised between good and evil, and with the legitimating structures that this matrix produced. They were all committed in response to a perceived threat or challenge to Aum, and the underlying pattern to each of these individual acts related to issues of authority. Each victim in his or her way represented a challenge, symbolic or real, to Asahara's sense of personal authority, which was incapable of tolerating challenges. Aum's violence, in other words, was not conceived or perpetrated in order to bring about a final war or to facilitate a coup, but in order to defend the name and ego of its guru, and to strike out at and punish those who had challenged him in any way.

IMMORTALITY, THE HISTORY BOOKS AND THE CREATION OF A MYTH

The subway attack, hitting at the nerve-centre of government and at the National Police Agency whose forces were about to raid Aum, could also be seen as a symbolic punitive strike against the Japanese state and people who had rejected Asahara, and as a blow in advance against the forces of law and order that were about to confront Aum. Clearly, too, on other levels it was a preventative measure aimed to defend the mission and hinder police investigations. However, I am doubtful whether these themes alone can account for the attack; nor am I convinced that even Aum's leaders could have been so deluded as to believe that the subway attack would deflect suspicion away from Aum or cause the police investigations to be postponed.

Aware of the evidence of its involvement in the Matsumoto case, Aum's leaders had managed a temporary cover-up, but as speculation about probable police raids continued to grow, and as Aum drew further attention to itself through the brazen kidnap of Kariya, they must have realised that a police move was inevitable. Moreover, because of the Japanese legal system which allows the police to keep suspects in de-tention for almost a month without access to lawyers, during which time detainees are placed under tremendous pressure to make confessions, they must have recognised that the police would be able to develop a case against them that would jeopardise the continuation of the move-ment. This is what did happen after 20 March 1995: much of the evidence that has since been used in the ensuing trials has been obtained through confessions made by followers who were detained in this manner.

In early spring 1995, aware that a raid was to occur, Aum faced the collapse of its mission in an ignominious manner as its leaders were arrested and incarcerated on a series of charges relating to Matsumoto and other offences. It is at this point that a possible further motive for the subway attack emerged. Rather than waiting for the police to come and carry out its raids, Asahara, I would suggest, seized the opportunity not to deflect attention *away* from Aum but, rather, to draw it *to* it. I have previously emphasised that Asahara had a history of making dramatic and attention-seeking gestures that would publicise his movement and mission. I would argue that the sarin attack, with its inevitable results – the immediate suspicion cast on Aum, the additional attention paid to the police raids and so on – fitted into this pattern and that it was, in a sense, Asahara's most dramatic action of this sort.

Before 20 March 1995 Aum was the focus of much discussion in the media, and a raid occurring before that date would have generated an appreciable amount of interest in Japan. The arrest of the leaders of a small religious group for incidents that occurred some months beforehand would not, however, have been a long-lasting story that captivated public attention for weeks and months, and it certainly would not have been the biggest media story in post-war Japan. Nor, indeed, would it have gained international attention: it might be noted on this score that the Matsumoto attack had hardly been a major international news story.

Conversely, by conducting a strike using chemical weapons on one of the world's largest mass transit systems, Aum became transformed from an item of national news, into the single biggest story not just in Japan but also, for a short time, internationally. It was the sarin attack and the singular drama and images it evoked, at the nerve-centre of Japan and in full view of the public and media gaze, that transformed Aum Shinrikyō from a murderous and deviant religious group into a movement of global notoriety, and made Asahara Shōkō into the best-known Japanese face on the planet, and the most (in)famous person in Japan.

It was because of the sarin attack, too, that Asahara Shōkō achieved a temporary yet massive degree of power. In the days and weeks when he was in hiding prior to his arrest, Asahara acquired the power to strike fear into a nation. I mentioned this in my previous book when I commented on Asahara's prophecy that something significant would happen in Tokyo on 15 April 1995. As I noted then, much of the city was brought to a standstill: shops and markets closed and major stations such as Shinjuku were deserted. The normally relentless city had been reduced to virtual silence by the mere words of a guru in hiding. Asahara had, as a result of the subway attack, achieved a level of power, attention and influence that he could never otherwise have gained, and that no post-war Japanese government has ever had. He no longer spoke to a small dedicated band of followers, but could seize the attention of a nation and, indeed, the world at large, and could influence the movements of millions of people.

I stress that this suggestion is speculative (the one person who could answer it would of course be Asahara himself) and I do not suggest that it was the only or even dominant factor behind the attack. However, given the constant frustrations that Asahara manifested because his movement did not get the attention he sought, it is not improbable that he might have thought in this way. He would not have been the first or last frustrated religious leader to carry out deeds that he knew would make his movement the focus of immense attention. As Jean-François Mayer has shown, in the period prior to the mass 'transit' of members of the Solar Temple, Joseph Di Mambro, speaking to Luc Jouret, a senior figure in the Temple, stated that what the members of the Order would do would be 'more spectacular' than what had happened at Waco.[55] When the transit occurred, Di Mambro and his fellow travellers sent videos containing their religious manifestos and doctrinest and recordings of their final ritual procession to journalists. Although they were, according to their beliefs, abandoning this world and leaving it behind in their journey to another realm, they made sure that their transit would be public knowledge and would receive, through the tapes they left and the manner of their departure, massive world-wide attention. As Mayer notes, the Solar Temple was a small and insignificant movement which had failed to acquire the support and attention it sought. However, its spectacular departure allowed it to project itself in a much larger sphere and to leave behind a myth. Rather than simply disappearing or continuing in existence as a small and little known movement, the Solar Temple was able to leave its name in the history books and, through the drama of its actions, to attain global significance.[56]

The way in which the members of Heaven's Gate departed from earth showed similar wishes to leave something behind and to attract attention. Although the members of Heaven's Gate were similarly abandoning or leaving this world behind in their celestial journey to other planets or realms, they saw fit to leave messages for the human beings whom they had abandoned and whose fate apparently no longer concerned them. The Heaven's Gate Internet site and the CD-ROM disks that they produced containing messages and explanations of their teachings, demonstrate the movement's need to have some continuing impact on earth and to attract attention that had not otherwise come to the movement.

Similarly, I would argue, the manner in which it acted in March 1995 brought Aum the attention and, indeed, the immortality it sought, just as had the actions of the Order of the Solar Temple before it and of Heaven's Gate afterwards. Aum already (like the Solar Temple) claimed to be the centre of world attention through the vast conspiracy directed at it: the subway attack gave it the opportunity to show that the attention was real. It also created an aura around the movement. Members, and even some former members whom I have talked to, even though they might feel uncomfortable about what their leaders actually did, have nevertheless exhibited a form of pride in being associated with a movement that had achieved such prominence. Indeed, when I first was able to make direct contact with members of Aum Shinrikyō in 1997, my initial contact there was extremely fascinated by the notion that someone living so far away from Japan, in Europe, had heard of and was interested in Aum Shinrikyō. It appeared to assure him that his movement was, after all, an important and internationally known one, and he was, of course, aware that what had brought this about was the sarin attack.

One devotee, a quite highly placed *shukkesha* who was in charge of an Aum centre which I visited, made this point in more striking terms. When I asked him for his opinion on the subway attack he uttered the words *subarashii ja nai ka* (wonderful, wasn't it?).[57] To my shocked reply – in which I pointed out that as a result the movement's leaders had been arrested, that Asahara was certainly never going to be free again, and that vast majority of followers had left the movement – he produced the following reason why he thought it was 'wonderful'. The movement, he felt, had been having problems; it was small and there were signs of fragmentation, and its teachings were barely known even in Japan. There was the danger, he felt, that it would die out as a result. The attack might have led to the immediate departure of a number of followers, but it had also made the movement widely known for the first time, and Asahara's teachings and his warnings about the state the world was in, had finally come to the attention of the world at large. The movement and his teachings would now not disappear: it was in the history books, and its teachings recorded for posterity.

While no other Aum follower has expressed anything like such positive opinions about the attack itself, there remains, amongst those whom I have talked to, a sense in which what happened on the subway was less important than the fact that Aum's teachings had become more widely transmitted. Even the massive loss of followers appeared not to cause much bother to the devotees I talked to who had remained faithful. Those who had stayed when the defections were going on were, they told me, the true and faithful core of the movement. Those who left had been less committed to Aum. My interviewees, in other words, while uneasy about the subway attack and unsure why it had been necessary to commit mass murder in this way, did not view it as an unmitigated disaster for the movement and felt in some ways that it had enabled the movement to achieve a global significance. While their responses are clearly those of people struggling to find meaning in an event that could otherwise appear unfathomable, and to read into this deed of their spiritual master and guru some evidence of his spiritual insight and power, they do appear to give some credence to my speculations about the underlying motives for the attack. Certainly as a result of it Aum Shinrikyō achieved a degree of prominence that its leader, when he established his yoga group in Tokyo barely 11 years beforehand, could hardly have dreamed of.

8 *Concluding Comments – Aum Shinrikyō and Religious Violence*

RESPONDING TO THE AFFAIR: DEALING WITH AUM IN LEGAL TERMS

In the months after the subway attack the Aum affair dominated Japanese society, the media and the political world. The enormous numbers of crimes committed by Aum, the public disquiet over the way in which the movement had seemingly been able to stockpile weapons and commit murders without the authorities taking much notice, and the apparent reluctance of the police to investigate an organisation because it was a registered religion, raised a number of political and legislative issues. The most important of these was how Aum, once its criminal nature had been established, ought to be treated, and whether the privileges and protections granted to religious groups in Japan were too liberal and needed to be amended.

On the first of these issues, there were moves from the government to proscribe Aum under the Anti-Subversive Activities Law (*Hakai katsudō bōshihō*, usually abbreviated in Japan as the *Habōhō*). Originally passed in 1952 to deal with the possible threat from communist groups at the time of the Korean War, this draconian act, which has never been used against any organisation or group in Japan, would have banned Aum and prohibited any activity by its members which related to Aum. They would not, for example, have been able to take part in spiritual practices led by religious teachers in Aum, produce materials promoting Aum's teachings or actively proselytise their faith. These proscriptions, which would have amounted to a basic restriction on the civil rights of existing Aum members who had not committed any crimes, caused many people in Japan to protest against the planned use of the act. Eventually, after investigations by a committee set up to judge this issue, and after Asahara had stepped down as leader of the movement in 1996 (a move designed to show that Aum no longer posed a danger to Japanese society), it was decided not to use this law against the movement.

Aum was, however, stripped of its protected status under the Religious Corporations Law, was declared bankrupt and had its assets (including its centres and commune) seized in order to pay compensation to its victims. Although a number of the faithful continue to be members of Aum, retaining a distanced and critical perspective on Japanese society, following their spiritual practices and continuing to regard Asahara as their true teacher, the movement has effectively been emasculated by its financial loss and by the massive exodus of followers.[1]

The debate extended beyond Aum to the position of religious movements in society in general. After the manipulation and repression of religions by the Japanese government in the first half of the twentieth century, the general assumption had been that, in a modern, secular and liberal society, religious movements needed to be protected from state interference. The constitutional reforms of post-war Japan were framed with this in mind, and the Constitution, which enshrines the separation of state and religion, affirmed the freedom of religion as a basic right and acknowledged that religious movements should be afforded strong protection against state interference. After Aum the focus of the debate turned to whether the state and its citizens required greater protection from religious groups, and whether laws needed to be brought in or strengthened to allow the state greater surveillance and control over religious groups in order to prevent them exploiting their privileges in the way Aum had. Eventually the Religious Corporations Law was amended to introduce some safeguards and to make it harder for movements to gain and retain their recognition under this act, although in the long run the changes were by no means as strict as originally proposed.[2]

EXPLAINING AUM: MEDIA RESPONSES AND JAPANESE EXPLANATIONS

After the subway attack every area of the media was for weeks afterwards saturated with coverage of Aum. Indeed, it was several weeks before anything other than an Aum story captured the front page of newspapers, while the main television companies devoted hour upon hour of prime-time television to the affair every day for weeks on end.[3] A lot of the coverage was sensationalised and there was profound disquiet in Japan at the lurid ways (which included peddling rumours, harassing members of Aum and their parents, and riding roughshod over the privacy of those associated in the affair) in which the media had behaved. This disquiet became stronger after the news broke that TBS had shown Aum officials the video incorporating Sakamoto Tsutsumi's criticisms of Aum.

The sensationalised coverage at first glance appeared to verify the frequent criticisms scholars have made of the media's treatment of new religious movements. There is an extensive academic literature on this topic, providing detailed analyses of how the mass media treat small religious movements outside the mainstream in unbalanced and inflammatory ways. The consensus has been that the mass media tend to discuss new religions in terms of deviance from mainstream attitudes or in terms of what some scholars have termed 'atrocity tales' – stories that depict such movements in a bad light, highlighting odd behaviour or alleging breaches of social norms. As some scholars have pointed out, these often turn out to be far less dramatic or 'atrocious' than initially portrayed.[4] However, the Aum case offers a cautionary warning that this is not always the case. In Aum, while many of the earlier 'atrocity tales' (besides those relating to the subway attack and suspicions about the murder of the Sakamotos) were highly sensational, such as stories of Hayakawa's fantasies about nuclear weapons, much of the later evidence that came out as result of investigations (such as the internal killings, uses of drugs, extortion and experiments with weapons designed to kill vast numbers of people) showed a far deeper culture of violence and criminality than even the early media stories appeared to suggest.[5]

Naturally, besides reporting the events relating to Aum and speculating about the movement's intentions, the biggest single question that ran through all the discussions of the affair in Japan was how a society that prided itself on its high levels of public safety and order could have produced such a movement, and what this said about the nature of Japanese society in general. These issues were discussed over and over in the weeks after the attack by social commentators and analysts, and their discussions tended to revolve around two interrelated themes.

One focused on the assumption that Aum was not a real religion, but a 'cult' (Japanese: *karuto*) established by an evil manipulator who was only out for power and money. The term *karuto* was used much in the ways the word 'cult' has been in the media in the West, to suggest a deviant, fanatical group led by a charismatic person who postures as a religious leader but who is in fact a self-serving individual who beguiles people into following him or her, and who manipulates and uses them for his or her own purposes. Aum was, in such a reading, a cult created by Asahara as a means to power and wealth: Asahara himself (aided by a small coterie of sinister accomplices) was evil, his evil manifested not only in the deeds he ordered but in his ability to draw naïve, impressionable and idealistic young Japanese into his web, 'brainwashing' and manipulating them to venerate him and kill to further his ambitions.[6]

I have already discussed why such an interpretation fails to explain adequately the reasons behind Aum's actions. I have also examined why it is problematic to utilise a model of religion which assumes that movements that display seemingly 'deviant' tendencies are not properly religious or are fraudulent. Equally, while Asahara demonstrated psychological imbalances, raw ambition, and a cruel and vindictive streak, these did not preclude him from being a charismatic religious teacher capable of inspiring people from a number of walks of life to join his movement, and adept at advising them in their practices. Of course, writing Asahara off as evil, besides providing a cathartic function for Japanese society in that it has a specific target at which to direct its anger, offers followers who recant their faith and claim that they have been manipulated by him the opportunity for reconciliation with society. This is a point that has been recognised by several formerly close disciples such as Ishii Hisako and Hayashi Ikuo who have turned against Asahara and denounced him.

The most common theme running through Japanese discussions of the affair focused on its national dimensions. In observing that the perpetrators of the affair were Japanese, it saw the seeds of their violence as being related to their discontent with their society, and their behaviour as reflecting and being produced by the Japanese system and cultural environment. Hence the affair was evidence of the breakdown of that society, and of the troubles and imbalances within it. This has been a predominant theme in virtually all subsequent Japanese analyses of the affair,[7] which have, perhaps unsurprisingly, treated Aum almost entirely as a Japanese phenomenon. According to such interpretations, the primary social problems that were highlighted by the Aum affair included: the inability of the established religions to answer the spiritual aspirations of the young; the failure of the education system to provide its students with the tools of analytical understanding; the pressures of Japan's oppressive work system and work ethic; and the excessive focus on materialism in modern Japanese consumer society. All of these had left a spiritual vacuum in Japan and had caused many young Japanese to seek alternative sources of comfort and to fall victim to manipulators such as Asahara who peddled a phoney spirituality. Particular criticism was levelled at the perceived failures of the education system, which was too concerned with hierarchy, status and the repetition of factual knowledge and rote learning to teach students to formulate their own opinions or help them to develop critical faculties.[8] Some critics (especially those with a Marxist bent) also used the affair to criticise religion in general as deviant and dangerous and out of place in a modern society.

The Aum affair, in other words, provided every critic of Japanese society with avenues through which to vent their particular grievances. The interpretation which relates the Aum affair primarily to the short-comings of the Japanese social and cultural environment clearly has some resonance. Aum was, after all, produced in the Japanese environment and, as has been seen in this book, many of the factors leading people to join it were related to general problems within mainstream society, such as the over-rationalised, stratified and pressurised education and work system, excessive materialism, and the familial demands for success coupled with the emotional deprivation that can be engendered by such a system.

In terms of social processes, too, the Japanese environment facilitated the development of violence in Aum and provided a legitimating cultural background for Asahara's uses of violence against his disciples. Japanese society and culture naturally served as the setting in which the drama of Aum Shinrikyō was played out. The social organisational patterns of that society left an indelible imprint on Aum, as did the religious influences of Japanese modern culture: these formed the background from which Aum emerged, while Asahara himself fitted into the broader mould of Japanese charismatic leaders in many ways. Aum's reactions to Japanese society were naturally voiced in a Japanese context because the members were Japanese and their immediate focus of unease and rejection related to that society.

However, it would be problematic to limit analyses of the Aum affair to such Japanese cultural-specific interpretations. What Aum, as a world-rejecting religious movement with a focus on internal spiritual develop-ment, reacted against and criticised most harshly was not Japanese society *per se* but contemporary materialism. Aum's antipathies had universal dimensions and its primary target of hate was materialism in general and the USA in particular. This was underscored by the views of one of my interviewees, who told me that, even if he did decide at some stage to leave Aum he would not want to return to the mainstream of Japanese society because he found it so corrupt and materialistic. He was also certain that he would not have felt better in any other society that was governed by materialism. Hence he felt most comfortable withdrawing from society and entering into a closed, world-rejecting order that focused on internal self-development.

It is, of course, understandable that Japanese commentators have been primarily concerned with the lessons and messages that the affair had in the Japanese social, cultural and political contexts, given the scale of the violence and the fear and horrors that the movement inflicted on the general Japanese public. However, for those who are not primarily specialists in the study of Japan, such cultural-specific interpretations are of little help in fully understanding the affair or, indeed, in making it in any way relevant to academic studies beyond the narrow confines of a single country. While the 'Japanese' interpretation highlights specific cultural factors that facilitated the ways in which Aum developed, it neglects the potentially universal dimensions of the affair. Moreover by emphasising local cultural factors and denying that Aum was a religion, it closes the door to any interpretation or understanding of the affair that makes use of the basic characteristics of Aum Shinrikyō itself.

Religion, Violence and Aum

The ramifications and implications of the Aum affair are not limited to Japan alone, or to the study of Japanese society and social processes. The Aum affair presents us with an example of how violence erupted in a new religious movement operating in a modern, highly developed society and led by a self-proclaimed charismatic leader. The manner in which the affair developed, and the factors that contributed to that violence, are highly relevant to scholars of religion in general, and especially to those who are interested in new religions and the inter-relationship between religion and violence. The Aum affair provides a Japanese example to add to the growing number of cases involving religious movements (and especially small and closed or communally based movements) with charismatic leaders and apocalyptic or millennial orientations that have been associated with violence or dramatic events in recent decades. In providing such an example, it offers some comparative dimensions to set alongside movements in other countries, such as the Rajneesh movement, the Peoples Temple and the Order of the Solar Temple. All of these show some similarities either in various aspects of their activities, or in the processes whereby they ran into difficulties, or in the ways in which they related to the world at large and which played a part in the turmoil that enveloped them.

Aum, in its polarisation of the world into good and evil, its images of a sacred war, and its emphasis on its enemies who (in its view) persecuted and conspired against it, provides an example of the relationship between religion and violence in terms expressed by scholars such as Rapoport, Schwartz, Smith and Juergensmeyer. Rapoport's comments about the violent dimensions of religion are substantiated throughout the narrative of the Aum affair, whether in its uses of violence to defend its mission or in the violent imagery within which it framed its conceptualisation of that mission. It thus also provides a Japanese affirmation of Juergensmeyer's view that violence is endemic to religion, and of the ways in which symbolically expressed violence and conflict can become transposed into actual violence and mayhem.

It illustrates, too, Schwartz's argument about the relationship between violence and identity formation and Smith's development of that concept. Aum is a striking example of how a religious movement can create a powerful sense of self-identity that is conditioned and strengthened through the formation of 'others' and that produces a potent form of authority that sanctifies and gives rise to actual violence. The powerful bonds of belonging and commitment created in Aum with its *sangha* of world renouncers who abandoned their families and jobs to pledge allegiance to a guru and cause were intensified by the creation of others – external enemies with whom Aum came into conflict or who, in the collective imagination of the movement, were oppressing and attacking it. While some of those enemies were real – parents who complained about the rupture of family relations, civil authorities who deplored Aum's lack of regard for civil law, local residents who did not want Aum as neighbours – many more were products of an imagined conspiracy and part of its polarised worldview in which the forces of good and evil were destined to fight. All of this conferred a powerful sense of authority within Aum. This was the authority of the guru and sacred master who, as leader of the forces of good and truth, had the right to use any means he felt necessary to promote the truth and to save people from falling into the realms of evil. It was reinforced also by the authority of his disciples, the 'true victors' who shared his beliefs and, through their attainment of the truth and their position of spiritual superiority, were entitled to commit acts of violence to punish the unworthy and protect the truth.

Aum Shinrikyō produced from within itself, its doctrines, its ways of looking at the world, and its experiences, an internalised sense of reality that, while strikingly different from the external reality of the society around it, contained its own internal logic. That logic was conditioned and stimulated not just by its worldviews, which produced such a distinct and implacable binary divide between Aum and the rest of the world, but by the paranoia that surrounded the movement.

Although Asahara from almost the outset of his movement was fired by the images of sacred war and of his own self-perception as a cosmic hero, it was through the experiences and unforeseen events that developed in Aum, such as the death of Majima Terayuki, that this worldview hardened into the rigidly hostile structure that took hold in Aum. Those experiences, unforeseen as they were, were nonetheless also products of Aum's worldview and of its basic religious orientations. Without its belief in the polluted nature of the body and world, without its insistence that ascetic practices were vital in order to transcend the evils of this world, and without its sanctioning of the guru's right to force people to perform such practices, these unforeseen (but perhaps, given the extremes of asceticism and the ready use of coercion, predictable) events would not have occurred.

THE PRODUCTION OF VIOLENCE IN AUM: PROCESS AND FACTORS

When Asahara Shōkō first set up his yoga group in 1984, the group he established had not set its aims on causing mayhem or mass murder, and its interests appear to have been primarily located in yoga, spiritual development and the attainment of psychic powers. Even when, from around 1985, its leader began to have visions of a sacred mission, Aum's orientations remained optimistic and its incipient message of salvation affirmed spiritual transformation rather than the destruction and violence that became paramount in later Aum teachings and actions. Within that optimistic vision, however, there were latently violent images of a sacred war which over the years became transformed into real conflict as Aum's view of the future turned dark and catastrophic. This change was conditioned by the gap between Aum's expectations and aspirations on the one hand, and the realities of its experience on the other. Asahara visualised himself and his movement in grand, messianic terms; however, its growth did not match these cosmic expectations, while the public response to his messages was, at the very least, indifferent. The contrast between expectations and realities demanded explanations and influenced Aum's view of the world at large. As a result Aum became more withdrawn and introverted, turning away from the optimism of world salvation, creating an internal religious hierarchy which progressively elevated the status and power of its guru (whose authority moved from being able to plead on behalf of the spirits of the dead to having the right to despatch people to their deaths) and his followers, and embracing catastrophic visions of the future. In this process it turned to violence, at first internally with the beatings administered to disciples, and then with an accidental death (caused by Aum's practices) and later with murders carried out to silence opponents. This path of violence was not so much a planned development as it was a process in which Aum reacted to events in ways that sought to bolster Asahara's authority in the face of setbacks. Such responses caused Aum to amend its doctrines in the light of these changing circumstances and to assume ever more confrontational postures.

One cannot, however, say that the violence was wholly accidental in origin. The various elements and factors that contributed to the formation of a culture of violence in Aum contained within them numerous violent images, in, for example, Asahara's visions of a sacred war, while its doctrinal stance provided a ready framework through which violence could emerge. Its guru had a violent side which, in the context of a movement that gave him absolute authority and sanctioned his acts as being beyond conventional morality, was transposed on to the movement as a whole, and made it aggressive and confrontational. The factors that contributed to this process were multiple and related to the nature of Aum as a religious movement, its doctrines, its visions of the future, its goals and ambitions, and of course the nature and personality of its founder and leader, as well as the ways in which his followers reacted with him, both in affirming his authority and in carrying out his orders.

The self-image Aum created was also critical. As a world-rejecting movement with millennialist and apocalyptic dimensions fired by a concept of sacred mission which revolved around images of conflict and war, Aum manifested a propensity towards the acceptance of confrontation and violence. This does not mean that all apocalyptic or world-rejecting movements can be categorised as being necessarily inclined or liable to engage in some form of violence; however, these were intrinsic elements of Aum's characteristic nature. Having such an orientation certainly meant that Aum did not have any in-built resistance to violence when this propensity began to surface in the movement, nor any clear way of putting a halt to such violence.

Aum's doctrinal leanings and its practices and goals were also influential in this process. Its basic concept of the structure of the universe and of its different realms, along with its emphasis on the inevitable dynamics of the laws of karma and the related *poa* concept, provided the framework through which early deaths and later murders could be explained and seemingly, from within Aum's enclosed world, justified and seen as worthy acts. The emphasis placed in Aum on extinction (of karma, of spiritual impurities, of desires) and its relationship to enlightenment was also critical in doctrinal terms. The cessation of desire was equated with enlightenment and with death – a view which provided a further viable framework through which to accommodate the deaths of practitioners and enemies alike.

The interrelated views of the body and world as polluted and in need of spiritual cleansing, coupled with the belief that one had to strive for transcendence and liberation through severe austerities, were also instrumental in fostering a climate in which coercion could occur and in which violence and even death could be condoned. It is relevant to suggest here that asceticism in general can have an innately violent dimension to it, especially when it involves or advocates extreme forms of bodily punishment and mortification. Certainly Aum's asceticism assumed such forms and gave impetus to its violent behaviour, and legitimated it further in the name of seeking the truth and striving for enlightenment. It also contributed to a number of deaths in Aum, including that of Majima, which was the most immediate catalyst precipitating Aum's direct slide into crime and murder.

The emphasis placed on detachment as a spiritual virtue, and on the primacy of inner experience and of one's own practice, also contributed to a climate whereby Aum's followers were free, from their moral standpoint, to participate in criminal activities or to disregard what was going on around them. This is a further example of how concepts and ideas with a seemingly spiritual meaning can function in ways that either facilitate violence or fail to provide any resistance to it. It is clear that many of the doctrines that Aum espoused and considered important – and that were by and large drawn from Buddhism – were readily adapted to legitimate its violence, while others (such as the belief that what transpired in the external world was not as important as inner spiritual development) fostered an environment within which violence could develop unchecked, with little opportunity for resistance. Rather than providing followers with a strong moral grounding through which to reject violence, its Buddhist-derived doctrines provided members with an avenue of escape through which they could turn their minds to their practice and their inner worlds, and disregard or remain blinkered to the behaviour of their leaders.

A POISONOUS COCKTAIL: CHARISMATIC AUTHORITY, ZEALOUS ELITES AND SILENT LAMBS

The single most critical element in the affair was the role of Asahara Shōkō. There is no need here to repeat the aspects of his charismatic

233

power, his personality, obsessions, sense of rejection and so on that were interwoven into the fabric of Aum's violence. One point that does, however, need to be commented upon is the transformation that Asahara appears to have undergone during the development of Aum. This has been one of the more striking images in the whole affair, with the young, slender, athletic-looking ascetic Asahara of the mid-1980s sitting cross-legged in meditation giving way to the Asahara of the mid-1990s, who appeared overweight with his face lined and bloated. The latter Asahara, having departed from the ideals of that earlier period, no longer performing ascetic practices and indulging in sexual relations with disciples, was portrayed in Aum as a supreme guru who had surpassed the constraints of this world and was no longer bound by its moral laws. This rationale was, of course, extremely dubious. Asahara was a guru and ardent practitioner who, for various reasons, had ceased ascetic practice and had become more and more elevated in status. Yet as he proceeded down this path of absolutism his mood turned to one of despair and pessimism, apparently being reduced to the hope that his 'true victors' would not fall to the hells. In a sense this physical deterioration – from a slim, inspired ascetic to an overweight, despairing guru – is both symbolic and symptomatic of Aum's descent from its early optimistic mission of world salvation to the murky depths of mass murder.

Asahara the sacred hero and leader of the forces of truth and righteousness wielded supreme authority in Aum, and it was because of this charismatic authority that his orders decreeing the death of an 'unworthy' enemy of the movement were enacted, and because of it that disciples were willing to risk their lives in acts of asceticism. Yet as he grew in status and received total obedience from his followers, he increasingly began to lose touch with reality; his behaviour became stranger (including a tendency to indulge himself in various luxuries and sexual affairs) and he became obsessed with ideas of conspiracies, with being poisoned and surrounded by spies. Whether one can say with certainty that Asahara, especially in the 1990s, had become mentally unstable is unclear although I tend to this view, especially in the light of his post-arrest behaviour. He had certainly become distanced from his earlier ascetic persona.

Such behaviour is not necessarily regarded as out of character for charismatic leaders. Their followers may be inclined to interpret odd or (in conventional terms) immoral behaviour as an example of their 'crazy wisdom' – and might, indeed, expect it as evidence of a different and advanced state of being, beyond the boundaries of ordinary morality.

The problem, however, is how such behaviour influences a movement in terms of violence. Charismatic authority is, according to Thomas Robbins and Dick Anthony, a highly contingent factor capable of affecting 'the volatility and violent potential of religious movements',[9] and they argue that emergent groups centred around charismatic leaders have a clear potential for instability, because they are so dependent on the whims of their leaders. Aum was, of course, a first-generation charismatic movement that had not yet settled down into a set structure or pattern of behaviour, and had as yet not systematised its doctrines.

Robbins and Anthony also look at how charismatic leaders respond to perceived threats to their authority and how they use stratagems and techniques in times of crisis in ways that 'embellish this authority and extrapolate it in increasingly authoritarian and absolutist directions'.[10] Using the examples of Jim Jones of the Peoples Temple and Charles Dederich of Synanon,[11] both of whom made numerous and growing demands on their followers to test their faith and commitment or to drive out potential threats to their authority, and who thus heightened the receptivity of their followers to extreme situations, Robbins and Anthony suggest that:

> The followers of a charismatic leader may be directly or indirectly prepared for future violence as the leader consolidates a disciplined cadre of devotees who have shed their inhibitions against taking extreme actions on behalf of the prophet's vision.[12]

In this process, too, they see the development of what they regard as a basic definitional quality of charismatic leadership: the absence of accountability and of inhibitions on the impulsivity of the leader.[13]

One can see in Asahara's demands on his disciples, in the use of dangerous and death-defying ascetic practices, in the various initiations, and in the development of a highly motivated elite dedicated to Asahara and perhaps vying for his attention and favours, much to substantiate Robbins and Anthony's argument. The Aum affair, indeed, is a good example of how charismatic authority may be developed, strengthened and used to sanction religious violence and contribute to the volatile nature of a new religious movement.

In emphasising the importance of charismatic authority, however, one should beware of focusing too much on the leader and his/her instability or strange behaviour. While Asahara underwent a transformation that ultimately involved him in paranoid visions, the crucial question to ask is how and why did his disciples accept these changes, and to what extent did they, through their support and devotion, acquiesce in, encourage, reinforce and facilitate them?

In the case of those who formed the senior hierarchy in Aum and who occupied positions of some influence around Asahara (the *kanbu*), there is clear evidence of a complicity not merely in the carrying out of acts of violence but in the creation of the mind-set that could legitimate them. At different times various senior members of the movement appear to have wielded particular influence with Asahara or to have been especially close to him. For example, Murai Hideo and others with a particular fascination for science (or, rather, science-fantasy) appear to have influenced the direction of Aum's thinking in the early 1990s. The keenness of Murai to try to implement every one of Asahara's wild ideas suggests a culture of supportive acquiescence which served to reinforce and encourage, rather than temper, Asahara's fantasies. Those who ascended to the top of Aum did so because of their loyalty and devotion to Asahara. They showed him that they deserved to enter into the spiritual elite through their austerities and total obedience. In offering that obedience and following his whims, of course, they created the conditions that encouraged his vicarious behaviour and reinforced his sense of power by acquiescing in every instruction, no matter how strange it might have seemed.

Those who reached the higher levels of Aum had to be zealous and highly committed, dedicated to the cause and ready to take on extreme practices. In entering these ranks they received affirmation of their spiritual transcendence through their holy names and titles, and through being admitted to an advanced spiritual guard above and beyond the rules of ordinary morality or law. Aum's *shukkesha* strove to enter these exalted ranks, a point emphasised by their commonly expressed desire for holy names, and by the elation of Nakagawa Tomomasa when he was chosen to join the Sakamoto death squad. This showed him that he had entered the elite, and in his eyes this was recognition of his devotion, loyalty to the truth, and high spiritual status. Like the materialist system they left behind, Aum's world rewarded followers with privileges and status for reaching its upper levels. As such, the *kanbu* joined with Asahara in creating a world of spiritual elitism and karmic righteousness that told them they were special. They, in effect, shared in his distancing from reality in creating the atmosphere of arrogance and hierarchic disdain that permeated Aum and in reinforcing Asahara's own delusions and paranoia. Rather than doing anything to stop them from escalating into violent realities, they appear to have encouraged them and, as the case of Ochi Naoki shows, willingly participated in a culture of punishment and violence while interpreting such activities within a framework of karmic righteousness that absolved them from any guilt and elevated even their criminal behaviour to a high spiritual plane.

Compared to those who reached the higher rungs of Aum's spiritual ladder, the ordinary *shukkesha* appear to have been largely unaware of the illegal activities of their leaders. In the aftermath of the affair, indeed, the general assumption was that they had been exploited and that they were victims of the movement, innocent parties who had given their money to Aum and had, as one commentator put it, been 'thoroughly fleeced'.[14] The sums of money that followers paid for initiations and the demand that they hand over all their wealth when renouncing the world certainly indicate that exploitation did occur in Aum, and some charges have been brought against senior members of Aum relating to the extortion and appropriation of funds from followers.

Yet I cannot consider that this model of unscrupulously self-serving leaders and exploited rank-and-file members is valid in Aum or, indeed, in other movements that have been associated with violence, murder or suicide. The relational nature of charisma not only means that one cannot treat the charismatic leader in isolation but that one cannot solely focus on those nearest the guru in terms of the construction of charisma. Asahara's status was not solely developed through interactions with those who became his closest disciples: it also depended (as did the senior disciples themselves) on the support of a wider group of people for sustenance. Asahara received support and homage not only from an inner elite of close disciples but from the movement as a whole, from whose ranks the *shukkesha* and *kanbu* were drawn. The eagerness with which Aum's disciples responded positively to Asahara when he spoke about seeking to *poa* all of humanity reflects a ready reinforcement and affirmation of Asahara's doctrines, even though they clearly contained potentially violent themes.

The people who joined Aum and especially those who became *shukkesha* did so because they had little emotional investment in the world they left behind. They appeared willing to break all links with their families and to distance themselves from a society they disdained. Consequently they were not necessarily committed to its laws, and they sought an alternative reality that emphasised inner development above all else. They could thus distance themselves from events in the external 'unreal' world while concentrating on the inner world which, for them, was immediate and real. Aum's cavalier disregard for the laws of the land, if it impinged on their consciousness at all, did not appear to concern them, a point illustrated by the fact that disciples such as A-san, and Takahashi Hidetoshi, both joined Aum and became *shukkesha* at times (1992 and 1994 respectively) when its public reputation was already poor and when suspicions that it had committed murders remained rife. Neither appeared concerned about whether Aum had broken the laws of a society in which they had little emotional investment. The interviews that I have had with current members of the movement illustrate a similar indifference: whether Aum did or did not commit a series of murders appears less important for people such as A-san and I-san than the scope that the movement provided for the fulfilment of their personal development.

A common theme in the testimonies of the three *shukkesha* in Chapter 4 was the importance of their own practice (*jibun no shugyō*). This notion was critically important for all three, who emphasised, when asked about their knowledge of, and feelings about, Aum's criminal behaviour, that this aspect of Aum had not entered their consciousness or had not concerned them, because their primary concern was to focus on their own spiritual development. The two interviewees who remain committed to Aum continue to emphasise that it is their spiritual practice and personal inner development, rather than the deeds committed by Aum, that are of primary importance to them and that keep them amongst the faithful.

There would appear to have been something of a culture of silence and acquiescence surrounding many of Aum's activities, which allowed the violence to grow unchallenged, and in which Aum members passively participated. This is shown by Takahashi Hidetoshi's admission that he and other *shukkesha* were aware of the violence being meted out at Kamikuishiki in 1994 to dissident (and suspected dissident) members. The 'lambs', however, remained silent. As Takahashi has subsequently acknowledged, they played a part in allowing the affair to develop as it did, by working for and supporting Aum.[15] H-san similarly recognised this point when speaking about his sense of complicity in the affair. Even though he overtly knew nothing about what the leaders were doing, he felt that he had passively contributed to the culture that developed in Aum and that he had chosen not to know what was really going on in the movement.[16]

Takahashi commented that the more Asahara made things difficult for his disciples, the more they felt drawn to him. They explained his demands on them, his creation of distance between himself and them, and his harshness towards them as examples of the guru's love.[17] They also appear to have found ways in which to explain behaviour that flouted Aum's strict asceticism. The disciple A-san was typical in his comments that although he was aware of Asahara's sexual and other hedonistic behaviour, he did not find this problematic on the grounds that this was how a guru was supposed to behave, since gurus were above or beyond normal laws of morality. Asahara, according to popular press reports, developed a liking for expensive melons (which can be a prized and expensive delicacy in Japan) which disciples purchased and offered to him.[18] While this sort of extravagance may not be of the same scale as Bhagwan Shree Rajneesh's collection of Rolls Royces, it represented a conflict with the ideals of asceticism and detachment from the material pleasures of the world that Aum claimed to uphold. Disciples nonetheless appeared capable of feeding Asahara's desires in this and other ways (the female disciples who, in a movement that affirmed a monastic-style order of celibacy, had sexual relations with Asahara also come to mind here) and hence of reinforcing his authority and reiterating the proposition that he had gone beyond the normative standards that other, ordinary human beings needed to observe. In freeing him from those bonds and explaining his whims in such ways, Asahara's disciples implicitly encouraged such behaviour. Rather than questioning the actions of their guru and perhaps keeping him in check through such means, they adopted a lens of interpretation that viewed such behaviour not as the sign of a fallen spiritual teacher but as one of immense power.

Such patterns of interpretation are well known in the study of charismatic groups, and appear to be especially prominent in movements that have encountered problems or become embroiled in turmoil. Again the Rajneesh movement offers a striking parallel. The followers of Rajneesh were able, despite the eccentric manner in which their guru began to behave (and despite a tide of criminality that developed in and beyond the commune, which ranged from intimidation and beatings, to conflicts with 'enemies' outside), to reinterpret these issues within the framework of their own worldviews. Having committed themselves to his commune (and also, often, having made considerable financial donations), members of the Rajneesh movement were confronted with his increasingly unpredictable behaviour – including complaints of illness and accusations against his followers – and his seeming obsession with an opulent lifestyle. While commune members were supposed to renounce the world and live simply, Rajneesh built up a fleet of Rolls Royces, and collected all manner of worldly goods. Simultaneously, large financial demands were made on his followers to help develop its commune, and since making donations was seen as a demonstration of faith, the pressure to concur was intense. Followers responded positively to such financial demands, and to the extraordinarily contradictory lifestyle of their guru who asked them to give up their luxuries and yet rode in a fleet of expensive cars, by seeing his actions as stratagems and devices intended to increase their spiritual consciousness by making them yield up their attachments and increase their surrender to, and ties with, their guru.[19]

There are similar patterns in the study by Alexander Deutsch, cited by Mark Galanter,[20] of the interactions of the American-born guru figure, Baba, and his small group of followers. Baba had travelled to India on a spiritual search, and when he returned to the USA he began to gather followers. He remained mute, communicating with his followers through sign language, but nevertheless built up a small cadre of devotees who met together in Central Park, New York. The group, which had developed a basic philosophy of detachment from desire, ambition and other worldly matters, then decided to move out of the city into the countryside, into a spartan setting with no electricity. It was at this juncture that serious problems began to manifest themselves in Baba's behaviour. Although it had been his wish that they move, he appears to have experienced difficulties as a result, and communication between him and the rest of the group faltered. He began using sign language in ways that his disciples could no longer comprehend, and engaged in bizarre and irrational behaviour, sexually abusing female members and subjecting other followers to physical violence.

Rather than fragmenting, however, his group of followers (whose sense of solidarity as a group had been intensified by their move to a rural environment), adapted to the new circumstances in ways that maintained their reliance on Baba as a source of leadership and inspiration, and that kept their group cohesive. They rationalised his odd behaviour: the purchase of an expensive and useless jacuzzi (useless since they had no electricity), which drained the group's finances, was justified as a lesson in how to renounce money, while the sexual abuse of a female follower was reinterpreted as a repercussion of her own repression about chastity. In this way members managed to convince themselves that his leadership remained positive and that, as Galanter puts it, his way was

> merely a 'hard trip,' requiring much faith and fortitude. Paradoxically, they even maintained that he was a model of freedom and his bizarre behavior was a reflection of not being trammeled by socially imposed conditions. They did not deny that Baba might be 'crazy' but insisted that this simply brought him closer to the expression of a 'divine energy' and that, in his behavior, he was 'teaching them a lesson'.[21]

I have touched on a number of guru figures or religious leaders who appear to have shown signs of disturbed behaviour; others include Jim

Jones of the Peoples Temple, with his loss of control due to drug abuse, and Joseph Di Mambro of the Solar Temple, with his paranoia about world police conspiracies and his own illness. What is evident in all these cases is that, rather than considering whether steps needed to be taken because their guru or leader was displaying manifestly problematic behavioural traits, or questioning the validity of their continuing adherence to their movements, followers (or at least a large proportion of them) chose not only to stay but to construct lines of reasoning which reinforced and thus encouraged further eccentric or disturbed behaviour.

In the cases of Aum, Rajneesh and Baba, as well as the Peoples Temple, a further striking point is that all had undergone moves from urban and accessible settings to more remote, rural ones in which the movement was enclosed in a communal setting. The Peoples Temple moved from San Francisco to the jungle of Guyana; Aum from its urban origins in Tokyo to communes in the Japanese countryside;[22] Rajneesh from the Indian city of Poona to the backwoods of Oregon; and Baba's group from Manhattan to a rural setting. This process contributed to internal solidarity in these movements as their members distanced themselves from society at large and joined together in the shared enterprise of creating a new world within their communal environments. However, the process of moving from a more familiar set of surroundings where alternative views and stimuli were available, to a closed and remote environment much more clearly under the authority of the guru/leader, also had its problems. It hardened the borderlines between the movement and the world at large, and made the followers who had committed themselves to such drastic changes of lifestyle more dependent on their guru.

It also increased the potential for volatility in these movements. Moving to rural areas in a sense represents a mode of escape, as evidenced not only by Aum's rejection of the world of Tokyo after the 1990 election, but also Rajneesh's move from Poona, where the movement had run into difficulties with the local authorities. Rather than providing a means of escape from tensions and problems, however, such rural moves can instead cause them to increase, especially if local conflicts arise. This was the case of course with Aum and Rajneesh. Indeed, this is likely to happen, given the generally divergent lifestyles of communal religious movements and rural communities. Moreover, compared to urban life, rural communal living gave followers less chance to hear alternative voices or to have contacts outside the group, and hence it made it that much harder for them to retain a sense of perspective on events, or to

241

maintain a point of view that was not wholly framed and conditioned by the internal logic of the movement.

Cognitive dissonance, or the way in which members of a group (and especially, I would add, of movements with a strongly introverted view of the world), manage to adjust their sense of reality and reinterpret events to conform to their movement's ideology, is a widely recognised social phenomenon. It is clear that this is what happened in all these aforementioned cases. By not questioning the oddities and apparent lapses of their leaders, and instead by casting them in a spiritually positive light, the followers were able to maintain their adherence to their movement and leader. More than that, they were able positively to reinforce their guru/leader's behaviour and, following the 'logic' of 'crazy wisdom', to open the doors to further, and crazier, 'wisdom'.

One cannot ascribe the process whereby Asahara (or indeed other charismatic leaders such as Rajneesh) increased their authority and began to manipulate, abuse or lead their disciples down a path of violence, solely to the cunning or the power-mad obsessions of a manipulative leader, or to the interactions between that leader and a close-knit set of leading disciples. The ways in which the wider membership, and in Aum's case this especially meant the *shukkesha* in general, tacitly accept and provide passive support to these processes is also crucial. We can see how the rank-and-file *shukkesha* vocally affirmed their support for concepts such as *poa*, how they reinterpreted their guru's unstable behaviour in ways that reinforced it, and how they disregarded, or *chose not to know*, what was going on around them at Kamikuishiki, even as recalcitrant members were being beaten and incarcerated, and instead turned inwards into their own world of practice.

One should also remember that those who did not possess the symbolic markers of status in the hierarchy, such as holy names, desperately sought or yearned for them. They wanted, in other words, to succeed and hence become members of the exclusive ranks in the movement. Aum, after all, preached a message that was elitist in tone: attain superhuman powers, be one of the true victors, be a bodhisattva, become part of the special movement that would save the world, and be superior to ordinary mortals. Those who embraced this message were also disaffected with modern society and held it in some contempt. They were keen to join the movement's upper echelons, and thus contributed immensely to the culture of elitism in Aum which helped foster the conditions in which violence could flourish.

RELIGIOUS ABSOLUTISM AND THE REFUSAL TO ACCOMMODATE TO THE LAW OF THE LAND

Aum represented a form of religious absolutism that was conditioned by its sense of righteousness, sacred mission and possession of the truth. It regarded the laws that were important to it (the law of karma and the laws of truth) as paramount, and answered only to an authority (its truth, mission and guru) that, it believed, was above the laws of the land. This type of attitude is not, of course, peculiar to Aum, but may be found in virtually any religion. Religions almost by definition have their own value systems, concepts of authority, codes of what is right and their own specific primary concerns.

The social reality is that for the most part the beliefs and orientations of religious movements are rarely if ever coterminous with the states or societies within which they operate. If religions are to function in such situations they inevitably have to work out some levels of compromise and accommodation between their belief system and the demands and expectations of the wider society. Equally, as is the general case with modern, liberal, secular societies, these tend to construct legal frameworks and adhere to policies of tolerance and acceptance that provide space for religious movements to function freely within them.

Problems may arise when religions are unable or unwilling to make such compromises or seek any form of accommodation. Again, this problem is perhaps most intense with movements that have a millennial bent, and especially during the earlier stages of their development when, in the first flushes of enthusiasm and inspired by a sense of mission and an overarching authority figure in the charismatic leader, they may be especially unwilling to subjugate their authority to the needs of a society that they believe is about to be swept away. Aum had clearly not worked out any viable strategy of accommodation to address the conflict between the laws it observed and the laws of the state. Indeed, the only strategy Aum appeared to have had was to regard itself above the law of the land and to pursue its own interests regardless of legal constraints. This had inevitable consequences, whether *vis-à-vis* the parents of minors who joined Aum, or with courts and local authorities who did not take kindly to Aum's disregard of statutory laws related to land purchase and use, or *vis-à-vis* people such as Sakamoto Tsutsumi who objected to Aum's false claims.

NO ONE WAS LISTENING: FAILURE, SUICIDE AND VIOLENCE

In its absolutist and polarising stance, Aum had failed to address the problem of the gap that would likely (if not inevitably) occur between its aspirations and the reception of its message. Again this problem is a common one that can be seen, for example, in the Order of the Solar Temple and in Heaven's Gate. Mayer noted when he first visited the former movement's premises in Switzerland that they had been prepared for much larger audiences than in fact attended Temple functions, and he considers that the movement was constantly beset by this great divide between expectations and reality.[23] Heaven's Gate, too, according to Richard P. Cimino and Don Lattin, experienced similar difficulties. It appears never to have attracted more than a handful of followers, and its leader, Marshall Applewhite, despaired because he felt his teachings drew mockery rather than support. As a result his teachings became increasingly paranoid and apocalyptic. In 1990s the movement attempted an advertising campaign and set up a Web site to attract more followers, before issuing a final appeal for people to join the group: however, as Cimino and Lattin put it, 'no one seemed to be listening'.[24] Applewhite gave up on earth, doomed because 'its inhabitants are refusing to evolve',[25] and, along with 38 followers, committed suicide – or, according to Heaven's Gate's doctrine, departed from earth by meeting up with a UFO that came in the shadow of the Hale Bopp comet in 1997, and left for another realm. There are strong parallels here with the Order of the Solar Temple and its members' departure for another realm, leaving the world behind mired in its delusions.

This sense of failure and the frustrations and reactions it provoked is one of the strongest themes of the Aum story. While Aum was not small by comparison with the Solar Temple or Heaven's Gate, there was a conspicuous sense of failure in terms of its expectations. Asahara's visions were grand and sweeping – world salvation, centres throughout the world, sacred leadership, turning the wheel of law again. They did not match with the reality of Aum's situation as a small, marginalised group greeted with opposition and derision, or of its leader, pilloried in the press for his demands on followers rather than being feted for his spiritual power.

This failure and the inability to achieve the sort of recognition, goals and status that Asahara sought, influenced the movement's development and resulted in repeated boosts of Asahara's personal status. In effect, the greater the degree of failure or lack of success in various aspects or phases of the movement's history, the more his authority inside the movement was expanded and shored up by doctrinal stances or titles. The sense of rejection that came from these repeated attempts to expand, along with Asahara's reactions to the world that rejected the truth, strengthened Aum's own sense of spiritual elitism and widened the gap between it and the world it criticised. Again, this was a dynamic that Aum appears to have shared with the Solar Temple and, so it would seem, with Heaven's Gate. For all three, their sense of spiritual superiority – whether as beings from another planet here temporarily in the hope of educating human beings, as gods on a journey to another realm, or as bodhisattvas and spiritual warriors destined to defeat evil in this realm – was reinforced by their lack of success, as were their views that the mass of humanity was unworthy of their attention or of salvation.

The Solar Temple and Heaven's Gate devotees abandoned this earth and committed suicide – or, in their terms, participated in a transit to another higher realm where they, as more evolved spiritual beings, belonged. In so doing, they punished the residents of earth for their refusal to listen to the movement and hence for their failure to receive and benefit from these higher teachings; the people of earth, not ready to evolve, deserved to be left behind. Heaven's Gate and the Order of the Solar Temple left behind messages that announced where they were going, both to create a myth about themselves and to show the people of this earth what they had missed out on. Failure and the fact that 'nobody listened' thus were reinterpreted in ways that heightened the sanctity and self-proclaimed authority of the practitioners of these movements.

Aum's response to rejection was of a different sort to that of Heaven's Gate and the Solar Temple, largely because of the ways in which its messages and visions were structured. Within the framework of its doctrines and beliefs, Aum's most viable response was to fight and confront rather than to commit suicide and depart. Aum, too, abandoned the world, but its rejection was played out in more overtly confrontational forms. Rather than punishing the world by abandoning it to its fate and departing to higher realms, Aum's true victors and its spiritual master, fired by the sense of karmic and spiritual righteousness that is frequently engendered in religious movements when their messages are rejected, punished the world for its ignorance and sins by venting retribution on it.

EXTERNAL PRESSURES AND PROBLEMATIC INTERPRETATIONS

While I have focused so far on the endogenous factors that contributed to Aum's violence, some consideration also needs to be paid to the role of exogenous factors. One of the prevailing themes in the study of new religious movements that have become embroiled in violence and/or suicide has been the part played by such exogenous factors as social pressure, hostility and antagonism directed at them from mainstream society. Many scholars have argued that the ways in which religious movements interpret or perceive opposition need to be taken into account in analysing violent episodes in such religions. This 'interpretive' approach, as Thomas Robbins has called it,[26] has been especially influenced by the Waco tragedy of April 1993, in which blunders, misinterpretations and overtly threatening actions by civil authorities pushed the Branch Davidians into a hostile defensive mode. External pressures affirmed and heightened the sense of apocalyptic tension within the Branch Davidian movement, placed extensive strains on its leader David Koresh (seemingly hastening his sense that the world was moving into an end-time), and strengthened the followers' resistance to the authorities. The Waco affair was, according to Robbins, a paradigmatic case for the interpretive approach[27], one in which external pressures on a religious group and the behaviour and mistakes made by civil authorities can be readily identified as primary causes of the violent destruction and deaths that ensued.

Robbins, while recognising that external provocation may be a factor in the violence of millennial groups,[28] is concerned about the possibility of scholars overemphasising the exogenous or external factors in analysing violent events related to new religions. Indeed, and here I extrapolate from his essay and add my own concerns, this gives rise to the concern that scholars will utilise it as a virtually universal mode of analysis, and will look immediately for the external factors behind any explosion of violence relating to new and apocalyptic movements. Shimada Hiromi was not the only one to make the immediate assumption that Aum either had not been guilty of the crimes of which it was accused, or that external forces were pressurising the movement and somehow responsible for its violence.[29] In such instances , the danger arises that scholars will, in seeking to explain a movement's activities through the lens of external pressure and exogenous factors, either vindicate or be seen as apologists for such movements, a danger that befell Shimada.

Robbins, in critiquing the interpretive approach, points to Aum Shinrikyō as well as the Order of the Solar Temple as cases where, he believes, external provocation was less of a factor in their activities than internal developments. Jean-François Mayer's study of the Order of the Solar Temple certainly places its emphasis on the movement's internal dynamics as the main factor in its implosion of murder and suicide.[30] My study of Aum Shinrikyō, if anything, shows that internal factors were even more emphatic in the production of Aum's violence.

246

Aum did face various external pressures. From relatively early on in its history it faced objections from parents whose offspring entered the movement and severed their family ties. Yet, despite the hostility inherent in such complaints, they were understandable within Japanese culture, especially in legal terms, given that some disciples were below the age of majority. The problem in terms of conflicts with parents was not so much that the parents or families took an aggressive or militant posture, as that Aum, because of its rejection of the parents' material culture, made no attempts to come to any form of accommodation with the parents. It therefore exacerbated such situations and increased the potential for conflict at every stage in its development.

Aum also, of course, faced other external pressures, whether in the context of media reports in 1989, the negative media coverage and the public humiliation that emanated from the 1990 election, and various criticisms from anti-Aum groups from that period onwards. Its experiences at Kamikuishiki and especially Namino also created difficulties for the movement. All of these inflamed the hostility that Aum felt towards the world at large, and were factors in pushing it into even more extreme confrontational stances. Such external opposition fed into Aum's perceptions about persecution, and gave added impetus to its development of conspiracy theories and the need to fight.

However, persecution and conspiracy were perceptions rather than realities. In every case in which Aum complained of persecution one can discern an Aum-generated cause, as with the arrests of Ishii and Aoyama in Namino, caused by their violation of (or contemptuous disregard for) the law of the land. In hindsight, the behaviour of the villagers at Namino, provoked as it was by the fear of a group that was suspected of murder, becomes understandable even if their refusal to respect the civil rights of Aum members remains reprehensible. Imagined persecution can certainly play a part in drawing a religious group further into a cycle of violence, as happened with Aum, but it has to be recognised as an internally generated factor, a product of the movement's paranoia rather than as an external factor.

In such contexts it is important for scholars to look closely and perhaps with an occasionally sceptical eye at complaints of persecution and at the ways in which religious movements use them. As we have seen in the case of Aum, an element in the use of such complaints and of the conspiracy theories that embellished them related to the internal problems of the movement and of its leader. Asahara used persecution and conspiracy as tropes to enhance his status as a sacred figure with the key to world salvation, to explain his and the movement's problems and failures, and as a means of holding it together and preventing defections. He was not the first religious leader to use such means or strategies (Di Mambro's complaints of world-wide police persecution of the Solar Temple had a similar dynamic) nor is he likely to be the last. The Aum case should be seen as a reminder that when religious groups complain of persecution, scholars need to consider and examine whether and to what extent, in so doing, they may be externalising their internal problems.

I do not argue that the Aum affair can be used as a paradigmatic case for the interpretation of violence in new or apocalyptic religious movements, or that endogenous factors will always be the main or dominant factor in such cases. However, the Aum affair, in showing how a new religious or apocalyptic movement which adopts a hostile and confrontational stance towards society can generate violence and conflict as a result of its own doctrines, nature and internal dynamics, serves as a reminder that one should not immediately look to external factors as the primary cause of that violence. The Aum affair informs us that violence can at least as readily be produced from within a movement.

CONCLUSION

Aum is an extreme example of a religious movement that, operating from a position of righteousness, set out on a grand mission that reflected the ambitions and visions of its leader and that was affirmed and strengthened by the beliefs, actions and commitment of its followers. That mission, although it also began with a promise of universal salvation, had an innately polarising dimension in its conceptualisation of a sacred war between good and evil. In its rejection of the external realities and the materialist orientations of the everyday world Aum rapidly set itself apart, creating a spiritual hierarchy that claimed superiority over the world at large. Due to the continuing failures of its mission – or rather, in Aum's terms, the refusal of the world to listen – its alienation from society increased, and as it did so, it constructed an alternative and self-directed view of morality. Its doctrines developed accordingly, sanctifying acts that were committed in order to protect the position and authority of its leader and to safeguard what it saw as its mission of truth. As it followed this path, Aum lost its grasp of external reality and turned inwards into a self-constructed world in which all who remained outside the movement were unworthy while those inside were transformed into sacred warriors who believed that they could kill with impunity and that in so doing, they could save in the spiritual sense those they killed.

The tragedy of Aum Shinrikyō is not just that its symbolic fight against evil and for world salvation was transformed into a real and brutal fight which resulted in indiscriminate murder, but that in claiming to operate on exalted spiritual ground beyond the boundaries of normal morality, it severed all links with the spiritual status to which it aspired. Asahara started with messages that resonated with the needs of many Japanese people and expressed ideas that have been at the heart of religions through the ages, such as the imbalances and problems of societies based on materialism and concepts of progress that fail to give due consideration to spiritual explanations and needs, and the affirmation of spiritual techniques and practices that can lead to happiness and liberation.

The tragedy and irony, of course, is that, in seeking to implement such messages, Asahara Shōkō and his disciples – the buddhas and bodhisattvas with the mission to create a Buddhist new age of Lotus villages and a Shambala kingdom – betrayed every one of their ideals, killing not only those outside the movement who symbolised the corruption against which they fought, but their own devotees. In setting out with a mission to save the world from disaster, Aum ended up by killing the very people, such as Ochi Naoki, it needed in order to carry out its mission. The process through which it reached this position was centred around religious themes, doctrines and images, and was linked closely to its self-image as a religious movement with a sacred mission. As such Aum Shinrikyō provides us with a salient example of the violence-producing dimensions of religion and reminds us of how religious movements can, through a confluence of circumstances, engender, legitimate and commit acts of violence in the name of their faith.

乱

Notes

INTRODUCTION

1.   The US Senate established an enquiry into Aum's arms-gathering and production activities as part of the remit of its committee on the proliferation of weapons
of mass destruction (Committee on Government Affairs 1996), as did the Canadian
intelligence services (their report is available at http://www. csis-scrs.gc.ca/eng/
miscdocs/postscre.html). Other law enforcement agencies, such as the Australian
Police Force, also displayed similar concerns: see the article by Penrose (1995).

2.   This phrase was the subtitle of Kaplan and Marshall (1996), the first journalistic book published in the English language about Aum.

3.   Although Asahara Shōkō, during his trial which began in April 1996, has
repeatedly denied that he gave the orders for the attack and has claimed that
he was not directly responsible for Aum's various criminal activities, all the
evidence, including testimonies from many of his disciples who committed the
crimes, indicates that he was deeply involved. In this book I, like others who
have written about Aum, depict Asahara as the main instigator of Aum's crimes,
and regard him as guilty of the various crimes with which he has been charged.

4.   In English, for example, Kaplan and Marshall (1996), while written from a
journalistic perspective that somewhat sensationalises the affair, provides much detail
about Aum's activities. This book differs greatly from my account in that it is not so
concerned with analysing Aum as in setting out accounts of its criminal activity.

5.   Besides the reports carried in various Japanese newspapers such as the *Asahi
Shinbun* and the *Yomiuri Shinbun*, there have been numerous books by reporters
detailing different trials and court appearances of the leading protagonists in the
affair. Amongst these, I have found the following of particular value: Egawa (1996,
1997, TSS (1995) and MNS (1996). A number of Internet sites also carry reports on
the trials: I have especially used the Asahi newspaper's site (http://www.
asahi.com/paper/aum). Aum Shinrikyō also continues to maintain an Internet site
that carries reports on various trials (http://www. aum-internet.org).

6.   Although a number of newspaper articles have appeared in the past year
or so claiming that Aum has been growing and now has several thousand
followers (Skelton 1997; Sullivan 1997; Watts 1998), my own information, based
on discussions with members of Aum in 1997 and 1998, and with colleagues in
Japan, is that the number of active followers was less than 1,000 as of January
1998 and that the numbers have not risen since then.

7.   An edited volume discussing such issues is being prepared by Robert
Kisala and Mark R. Mullins.

8. Reader (1996).
9. Ibid., p. i
10. In particular, the reviews by Gardner (1996), Metraux (1997) and Watt (1998) have pointed to aspects and issues which I had either neglected or had not taken adequate account of. Moreover Shimazono (1997, esp. pp. 70–78), in his detailed critique of my work, alerted me to my neglect of the doctrinal aspects of Aum which, as he amply demonstrates, played an important part in the affair.
11. Hubbard (1998, pp. 59–92).

CHAPTER 1

1. The new religions (*shin shūkyō*) of Japan are a broad and diverse phenomenon: the term refers to movements outside the mainstream religious traditions of Buddhism and Shinto that have usually, though not always, been founded by charismatic individuals. Numerous such movements have emerged in Japan since the first half of the nineteenth century, with different eras seeing the rise of new waves of new religions. The term 'new' new religion is a translation of the Japanese *shin shin shūkyō*, which has come into use in recent years to refer to movements that either emerged in the late 1970s and 1980s, or came into prominence in this era. In Chapter 2 I shall discuss some of the prevailing religious themes that formed the backdrop to the emergence of Aum and these other movements, but in general, for further information on the new religions, see Inoue *et al.* (1991), Hardacre (1984, 1986), Reader (1991, pp. 194–233) and Earhart (1989). For the 'new' new religions, see also Nishiyama (1988), Reader (1988) and Shimazono (1992, 1996).

2. In addition Aum had, according to estimates, around 30,000 followers in Russia, although these do not appear to have had any connection with the movement's nefarious activities in Japan (see below, Chapter 6).

3. Asahara (VK 1, p. 16).

4. This was established in June 1994: see below, Chapter 7.

5. The term *kundalini* in yoga and Hindu systems refers to the inherent spiritual energy latent within humans, that is found at the base of the spine and that, when awakened via yoga techniques, rises through the body and empowers the individual. Aum based many of its practices and concepts on Hindu and yoga systems, a point that will be discussed further in Chapter 3.

6. The English titles given here are the ones Aum used in its English publications to translate Asahara's Japanese titles.

7. These were, besides Ishii: Asahara's wife Tomoko; his third daughter, Achari, who was considered to have inherited Asahara's spiritual power; Murai Hideo, who was one of the chief architects of Aum's programme of weapons building; and Jōyu Fumihiro, who for a time headed Aum's activities in Russia and who, after the subway attack, acted as Aum's chief spokesman.

8. See, for example, Maha Khema Taishi (Ishii Hisako) (1989, 1991a, 1991b).

9. Egawa (1996, pp. 158–161) discusses Ishii's position in the movement, including her closeness to Asahara, but notes that she was scarcely seen by members for a number of years (apparently from the early 1990s onwards) during which time she bore three children. Asahara appeared to confirm this in a court outburst on 22 May 1998, when he bemoaned the fact that Ishii had denounced him and asked

aloud how she could have done so, after bearing him three children (http://
www.asahi.com/paper/aum/kouhan80.html). According to Arita (1995, pp. 191–
192), Ishii had twin girls in or around May 1991 and another girl in early 1992. It
appears that Ishii had been replaced in Asahara's affections by other women shortly
before the subway attack, while her place as second in Aum's de facto hierarchy had
been taken over by Murai Hideo in 1994.

10. See, for example, his comments made in September 1989 in Asahara (VK 9,
p. 71).

11. This comment by Noda Naruhito was reported in the Japanese magazine
Shûkan Asahi, 13 Oct. 1995; see also Reader (1996, p. 9).

12. Asahara (VK 19, p. 138),

13. Asahara (1992d, p. 33).

14. See, for example, Asahara (VK 50, p. 322).

15. The prosecution indictment outlining this incident is given in KTS (1997,
pp. 288–290).

16. Takimoto and Nagaoka (1995, p. 129).

17. See, for example, Aum Translation Committee (1992, pp. 14–64) and Asahara (1991a, 1991b) for general discussions of the different realms.

18. See, for example, Aum Translation Committee (1992, pp. 154–155.

19. See below Chapter 4 for examples of followers who were attracted to Aum
for such reasons.

20. See below Chapter 2 and also the book by Kiriyama Seiyū, the founder of
Agonshū, who claimed that Aum had merely copied many of its teachings (Kiriyama
1995). On Agonshū, see Reader (1988, 1991, pp. 194–233, 1994). Miyazaka (1996),
in discussing Aum's basic doctrinal themes, also draws particular attention to the
influences it imbibed from Agonshū, as does Shimazono (1997, pp. 124–138).

21. See, for example, Asahara (1992a, pp. 70–74).

22. See, for example, Asahara (VK 49, p. 315; VK 53, pp. 339–341).

23. Asahara (VK 38, p. 250).

24. Asahara (1992e, p. 11).

25. Asahara (VK 23, pp. 163–164; 1991g, pp. 120–129).

26. This phrase was used in Asahara (VK 2, p. 22), in a sermon which expressed
the importance of the disciple assuming or taking on the spiritual imprint of the
guru. In Asahara (1986b, pp. 148ff.) accounts are given of how disciples, through
their spiritual practice, seek to copy and implant the guru's spiritual force within
themselves.

27. In October 1997 and January 1998 I interviewed three devout Aum members who had their own PSI units and who wore them from time to time. They
all affirmed to me that they felt great benefits from them.

28. The allegation of brainwashing was used in many media reports and in the
writings of people involved with the anti-cult movement in Japan. For a fuller
discussion of this point see Watanabe (1997). Among commentators on the
affair who assert that Aum brainwashed its followers are Takimoto and
Fukushima (1996, p. 3), and Setagawa (1997 pp. 103–140).

29. Academic studies of conversions to new religious movements have firmly
rejected the idea that these occur because of 'brainwashing': see Barker (1984).

The debate over 'brainwashing' has been discussed further by Zablocki (1997) and Bromley (1998).

30. See, for example, Asahara (VK 29, p. 193).

31. Asahara, for example, was highly critical of the rival new religion Kōfuku no Kagaku and its leader Okawa Ryūhō, for not emphasising ascetic practice (Asahara 1991m), and he and other Aum figures criticised established Buddhist movements in Japan on similar grounds. Aum members interviewed in October 1997 were highly critical of people who fail to understand Aum because, as one put it to me, they have no experience of ascetic practice.

32. This manner of persecuting and coercing missionaries to renounce their faith is discussed in Boxer (1951, pp. 353–354).

33. There is a very transitory usage of upside-down suspension in mountain ascetic practice, in which ascetics are briefly suspended over a precipice to awaken them to the intransience of life (see Swanson 1981, p. 71 for a description) but apart from this I am unaware of its use in Japan.

34. See, for example, Asahara (1994a). Japanese ideograms can be read or pronounced in various ways depending on context and meaning, and may be amended by the addition of *furigana*, or phonetic syllabary, which indicates how an ideogram should be read in a particular context. In Aum *shi* was at times given with the *furigana* for *samadhi* by its side, thus indicating this gloss between the two.

35. This account of the death of Ochi is taken from Egawa (1997, pp. 160–162). It was, in fact, Ōuchi who made this incident known when, arrested on another charge of extorting money from a female believer for the movement, she confessed it to her lawyer.

36. Egawa (1997, p. 162).

37. This latter is the romanised version found in some of Aum's English publications, e.g. Aum Translation Committee (1992, p. 156).

38. Ibid., p. 157.

39. Testimony by Iida Erika in Asahara Shōkō (1992b, pp. 129–132).

40. Kanai (1991, pp. 190–198).

41. For further discussion see Reader (1991, esp. pp. 77–106).

42. This argument is outlined in many of Asahara's later sermons: see, for example, in Asahara (VK 44, esp. p. 286). An example of Ashara using the term *poa shika nai* as a de facto order to kill someone may be found in Egawa (1996, p. 114).

43. Egawa (1997, pp. 162–165).

44. Tabor and Gallagher (1995, p. 142).

45. Ishii, for example, was able to conduct an affair with Asahara although the movement emphasised celibacy for its world renouncers, while other senior figures in the movement, it appears, were able to disregard Aum's normally austere lifestyle.

46. Asahara (1993b, p. 124).

47. Asahara (VK 45, p. 288).

48. Original reports suggested 5,000–6,000 casualties, although court indictments in the trial of Asahara originally listed 3,786 people injured in the attack. The *Asahi Shinbun* of 19 November 1997 gives details of a survey carried out one year after the attack on those who were injured. The survey shows that many

were suffering from long-term psychological problems stemming from the ingestion of gases. A detailed account of the effects of the subway attack itself, and its aftermath on victims, can be found in Murakami (1997).

49. I was informed quite unequivocally of Aum's involvement by a television journalist who telephoned me some hours after the attack on 20 March 1995 and told me that unofficial police briefings in Tokyo had blamed Aum.

50. See Reader (1996, p. 83).

51. See Reader (1996, pp. 84–85) and Shimosato (1995, p. 239).

52. Detailed accounts of Aum's activities in areas such as the acquisition of weapons and materials for making them are recounted in the US Senate report on the global proliferation of weapons of mass destruction (Committee on Government Affairs 1996): a recent article in the *New York Times Online* service by William J. Broad *et al.* (1998) also goes into details about these activities.

53. The death penalty can be given in Japan for crimes that are considered horrendous, and normally this occurs when more than one death has resulted from a person's actions. Hayashi, although participating in a crime that killed 12 people, was sentenced to life imprisonment rather than death because of his cooperation with the authorities and because it was deemed that he had shown sincere remorse and repentance. Okazaki, guilty of three particularly brutal murders, was considered not to have shown remorse and was sentenced to death.

54. Hoffman (1996, 1998).

55. I am grateful for Paul L. Swanson for pointing out this symbolism to me.

56. *Vajrayāna Sacca* (1995, no. 8, p. 14). Similar themes are expressed in Asahara (1995c, p. 135).

57. This comment is given in Asahara (1995a, p. 238; 1995c, p. 198). Toyoda, in these publications, is cited as Vajrapani (his holy name in Aum).

58. Indeed, not long after Toyoda's comment, the poor response of the Japanese government to the devastating earthquake of 17 January 1995 in the Kōbe region appeared to confirm this commonly held view of the government's lack of concern for its ordinary citizens, and to undermine the average citizen's confidence in the government and its bureaucracy.

59. See, for example, Pye (1996, p. 262).

60. The Japanese scholar of religion Yamaori Tetsuo, for example, made some comments suggesting Aum was not a religious group early on, and describing Aum's leaders as 'political technocrats' (Yamaori 1995, p. 11, quoted in Metraux 1995, p. 1148). Various opinions were posted on a number of Religious Studies and Buddhist Studies Internet discussion groups in 1995 expressing similar views or questioning whether it was correct to consider Aum as a religious movement.

61. See Watanabe (1997) for further details about such discussions.

62. Rapoport (1992, p. 118).

63. Shimazono (1997).

64. Smith (1998, p. 404).

65. Juergensmeyer (1992a, p. 1).

66. Ibid., p. 1. The theme of symbols of violence in religious contexts is developed further in Juergensmeyer (1992b, pp. 106–111).

67. Juergensmeyer (1992b, p. 111). Juergensmeyer's essays cited here were written in the context of a conference discussing the work of René Girard (1977), whose theoretical analysis of violence, most particularly centred around the ritual and symbolism of sacrifice, has been influential in pointing to the deep relationship between religion and violence, albeit largely in functionalist terms suggesting the positive functions of religion as a means of deflecting violent impulses into symbolic ritual formats.

68. Ibid., pp. 112–114.

69. Schwartz (1997).

70. Smith (1998, pp. 405–406).

CHAPTER 2

1. See Chapter 3 for a discussion of Aum's beliefs in the existence of a number of different worlds or realms (including what it called the astral and causal worlds) beyond this one, and in the existence of spiritual bodies relating to these worlds.

2. Shanti Taishi (Ōuchi Sanae) (1988, p. 227).

3. These two concepts are important in various branches of Japanese Buddhism as well as in some of the Buddhist-inspired new religions. Aum's understanding of these terms is discussed particularly in Asahara's earlier works (see Asahara 1986b, 1987). There are good accounts of how these two terms were used in Aum, in Shimazono (1995b, pp. 389–393) and Yumiyama (1997, pp. 337–338). One should note also that *gedatsu* itself did not refer to just one state of being in Aum, but had numerous levels, the final one of which (complete, ultimate liberation) had only been attained by Asahara. According to Shimazono, the vagueness of the concept and state of *gedatsu* caused its followers a certain amount of difficulty, especially in the early days of the movement (Shimazono 1995b, p. 392).

4. For further details on the new religions, and on the importance of charismatic founders in the new religions, see the various works cited in Chapter 1, note 1, and also Shimazono (1979).

5. See, for example, Egawa Shōko (1997, p. 342). Egawa is also highly critical of the lack of access allowed to ordinary people in the trials themselves (ibid., pp. 339–342).

6. I do not know why no attempt has been made to examine Asahara from a psychiatric viewpoint to determine his mental state. Certainly in British court cases, debates over the mental well-being of defendants are often critical in determining the degree of culpability. More than one person has speculated to me that the Japanese authorities do not *want* to have Asahara studied from psychological or psychiatric angles because these might show him to be mentally unbalanced and hence unfit to be tried. Given the public mood in Japan, this outcome would be highly problematic for the courts.

7. See above, Chapter 1, note 29.

8. This court statement was reported on the web pages of the *Yomiuri Shinbun* on 24 April 1997 (http://www.yomiuri.com) and CNN (http://cnn.com).

9. See *Asahi Shinbun*, 25 April 1996. An English translation of his opening statement is available on Aum's web pages at http://www.aum-shinrikyo.com/english/master/trial.htm.

10. This public anger was very visible on the first day of his trial in comments made by spokespeople for the victims of the subway attack who were interviewed on television on 24 April 1996 and in response to Asahara's original court statement. One woman, speaking on behalf of families who had lost relatives in the attack, could barely contain her anger as she stated that they had hoped he would take responsibility for the attack and make some form of apology to the public: this view has if anything become stronger the longer he has appeared to evade responsibility for the crimes.

11. Accounts of Asahara's erratic court behaviour are found throughout the various volumes reporting his ongoing court case, such as Egawa (1996, 1997) and KDT(1997).

12. Tamura (1996).

13. Perhaps this was nowhere more evident than in a somewhat ludicrous and unwittingly funny 'non-fiction novel' (Matsuda 1995) that claimed to portray, in fictional form, life inside Aum, in which Asahara appeared to spend most of his time inviting nubile young women into his room, plying them with wine and engaging in dialogues ('Master, is it really me that you like best?' 'Yes, of course' [p. 129]) that came straight out of the genre of cheap romantic novels.

14. This is another recurrent theme of Tamura (1996).

15. For example, shortly before the subway attack, in February 1995, Asahara and his family embarked on a vacation trip around western Japan in which they stayed at expensive inns, visited tourist attractions and generally lived extremely well. An account of this trip is given in TSS (1995, pp. 91–92).

16. Egawa (1995, pp. 158–160) details how he lived in a manner beyond those of disciples, and engaged in sexual relations with female followers, while TSS (1995, esp. pp. 91–92, 101) details Asahara's seeming indulgence in good food.

17. See, for example, the series of interviews between Asahara and personalities such as Beat Takeshi (the actor, comic and film director) and others (Oumu Shuppan 1993). In the interview between the scholar Yamaori Tetsuo and Asahara (which is quoted later in this chapter), Yamaori also appears to be quite impressed with Asahara and makes several positive comments about him as a religious leader and as a person (Asahara and Yamaori 1992).

18. The Dalai Lama was one of a number of Buddhists (others included prominent Sri Lankan and Tibetan priests) who met Asahara and who wrote or spoke positively about his work in promoting Buddhism in Japan. However, there may well have been a level of politeness and diplomatic formality in such greetings and gestures of friendship. As I have pointed out elsewhere, Japanese new religious leaders in general have been extremely adept at developing contacts with and acquiring recognition from world religious leaders such as the Dalai Lama (Reader 1988). However, the fact that Asahara was able to secure a positive endorsement is in itself a criticism of the Dalai Lama who, as Michael Pye (1996, p. 268) has rightly commented, allowed himself to be used by Aum and displayed a lack of critical judgement.

19. Such accounts can be found in numerous Aum publications, for example, Asahara (1986b, 1987) and Kanai (1991).

20. See, for example, Serizawa (1995, pp. 73–74) and the comments by Jōyu Fumihiro writing under his holy name in an Aum magazine (Maitreya Seigoshi 1991, p. 75).

21. Takahashi (1996, pp. 155, 182).

22. For a brief introduction to the rivalry between Aum and Kōfuku no Kagaku, see Reader and Tanabe (1994) and Astley (1995, pp. 16–17). Asahara (1991m) is a volume dedicated to an attack on Kōfuku no Kagaku and its leader, while Astley (1995) is the most comprehensive work available in English on Kōfuku no Kagaku.

23. KDT (1997, p. 23).

24. TSS (1995, p. 170).

25. I base this on my court notes from Hayashi's trial on 22 January 1998. See also *Asahi Shinbun*, 23 January 1998.

26. There is perhaps an irony here in that Asahara himself appeared devoted to his children and placed his family members in high positions in Aum.

27. See Reader (1996, esp. pp. 42–43), for some preliminary comments on the issue of failure and rejection.

28. The data in this section come from TSS (1995, p. 171).

29. Egawa (1997, pp. 260–262).

30. This testimony comes from an interview conducted by Robert Kisala with N-san on 28 January 1996. I am grateful for Robert Kisala for kindly allowing me use of his interview notes.

31. Aum Translation Committee (1992, pp. 130–131).

32. Serizawa (1995, p.149).

33. Takahashi (1996, pp. 154–156). Takahashi records, for example, an occasion when Asahara hurled a dish of curry over a member who annoyed him, while the *Asahi Evening News* (30 October 1995) states that Murai Hideo, one of Asahara's closest disciples, reported that Asahara often threw things at him in rage.

34. Kisala (1998, p. 35).

35. Kanai (1991, pp. 160–172).

36. Egawa (1995, p. 153) quotes Asahara making such statements: Asahara has spoken in various sermons (for example VK 16, pp. 111–112) on similar lines.

37. The same terms were mentioned by a Japanese colleague in Tokyo when discussing her interviews with Aum members.

38. See, for example, the various disciples' testimonies in Asahara (1991c, pp. 121–122).

39. Asahara (VK 37, p. 241).

40. Interview with Asahara (KNS 1992, pp. 187–188).

41. TSS (1995, p. 171) and KTS (1997, p. 215).

42. Arita (1995, p. 34).

43. Kashima (1996, pp. 65–66).

44. Arita (1995, p. 37).

45. TSS (1995, p. 171).

46. Asahara and Yamaori interview (1992, p. 94). According to TSS (1995, p. 172), he began to engage in spiritual practices in 1977, although dates are a little unclear. Asahara's own comments to Yamaori seem to put the date as a little later than this.

47. Asahara (1993a, pp. 25–26). This book was originally published in 1986. References in the present volume are to the 1993 edition.

48. Asahara and Yamaori (1992, p. 94).

49. Ibid., p. 94.

50. See, for example, Asahara's comments in Oumu Shuppan Kōhō Henshūbu (1992c, pp. 18–21), where he says that Buddhist institutions in the present day are worthless.

51. This comment by an Aum member is reported in TSS (1995, pp. 302–303). On the general issue of the social and customary roles of Japanese Buddhism, see Reader (1991, esp. pp. 77–106).

52. Many Japanese new religions first developed around healing and related practices: Nakayama Miki, the foundress of Tenrikyō, for example, first gathered followers because of her apparent power to grant safe childbirth. The importance of healing practices in Japanese new religions has been discussed in numerous volumes, including Davis (1980) and Hardacre (1986).

53. Aum produced numerous volumes of testimonies and stories relating to the spiritual healing of illnesses, such as Atarashii Iryō Kenkyūkai (1991a, 1991b, 1992).

54. Takahashi (1996, pp. 184–189).

55. Oumu Shuppan Kōhō Henshūbu (1992c, pp. 147–148). The concept of changing one's name (or indeed the ideograms of one's name) in order to change one's luck is found quite frequently in Japan: Sumō wrestlers, for example, may change their fighting names in the belief (or hope) that a new name might bring them better luck, especially if they have been on a losing streak.

56. The account given here of the spiritual themes and influences of the 1980s is, of necessity, brief: fuller accounts can be found in Shimazono (1992, 1996), Shimada (1995) and Numata (1995).

57. Nishiyama (1988).

58. Kiriyama (1971). This book became a best-seller in Japan in the 1970s and remained popular in the 1980s. It contributed immensely to the growth of Kiriyama's religious movement.

59. See Numata (1995).

60. Strozier (1994, pp. 227–232).

61. Yamashita (1997, esp. pp. 128–130).

62. Kisala (1998, pp. 144–145).

63. See, for example, Kiriyama (1981), Ōkawa (1988, 1991) and Asahara (1991n).

64. Shimada (1995, pp. 106–107).

65. Serizawa (1996, pp. 9–10).

66. This issue is discussed by Susan J. Napier (1996, esp. pp. 181–222) and Napier (n.d.). Napier discusses these issues further in a book currently in progress: I am grateful to her for sharing her thoughts on this issue with me. Images of imminent apocalypse and millennial scenarios can be found also in Japanese pop songs, such as 'Countdown 1999' by the Alfee. I am grateful to Carolyn Stevens of the University of Melbourne for bringing this song to my attention.

67. Takahashi (1996, p. 160).

68. See Miyazaka (1996, p. 3) for further comments on this issue: on Ōkawa's proclamations of Buddhahood see Astley (1995, p. 343), Numata (1995, p. 195) and Ōkawa (1995). Asahara's claims are repeated in numerous of his books and sermons (e.g. Asahara 1991i and 1991j).

69. Ōkawa (1995, p.19).

70. See, for example, Asahara (VK 22, p.154).

71. Agonshū itself, after the subway attack, did as much as it could to distance itself from Asahara, initially denying that he had been a member, and when that denial was found to be incorrect, claiming that his membership records had inadvertently been misplaced. It further argued that he had been a member in name only, and that he had not really participated in or followed Agonshū teachings or practices. Kiriyama himself wrote a book denouncing Asahara, denying that he had been a genuine member of the movement, and arguing that if he had truly followed Agonshū's practices he would never have taken the path he did (Kiriyama 1995). When I attempted to investigate the Asahara connection with Agonshū further in 1996, officials of the movement refused to speak to me or to meet me. It is clear, however, that there was a substantial link between Agonshū's teachings and those that developed in Aum, while a number of Asahara's close followers, including Hayashi Ikuo, had originally also been in Agonshū.

72. Fujita (1995, p. 82).

73. Shimazono (1997, pp. 138–141).

74. MNL, no. 13, Sept. 1989, pp. 45–50. Shimazono (1997, p. 138) also states that Asahara was frustrated by the lack of practice in Agonshū and took up yoga on his own.

75. For example, he claims to have experienced the awakening of the *kundalini* in 1981 (Shimazono 1995b, pp. 387–388) although most of the major religious experiences he had appear to have come after he left Agonshū.

76. MNL (no. 13, Sept. 1989, pp. 45–50).

77. This is the case, for example, with two of his closest disciples on trial on capital charges, Tsuchiya Masami (accused of conspiracy to murder, because he was one of those who made the sarin used in the Matsumoto and Tokyo attacks) and Niimi Tomomitsu, accused of murders and of conspiracy in the subway case.

78. Interview in Tokyo on 19 Oct. 1997.

79. Interview 20 Oct. 1997.

80. These testimonies are taken from Asahara (1992b, 1992c). The one relating to the phone call is given in Asahara (1992c, p. 121). The disciple states that Asahara even knew the title of the song ('Let It Be') that he was listening to on his headphones. A number of similar testimonies can be found in English on Aum's web site at http://www.aum-internet.org/aum2/choetu/index_e.html.

81. These images recur throughout Asahara's teachings and books: they are central, for example, to Asahara (1991b, 1992c, 1992d).

82. Asahara (1992d, p. v.).

83. Aum Translation Committee (1992, pp. 180–181).

84. Asahara and Yamaori (1992, p. 95). Similar claims are made in Asahara (1992c, pp. 26ff.) and Aum Translation Committee (1992, pp. 206–208).

85. See Reader (1996, pp. 15–16).

86. Kaplan and Marshall (1996, p. 281).

87. Takahashi (1997, p. 237).

88. See, for example, MNLAsahara (1991i, 1991j).

89. Asahara (1992f).

90. (1989, no. 14, pp. 46–52), Asahara (1989a) and Asahara (VK, *passim*).

91. See, for example, the interview with Asahara in *Truth Monthly* (Nov. 1992, no. 11, p. 10).

92. This tendency to explain cases of religious violence and controversy involving devotional religious groups centred around a charismatic leader, as externalised expressions of such leaders' internal troubles, has been expressed, in the case of Aum, by various 'psychological' interpretations of the affair in the Japanese media. Comments along similar lines were also made by Dr Jerrold Post, a psychologist specialising in issues such as terrorism and violence, in response to a presentation I made on the Aum affair at the FBI Academy in Quantico, Virginia, 26 March 1998. Post's point was that Asahara was tormented by an internal paranoia that he projected on to a wider stage. While I recognise Post's point (and, as this chapter and subsequent discussions of Asahara's teachings will show, the leader had severe psychological imbalances), I do not go so far as to share Post's interpretation of the affair largely in terms of the forceful externalised projections of a troubled leader that were imbibed by weak disciples incapable of establishing their own criteria and views. As the rest of this book will show, while there is some element of validity in this perspective, in that it points to the importance of Asahara's internal states of mind in determining the ways in which events unfolded, it is ultimately too one-dimensional to give a full picture of what went on in Aum.

93. Indeed, some writers had levelled such charges before the subway attack: Asami (1992; republished in 1995 after the attack), for example, seeks to investigate what its author considers as phoney prophets and religious leaders, amongst whom is included Asahara.

94. On Deguchi Nao, see the study by Ooms (1993) and on Kitamura Sayo see the biography produced by her movement, Tenshō Kōtai Jingūkyō (1964) which makes little attempt to conceal her fiery and abrasive nature.

95. See Davis (1995, pp. 708–709) for comments on Deguchi's activities and similarities with Asahara.

96. Reader (1991, p. 209).

97. Sakashita (1998, p. 41).

98. Bell (1998, esp. pp. 62–63).

CHAPTER 3

1. Asahara (1991k, p. 2).

2. *Asahi Shinbun*, 6 June 1995, p. 18.

3. This type of pattern can be discerned frequently in the histories of new religious movements, both in Japan and elsewhere. Similar voyages and changes in direction (and even geographical location) can be found in the histories of several other new religions that will be mentioned at various points in this book, such as the Rajneesh movement (Gordon 1987), the Order of the Solar Temple (Mayer 1996) and the People's Temple (Maaga 1996). In Japan examples of the shifts in direction can be seen in, for example, the ways in which new movements such as Agonshu (see Reader 1988, 1991, 1994) grew, adopted new teachings and changes in orientation as its leader Kiriyama had numerous new experiences and visions.

4. Davis (1980, p. 73).

5. See, for example, Gordon (1987).

6. Shimazono (1992, 1996).

7. Accusations that he had merely copied everything Agonshū said, were at the heart of the book by Agonshū's leader Kiriyama Seiyū, which denounced Asahara and Aum (Kiriyama 1995).

8. See the photograph in Asahara (1988b, p. 35).

9. See, for example, the colour photograph section at the front of Asahara (1987).

10. Such a relationship, between a charismatic religious founder and a deity who serves as a personal guide and source of spiritual energy, is not uncommon among the founders of new religions, although the choice of a deity from outside the Japanese realm is somewhat rare in the Japanese tradition. Asahara's dress, especially in the early days of Aum when he was photographed dressed like an Indian sadhu, especially demonstrates a close identification with Shiva.

11. MNL (no. 13, 1989, p. 49).

12. See, for example, Asahara (1992e, p. 104).

13. Asahara (VK 52, p. 336).

14. Asahara (1992e, pp 105–106).

15. Asahara (1991o, p. 7).

16. Asahara (1988b, p. 222).

17. Nishiwaki (n.d., but probably 1997, pp. 18–20).

18. Nishiwaki (n.d., pp. 4–12).

19. As Kisala (1998, p. 36) notes, Asahara's first book (1986a) barely provides any discussion of Buddhist doctrines and is largely focused on psychic powers.

20. Asahara (1986b, pp. 25–26, 133–146).

21. Out of the 100 or so Aum books in my own collection, around 80 have some Buddhist theme in their title, including Asahara 1988b (*Mahāyāna sūtora*), 1992a (*Haiesuto danma*) and 1994c (*Bōdisattova sutora*).

22. See Asahara (1991a, 1991b, 1992c, 1992d).

23. See, for example, Asahara (1991q) for the description of an Aum pilgrimage to Indian Buddhist sites.

24. Various scholars have argued that Aum should not be considered Buddhist because of its eclecticism (see Pye 1996, p. 268) or because of its violence. In her study of Aum in Russia, Yulia Mikhailova (1996, pp. 29–30) draws attention

to misreadings and errors in Aum's use of Buddhist terms and teachings, to suggest that its Buddhist claims were erroneous.

25. Asahara (1992e, pp. 11–13).

26. Shimazono (1997, p. 143).

27. Serizawa (1997, pp. 143–144).

28. I base this remark on interviews that I conducted in Tokyo in October 1997 and January 1998. An interview conducted by Robert Kisala with a former Aum member in January 1996 expressed similar themes, while there are numerous accounts of believers' testimonies throughout Aum's publications, many of which (as in other new religions) devote numerous pages to disciples' experiences (*taiken*). On the issue of followers' testimonies and experiences in the new religions in general, see Anderson (1988); for some representative examples of these in Aum, see Asahara (1993a, pp. 248–365; 1987, pp. 136ff.).

29. Takahashi (1997, pp. 124–128).

30. Asahara (VK 21, p. 151).

31. See, for example, Asahara (1991d, pp. 258–263; 1994c, pp. 212–229).

32. Takahashi (1997, p. 76).

33. MNL (no. 13, Sept. 1989, p. 46).

34. MNL (no. 13, Sept. 1989, p. 46). For a fuller description of this initiation and its importance in Aum, see Oumu Shuppan Kōhō Henshūbu (1992c) and Oumu Shinrikyō (n.d., p. 7).

35. There are frequent references in Aum magazines and books to Asahara breaking down or becoming sick because of performing too many *shaktipat* initiations: see, for example, MNL (no.13, 1989, p. 48) and MNL (no. 14, 1989, p. 50).

36. See Reader (1994) for a fuller discussion of this issue.

37. See, for example, the photograph in Takimoto and Fukushima (1996, p. 44).

38. Asahara (1993a, pp. 16–21).

39. See, for example, the various testimonies by followers in Asahara (1992b), including that by Ishii Hisako, who claims to have seen Asahara levitating peacefully. One disciple describes how he saw Asahara, during meditation, begin to float a few centimetres off the ground initially for a few seconds: gradually the periods became longer. The disciple also firmly rebuffs the suggestion that these could have been leaps because, he states, the landings were gentle and peaceful, not violent bumps as would be the case with a deliberate leap (Asahara 1992b, pp. 17–18). Asahara (1993a) also has a section of photographs of disciples levitating: not all appear to be in pain and the faces of at least two seem relatively calm and relaxed.

40. Asahara (1991c, pp. 1–2).

41. Asahara (1992b, pp. 14–15).

42. Asahara (1991c, pp. 1–2).

43. Ibid., pp. 92–93.

44. In Asahara (1993a, p.112), for example, he claims to have foreseen the crash in 1985 of a Japanese Air Lines jumbo jet in Gunma prefecture which cost over 500 lives.

45. Asahara (1988b, p. 37).

46. See, for example, Oumu Shinrikyō (n.d.) as an example of the various courses and forms of practice that could be undertaken.

47. Asahara (1992c, p. 47). This discussion of Aum's concepts of the realms of existence is based primarily on Asahara (1992c, pp. 19–48). The existence of a number of other realms of existence which are interconnected with this world is an idea found in a number of new religions: Mahikari, for example, talks of the Divine World, Astral World and Earthly World (Davis 1980, p. 34), while GLA, the works of whose founder Takahashi Shinji (d.1976) Asahara read, and other new religions such as Kōfuku no Kagaku that have been influenced by GLA, display some similarities in terms of cosmology, realms of existence and spiritual hierarchies.

48. Using classic Buddhist terms, Asahara likened this world to the world of emptiness (Sanskrit: sūnyatā) (Asahara 1992c, p. 44).

49. Truth Monthly, May 1993, p. 46. An Aum flyer produced by its centre in New York speaks of 'Astral Music' as 'reproduction of the holy sound vibrations that the Master Asahara has perceived in the higher Astral Worlds'. Such music allows one to enter into meditation and purifies the consciousness. (Aum leaflet, nd., published in New York).

50. Maha Khema Taishi (Ishii Hisako) 1991a and 1991b.

51. Asahara (1992e p. 57).

52. Shanti Taishi (Ōuchi Sanae) (1988, p. 227).

53. Asahara (1992g, pp. 56–58).

54. See, for example, Maha Kheema Taishi (Ishii Hisako) (1991a, pp. 94–101).

55. The assertion that his prophecies are accurate and that the world was developing exactly as he predicted, is a claim that was made in numerous Aum publications: see Reader (1996, pp. 58–59) and Asahara 1993b, p. 1.).

56. Asahara (1986b, p. 2).

57. Asahara (1986b, pp. 3– 4). I have been informed that in a Japanese television documentary about Asahara's visit to India, various Indian practitioners testified that Asahara had in fact spent a two-month period performing austerities in the mountains, although they suggested also that he had failed to achieve the levels of spiritual attainment he later claimed. I have not been able to verify this point, or to see the documentary in question, but it appears to indicate that Asahara did at least undergo a certain degree of ascetic training.

58. Asahara (1988b, p. 2).

59. Ibid., p. 4.

60. These themes are developed in works such as Asahara (1986b, 1987, 1988a). See also MNL (no.15, 1989, pp. 1–12) for a brief historical summary of the development of Aum's teachings.

61. The Japanese terms used here are the standard ones used in Japanese Buddhism to denote the six disciplines in the Buddhist path: the English terms are those that Aum used in its English language volumes (e.g. Asahara 1988a, p. 63).

62. Interview on 20 October 1997. See also Takahashi (1997, p. 88), who was a student with little money when he renounced the world.

63. Asahara (1992a, pp. 197–199): see also Shimazono (1995b, pp. 409–410) for an English translation of Asahara's discussion of detachment.

64. Shimazono (1995b, p. 410).

65. See, for example, Kaplan and Marshall (1996, p. 263) which comments on Murai's 'calm and confident manner' and of how 'nothing seemed to faze him' when facing the media in the days after the subway attack.

66. Takahashi (1997, p. 55).

67. Asahara (1991a, pp. 51–52; 1992c, pp. 35–36).

68. MNL (no.14, 1989, p. 48).

69. Shimazono (1995a, p. 6).

70. See Hurvitz (1976) for a translation of the Lotus Sutra and its future predictions of buddhahood.

71. Jōyu was convicted and incarcerated for perjury but has not been charged with offences relating to the violence Aum committed.

72. KNS (1992, p. 26).

73. These terms appear throughout Aum's publications: see Aum's final magazine *Anuttara Sacca* (no. 1, 1995, pp. 10–11) for an outline of these various stages.

74. One should note that giving one's time to and voluntarily working for the religious group is a concept widely found among the Japanese new religions, whose members are expected to perform such tasks for the sake of their religion. It is, indeed, regarded as an important religious practice, as it is in Zen Buddhism where it is called *samu*. For monks and inhabitants of Zen temples, *samu* generally involves such tasks as cleaning the corridors and floors, sweeping the gardens and so on (see Reader 1995 for a general outline of these issues).

75. Kisala (1998, pp. 39, 46–47, fn. 6).

76. See, for example, Shimazono (1995b, pp. 391–395) and Kisala (1998, p. 39).

77. Shimazono (1995b, p. 393).

78. Recruiting new members gained members points which contributed to their advance in status (see Egawa 1995, pp. 84–85).

79. Like many terms used in Aum, this was derived from Sanskrit.

80. I have devised this table based on *Anuttara Sacca* (no. 1, 1995, p. 11).

81. Takahashi (1997, p. 52).

82. It should be noted that the term Hinayāna has pejorative connotations, and is a product of Mahāyāna thought, which seeks to belittle the form of Buddhism it represents. The term is widely used to such ends in Japanese Buddhism which has been greatly influenced by and adheres to the Mahāyāna path.

83. See Asahara (VK 1, pp. 1–4).

84. Asahara shifted focus between the two terms Tantra-Vajrayāna and Vajrayāna throughout the Vajrayāna course lectures. I use Vajrayāna for reasons of clarity.

85. Here, of course, I am referring to Asahara's conception of what the Vajrayāna path was, rather than outlining what it is in classic Buddhist thought.

86. This is clearly the name of a Shinto deity (*nomikoto* being a common Shinto suffix).

87. This account of Asahara's vision is taken from an Aum's history of the movement (MNL no. 13, 1989, pp. 46–47).

88. Shimazono (1995b, p. 388). Shimazono states that the deity who spoke to Asahara was Shiva. However, although Shiva plays a major role as an inspirational

deity and spiritual guide for Asahara, the Aum account cited above does not name Shiva as the deity who speaks to Asahara.

89. Shimazono (1995b, p. 395).

90. MNL (no. 13, 1989, p. 47). In this account the name of the nationalist is given as Sakai Katsuisa.

91. Ibid., p. 48.

92. MNL (no. 13, 1989, p. 50).

93. Asahara (1987, pp. 87–88).

94. This is also a basic theme of Agonshū's teaching (see Reader 1991, pp. 212–215).

95. While I have been unable to find a reference to this figure in Asahara's published sermons, it is cited in Mainichi Shinbun Shūkyō Shuzaihan (ed) 1993 (p. 131) and in Inoue *et al.* (1991), and was confirmed in the interview cited here and conducted in October 1997 with an Aum *shukkesha*.

96. See Shimazono (1995b, pp. 395–397) for the translation of an Aum pamphlet of 1988 on this topic.

97. On this question see Newman (1995, p. 285).

98. See Numata (1996, pp. 44–45) and Shimazono (1995b, p. 388).

99. The term Asahara used for this was '*Shanbaraka keikaku*' (Asahara VK 19, p. 139).

100. Shimazono (1995b, p. 397).

101. Ibid., p. 397.

102. See for example Asahara (1988a, p. 88).

103. Numata (1996, p. 57).

104. This comment from Asahara's *Twilight Zone* interview is reprinted in Asahara (1995c, p. 248).

105. I have taken this term 'catastrophic millennialism' from the work of Catherine Wessinger (e.g. Wessinger 1997: see also Wessinger 1999 forthcoming) which Wessinger uses to refer to movements that believe that any millennial occurrence such as the dawning of a new spiritual era must be presaged by a catastrophe or massive cataclysm that will eradicate much of the material world, thereby wiping away the traces of the corrupt world and paving the way for the emergence of a new way.

106. This equation of materialism and the devil first surfaces in Asahara (VK 5, pp. 50–51), in the course of a sermon delivered in April 1989.

107. Asahara (1995b, *passim*, but esp. pp. 262–263).

108. Asahara (VK 22, p. 154).

CHAPTER 4

1. Shimazono (1995a, p. 6) replicates the graph of membership ages given by the *Mainichi Shinbun*. Figure 1 is based on this graph.

2. See Reader (1996, p. 82).

3. KNS (pp. 26–28). See also Aum Press (1995, pp. 161–172) which relates the stories of a number of other older Aum *shukkesha*, including a woman of 83.

4. Richard Young, for example, has commented upon how, when watching a video of a sermon by Asahara, he felt Asahara sparkled with wit, humour and

insight – a stark contrast to the printed text of his talks, which tended to be rather uninspiring and flat (Young 1995, pp. 234–235).

5.   Takahashi (1996, *passim*, esp. pp. 41–46 on Inoue and pp. 107–111 on Murai).

6.   As soon as it became clear that Aum had been involved in this, bookshops throughout Japan removed its books from their shelves.

7.   See, for example, Hayashi's account in Oumu Shuppan Kōhō Henshūbu (1991, pp. 92–118). Various other accounts of the experiences of other Aum members and ex-members also mention books as the initial point of contact with the movement: see, for example, Takimoto and Nagaoka (1995, p. 136).

8.   In this chapter I refer to several members by their initials (with the polite Japanese title *san* as a suffix). This particular member was referred to as NF-san in KNS (1995).

9.   KNS (1995, pp. 29–30).

10.   KNS (1995, pp. 137–144). One should note that the reporters clearly were under the impression much emphasised in the Japanese media in the earlier part of the post-war era that people who joined new religions did so because of material deprivation and because they were marginalised in society.

11.   Ibid. (pp. 137–144).

12.   Ibid. (pp. 101–102).

13.   Takimoto and Nagaoka (1995, pp. 128–129).

14.   Egawa (1995, pp. 114–115).

15.   See KNS (1995, pp. 37–38) for two such examples.

16.   None of the three interviewees mentioned here has been charged or associated with any criminal actions. Since they are all trying to adjust their lives to the post-March 1995 situation, where their lives as Aum *shukkesha* were dramatically interrupted, I have not revealed their names but refer to them instead by initials.

17.   This was almost certainly the sermon that he gave on 23 November 1992 at Kyoto University. Many of Asahara's sermons at this period were at university campuses.

18.   By examining the dates and locations of Asahara's sermons in this period, I have ascertained that the sermon A-san heard was Asahara (VK 27, pp. 181–184).

19.   In Buddhism, the evil passions (Japanese: *bonnō*) are at the root of the desire that causes suffering, and the purpose of spiritual practice is to eradicate them.

20.   See, for example, Takimoto and Nagaoka (1995, pp. 86–93).

21.   Motoyama has written numerous books about yoga and psychic powers, and has established a society for the study of parapsychology (*chōshinrigaku*) in Tokyo. See Motoyama and Motoyama (1983) for further details about his teaching and the organisation he runs.

22.   Of the two, Hayashi actually released sarin on the subway while Inoue was deeply involved in planning and coordinating the attack.

23.   Hayashi's story is given in Oumu Shuppan Kōhō Henshūbu (1991, pp. 92–118).

24.   Ibid. (p. 98).

25.   Ibid. (p. 101).

26.   Ibid. (pp. 102–103).

27. Ibid. (pp. 102–103).

28. These were Asahara (1986b, 1988b).

29. Oumu Shuppan Kōhō Henshūbu (1991, pp. 108–109).

30. Ibid. (p. 111).

31. Ibid. (p. 116).

32. Ibid. (p. 117). The techniques included hot water immersions and other therapies that are believed to have caused the deaths of several patients (see Egawa 1997, pp. 162–165).

33. Oumu Shuppan Kōhō Henshūbu (1991, p. 118).

34. See Kaplan and Marshall (1996, p. 209). Elsewhere (p. 154) Kaplan and Marshall describe him as one of Aum's 'ruthless killers'; he has been similarly portrayed in much of the Japanese media as well.

35. Takahashi (1996, *passim*, but esp, pp. 41–46).

36. KDT (1997, p. 24) and Oumu Shuppan Kōhō Henshūbu (1992a, p. 95).

37. This account of Inoue's life and experiences is based on Oumu Shuppan Kōhō Henshūbu (1992a, pp. 95–140), supplemented by information from Kisala (1998), Arita (1995), and KDT (1997, pp. 22–27).

38. Oumu Shuppan Kōhō Henshūbu (1992a, p. 103).

39. Ibid. (p. 105).

40. Ibid. (pp. 107–109).

41. Ibid. (pp. 113–117).

42. Ibid. (p. 128).

43. Ibid. (pp. 133–134).

44. Ibid. (pp. 139–140).

45. KDT (1997, pp. 10–20).

46. KNS (1995, pp. 39, 46–48). See also Reader (1996, pp. 33–34) for further comments on this issue and examples of those who gave large sums to Aum.

47. Oumu Shuppan Kōhō Henshūbu (1992b, p. 23). The austerity itself was derived, it appears, from practices in Tibetan Buddhism which Asahara encountered while in India (Shimazono 1995b, pp. 391–392).

48. This account is taken from Oumu Shuppan Kōhō Henshūbu (1992a, pp. 56–89).

49. Ibid. (pp. 56– 57). He renounced the world in August 1989 (p. 58).

50. Ibid. (pp. 60–62).

51. Ibid.

52. Ibid. (pp. 81–82).

53. Ibid. (p. 89).

54. See, for example, Oumu Shuppan Kōhō Henshūbu (1992b) for the accounts of Jōyu's, Murai's and Tomoko's practices.

55. Takahashi (1996, p. 64).

56. KDT (1997, p. 27).

57. Ibid.

NOTES

CHAPTER 5

1. Asahara (VK 1, pp. 4–17). Asahara used both these terms almost inter-
changeably, although more commonly using simply Vajrayāna, which he appeared
to regard as the higher manifestation of this path. For brevity I shall use the
term Vajrayāna to refer to this path.

2. Miyazaka (1996, p. 20), for example, has described the Vajrayāna sermons
as containing the 'real essence' of Asahara's teachings. Much of Shimazono's
(1997) analysis of Aum and of Asahara's teaching is based on this text.

3. Takahashi Hidetoshi, for example, states that he was given this text to read
when he became a *shukkesha* in the summer of 1994 and was told that it was a
key teaching (1996, p. 157). Indeed, access to the text as a whole appears to have
been highly restricted even after the subway attack and the mass investigations
into Aum: several scholars who have written about Aum have commented that they
have been unable to get access to these lectures (see, for example, Setagawa
1997, p. 33). It was not until almost two years after the subway attack that I was
able, through a colleague, to get a copy of this text.

4. Many of these themes were, of course, also highlighted in various terms in
other of his published works in this period, such as Asahara (1989a, 1989b,
1991n, 1992g, 1993b, 1995a, 1995b, 1995c).

5. Asahara (1991c, pp. 92–93).

6. Asahara (VK 1, pp. 4–17).

7. Asahara (VK 2, p. 21).

8. See, for example, MNL (14, 1989, pp. 41–42) where Asahara, in response
to a disciple's question, suggests that lying, from a Tantric perspective, could be
acceptable if it is done to further the truth.

9. In Asahara (1986b, pp.148 ff.), which discusses the practices of the followers
and their experiences, the term used is to 'copy' (*kopii*)) the guru rather than
'clone' (*kurōnu*) as in this sermon.

10. Shimazono (1995b, pp. 394–395).

11. Egawa (1995, p. 81).

12. For an outline of the various chemicals used in Aum initiations in this
later period, see Setagawa (1997, pp.104–105).

13. Douglas (1984 [1966]; citing Harper, p. 9).

14. On the cult of relics in Buddhism, see Faure (1991, pp.132–147) and
Schopen (1997). On Christianity, see Geary (1990, 1994, esp. pp. 177–218).

15. At the current (1999) rate of approximately ¥125 yen to US$1, this was
around US$2,400.

16. See my comments in Reader (1996, pp. 33–34). Kanai Ryōko, for example,
records that her father, when dying from cancer, received relief from pain as a
result of drinking the 'Miracle Pond' liquid. Her testimony is cited in Oumu
Shinrikyō (n.d., p. 9).

17. Egawa (1995, p. 84).

18. Ibid. (pp. 78–86).

19. This claim was made in an Aum publication cited by Egawa (1995, p. 13).

269

20. KDT (1997, p. 270).

21. Kaplan and Marshall (1996, p. 37).

22. These thoughts were first expressed publicly in Asahara (1989a), which was compiled in autumn 1988 and which will be discussed at greater length later in this chapter.

23. On Kiriyama's prophecies see, for example, Kiriyama (1995).

24. See, for example, Ōkawa (1990a, 1990b, 1991). On this score, a comparative study of the catastrophic prophecies of Asahara and of Ōkawa Ryūhō of Kōfuku no Kagaku would be most interesting, although this is unfortunately beyond the scope of the present study.

25. Shimazono (1997, p. 86) argues that the uses of apocalyptic ideas such as Armageddon were, for Asahara, a stratagem or 'skilful means' (hōben) aimed at getting new members. While I agree that Asahara used these ideas to attract members, I do not concur that he viewed it solely in such terms: in the Vajrayāna sermons in particular, Asahara's visions of a potential apocalypse were extremely intense and leave me in little doubt that this scenario was, for Asahara, a very real one.

26. Arita (1995, pp. 184–190).

27. Even those senior disciples who performed initiations could only do so because Asahara had permitted it, and as a result of attainments that they had achieved through his teaching.

28. Serizawa (1996, pp.74–75, 145–146).

29. Asahara (1989a, pp. 1–3).

30. Ibid. (pp.74–75).

31. It also provided his followers with the means to explain or rationalise such behaviour by their guru, an issue to be discussed in Chapter 8.

32. These are the implications of her earlier interviews on the subject of being forced into practice, as reported in Fujita (1995, pp. 120–121) and Arita (1995, p. 68).

33. Tomoko's comments, in which she claims that she, too, was a victim of her husband's brutality, were made during her 27 October 1997 court appearance and were reported on http://www.asahi.com on 28 October 1997.

34. Serizawa (1996, p. 149).

35. Egawa (1995, p. 153), citing an interview in Mahāyāna, no. 26.

36. Asahara (VK 15, pp.109–113). Among other senior figures in Aum who received similar treatment was Inoue Yoshihiro who was punished in July 1990 for offending Tomoko (Egawa 1996, p. 200).

37. Asahara (VK 8, pp. 63–67).

38. Ibid. (p. 65).

39. During the years that I lived in Japan in the 1980s I saw numerous programmes and documentary films focusing on Zen Buddhism on Japanese television, particularly on the national channel NHK. These documentaries invariably put great emphasis on the strictness of Zen temple life, and one of the recurrent symbols used to emphasise this point was the use of the kyōsaku. It is an image often used by the Zen sects themselves in publications designed to promote Zen and to portray it as an austere tradition, but which implicitly glorify the ritualised use of violence (see, for example, Sōtōshū 1981).

40. This incident was reported in the *Asahi Shinbun* (6 and 7 July 1995). I would like to thank Clark Chilson for bringing this incident to my attention.

41. This comment was made by Hattō Masami, a former soldier interviewed during *The Real Tojo*, a programme about the Japanese Army and General Tojo during the war years (Channel 4, 12 Dec. 1998).

42. Steinhoff (1992, p. 205).

43. Ibid.

44. Asahara (1989a, pp.1–3).

45. Tabor and Gallagher (1995, p. 8).

46. Ibid.

47. Asahara (1989a, pp. 3, 18).

48. Asahara made frequent references to the devil (*akuma*) in sermons from spring 1989 onwards: see, for example, the sermon on 28 April 1989 (Asahara VK 6, pp.50–51).

49. Asahara (1989a, p. 46).

50. Shimazono (1997, pp. 79–80).

51. KDT (1997, p. 272).

52. Ibid. (p. 273).

53. Ibid.

54. Asahara (VK 3, pp. 31–33).

55. Asahara (VK 10, p. 83).

56. Mullins (1997, p. 38).

57. Asahara (VK 4, pp.35–36).

58. Asahara (VK 9, p. 71).

59. Interview, Tokyo, 19 Oct. 1997.

60. Sakamoto had been introduced to some parents with complaints against Aum by a colleague, the journalist Egawa Shōko, because Sakamoto had previous experience of dealing with similar disputes relating to the Unification Church.

61. The actions of TBS in showing the programme to Aum representatives only came to light well after the subway attack. In fact TBS had covered the whole matter up; it had never alerted the police about a possible Aum connection at the time of the disappearance of the Sakamoto family, and perhaps more shockingly, had not warned Sakamoto that Aum officials had seen his interview and were incensed by it. As a result, when the details of this affair emerged in 1996, TBS received much, amply deserved, public criticism. Whether its actions in some way contributed to the subsequent murder of the Sakamotos is unclear. Its behaviour, however, was cowardly and reprehensible.

62. This statement was made by Asahara during hearings into whether Aum should be proscribed under the Subversives Prevention Act (Habōhō) in late 1995. In it Asahara, for perhaps the only time, takes on some responsibility for Aum's actions, although he has subsequently retreated from this position: for a fuller account of his statement on this issue see KDT (1997, pp. 51–53).

63. Reported on 16 January 1998 on http://www.asahi.com.

64. Cited by Pye (1996, p. 265).

65. I was later to catch a glimpse of similar sentiments when talking to a former Aum member in Tokyo in October 1997. He had been close to Toyoda Tōru, one

of the subway attackers, and spoke of his shock at Toyoda's involvement in the affair. However, underneath his seeming dismay and concern that a friend had been involved in that attack (and had not told him, a close colleague, about it) I sensed that another emotion was also at play. In effect, the former member seemed to be asking himself the question: Why was it Toyoda who was chosen and not me?

66. So, too, was that of Sakamoto's wife. However I have not come across any attempts by Asahara or the actual killers to legitimate her murder: I assume that this is because she, as an adult married to Sakamoto and hence associated with his activities, was regarded as being complicit in his 'sins'.

67. KDT (1997, pp. 51–53).

68. This statement was reported on http://www.asahi.com/paper/aum.html.

69. I heard comments along these lines not just from Japanese friends but also from Western friends living in Japan.

70. It has widely been suggested that they did not follow matters up for two reasons: one, because Sakamoto was a left-wing activist who had previously conducted civil rights cases against the police, and the other because the police, mindful of Japan's past history of police suppression of religious freedoms in Japan's pre-war fascist era, were reluctant to investigate a religious group. For a full account of police investigations of Aum, and of problematic issues involved in them, see Asō (1997).

71. Egawa (1995; originally published in 1992) is an example of her crusading journalism against Asahara. Takimoto has also published widely on the Aum affair and been involved in campaigns to persuade Aum members to leave the movement: see for example Takimoto and Nagaoka (1995), and Takimoto and Fukushima (1996).

72. I first became aware of the suspicions against Aum during a visit to Japan in March 1990 when I came across an article in the *Sunday Mainichi* (11 March 1990, pp. 204–207) which quite openly discussed the disappearance of the Sakamotos and clearly insinuated that Aum was guilty in this matter.

73. Interview in Tokyo, 22 January 1998. Apparently Jōyu Fumihiro was one of those most opposed to the idea.

74. Asahara (VK 9, p. 71).

75. Constituencies in Japanese parliamentary elections elect a number of candidates, rather than simply one, and hence it is normal for parties to put up more than one candidate in each area.

76. According to an interviewee, all at Aum's headquarters gathered to hear the results, and when the news of the defeat came through, Asahara simply uttered the words '*kanpai datta*' ('it's a total defeat') (interview, Tokyo, 22 January 1998).

77. TSS (1995, pp. 214–215).

78. Ibid. (p. 215).

79. Aum spent US$7 million on the campaign, while Okazaki stole US$1.5 million from it, according to evidence that came to light in investigations into Aum following the subway attack. In March 1990 the *Sunday Mainichi* magazine ran an article suggesting that funds had been stolen from the Shinritō offices during the campaign and suggesting some tenuous links between this incident and the disappearance of the Sakamotos.

80. Kaplan and Marshall (1996, p. 47) suggest that 'dozens' of commune members left at this time.

81. Interview in Tokyo, October 1997: the interviewee also confirmed that there were many defections at this time.

82. Interview in Tokyo, October 1997.

83. Young (1995, pp. 232–233).

84. KNS (1995, p. 32).

85. Asahara (VK 12 and 13, pp. 97–102).

86. In Asahara (1991l p. 183; 1992f, p. 153) there are chronologies of Aum's history, from the Aum perspective, which date the beginning of what was later to be seen as an organised conspiracy against Aum, to these articles of October 1989. Here Asahara used the term 'Aum-bashing': in VK 14 (p. 103) he states that Aum has been used as a 'punch-bag' by the media.

87. Asahara (VK 14, pp.103–104). This sermon is the earliest one in the VK series to mention the Jews and Freemasons as participants in a conspiracy against Aum. There is, on the fringes of Japanese popular culture, a recurrent strand of anti-Semitism in which the Jews have been portrayed in sinister terms, and Asahara was clearly playing on this sentiment. On the issue of Jews as a focus of discrimination and a target of such ideas in Japan, see Goodman (1997).

88. Asahara (VK 13, p. 102).

89. Asahara (VK 15, pp. 108–114).

90. Ibid. (pp. 113–114).

91. Asahara (VK 19, pp. 138–139).

92. Ibid.

93. TSS (1995, p. 215).

94. Ibid. This source states that 500 people took this step at Ishigaki, although this may well be an overestimate: Kaplan and Marshall (1996, p. 59) have a more conservative 125 people taking this step in the month after the seminar.

95. These speculations persisted among the media afterwards as well: in interviews with journalists in Namino later in 1990 Asahara was forced to deny that the group had plans for mass suicide at its commune (KNS 1995, p. 189).

96. The botulinus toxin loses its effect when it comes into contact with oxygen (i.e. it cannot be ingested, it would appear, through the air but requires some other medium, such as food through which to be transmitted. Failing to understand this was one of the many elementary errors Endō and his colleagues made.

97. On Aum's manufacture and attempted use of botulism at this time, see Kaplan and Marshall (1996, pp. 57–59).

98. Hall and Schuyler (1997, p. 297).

CHAPTER 6

1. The prosecution's case against Asahara (outlined in detail in KDT 1997, pp. 232–298) mentions the manufacture of biological weapons in the context of Aum's attempts to arm itself but it does not bring any charges against Asahara on this score, possibly because tangible evidence beyond the statements of those involved could not be found by the time Asahara was arrested.

2.   Gordon (1987, p. 105).

3.   Reader (1996, pp. 101–107).

4.   KNS (1995, p. 49).

5.   In a chronology of the Aum affair published in the *Shûkan Yomiuri* (1 June 1995, pp. 64–65) there are numerous references to such fights and conflicts at Namino in 1990 and 1991. On 12 August 1990, for example, a fight broke out involving 400 villagers and commune members.

6.   KNS (1995, p. 163).

7.   Maha Khema Taishi (Ishii Hisako) (1991a, p. 100).

8.   Aoyama (1990, p. 148). See also Aoyama (1991, pp. 206–332) for a detailed account of his view of the Namino affair, which further emphasises the issue of 'persecution'.

9.   These issues are discussed at length in KNS 1995 (originally published in 1992).

10.   His opposition was not only based in his intense commitment to the area and his wish that control of the region should not fall into the hands of a problematic religious movement, but because he was a member of the Japanese Communist Party and had a strongly critical view of religions in general. This is an issue that cannot be dealt with in the context of this volume, but is one that requires some further exploration, for many of those who were actively opposed to Aum (such as for example, Sakamoto Tsutsumi) had similar left-wing and anti-religious leanings.

11.   The dispute between the movement and locals in Kamikuishiki is covered, albeit partially, by Takeuchi (1995).

12.   These issues are discussed in KNS (1995, esp. pp. 172–175).

13.   Asahara (1991i, 1991j, 1992f).

14.   Asahara (1992f, p. ix).

15.   Ibid. (pp. ix, 153).

16.   Ibid. (pp.115–116).

17.   Ibid. (p. 44).

18.   Asahara (VK 50, pp. 324–325).

19.   Asahara (1992f, pp. 28–29, 79).

20.   See, for example, Asahara (VK 45, p. 288; VK 46, p. 294).

21.   Interviews, Tokyo, Oct. 1997 and Jan. 1998. Takahashi (1996, p. 76) also states that Asahara seemed unwell and that his voice sounded cracked and hoarse around this time.

22.   See, for example, Egawa (1997, p. 55).

23.   The illness in 1994 might well have been real but caused inadvertently by the incompetence of those involved in making Aum's chemical weapons. As will be noted in Chapter 7, they appear to have experienced a number of leaks of poisonous gases.

24.   Gordon (1987, pp. 116–117).

25.   Maaga (1996, pp. 88–89).

26.   See Introvigne (forthcoming).

27. The case of Michi no Tomo ('Friends of the Way') is discussed by Serizawa (1995, pp. 222–238).

28. I use the male pronoun here because the leader figure has been male in all the recent cases that I discuss here and that have been associated with violent denouements.

29. On this debate see Astley (1995, p. 372) and Shimazono (1995b, p. 401).

30. Shimada (1992, 1995). See also Astley (1995, pp. 368–369).

31. For details of this incident, see Astley (1995, pp. 369–372).

32. In the interview with the scholar Yamaori Tetsuo, cited in Chapter 2, for example, Yamaori comes across as being quite impressed with Asahara's religious abilities. The interviews with personalities such as Beat Takeshi, the television personality and film director, published in Oumu Shuppan (1993), also manifest similar themes.

33. Asahara (n.d.) *The Art of Wish Fulfilment* (Fujinomiya: Aum Supreme Truth); undated English language publication, giving the texts of talks from early 1991.

34. Asahara (1992b, pp. 157–166).

35. Asahara (VK 21, p. 145).

36. Ibid. (p. 147).

37. Asahara (1995c, pp.155–156).

38. Mikhailova (1996, p. 15). The term 'rush hour of the gods' comes from the title of McFarland (1967).

39. This account is based in large part on Mikhailova (1996). I am grateful to Yulia Mikhailova for giving me a copy of her article, which is the best and clearest account I have come across on this topic. Overall, details of Aum's activities in Russia remain scarce. While there have been a lot of media-driven speculative accounts, there has been relatively little academic study, apart from Mikhailova's, of the movement's activities there or, crucially, of the political interactions which clearly enabled Aum to gain a footing in Russia.

40. Mikhailova (1996, p. 22).

41. 30,000 is the figure most widely given in publications about Aum, although Mikhailova says that the number was 40,000 (p. 26).

42. Mikhailova (1996, p. 25).

43. Ibid. (p. 32).

44. Asahara (VK 41, pp. 271–272). The person sent to head the Russian mission of Aum was Jōyu Fumihiro.

45. Asahara (VK 51, pp. 321–322).

46. Mikhailova (1996, p. 22, fn.14) suggests that the movement was in search of military technology because of the locations it chose for the centres it opened, which were in areas of the country with a heavy military presence. However, she does not provide any further evidence for her argument.

47. KDT (1997, p. 257).

48. See, for example, Fujita (1995, p. 19). Asahara (VK 46, p. 294) confirms that Russia was a source of equipment for Aum, stating that the movement had acquired a machine for detecting poisonous gases there, in order to defend itself against attacks that, he alleged, were being made on it.

49. *Truth Monthly* (1992, no. 3, pp. 6–20).
50. Kaplan and Marshall (1996, p. 97).
51. Asahara (1992g). See Reader (1996, pp. 56–60) for a detailed outline of the contents of this publication.
52. Asahara (VK 23, p. 160).
53. Asahara (VK 24, pp. 167–170).
54. Asahara (VK 27, pp. 183–184).
55. See, for example, Asahara (VK 37, pp. 243–245; VK 38, pp. 250–251).
56. Asahara (VK 29, pp. 190–191).
57. Asahara (VK 32, p. 222).
58. Asahara (1995a, pp. 1–8).
59. See, for example, Shimazono (1995b, pp. 402–403).
60. Asahara (VK 23, p. 160).
61. Shimazono (1995b, p. 403).
62. Maaga (1996, p. 114; see also pp. 111–132).
63. Gordon (1987, esp. pp. 134–137). For a summary of this issue see also Reader (1996 pp.104–105).
64. Mayer (1996, pp. 71–72).
65. Ibid. (pp. 70–78).
66. Ibid. (pp.74–75; on its hopes of attracting a mass audience see p. 34).
67. Shimazono (1995a, p. 6), based on figures from the *Mainichi Shinbun*.
68. See, for example, Asahara (VK 29, p 190).
69. Astley (1995, p. 370).
70. Interview, Tokyo, 20 Oct. 1997.
71. Takahashi (1996, pp. 109–115).
72. Arita (1995, pp. 190–192).
73. Kaplan and Marshall (1996, p. 161) suggest also that, after having had the children, she lost her place in Asahara's favours to a younger rival.
74. See, for example, Asahara (1992a), which claims to be able to 'prove' the truth of Buddhism in scientific terms.
75. See, for example, Asahara (1994a, 1994b, 1994c).
76. Asahara (1992f, p. 152). This apparently was developed in 1988.
77. See Takashashi (1996, pp. 187–189).
78. Asahara (VK 24, p. 169).
79. The first mention of the USA in this capacity came, as far as I have been able to discover, in November 1992 in Asahara (VK 27, p. 181).
80. See, for example, Asahara (VK 36, p. 238).
81. Asahara (VK 35, p. 234).
82. Ibid. (p. 231).
83. Asahara (VK 45 p. 288).
84. See also Shimosato (1995, pp. 248–249) for similar speculations on this issue.
85. See, for example, Asahara (VK 46, p. 295) (delivered in October 1993).
86. Asahara (VK 49, p. 299; VK 50, p. 322).

87. Asahara (VK 49, p. 314).

88. These names and groups are mentioned in various of the VK sermons and were 'exposed' in Aum's monthly magazine *Vajrayāna Sacca* in 1994. See Reader (1996, pp. 67–68) and Fujita (1995, pp. 60–64) for further details.

89. Asahara (VK 46, p. 299).

90. Accusations on this score permeate many of the Vajrayāna sermons in autumn 1993 (VK 45, p. 288; VK 46, p. 290; VK 50, p. 322).

91. Asahara (VK 46, pp. 294–295).

92. See Asahara (1995a, pp. 122–123), which also contains photographs allegedly of American planes conducting such missions. One Aum follower whom I interviewed and who was resident at the commune in 1994–1995, clearly believed these allegations, and stated that he noticed many such planes in this period and that he was sure they were spying on Aum.

93. See, for example, *Vajrayāna Sacca* (1995, no. 9, esp. p. 38).

94. Ibid. (*passim*, but esp. pp. 6–20).

95. See Reader (1996, pp.104–105) and Gordon (1987, pp. 137, 164).

96. See Introvigne (forthcoming).

97. Mayer (1996, p. 100).

98. Asahara (VK 40, pp. 267–268).

99. See, for example, Kinman 1995, who also suggests that the Waco tragedy of April 1993 was part of the conspiracy – as indeed, are plans to implant microchips into the foreheads of all the citizens of earth by the year 2000 so that the new world government can control everyone. This is just one example of such survivalist literature which I found on the shelves of a prominent New York bookshop in March 1998: one can find numerous 'conspiracy theory' sites on the Internet as well.

100. Mayer (1996, esp. pp. 79–103). I am grateful to Jean-François Mayer also for discussing this issue with me during private correspondence which has helped me further clarify my thoughts on this matter.

101. See, for example, Asahara (VK 46, p. 299).

102. Takimoto and Fukushima (1996, pp. 4–6). Takimoto's warning was issued in November 1994 – a time at which he was under police protection because of fears that Aum would attack him.

103. Wojcik (1997, p. 10).

104. See Kaplan and Marshall (1996, pp. 126–133) for details of Aum's operation in Australia.

105. Asahara (VK 24, p. 169; VK 25, p. 175; VK 27, p. 180).

106. Asahara (VK 36, pp. 237–240).

107. Asahara (VK 27, p. 184).

108. Ibid. (p. 184).

109. Asahara (VK 33, p. 225).

110. See, for example, Asahara (VK 35, p. 235; VK 38, pp. 251–252).

111. Asahara (VK 47, p. 305).

112. Asahara (VK 22, p. 154).

113. Ibid. (p. 154).

114. Asahara (VK 38, pp. 249–250).

115. Asahara (VK 39, p. 261).

116. Asahara (VK 40, p. 270).

117. Asahara (VK 43, p. 280).

118. Asahara (VK 44, p. 286).

119. Asahara (VK 46, p. 293).

120. Asahara (VK 53, p. 345).

121. Asahara (VK 49, p. 317).

122. Asahara (VK 52, pp. 337–338).

123. Cohn (1970, p. 150) (cited in Wojcik 1997, p. 15).

CHAPTER 7

1.   *Oumu tatakai ka hametsu ka,* Oumu Shinrikyō (ed.) Video 1 (n.d. but probably late 1994).

2.   Kaplan and Marshall (1996, pp. 217–218).

3.   For a fuller outline of Aum's activities in such areas, see Kaplan and Marshall (1996, *passim,* but esp. pp. 206–229).

4.   This phrase is of course the title of Aldous Huxley's famous book (1954) about his experiences of taking hallucinogens, and indicates the consciousness-expanding potential that Huxley considered such drugs to have. The belief that LSD and other drugs could have such effects were widely affirmed in the counter-culture movement of the 1960s, which was a precursor of the New Age movement.

5.   For example, see Kaplan and Marshall (1996, pp. 162–166) and Setagawa (1997, pp. 103–108).

6.   See Miyadai (1995, p. 30) for an interview with a former follower who had been working under Murai's supervision and who, when he asked what he was involved in making, was told by Murai not to concern himself about such things but just to get on with his work.

7.   Takahashi (1996, pp. 101–102).

8.   Interview with H-san, 19 Oct. 1997.

9.   Rajneesh had not been able to get the appropriate visa when he entered the USA which would have allowed him to teach his disciples or conduct religious activities in public, and hence had to use intermediaries if he wanted to impart messages to the faithful.

10. Gordon (1987, p. 100).

11. Maaga (1996, p. 94).

12. Takahashi (1997, pp. 162–163; my translation).

13. Hall (1995, p. 208).

14. Ibid. (pp. 208–209).

15. Reader (1996, pp. 81–82).

16. *Asahi Shinbun,* 8 August 1995, cited in Hardacre (1995, p. 17).

NOTES

17. Takahashi (1997, p. 148).

18. This imagery was prevalent in the Japanese media coverage especially by the various weekly magazines (ranging from *Flash* and *Focus* on the one hand to the *Shûkan Asahi* and *Shûkan Yomiuri* on the other, as well as in some English language coverage of the affair: Kaplan and Marshall (1996, *passim*, but especially pp. 28–29), for example, portray them in such terms: as 'brilliant', as Asahara's 'young brains' and so on.

19. Indeed Kaplan and Marshall (1996, p. 140) state that 'Aum's senior chemist' (presumably Endō) had telephoned a friend in June 1994 to warn him that Aum was 'out of control'.

20. Asahara (VK 57, p. 361).

21. See, for example, Asahara (VK 45, p. 288), delivered on 25 Oct. 1993, which was the first occasion when Asahara spoke publicly of sarin attacks against Aum. See also my comments in Chapter 6 where I suggest reasons why Asahara might have spoken publicly about sarin at a time when his movement was making it.

22. See Kaplan and Marshall (1996, pp. 139–141). Moreover, as tangible evidence of Aum's involvement in the attack, it had to be dismantled and disposed of immediately so as to cover Aum's tracks.

23. Takahashi (1996, pp. 100–116).

24. Ibid. (p. 99).

25. Kashima (1996, pp. 105–106).

26. Takahashi (1996, pp. 117–118).

27. Her statement was made on 6 November 1995 during questioning: the text of her statement was made available to me by Takeda Michio from his collection of Aum materials and trial transcripts (Takeda n.d.).

28. Moore (forthcoming).

29. KDT (1997, pp. 286–288).

30. Ibid. (pp. 292–293).

31. These plans were reported in various newspapers in June and July 1995: see Astley (1995, p. 373). Kaplan and Marshall (1996, p. 132) mention the plot to kill Ikeda.

32. Astley (1995, pp. 343, 360.

33. See Astley (1995, pp. 352–354). As Astley rightly comments, the figures given by Kōfuku no Kagaku for its membership in this period overstate its size considerably. Astley comes up with what he terms a 'conservative' estimate of size for Kōfuku of around 100–300,000 members in the early 1990s, but points out that this still represents a 'phenomenal rate of growth for a group that started with only four members in 1986' (p. 354). By any comparison this shows a far greater degree of success than Aum.

34. On Sōka Gakkai's split with Nichiren Shōshū and on its general orientations, see Stone (1994).

35. Asahara (VK 41, 42 and 43, esp. VK 41, pp. 272–273).

36. Asahara (VK 41, p. 273; VK 42, p. 276).

37. *Vajrayāna Sacca* (nos 8 and 9, 1995); see also Kaplan and Marshall (1996, p. 218).

38. These were the comments of the American chemical warfare expert Kyle Olson whose comments on the Matsumoto attack are reported in Committee on Government Affairs (1995, p. 66). Tsuchiya Masami also apparently confirmed to the police that the Matsumoto attack was a test run, since the movement had never tested sarin out in public before (Ibid.).

39. Asahara (VK 28, pp. 186–189).

40. Ibid. (p. 186).

41. Shimosato (1995, pp. 73–84).

42. The Aum case has had some profound repercussions for academics in Japan, who have come into criticism for, as the media would have it, failing to spot the dangers of Aum. These issues cannot be discussed here but further comments on the Shimada affair and its repercussions can be found in Watanabe (1997, pp. 46–48) and in Reader (forthcoming).

43. Murakami (1997, pp. 686–687).

44. Shimosato (1995, pp. 238–239).

45. Astley (1995, p. 373).

46. See Reader (1996, p. 85). Shimosato (1995, p. 239) says that a media colleague of his had been told about the raids on 19 March and had spent that night outside the Kamikuishiki commune waiting for them to materialise.

47. There had been a number of incidents in the days before in which devices had been left on trains and in public places, which were, according to Kaplan and Marshall (1996, pp. 235–236), earlier attempts by Aum to cause mass disruption and head off the police investigations by spreading toxins in public. None of these had worked.

48. Egawa (1996, p. 111) cites Nakagawa Tomomasa, who assisted in preparing the sarin, as saying that he thought that it was Murai's plan to carry out this attack.

49. See *Vajrayāna Sacca* (no. 9, 1995).

50. Among the protagonists of these attempted atrocities were Inoue Yoshihiro, Nakagawa Tomomasa and Toyoda Tōru, all of whom had managed to absent themselves from Kamikuishiki when the first raids occurred, and who had subsequently been on the run.

51. Shirakawa (1995, pp.104–110).

52. See Reader (1996, p. 3).

53. Inoue's remarks are reported in Kisala (1998, p. 33).

54. Reader (1996, esp. p. 93).

55. Mayer (1996, p. 18).

56. Ibid. (pp. 18–20, 103–106).

57. Interview, Yokohama, 23 Jan. 1998.

CHAPTER 8

1. As I indicated in the Introduction, there is a pressing need for a study of the retention of faith by Aum members in the face of the evidence of what the movement actually did, in order to answer such questions as why people retain faith in movements and teachers who appear (to the outside eye) to be thoroughly compromised or discredited due to their actions.

2.   For fuller discussion of the political and legal responses to the affair, see Mullins (1997).

3.   For discussion of the extent of media coverage of the Aum affair, see Ishii (1997).

4.   On the question of 'atrocity tales' see Barker (1989, pp. 39–51), Bromley and Shupe (1981) and Beckford (1985).

5.   This point is also worth mentioning in the Aum case because some academics did, when Aum became the target of police investigations and media stories, travel to Japan at Aum's request, to examine the possibility that Aum had been set up and that the media stories were false, an incident which caused strong media reaction in Japan. Ssee my comments in Reader (forthcoming) for further discussion of this issue.

6.   Among the numerous volumes and writings that affirmed these lines of argument, see Asami (1995) and Takimoto and Nagaoka (1995).

7.   Among the exceptions to this has been the work of Shimazono Susumu (1995a, 1995b, 1997) which, while recognising that Aum emerged out of the Japanese social environment, shows that its violence was related to its nature as a religious movement and that its espousal of violence demonstrates the potential for religions to act violently. A further exception is the work of Serizawa Shunsuke (1995), which locates Aum firmly within the broader phenomenon of the Japanese new religions.

8.   The Japanese literature on these themes has been immense in the period since spring 1995. Besides the works of Asami and of Takimoto and Nagaoka, mentioned in note 6, see Setagawa (1997), whose book title translates as 'The Sickness of Japanese Society and Aum Shinrikyō'.

9.   Robbins and Anthony (1995, p. 244).

10.   Ibid. (pp. 245–246).

11.   This was a community using therapeutic techniques to provide treatment for drug abuse. It developed in the 1950s in California and took on the appearance of a charismatic healing movement (see Galanter 1989, pp. 187–190).

12.   Robbins and Anthony (1995, p. 246).

13.   Ibid.

14.   Davis (1995, p. 710).

15.   Takahashi (1996, p. 233).

16.   Interview, Tokyo, 19 Oct. 1997.

17.   Takahashi (1996, p. 237).

18.   TSS (1995, p. 101).

19.   Gordon (1987, p. 81).

20.   Deutsch (1980), discussed in Galanter (1989, pp. 19–20), on which my account is based.

21.   Galanter (1989, p. 20).

22.   It should be noted that Aum continued to maintain centres in Tokyo and other cities. However, its main centres of operation revolved around the communes from around 1988 onwards.

23. Mayer (1996) and also personal communication.

24. Cimino and Lattin (1998, p. 172)

25. Applewhite, quoted in Cimino and Lattin (1998, p. 172).

26. Robbins (1997, pp. 13, 17). It should be emphasised that Robbins' essay does not support so much as provide what he calls a 'friendly critique' of this approach. See also the essay in the same volume by Jeffrey Kaplan (1997), which presents an alternative view.

27. Robbins (1997, p. 17).

28. It should be noted here that his essay (and Kaplan's, mentioned in note 26) is concerned with this issue in relation primarily to millennial and apocalyptic movements.

29. See Reader (forthcoming) for a fuller discussion of this point. I noted an immediate assumption among a number of colleagues with whom I discussed this affair in the period after the subway attack that some form of direct provocation and pressure from the Japanese authorities must have provoked Aum's behaviour. While clearly, as details emerged, these positions changed, nevertheless it is indicative of the paradigms operative in the field in general that such assumptions could have arisen at the outset.

30. Mayer (1996); also personal communication. Introvigne's (forthcoming) chapter on the Solar Temple places more emphasis on external factors but recognises the internal dynamics that contributed to the suicides and murders.

References

This list of references is divided into two sections, one representing Aum Shinrikyō primary sources (sub-divided into works by or attributed to Asahara Shōkō, and publications by other members or by the organisation) published by Aum, the second other sources and references cited.

AUM SHINRIKYŌ PUBLICATIONS AND MATERIALS

1. Works by or Attributed to Asahara Shōkō

Asahara Shōkō (n.d.; c.1994). *Vajrayāna kōsu. Kyōgaku shisutemu kyōhon.* Internal Aum document (referred to in text as Asahara VK).

—— (1986a) *Chōnōryoku: himitsu no kaihatsuhō.* Tokyo: Oumu Shuppan (republished 1993 and referred to in the text as Asahara 1993a).

—— (1986b) *Seishi o koeru.* Tokyo: Oumu Shuppan.

—— (1987) *Inishieeshon.* Tokyo: Oumu Shuppan.

—— (1988a) *Supreme Initiation.* Tokyo: Aum USA Co.

—— (1988b) *Mahāyāna sūtora* Tokyo: Oumu Shuppan.

—— (1989a) *Metsubō no hi.* Tokyo: Oumu Shuppan.

—— (1989b) *Metsubō kara kokū e.* Tokyo: Oumu Shuppan.

—— (1991a) *Tatāgata abidanma: shinri shōsha zettai saishō no hōsoku,* vol. 1 *Daiuchū no jissō.* Tokyo: Oumu Shuppan.

—— (1991b) *Tatāgata abidanma: shinri shōsha zettai saishō no hōsoku,* vol. 2 *Shinri shōsha no kyūsai keikaku.* Tokyo: Oumu Shuppan.

—— (1991c) *Chōetsu jinriki* (Part 3) *Kanzen naru zettai naru kami no eichi, rōjintsū.* Tokyo: Oumu Shuppan.

—— (1991d) *Asahara Shōkō no sekai,* vol. 1. Tokyo: Oumu Shuppan.

—— (1991e) *Sonshi Asahara Shōkō ga kiru! Asahara Shōkō no sekai* (Part 2). Tokyo: Oumu Shuppan.

—— (1991f) *Shinjitsu! rokudō rinne Asahara Shōkō no sekai* (Part 3). Tokyo: Oumu Shuppan.

—— (1991g) *Zettai no shinri: Asahara Shōkō no sekai* (Part 5). Tokyo: Oumu Shuppan.

—— (1991h) *Genbō jōjū no hihō: Asahara Shōkō no sekai* (Part 6). Tokyo: Oumu Shuppan.

—— (1991i) *Kirisuto sengen: kirisuto no oshie no subete o akasu.* Tokyo: Oumu Shuppan.

—— (1991j) *Kirisuto sengen 2: sairin, sabaki, shūmatsu.* Tokyo: Oumu Shuppan.

—— (1991k) 'Beyond the Impermanence of Things: The Path to Being a Great Winner of the Truth'. *Mahayana Newsletter,* no. 24, pp. 1–8.

—— (1991l) *Asahara Shōkō za samadi (The Samadhi).* Tokyo: Oumu Shuppan.

—— (1991m) *Shinjitsu no budda no oshie wa kō da!* Tokyo: Oumu Shuppan.

—— (1991n) *Nosutoradamusu jimitsu no daiyogen.* Tokyo: Oumu Shuppan.

—— (1991o) *The Art of Wish Fulfilment.* Tokyo: Aum Supreme Truth.

—— (1991p) *Mahāyāna sūtora* (Part 2). Tokyo: Oumu Shuppan.

—— (1991q) *Sonshi seichi Indo o iku.* Tokyo: Oumu Shuppan.

—— (1992a) *Haiesuto danma.* Tokyo: Oumu Shuppan.

—— (1992b) *Chōetsu jinriki* (Part 4). *Watashi wa mita! kore ga sonshi no chōetsujinriki.* Tokyo: Oumu Shuppan.

—— (1992c) *Tathāgata Abhidhamma: The Ever-Winning Law of the True Victors. Book 1 The Reality of the Universe* (trans. and edited by the Aum Translation Committee). Tokyo: Aum Publishing.

—— (1992d) *Tathāgata Abhidhamma: The Ever-Winning Law of the True Victors. Book 2 The Salvation of the True Victors* (trans. and edited by the Aum Translation Committee. Tokyo: Aum Publishing.

—— (1992e) *Shūkyō no jōken* (*Asahara Shōkō no sekai* Part 14). Tokyo: Oumu Shuppan.

—— (1992f) *Declaring Myself the Christ: Essential Teachings of Jesus Christ's Gospel.* Tokyo: Aum Publishing Co.

—— (ed.) (1992g) *Risōshakai Shambala.* Tokyo: Oumu Shuppan.

—— (1993a) [1986] *Chōnōryoku: himitsu no kaihatsuhō.* Tokyo: Oumu Shuppan.

—— (1993b) *Asahara Shōkō, senritsu no yogen.* (*Asahara Shōkō no sekai* Part 20). Tokyo: Oumu Shuppan.

—— (ed.) (1994a) *Kenshō: Samadī (shi).* Tokyo: Oumu Shuppan.

—— (ed.) (1994b) *Chakura no kagaku.* Tokyo: Oumu Shuppan.

—— (1994c) *Bōdisattova sūtora: kanzen tariki hongan no michi o toku.* Tokyo: Oumu Shuppan.

—— (1995a) *Hiizuru kuni wazawaichikashi.* Tokyo: Oumu Shuppan.

—— (1995b) *Bōkoku Nihon no kanashimi.* Tokyo: Oumu Shuppan.

—— (1995c) *Disaster Approaches the Land of the Rising Sun.* Tokyo: Aum Publishing Co.

Asahara VK (See Ashara Shōko n.d.).

REFERENCES

2. Works by Other Aum Members

Aoyama Yoshinobu (1990) *Shinri no bengoshi ganbaru zo!* Tokyo: Oumu Shuppan.

—— (1991) *Naze watashi wa taiho sarenakute wa naranakatta no ka.* Tokyo: Oumu Shuppan.

Atarashii Iryō Kenkyūkai (ed.) (1991a) *Arerūgi kaishōhō.* Tokyo: Oumu Shuppan.

—— (ed.) (1991b) *Asahara Shōkō aa gan ga kieta!* Tokyo: Oumu Shuppan.

—— (ed.) (1992) *Kōketsuatsu wa naoru: Asahara Shōkō no kiseki no yoga hihō kōkai.* Tokyo: Oumu Shuppan.

Aum Press (ed.) (1995) *Oumu Shinrikyo wa ima.* Tokyo: Aum Press.

Aum Public Relations Staff (ed.) (1992) *Sonshi ni kiku,* vols 1 and 2. Tokyo: Oumu Shuppan.

Aum Translation Committee (ed.) (1992) *Your First Steps to Truth.* Fujinomiya: Aum Publishing Co.

Kanai Ryōko (1991) *Otōsan, ikite!* Tokyo: Oumu Shuppan.

Maha Khema Taishi (Ishii Hisako) (1989) 'Welcome to the Astral World: Heaven Is Glorious with the Flowers in Bloom'. *Mahayana News Letter,* no. 15, pp. 38–47.

—— (1991a) 'Welcome to the Astral World: Visions which Forecast the Future'. *Mahayana News Letter,* no. 24, pp. 94–110.

—— (1991b) *Hishō: fuse. asutoraru e no tabi.* Tokyo: Oumu Shuppan.

Maitreya Seigoshi (Jōyu Fumihiro) (1991) 'Idai naru guru no shōzō'. *MahāyānaNew Letter,* no. 38, pp. 75–79.

Oumu Shinrikyō (ed.) (n.d.) *Shugyō.* Tokyo: Aum Shuppan.

Oumu Shinrikyō Tōdaisei Gurūppu (1991) *Nōryoku kakusei no hihō o toku.* Tokyo: Oumu Shuppan.

Oumu Shuppan Kōhō Henshūbu (ed.) (1991) *Kokoro no rurō no hate ni: ima naze Oumu Shinrikyō ka?* Tokyo: Oumu Shuppan.

—— (ed.) (1992a) *Jintsūrikisha e no michi.* Tokyo: Oumu Shuppan.

—— (ed.) (1992b) *Yomigaeru seisha densetsu.* Tokyo: Oumu Shuppan.

—— (ed.) (1992c) *Genbaku kakusei: seishin no honō o mezamesaseyo!* Tokyo: Oumu Shuppan.

—— (ed.) (1993) *Sonshi taidanshū.* Tokyo: Oumu Shuppan.

Shanti Taishi (Ōuchi Sanae) (1988) 'Gedatsu – hikarikagakyaku shinjitsu no michi e'. In Asahara Shōkō *Mahāyāna sutora,* Tokyo: Oumu Shuppan, pp. 219–242.

Shūkyō Hōjin Oumu Shinrikyō (March 1995 broadsheet) *Rachi shita no wa keisatsu!*

Aum magazines and periodicals

(*Note: published in English)
Anuttara Sacca

285

Mahāyāna
Mahāyāna Newsletter (MNL) *
Truth Monthly *
Vajrayāna Sacca

Videos

Oumu Shinrikyō (ed.) Video 1 (n.d.) *Oumu tatakai ka hametsu ka.* Tokyo: Oumu Shinrikyō.

Oumu Shinrikyō (ed.) Video 2 (1995) *Hofurareta kohitsuji.* Tokyo: Oumu Shinrikyō.

Aum Web Sites

http://www.aum-internet.org
http://www.aum-shinrikyo.com

OTHER NON-AUM SOURCES

Books, Articles, etc.

Anderson, Richard (1988) 'Taiken: Personal Narratives and Japanese New Religions'. PhD dissertation, Indiana University, Bloomington.

Arita Yoshifu (1995) *Ano ko ga Oumu ni.* Tokyo: Kōbunsha.

Asahara Shōkō and Yamaori Tetsuo (1992) Interview. In *Bessatsu Taiyō,* pp. 94–101.

Asami Sadao (1992) *Nise yogensha ni kokoro seyo.* Tokyo: Bansosha.

Asō Iku (1997) *Gokuhi sōsa: keisatsu.jietai no 'tai Oumu fairu'.* Tokyo: Bungei Shunjū.

Astley, Trevor (1995) 'The Transformation of a Recent Japanese New Religion: Okawa Ryūhō and Kōfuku no Kagaku'. *Japanese Journal of Religious Studies,* vol. 22, nos 3–4, pp. 343–380.

Barker, Eileen (1984) *The Making of a Moonie: Choice or Brainwashing?* Oxford: Basil Blackwell.

—— (1989) *New Religious Movements: A Practical Introduction.* London: HMSO.

Beckford, James (1985) *Cult Controversies: The Societal Response to the New Religious Movements.* London: Tavistock.

Bell, Sandra (1998) '"Crazy Wisdom", Charisma, and the Transmission of Buddhism in the United States'. *Nova Religio,* vol. 2, no. 1, pp. 55–75.

Boxer, C.R. (1951) *The Christian Century in Japan.* Berkeley: University of California Press.

Broad, William J. *et al.* (1998) 'When a Cult Turns to Germ Warfare'. *New York Times Online,* 26 May 1998.

Bromley, David (1998) 'Listing (in Black and White) Some Observations on (Sociological) Thought Reform'. *Nova Religio,* vol. 1, no. 2, pp. 250–266.

REFERENCES

Bromley, David G. and Anson D. Shupe 1981 *Strange Gods: The Great American Cult Hoax*. Boston, MA: Beacon.

Cimino, Richard P., and Don Lattin (1998) *Shopping for Faith: American Religion in the New Millennium*. San Francisco: Jossey-Bass.

Cohn, Norma (1970) *The Pursuit of the Millennium: Revolutionary Millenarians and Mystical Anarchists of the Middle Ages*. New York: Oxford University Press.

Committee on Government Affairs, United States Senate (1996) *Global Proliferation of Weapons of Mass Destruction: Hearings before the Permanent Subcommittee on Investigations. First Session*. 31 October and 1 November 1995. Washington: US Government Printing Office.

Davis, Winston B. (1980) *Dojo: Magic and Exorcism in Modern Japan*. Stanford, CA: Stanford University Press.

—— (1995) 'Dealing with Criminal Religions: the Case of Om Supreme Truth'. *The Christian Century*, 19–26 July 1995, pp. 708–709.

Deutsch, Alexander (1980) 'Tenacity of Attachment to a Cult Leader: a Psychiatric Perspective'. *American Journal of Psychiatry*, no. 137, pp. 1569–1573.

Douglas, Mary (1984) [1966] *Purity and Danger: An Analysis of the Concepts of Pollution and Taboo*. London: Ark.

Earhart, H. Byron (1989) *Gedatsukai and Religion in Contemporary Japan*. Bloomington, IN: University of Indiana Press.

Egawa Shōko (1995) [1991] *Kyūseishu no yabō*. Tokyo: Kyōikushiryō Shuppankai.

—— (1996) *Oumu Shinrikyō saiban bōchōki*, vol. 1. Tokyo: Bungei Shunjū.

—— (1997) *Oumu Shinrikyō saiban bōchōki*, vol. 2. Tokyo: Bungei Shunjū.

Faure, Bernard (1991) *The Rhetoric of Immediacy: A Cultural Critique of Chan/Zen Buddhism*. Princeton, NJ: Princeton University Press.

Fujita Shōichi (1995) *Aum Shinrikyō jiken*. Tokyo: Asahi News Shop.

Galanter, Mark (1989) *Cults: Faith, Healing, Coercion*. Oxford and New York: Oxford University Press.

Gardner, Richard (1996) Review Article on Reader *A Poisonous Cocktail?* and other works. *Monumenta Nipponica*, vol. 51, no. 3 (Autumn), pp. 402–405.

Geary, Patrick J. (1990) *Furta Sacra: Thefts of Relics in the Central Middle Ages*. Princeton, NJ: Princeton University Press.

—— (1994) *Living with the Dead in the Middle Ages*. Ithaca, NY: Cornell University Press.

Goodman, David G. (1997) 'Anti-Semitism in Japan: Its History and Current Implications'. In Frank Dikotter (ed.) *The Construction of Racial Identities in China and Japan*. London: Hurst & Co., pp. 177–198.

Gordon, James S. (1987) *The Golden Guru*. Lexington, VA: Stephen Greene Press.

Hall, John R. (1995) 'Public Narratives and the Apocalyptic Sect: from Jonestown to Mt. Carmel'. In Stuart A. Wright (ed.) *Armageddon in Waco: Critical Perspectives on the Branch Davidian Conflict*. Chicago: University of Chicago Press, pp. 205–235.

—— and Philip Schuyler (1997) 'The Mystical Apocalypse of the Solar Temple'. In Thomas Robbins and Susan Palmer (eds) *Millennium, Messiahs, and Mayhem*. New York: Routledge, pp. 285–311.

Hardacre, Helen (1984) *Lay Buddhism in Contemporary Japan: Reiyūkai Kyōdan*. Princeton,. NJ: Princeton University Press.

—— (1986) *Kurozumikyō and the New Religions of Japan*. (Princeton, NJ: Princeton University Press.

—— (1995) *Aum Shinrikyō and the Japanese Media: The Pied Piper Meets the Lamb of God*. Columbia University, New York : East Asian Institute Report.

Hoffman, Bruce (1996) 'Holy Terror: the Implications of Terrorism Motivated by a Religious Imperative'. *Studies in Conflict and Terrorism*, vol. 18, pp. 271–284.

—— (1998) *Inside Terrorism*. London: Indigo.

Hubbard, Jamie (1998) 'Embarrassing Superstition, Doctrine and the Study of New Religious Movements'. *Journal of the American Academy of Religion*, vol. 66, no. 1, pp. 59–92.

Hurvitz, Leon (1976) (trans.) *Scripture of the Lotus Blossom of the Fine Dharma (The Lotus Sutra)*. New York: Columbia University Press.

Huxley, Aldous (1954) *The Doors of Perception*. London: Chatto & Windus.

Inoue, Nobutaka *et al.* (1991) *Shin shūkyō jiten*. Tokyo: Kōbundō.

Introvigne, Massimo (forthcoming) 'The Magic of Death: The Suicides of the Solar Temple'. In Catherine Wessinger (ed.) *Millennialism, Persecution, and Violence: Historical Cases*. Syracuse: Syracuse University Press.

Ishii Kenji (1997) 'Jōhōka to shūkyō'. In Shimazono Susumu and Ishii Kenji (eds) *Shōhi sareru shūkyō*. Tokyo: Shunjūsha, pp. 185–208.

Juergensmeyer, Mark (ed.) (1992) *Violence and the Sacred in the Modern World*. London: Frank Cass.

—— (1992a) 'Introduction: Is Violence Symbolic or Real?' In Juergensmeyer (ed.) *Violence and the Sacred in the Modern World*. London: Frank Cass, pp. 1–8.

—— (1992b) 'Sacrifice and Cosmic War' in Juergensmeyer (ed.) *Violence and the Sacred in the Modern World*. London: Frank Cass, pp. 101–117.

Kaplan, David E., and Andrew Marshall (1996) *The Cult at the End of the World: The Incredible Story of Aum*. London: Arrow Books.

Kaplan, Jeffrey (1997) 'Interpreting the Interpretive Approach: A Friendly Reply to Thomas Robbins'. *Nova Religio*, vol. 1, no. 1, pp. 30–49.

Kashima Tomoko (1996) *Oumu no onibaba to yobarete*. Tokyo: Kindai Eikakusha.

Kinman, Dwight L. (1995) *The World's Last Dictator*. Canby, OR: Whitaker House.

Kiriyama Seiyū (1971) *Henshin no genri*. Tokyo: Kadokawa Bunsho.

—— (1981) *1999 nen karuma to reishō kara no dasshutsu*. Tokyo: Hirakawa Shuppansha.

—— (1995) *Oumu Shinrikyō to Agonshū*. Tokyo: Hirakawa Shuppan.

Kisala, Robert (1997) '1999 and Beyond: The Use of Nostradamus' Prophecies by Japanese Religions'. *Japanese Religions*, vol. 23, no. 1, pp. 143–157.

——— (1998) 'The AUM Spiritual Truth Church in Japan'. In Anson Shupe (ed.) *Wolves within the Fold: Religious Leadership and Abuses of Power.* New Brunswick: Rutgers University Press, pp. 33–48.

Kumamoto Nichinichi Shinbun (ed.) (KNS) (1995) [1992] *Aum Shinri Kyō to mura no ronri.* Fukuoka: Ashi Shobō.

Kyōdō Tsūshinsha Shakaibu (ed.) (KDT) (1997) *Sabakareru kyōso.* Tokyo: Kyōdō Tsūshinsha.

Maaga, Mary McCormick (1996) *Triple Erasure: Women and Power in People's Temple.* PhD dissertation, Drew University, New Jersey.

Mainichi Shinbun Shakaibu (ed.) (MNS) (1996) *Sabakareru 'Oumu no yabō'.* Tokyo: Mainichi Shinbunsha.

Matsuda Michiko (1995) *Oumu no onna.* Tokyo: Waseda Shuppan.

Mayer, Jean-François (1996) *Les Mythes du Temple Solaire.* Geneva: Georg.

——— (1999) 'Our Terrestrial Journey Is Coming to an End': The Last Voyage of the Solar Temple'. *Nova Religio,* vol. 2, no. 2, pp. 172–196.

McFarland, H.N. (1967) *The Rush Hour of the Gods: a Study of New Religions in Japan.* New York: Macmillan.

Metraux, Daniel (1995) 'Religious Terrorism in Japan: The Fatal Appeal of Aum Shinrikyō'. *Asian Survey,* vol. 35, no. 12, pp. 1140–1154.

——— (1997) Review of Reader 1996 (and others), *Japanese Journal of Religious Studies,* vol. 24, nos. 1–2, pp. 207–210.

Mikhailova, Yulia (1996) 'The Aum Supreme Truth Sect in Russia' *Bulletin of the Japanese Studies Association of Australia,* vol. 16, nos. 2–3, pp. 15–34.

Miyadai Shinji (1995) Ryōshin no hanzaisha, *Takarajima,* no. 30, pp. 28–39.

Miyazaka Yūshō (1996) Oumu Shinrikyō to wa nanika: kyōri no jittai ni tsuite. *Bukkyō. Bessatsu,* no. 8, pp. 10–42.

Moore, Rebecca (forthcoming) '"American as Cherry Pie:" Peoples Temple and Violence'. In Catherine Wessinger (ed.) *Millennialism, Persecution, and Violence: Historical Cases.* Syracuse: Syracuse University Press.

Motoyama Kinue and Motoyama Hiroshi (1983) *Kiseki to shūkyō taiken.* Tokyo: Shūkyō Shinrigaku Kenkyūjo Shuppan.

Mullins, Mark R. (1997) 'The Political and Legal Response to Aum-Related Violence in Japan'. *Japan Christian Review,* no. 63, pp. 37–46.

Murakami Haruki (1997) *Andāguraundo.* Tokyo: Kōdansha.

Napier, Susan J. (1996) *The Fantastic in Modern Japanese Literature: The Subversion of Modernity.* London: Routledge).

——— (n.d.) 'Waiting for the End of the World: Images of Apocalypse in Japanese Animation' (unpublished paper) 32 pp.

Newman, John (1995) 'Eschatology in the Wheel of Time Tantra'. In Donald S. Lopez, Jr. (ed.) *Buddhism in Practice.* Princeton, NJ: Princeton University Press, pp. 284–289.

Nishiwake Kei (n.d.) 'Oumu Shinrikyō no taikei'. Unpublished paper in possession of the author, probably produced by Aum Shinrikyō in 1997, 23 pp.

Nishiyama Shigeru (1988) 'Gendai no shūkyō undō'. In Ōmura Eishō and Nishiyama Shigeru (eds) *Gendaijin no shūkyō*. Tokyo: Yuhikaku.

Numata Kenya (1995) *Shūkyō to kagaku no neoparadaimu*. Osaka: Sōgensha.

—— (1996) 'Oumu Shinrikyō no kenkyū- kagaku to shūkyō no kankei ni kanren shite'. *Momoyama Gakuin Daigaku Sōgō Kenkyūjo Kiyō*, vol. 22, no. 1, pp. 93–128.

Ōkawa Ryūhō (1988) *Nosutoradamusu no shinyogen*. Tokyo: Kōfuku no Kagaku Shuppan.

—— 1990a *Taiyō no hō*. Tokyo: Kōfuku no Kagaku Shuppan.

—— 1990b *The Laws of Gold* Tokyo: Kōfuku no Kagaku Shuppan.

—— (1991) *Nosutoradamusu senritsu no keiji*. Tokyo: Kōfuku no Kagaku Shuppan.

—— (1995) *Buddha Speaks: Discourses with the Buddha Incarnate*. Tokyo: Kōfuku no Kagaku Shuppan.

Ooms, Emily Groszos (1993) *Women and Millenarian Protest in Meiji Japan*. Ithaca, NY: Cornell East Asia Series.

Penrose, Commander Jeff (1995) 'Western Australian Link to Japanese Doomsday Cult'. *Platypus Magazine*, no. 49, pp. 2–7.

Pye, Michael (1996) 'Aum Shinrikyō: Can Religious Studies Cope?'. *Religion*, vol. 26, pp. 261–270.

Rapoport, David C. (1992) 'Some General Observations on Religion and Violence'. In Mark Juergensmeyer (ed.) *Violence and the Sacred in the Modern World*, London: Frank Cass, pp. 118–140.

Reader, Ian (1988) 'The "New" New Religions of Japan: an Analysis of the Rise of Agonshu'. *Japanese Journal of Religious Studies*, vol. 15, no. 4, pp. 235–261.

—— (1991) *Religion in Contemporary Japan*. Basingstoke, UK: Macmillan.

—— (1994) 'Appropriated Images: Esoteric Themes in a Japanese New Religion'. In Ian Astley (ed.) *Esoteric Buddhism in Japan*. Copenhagen and Aarhus: Seminar for Buddhist Studies, pp. 36–63.

—— (1995) 'Cleaning Floors and Sweeping the Mind: Cleaning as a Ritual Process'. In Jan van Bremen and D.P. Martinez (eds) *Ceremony and Ritual in Japan: Religious Practices in an Industrialized Society*. London: Routledge, pp. 227–245.

—— (1996) *A Poisonous Cocktail? Aum Shinrikyō's Path to Violence*. Copenhagen: NIAS Books.

—— (forthcoming) 'Scholarship, Aum Shinrikyō and Academic Integrity'. *Nova Religio*.

—— and George J. Tanabe Jr. (1994) 'Introduction'. In I. Reader and G.J. Tanabe Jr. (eds.) 'Conflict and Religion in Japan'.Special Edition of the *Japanese Journal of Religious Studies*, vol. 21, nos 2–3, pp. 123–136.

Robbins, Thomas (1997) 'Religious Movements and Violence: A Friendly Critique of the Interpretive Approach'. *Nova Religio*, vol. 1, no. 1, pp. 13–29.

Robbins, Thomas, and Dick Anthony (1995) 'Sects and Violence: Factors Enhancing the Volatility of Marginal Religious Movements'. In Stuart A. Wright (ed.) *Armageddon in Waco: Critical Perspectives on the Branch Davidian Conflict*. Chicago: University of Chicago Press, pp. 236–259.

Sakashita, Jay (1998) 'Shinnyoen and the Transmission of Japanese New Religions Abroad'. University of Stirling, Scotland, unpublished PhD dissertation.

Schopen, Gregory 1997 *Bones, stones and Buddhist monks : collected papers on the archaeology, epigraphy and texts of Monastic Buddhism in India*. Honolulu : University of Hawaii Press.

Schwartz, Regina M. (1997) *The Curse of Cain: The Violent Legacy of Monotheism*. Chicago: University of Chicago Press.

Serizawa Shunsuke (1995) *Oumu genshō no kaidoku*. Tokyo: Chikuma Shōbo.

Setagawa Masahiro (1997) *Nihon shakai no byōri to Oumu Shinrikyō*. Tokyo: Byakujunsha.

Shimada Hiromi (1992) *Kamisama no tsugō*. Kyoto: Hōzōkan.

—— (1995) *Shinji yasui kokoro: wakamono ga shinshin shūkyō ni hashiru riyū*. Tokyo: PHP Kenkyūjo.

Shimazono Susumu (1979) 'The Living Kami Idea in the New Religions of Japan'. *Japanese Journal of Religious Studies*, vol. 6, no. 3, pp. 389–412.

—— (1992) *Shinshin shūkyō to shūkyō būmu*. Tokyo: Iwanami Booklets No. 237.

—— (1995a) *Aum Shinrikyō no kiseki*. Tokyo: Iwanami Booklets No. 379.

—— (1995b) 'In the Wake of Aum: The Formation and Transformation of a Universe of Belief'. *Japanese Journal of Religious Studies*, vol. 22, no. 3–4, pp. 343–380.

—— (1996) *Seishin sekai no yukue: gendai sekai to shinreisei undō*, Tokyo: Tōkyōdō Shuppan.

—— (1997) *Gendai shūkyō no kanōsei: Oumu Shinrikyō to bōryoku*. Tokyo: Iwanami Shoten.

Shimosato Masaaki (1995) *Akuma no shiroi kiri*. Tokyo: Pocket Books Ltd.

Shirakawa Tadashi (1995) 'Busō kūdetā keikaku no zenyō'. *Bungei Shunjū*, no.6, pp. 104–110.

Skelton, Russell (1997) 'Second Coming of the Doomsday Cult'. *The Age* (Melbourne Online) 11 Oct. 1997.

Smith, Brian K. (1998) 'Monotheism and Its Discontents: Religious Violence and the Bible'. *Journal of the American Academy of Religion*, vol. 66, no. 2, pp. 403–411.

Sōtōshū Shūmuchō (ed.) (1981) *Zen no kaze*. Tokyo: Sōtōshū Shūmuchō.

Steinhoff, Patricia G. (1992) 'Defeat by Defeatism and Other Fables: the Social Dynamics of the Rengō Sekigun Purge'. In Takie Sugiyama Lebra (ed.) *Japanese Social Organizations*. Honolulu: University of Hawaii, pp. 195–224.

Stone, Jacqueline (1994) 'Rebuking the Enemies of the Lotus: Nichirenist Exclusivism in Historical Perspective'. *Japanese Journal of Religious Studies*, vol. 21, nos 2–3, pp. 231–259.

Strozier, Charles B. (1994) *Apocalypse: On the Psychology of Fundamentalism in America*. Boston, MA: Beacon Press.

Sullivan, Kevin (1997) 'Japan Cult Thrives while Guru Is Jailed'. *Washington Post*, 28 Sept. 1997, p. A21.

Swanson, Paul L. (1981) 'Shugendō and the Yoshino–Kumano Pilgrimage: An Example of Mountain Pilgrimage'. *Monumenta Nipponica*, vol. 36, no. 1, pp. 55–94.

Tabor, James D., and Gallagher, Eugene V. (1995) *Why Waco? Cults and the Battle for Religious Freedom in America.* Berkeley and Los Angeles: University of California Press.

Takahashi Hidetoshi (1996) *Oumu kara no kikan,* Tokyo: Sōshisha.

Takeda Michio (ed.) (n.d.) Unpublished collection of statements by Aum defendants taken from the media and from trial transcripts, in possession of the author.

Takeuchi Seiichi (1995) *Fujisan fumoto no tatakai: Oumu 2000 nichi sensō.* Tokyo: KK Besuto serazu.

Takimoto Tarō and Fukushima Mizuho (1996) *Habōhō to Oumu Shinrikyō.* Tokyo: Iwanami Booklets No. 398.

Takimoto Tarō and Nagaoka Tatsuya (1995) *Maindo kontorōru kara nigerete: Oumu Shinrikyō dakkaishatachi no taiken.* Tokyo: Kōyū Shuppan.

Tamura Tomo (1996) *Asahara wa tada no ossan da!* Tokyo: Sakura Shobō (cartoon version: illustrated by Kai Naohito).

Tenshō Kōtai Jingūkyō (ed.) (1954) *The Prophet of Tabuse.* Tabuse, Japan: Tenshō Kōtai Jingūkyō.

Tōkyō Shinbun Shakaibu (ed.) (TSS) (1995) *Oumu soshiki hanzai no nazo.* Tokyo: Tokyo Shinbun Shuppankyoku.

Watanabe Manabu (1997) 'Reactions to the Aum Affair: The Rise of the Anti-Cult Movement in Japan'. *Bulletin of the Nanzan Institute for Religion and Culture,* vol. 21, pp. 32–48.

Watt, Paul B. (1998) Review of Ian Reader *A Poisonous Cocktail? Aum Shinrikyō's Path to Violence.* In *Journal of Asian Studies,* pp. 802–803.

Watts, Jonathan (1998) 'Resurgent Cult Lures Disaffected Youth'. *The Guardian,* 13 October 1998, p. 17.

Wessinger, Catherine (1997) 'Millennialism with and without the Mayhem'. In Thomas J. Robbins and Susan J. Palmer (eds) *Millennium, Messiahs, and Mayhem.* New York: Routledge, pp. 47–59.

—— (ed.) (forthcoming) *Millennialism, Persecution, and Violence: Historical Cases.* Syracuse: Syracuse University Press.

Wojcik, Daniel (1997) *The End of the World as We Know It: Faith, Fatalism, and Apocalypse in America.* New York: New York University Press.

Wright, Stuart A. (ed.) (1995) *Armageddon in Waco: Critical Perspectives on the Branch Davidian Conflict.* Chicago: University of Chicago Press.

Yamaori Tetsuo (1995) 'Atheists by Default', *Look Japan,* vol. 41, no. 3, p. 11.

Yamashita Akiko (1997) 'The Eschatology of Japanese New and New New Religions: From Tenri-kyo to Kōfuku no Kagaku'. *Japanese Religions,* vol. 23, no. 1, pp. 125–142.

Young, Richard Fox (1995) 'Lethal Achievements: Fragments of a Response to the Aum Shinrikyō Affair', *Japanese Religions,* vol. 20, no. 2, pp. 230–245.

Yumiyama Tatsuya (1997) 'Oumu Shinrikyō ni okeru "satori" to "gedatsu"', *Shūkyō kenkyū*, vol. 70, no.4, pp. 337–338.

Zablocki, Benjamin (1997) 'The Blacklisting of a Concept: The Strange History of the Brainwashing Conjecture in the Sociology of Religion'. *Nova Religio*, vol. 1, no. 1, pp. 96–121.

Web Sites

http://www.csis-scrs.gc.ca/eng/miscdocs/postscre.html

http://www.asahi.com/paper/aum

http://www.aum-internet.org

http://www.aum-shinrikyo.com/english.master/trial.htm

http://www.cnn.com

http://www.yomiuri.com

Japanese language newspapers

Asahi shinbun

Mainichi Shinbun

Yomiuri Shinbun

English language newspapers

Asahi Evening News

Daily Yomiuri

The Guardian

Japan Times

Mainichi Daily News

New York Times

Japanese Magazines

Aera

Shūkan Asahi

Shūkan Yomiuri

Sunday Mainichi

世

Index

Asahara Shōkō *(continued)*

distancing from reality and projection of blame for failures onto others 35–37, 55–56, 92, 155, 134, 177, 236

dualistic personality of 33–39, 41–43

exhaustion of, due to excessive practices and initiations 72, 130, 136–137

fears, obsessions, and preoccupations with death of 46, 171, 193, 202

feels rejected as a child 40–41

fined for assault and for fraud 41, 53

forces disciples to perform ascetic practices 9, 13, 137

frustrated ambitions and failure to enter university 44

gives up initiations and asceticism: reasons and repercussions 130, 136–138, 142

guilt and responsibility for Aum's crimes 20, 25

identifies with Shiva and Jesus 52, 66–67, 141–142

inability to compromise or handle challenges to his authority 41–43

joins and leaves Agonshū 53–54

kindness and warmth of 38, 42–43, 174–175

lack of prior spiritual training of 70–71

levitation claims of 72–73

links world salvation to Aum's growth 89–93

marries Tomoko 45

masochistic inclinations of 42

orders and uses beatings, punishments and killings 1–2, 12, 16, 22–23, 137–138, 144–145, 149–151, 159–160, 206–213

parallels with other religious leaders in Japan 57–60

paranoia, doubts, fears and insecurity of 10, 35, 56–57, 63, 135–136, 142–143, 147, 171, 236

past lives of 55

preaches against taking life 79

psychological disturbance and collapse of 35–36, 119, 173, 202–203

public and media images of as fraud and evil manipulator 33–39, 57, 132, 226–227

receives revelations from Shiva 66–77

rejection of past and of original name 39–40

religious background of and religious influences on 45–47, 65–66

rivalry with and resentment against more successful religious leaders 206–208

sense of mission of 10, 26, 53, 141

sexual excess and gluttony of 36

surrounded by inner elite clique of disciples 198–199

transformation from ascetic to overweight hedonistic guru 137

travels to India 89–90

use of publicity and public demonstrations of austerities 73

see also apocalypse, Armageddon, asceticism, Aum, cloning the guru, conspiracy theories, defections, disciples, guru, hell(s), hierarchy and status, illness, initiation, karma, karmic retribution, karmic righteousness, killing for salvation, millennialism, mission, persecution, *poa*, subway attack, violence, weapons

asceticism in Aum 9, 15, 113, 116, 118–119, 121–128

as means of ascending the hierarchy 123–124

as means of eradicating karma 14, 71

as means of surviving apocalypse 193

relationship with violence 232–233

astrology and divination in Aum 46–47

'atrocity tales' about new religions 226

Aum (Aum Shinrikyō, Aum Supreme
    Truth)
  affair as a case of religious violence
    28–29
  attacks, murders and crimes of 1–2,
    22–23, 144–145, 149–151, 159–
    160, 206–216
  attitudes to civil law 132–133, 166–
    167
  attitudes to science, technology and
    scientific rationalism 47–50, 186
  attractions of for disciples 99–103
  as bad and aggressive neighbour
    163–168
  bond of criminality in 143–146, 153
  Buddhism as primary frame of
    reference in 67–69
  campaign to register as religious
    organisation 146–147
  commercial activities of 64
  conceptualisation of enemies 31,
    93–95
  concepts of challenge and struggle
    9, 71, 84–85, 94, 192
  confrontational nature of 127, 147,
    188, 200, 232
  cosmology and views of other
    worlds 12, 76–77
  courts and civil liberties groups
    support of at Namino 168, 173
  criticisms of other religions by 15,
    46, 74
  culture of fear, paranoia and
    violence in 10–11, 19–20, 24,
    147, 153, 190, 202–204
  develops myth of self-importance
    231–232
  disorganisation, chaos and incom-
    petence of 202–204, 215
  eclectic nature and roots of 61–69,
    142
  elitism and hierarchic nature of 9–
    10, 15, 56, 51, 84–88, 134, 242
  establishes political party and runs
    disastrous election campaign
    153–156

  exists in its own paranoid and
    closed thought world 20–21
  experimental nature of spiritual
    training in 70–71, 198
  exploitative aspects of 14, 25, 237
  factors contributing to its violence
    230–248
  fantasies and unrealistic projects
    of 186, 192–193, 197–198
  fighting for the truth as key concept
    in 164, 168, 179, 187, 195, 196, 200
  forms alternative government 9, 26,
    97, 198, 200
  foundation and turbulent history
    of 61–65
  importance of asceticism in 138,
    139
  internal dissent in Aum over
    election campaign 153–155
  lack of co-ordinated strategy in
    violence 24, 217–218
  lack of political orientation 26–27
  meaning of name 61
  nature as religious movement 67–
    69, 85–86 93–94, 231–233
  organisational development and
    structure of 8, 64, 82–84, 136
  preparations for war 201
  public images of as criminal and
    bizarre 23, 79, 81, 131–132
  religious absolutism of 243
  Russia, Aum's activities in 175–178
  salvation plans of 2, 142
  sangha (Buddhist monastic order)
    in 82–84
  science-fictional fantasy world of
    185–187
  Sri Lanka, Aum's activities in 175
  views of karma and transmigration
    20
  world-rejection of and views of
    world as evil 10–12, 142, 161
  worldview, polarised nature of 10–
    12, 20, 31, 142, 161, 170, 218,
    248
  yoga and mediation in 9, 47, 66–
    67, 79
Zaire, Aum's activities in 178

detachment (*seimutonjaku*) 80–82
  and freedom from karmic reper-
    cussions for one's deeds 81–82
  cultivation of in Aum practice 80–82
  shown by disciples during crimes
    and after subway attack 81
devil
  as symbol of and synonymous with
    evil and materialism in Aum 93,
    142
  see also Satan
Di Mambro, Joseph 172–173, 191, 248
  paranoid behaviour of 241
disciples of Asahara 95–125
  ambitions to acquire psychic powers
    74, 103
  appeal of Aum for and reasons for
    joining 96–101, 124–125
  complicity in and responsibility for
    violence 21–22, 114, 205–206,
    234–242
  desire for holy names 84, 236, 242
  devotion to Asahara and role in
    creation of his authority 21–22,
    54, 63, 124–125
  emphasise personal practice and
    inner experience over external
    issues 237–238
  general profile of 96–99
  hostility to Japanese society and its
    laws 101–103, 237
  pretentious nature of 83–84
  readiness to fight and kill for the
    'truth' 95, 140–141, 147, 150–
    151, 194, 236–237
  testimonies, experiences and ascetic
    practices of 104–124
  zealous nature and readiness to
    give up everything for Aum 95,
    119–121, 124–125
  see also individual disciples' names
doctrine, importance of in new
  religions 4–5
drugs made and used in Aum 70–71,
  198
  see also LSD

Egawa Shōkō 20, 152, 206
Endō Seiichi 22, 83, 97, 129
  as source of claims about Asahara's
    DNA 131
  manufactures biological and
    chemical weapons and drugs
    159, 163, 188, 198
  manufactures sarin for use in
    subway attack 21

failure
  of Aum to deal with gap of ambition
    and reality 243–244
  of Aum to develop strategies for
    dealing with society 243
  of Aum to meet aspirations and
    targets for growth 63, 92, 133–
    134, 183–184, 231
  Aum's explanations of failure of
    election campaign 153–157
  of Aum's overseas ventures 63,
    175–178
  of Aum's proselytisation campaigns
    173, 174–175, 184
  as a factor in religious violence 63,
    183–184, 248
  as a factor in the Heaven's Gate
    and Order of the Solar Temple
    affairs 244–245

gedatsu (liberation) 32, 85
gedatsusha (liberated being), Asahara
  as 78–79
gekō ('going down' i.e. leaving Aum)
  12, 17
genshi bukkyō (original Buddhism)
  xiii, 79
guru (as used in Aum and referring to
  Asahara)
  absolute authority of and need for
    absolute devotion to 20, 127–
    130, 140
  as being beyond the bounds of
    conventional morality 107–108,
    238–239

Ishii Hisako 8–9, 62, 91, 100, 247
arrested and complains of persecution at Namino 165–166
ascetic reputation and charismatic nature of 10, 101, 109
bears Asahara's children 10
challenges death in underground *samadhi* 121, 123
disposes of Ochi's body 17
as first disciple and first *shukkesha* 9, 83
parents campaign against Aum 135
performs *shaktipat* initiations in Aum 72, 112, 130
power wanes inside Aum 185
powers of spirit travel and prophecy 77–78
renounces faith in Asahara 231
as senior figure in Aum and controller of finances 10

Japan
as deserving punishment 184
as focus of salvation and Aum's mission 89–90
as needing to manufacture sarin and fight against USA 187
Jesus 52, 57, 169–170
Jones, Jim 171–173, 199, 201, 241
Jōyu Fumihiro 17, 21, 81, 83, 97, 123, 155
denies Aum carried out subway attack 215
underground *samadhi* of 174–175

Kālacakra Tantra (Buddhist millennial text) 91
Kamikuishiki, Aum's commune at 8, 23, 126
and conflicts with locals at 166–168, 247
police raids on 215
kanbu (upper elite in Aum) 22, 236–237
Kariya Kiyoshi
abducted and killed by Aum 23–24, 80 213–214, 219

karma
in Aum's thought 12–13, 17,72, 77–79, 128, 169–170, 180, 193, 232
casting off and eradication of 14–15, 66, 71, 138
as negative force pulling the spirit down to the hells 71, 128, 169–170, 194
karmic retribution on those who attack or fail to support Aum 43, 175, 193–195
karmic righteousness of Aum 168, 195, 236–237, 245
Kashima Tomoko 44, 204
Kasumigaseki (station at centre of subway attack) 22, 26, 27, 214–215
ketsui (determination) tapes and chants 200
killing for salvation 19, 145, 160, 200
as moral obligation in Aum 194–195
as sign of spiritual attainment 150–152
see also legitimation of violence, *poa*
Kiriyama Seiyū 39, 48, 50, 59, 73, 135
Kōfuku no Kagaku 39, 100, 135, 214
conflicts with Aum 173–174
conflicts with media 174
see also Ôkawa Ryūhō
Kômeitô (political party) 153–154, 208
Koresh, David 141–142, 201, 246
kundalini 9, 66

legitimation of violence in Aum
doctrines 128, 137–138, 145–146, 161, 217–218, 232–233
as drawn from Tibetan Buddhist sources 139
as having a basis in Japanese cultural contexts 139–140
levitation in Aum and its meaning 71–74
Lobov Oleg 176
Lotus Villages 91
LSD, Aum's manufacture and use of 20, 70–71, 81, 131, 163